Praise, Praise, Praise for Cats For Dummies!

"*Cats For Dummies* is an excellent, engaging, encyclopedic primer and reference book for the person about to be adopted by a cat. This is a book that readers will undoubtedly pull off the shelf again and again."

— Margie Scherk-Nixon DVM, DABVP (Feline Practice)

"*Cats For Dummies* is catnip for the feline fanatic. It offers sound advice on cat care, behavior issues, products, services, and fascinating feline trivia, all served up with wry humor that entertains, even as it educates."

— Amy Shojai, Pet Author and President, Cat Writers' Association

"*Cats For Dummies* is terrific. It's an educational and fun read for all cat owners — new and experienced."

— Dr. Colleen Currigan, DVM, Veterinary Homecare For Cats

"All the questions you have about owning a cat are answered in *Cats For Dummies*. This book is a must-read for the new kitten owner."

— Sandi Pergande, Country Paws - Burmese Cats

Praise, Praise, Praise for Dogs For Dummies!

"Gina Spadafori is one of the most knowledgeable dog writers I know. Her talents as a journalist combined with her passion for all things canine make her uniquely qualified to educate and motivate new dog owners."

— Joseph McGraw, attorney, Georgia

"I am really excited about Gina's book! This is a book I recommend to all my clients, and to anyone who has a dog. Gina's enthusiasm, knowledge, and compassion show on every page."

— Linda Randall, DVM, Dipl. American Board of Veterinary Practitioners

"Gina is extremely perceptive when it comes to dogs and people, and is able to communicate ideas in a clear, insightful, and humorous manner."

— Mary Young, top dog trainer, Texas

"An intriguing book filled with a wealth of practical information for dog owners that stands tails above the rest – two paws up!"

— Darris O. Hercs, Executive Assistant Director, Oakland SPCA

"Owning a copy of this delightful book is one of the best things you can do for your dog."

— Maria Goodavage, author, *The California Dog Lover's Companion*

"This book is my current favorite and most up-to-date volume on dog ownership, especially for the novice owner, although there is something for everyone here. Gina's experience and helpful advice comes through in every page on this book."

— Cindy Tittle Moore, `rec.pet.dogs` newsgroup

"No matter what you're looking for, a sporting breed, a working breed, or a house pet, a puppy or an adult, male or female, this reference covers the basics for all. This is a thoroughly researched, wittily written guide for new dog owners."

— *Sports Afield Magazine*

Praise, Praise, Praise for Gina's Columns!

"Gina's Pet Connection column comes from the mind of a journalist who knows pets and from the heart of a pet owner who loves them. And her readers benefit greatly."

— Gregory Favre, executive editor, *The Sacramento Bee* newspaper

"THE PET CONNECTION: pet protection, pet reflection, pet selection, pet perfection, pet correction, pet direction, pet affection, pet inspection, pet collection and pet retrospection. Where else can you find all this but in Gina Spadafori's entertaining and indispensable column, The Pet Connection. I love it."

— Mordecai Siegal, editor of *The UC Davis Book Of Dogs* and president of the *Dog Writers Association of America*

"I am impressed by the breadth of Gina Spadafori's knowledge, the extent of her research, and the depth of her sincerity. Her columns are a labor of love and anyone who has known, and loved, a dog should never miss them."

— Margaret Gavel, Georgia

"Gina Spadafori captured the attention of the online world when her Pet Connection appeared in the Pet Care Forum on America Online. Her personable writing style and great knowledge of dogs make her column a regular favorite with AOL members."

— Mike Richards, D.V. M., former head of the America Online Pet Care Forum

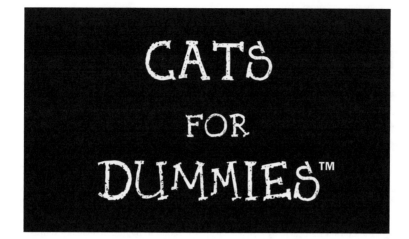

CATS
FOR
DUMMIES™

by Gina Spadafori
and
Paul D. Pion, DVM, DACVIM

Foreword by
Lilian Jackson Braun

IDG
BOOKS
WORLDWIDE

IDG Books Worldwide, Inc.
An International Data Group Company

Foster City, CA ♦ Chicago, IL ♦ Indianapolis, IN ♦ Southlake, TX

Cats For Dummies™

Published by
IDG Books Worldwide, Inc.
An International Data Group Company
919 E. Hillsdale Blvd.
Suite 400
Foster City, CA 94404
www.idgbooks.com (IDG Books Worldwide Web site)
www.dummies.com (Dummies Press Web site)

Library of Congress Catalog Card No.: 97-72425

ISBN: 0-7645-5037-3

Printed in the United States of America

10 9 8 7 6 5 4 3 2 1

1E/TR/QX/ZX/IN

Distributed in the United States by IDG Books Worldwide, Inc.

Distributed by Macmillan Canada for Canada; by Transworld Publishers Limited in the United Kingdom; by IDG Norge Books for Norway; by IDG Sweden Books for Sweden; by Woodslane Pty. Ltd. for Australia; by Woodslane Enterprises Ltd. for New Zealand; by Longman Singapore Publishers Ltd. for Singapore, Malaysia, Thailand, and Indonesia; by Simron Pty. Ltd. for South Africa; by Toppan Company Ltd. for Japan; by Distribuidora Cuspide for Argentina; by Livraria Cultura for Brazil; by Ediciencia S.A. for Ecuador; by Addison-Wesley Publishing Company for Korea; by Ediciones ZETA S.C.R. Ltda. for Peru; by WS Computer Publishing Corporation, Inc., for the Philippines; by Unalis Corporation for Taiwan; by Contemporanea de Ediciones for Venezuela; by Computer Book & Magazine Store for Puerto Rico; by Express Computer Distributors for the Caribbean and West Indies. Authorized Sales Agent: Anthony Rudkin Associates for the Middle East and North Africa.

For general information on IDG Books Worldwide's books in the U.S., please call our Consumer Customer Service department at 800-762-2974. For reseller information, including discounts and premium sales, please call our Reseller Customer Service department at 800-434-3422.

For information on where to purchase IDG Books Worldwide's books outside the U.S., please contact our International Sales department at 415-655-3200 or fax 415-655-3295.

For information on foreign language translations, please contact our Foreign & Subsidiary Rights department at 415-655-3021 or fax 415-655-3281.

For sales inquiries and special prices for bulk quantities, please contact our Sales department at 415-655-3200 or write to the address above.

For information on using IDG Books Worldwide's books in the classroom or for ordering examination copies, please contact our Educational Sales department at 800-434-2086 or fax 817-251-8174.

For press review copies, author interviews, or other publicity information, please contact our Public Relations department at 415-655-3000 or fax 415-655-3299.

For authorization to photocopy items for corporate, personal, or educational use, please contact Copyright Clearance Center, 222 Rosewood Drive, Danvers, MA 01923, or fax 508-750-4470.

 is a trademark under exclusive license to IDG Books Worldwide, Inc., from International Data Group, Inc.

About the Authors

Gina Spadafori: Gina writes an award-winning column on pets and their care, which appears in newspapers across the United States through the Universal Press Syndicate and in the Pet Care Forum on America Online, the world's largest commercial online service. She is the author of the best-selling *Dogs For Dummies,* which was given the President's Award for the best writing on dogs and the Maxwell Medallion for best general reference book, both by the Dog Writers Association of America.

Gina has served on the board of directors of both the Cat Writers' Association and the Dog Writers Association of America. She is a three-time recipient of the DWAA's Maxwell Medallion for best newspaper column, and her column has also been honored with a certificate of excellence by the CWA. She has been given the Geraldine R. Dodge award for writing on animal-welfare issues, as well as the Pedigree Dog Food Outstanding Journalist Pet Care Award for excellence in writing on animals over a five-year period.

Gina is affiliated with the Veterinary Information Network, Inc., of Davis, California, an international online service for veterinary professionals and the owner of the Pet Care Forum on America Online. She lives in Sacramento, California, with her dogs Andy and Benjamin and is waiting for the right cat to come along.

Paul D. Pion, DVM, DACVIM: Paul is co-founder, president, and CEO of the Veterinary Information Network, Inc., and a board-certified veterinary cardiologist. Paul's company is a pioneer in the field of information technology, providing veterinary professionals with online access to top consultants, searchable databases, continuing education in a variety of specialities, and the opportunity to share views and ideas with others in the profession. Paul has been awarded a Physician's Scientist Award by the National Institutes of Health, a Small Animal Research Award by Ralston Purina, National Phi Zeta Award for the one of the two most outstanding manuscripts in 1989, and a Special Recognition Award by the American Animal Hospital Association for innovations in the field of veterinary medicine.

Paul graduated from the veterinary college at Cornell University and has taught in the veterinary school at the University of California, Davis. While at UCD, he made an important research discovery that has touched the lives of every cat in the world: He proved that deficiency of a single amino acid, taurine, in commercial cat food was causing heart disease in cats. His discovery was published as a cover article in *SCIENCE,* one of the most competitive and respected research journals, and, more important, led to the reformulation of the world's cat foods and virtual eradication of a fatal heart disease that afflicted tens of thousands of cats annually in the late '80s. He is also a veterinary consultant to the Winn Feline Foundation, a nonprofit organization that raises money and grants research funds for feline health studies.

Paul lives in Davis, California, with his wife, Carla, also a veterinarian, son Luca, dogs Wes and Barney, birds Sunny and Bird, hedgehog Bashful, and cat PC (for Prayer Cat), an uncommon tabby who sits up and prays for what she wants, a trait so endearing that Paul says his wife fell in love with the cat first.

ABOUT IDG BOOKS WORLDWIDE

Welcome to the world of IDG Books Worldwide.

IDG Books Worldwide, Inc., is a subsidiary of International Data Group, the world's largest publisher of computer-related information and the leading global provider of information services on information technology. IDG was founded more than 25 years ago and now employs more than 8,500 people worldwide. IDG publishes more than 275 computer publications in over 75 countries (see listing below). More than 60 million people read one or more IDG publications each month.

Launched in 1990, IDG Books Worldwide is today the #1 publisher of best-selling computer books in the United States. We are proud to have received eight awards from the Computer Press Association in recognition of editorial excellence and three from *Computer Currents'* First Annual Readers' Choice Awards. Our best-selling *...For Dummies®* series has more than 30 million copies in print with translations in 30 languages. IDG Books Worldwide, through a joint venture with IDG's Hi-Tech Beijing, became the first U.S. publisher to publish a computer book in the People's Republic of China. In record time, IDG Books Worldwide has become the first choice for millions of readers around the world who want to learn how to better manage their businesses.

Our mission is simple: Every one of our books is designed to bring extra value and skill-building instructions to the reader. Our books are written by experts who understand and care about our readers. The knowledge base of our editorial staff comes from years of experience in publishing, education, and journalism — experience we use to produce books for the '90s. In short, we care about books, so we attract the best people. We devote special attention to details such as audience, interior design, use of icons, and illustrations. And because we use an efficient process of authoring, editing, and desktop publishing our books electronically, we can spend more time ensuring superior content and spend less time on the technicalities of making books.

You can count on our commitment to deliver high-quality books at competitive prices on topics you want to read about. At IDG Books Worldwide, we continue in the IDG tradition of delivering quality for more than 25 years. You'll find no better book on a subject than one from IDG Books Worldwide.

John Kilcullen
CEO
IDG Books Worldwide, Inc.

Steven Berkowitz
President and Publisher
IDG Books Worldwide, Inc.

Eighth Annual Computer Press Awards ≥1992

Ninth Annual Computer Press Awards ≥1993

Tenth Annual Computer Press Awards ≥1994

Eleventh Annual Computer Press Awards ≥1995

Dedication

Gina: For my family and friends, two-legged and four-legged, especially my parents, Louise and Nino, and my brothers, Pete and Joe. And to my first cat, Calico, who was really a tabby, and to the two geniuses, Bruce and Paul.

Paul: To my parents, Howard and Libby, who shaped my soul; my sister, Jodi, who nurtured my soul; my brothers Danny and Michael, who are always there; my wife, Carla, who makes it all so wonderful. And to my son, Luca, who those who love me should thank for teaching me to love and to look for more in life than work.

To my mentors, especially Bill Hornbuckle, Art Hurvitz, Quinton Rogers, Ryan Huxtable, and Margarethe Britton, who let me learn; to my colleagues, especially Mark Kittleson, Duncan Ferguson, Alice Wolf, David Bruyette, Roy Brenton Smith, Nicky Mastin, and Steve Moore, who let me grow; to my students, who taught me more than I ever hoped to teach them; to my staff and colleagues at the Veterinary Information Network and Pet Care Forum who live my dream daily; and to Gina, who truly wrote this book.

Authors' Acknowledgments

So many people contributed to this book we feel fortunate this isn't the Academy Awards, where the music starts and the pretty women come on stage to hustle us off before we can name them all.

Our first thanks must be to the many experts who read over our shoulders and made suggestions that helped us realize our dream of making *Cats For Dummies* a complete, cutting-edge reference that will improve the lives of cats and those who love them. William G. Porte, MBA, DVM, of Sacramento Veterinary Surgical Services, repeated his role from *Dogs For Dummies* as our lead technical reviewer and again brought his keen observations to bear on the text.

To date only two dozen board-certified feline practitoners are in the United States and Canada, and we are thankful to have had two of them review parts of this book: Margaret A. Scherk-Nixon, DVM, DABVP, of Cats Only in Vancouver, British Columbia, Canada's Veterinarian of the Year for 1997; and Alice M. Wolf, DVM, DACVIM, DABVP, of the Texas A&M University's College of Veterinary Medicine and one of two lead consultants for the Veterinary Information Network (VIN). Two of our VIN colleagues also contributed greatly: Monica M. Mastin, DVM, head of VIN database services, and Stuart W. Turner, DVM, head of the Pet Care Forum on America Online and an emergency-care practitioner at the Solano Pet Emergency Clinic in Cordelia, California.

Other veterinarians who helped us include David Bruyette, DVM, DACVIM, chief of staff of the VCA West Los Angeles Animal Hospital and the other lead consultant for VIN; James H. Sokolowski, DVM, Ph.D., Professional Services Manager, Waltham USA, Inc; Duncan Ferguson, VMD, PhD, DACVIM, DACVCP, Professor, Department of Veterinary Pharmacology and Physiology, the University of Georgia College of Veterinary Medicine; Roger Gfeller, DVM, DACVECC, chief of staff of the Veterinary Emergency Service, Inc., Fresno, California; Gary Landsberg, DVM, Doncaster Animal Clinic, Thornhill, Ontario; Ilana Reisner, DVM, Ph.D, DACVB of Ithaca, New York, and David Aucoin, DVM, DACVCP, Director, Veterinary Services, for Innovative Veterinary Diets. We need to acknowledge the assistance of the American Association of Feline Practitioners and the Academy of Feline Medicine, and the more than 4,500 members of the Veterinary Information Network, who through daily contributions of their expertise and experience to the VIN community online continue to shape our understanding of the medical and ethical challenges of caring for cats. Finally, a note of thanks to another important veterinarian, Paul's wife, Carla L. Weinberg, MS, DVM.

We also wish to thank Steve Aiken, the Pet Care Forum on America Online's resident feline behaviorist, and Michael Brim of the Cat Fanciers' Association, as well as researchers Janine Adams and Audrey Pavia. Kirsten Baitis, a student in the Veterinary School at U.C. Davis, was invaluable in helping us with the final stages of the manuscript.

The staff at IDG Books Worldwide has to have one of the biggest concentrations of cat lovers at any company in the world, led by Dummies Trade Press Vice President and Publisher Kathy Welton, who has a soft spot in her heart for all cats, but especially the Burmese. The unflappable Jennifer Ehrlich, who has an amazing double-coated cat, Charlie, was again the best project editor any authors could wish for, and cat lover Bill Barton did a fine job as copy editor. Others who deserve mention are Michelle Vukas, Jamie Klobuchar-Medgyesy, Ann Miller, Nickole J. Harris, Tammy Castleman, Sherry Gomoll, Brent Savage, Angie Hunckler, Elizabeth Cárdenas-Nelson, Pamela Emanoil, and Nancy Price. The contributions of illustrator Jay Gavron are second to none, and we're still smiling at Rich Tennant's "The 5th Wave" cartoons. Thanks to all those who contributed photographs, especially Dick Schmidt and Michael Brenton. We still can't believe our good fortune at having Lilian Jackson Braun write our foreword, and we can't thank her enough for her generosity.

We also would like to thank a few of our family and friends for their help: Carol Benjamin, Ann Cony, Peggy Conway, Gay Currier, Kerry Drager, Audrey Fitzgerald, Joan Frazzini, Peg Gavel, Robin Glass, Jan Haag, Marion Knoll, Carrie Peyton, Gene and Susan Lock, Stan and Louella Lourimore, Tonya Machen, Ellen O'Connor and Darryl Young, Morgan Ong, Bruce Rubin, Amy Shojai, Mordecai Siegal, and Kate, Sally, and Steven Spatafore. Thanks again to Robin Shapiro, proud father of Marissa, who kept backups of the chapters in progress on his hard drive and helped us find our ace attorney, Patricia Crown. Gina owes a great deal to her colleagues at *The Sacramento Bee,* especially Mort Saltzman, Bob Shallit, Terry Hennessy, Rick Nelson, and Tom Couzens, as well as to the folks at the Universal Press Syndicate, especially Bill Mitchell and Lee Salem.

Of course, we couldn't close without acknowledging the difference cats and other animals have made in our lives. They have led us every step of the way, teaching us some of the most significant of life's lessons, including the importance of unconditional love and the value of a really good afternoon nap.

Publisher's Acknowledgments

We're proud of this book; please send us your comments about it by using the IDG Books Worldwide Registration Card at the back of the book or by e-mailing us at feedback/dummies @idgbooks.com. Some of the people who helped bring this book to market include the following:

Acquisitions, Development, and Editorial

Project Editor: Jennifer Ehrlich

Acquisitions Editor: Kathleen Welton, Vice President and Publisher

Associate Permissions Editor: Heather H. Dismore

Copy Editor: William A. Barton

Technical Editor: William G. Porte, M.B.A., D.V.M.

Editorial Manager: Leah P. Cameron

Editorial Assistant: Ann Miller

Production

Project Coordinator: Sherry Gomoll

Layout and Graphics:
Elizabeth Cárdenas-Nelson, Angela F. Hunckler, Jane E. Martin, Brent Savage

Proofreaders: Henry Lazarek, Carrie Voorhis, Christine Berman, Rachel Garvey, Nancy Price, Rob Springer

Indexer: Sherry Massey

Special Help: Jay Gavron, Illustrator; Diana R. Conover, Dwight Ramsey, Darren Meiss, Michael D. Sullivan, Donna Love, Linda Stark

General and Administrative

IDG Books Worldwide, Inc.: John Kilcullen, CEO; Steven Berkowitz, President and Publisher

IDG Books Technology Publishing: Brenda McLaughlin, Senior Vice President and Group Publisher

Dummies Technology Press and Dummies Editorial: Diane Graves Steele, Vice President and Associate Publisher; Judith A. Taylor, Product Marketing Manager; Kristin A. Cocks, Editorial Director; Mary Bednarek, Acquisitions and Product Development Director

Dummies Trade Press: Kathleen A. Welton, Vice President and Publisher

IDG Books Production for Dummies Press: Beth Jenkins, Production Director; Cindy L. Phipps, Manager of Project Coordination, Production Proofreading, and Indexing; Kathie S. Schutte, Supervisor of Page Layout; Shelley Lea, Supervisor of Graphics and Design; Debbie J. Gates, Production Systems Specialist; Robert Springer, Supervisor of Proofreading; Debbie Stailey, Special Projects Coordinator; Tony Augsburger, Supervisor of Reprints and Bluelines; Leslie Popplewell, Media Archive Coordinator

Dummies Packaging and Book Design: Patti Sandez, Packaging Specialist; Lance Kayser, Packaging Assistant; Kavish + Kavish, Cover Design

♦

The publisher would like to give special thanks to Patrick J. McGovern, without whom this book would not have been possible.

Contents at a Glance

Table of Contents

Foreword

1, too, was once a dummy when it came to cats, believe it or not. How did I ever get to be 35 years old without ever having had a pet? It happens.

True, I liked cats. Friends' cats sat on my lap at cocktail parties. Strays followed me on the street. And in my apartment I had a Goldscheider porcelain figurine of a Siamese, almost life size. But no cat!

Then I received a Siamese kitten for a gift. I panicked! How does one take care of a cat? What do they . . . *do?* What am I supposed to . . . *do?* The first night with that tiny furry bundle under my roof . . . well . . . I slept not a wink.

I looked for cat-care books, but they all assumed I knew more than I did. Which end of the cat is the front? (Not really. I exaggerate, but not much.)

Somehow we muddled through, Koko and I. He was my first Koko. I adored him, and — if I may say so — he adored me. Since then, I have had a dynasty of Siamese, and I write mystery novels that fool readers into thinking I'm an expert on felines. I love them, that's all. I empathize with them: I know what they're thinking . . . they know what I'm thinking.

If only I had had a nice, easy-to-read, easy-to-understand book "way back then" when I was a dummy.

— Lilian Jackson Braun, Author of *The Cat Who...* Mystery Novels

Introduction

· ·

Welcome to *Cats For Dummies,* the most easy-to-use, up-to-date reference available on one of the world's most remarkable animal companions, the cat.

We wanted to start this book with an overview of what's in its pages, why you should buy the book, and how much of a difference its information can make in your life. As so often happens if you live with a cat, however, the cat had a better idea.

The cat in question is Paul's cat, PC, and she *always* has a better idea. So it came as no surprise to us that this book is no exception.

We started organizing what we wanted to say months ago in Paul's home office, the heart of the Veterinary Information Network, Inc., the world's largest online service for veterinary professionals and the content provider for the Pet Care Forum of America Online. A converted bedroom, Paul's office is a cluttered space with signs everywhere of three of the great loves of his life: animals, computers, and medicine. (Gina's home office, in another converted bedroom some 20 miles away, has a slightly different theme to its decor: animals, computers, and writing.)

In Paul's office, colorful fish zip around in the tank that accents one wall; a sophisticated ultrasound machine — with all the bells and whistles, please note — nestles between two computer desks on another wall. Add a fax machine, a pair of desktop computers, and usually a laptop or two. Files are everywhere: in stacks on the floor, in stacks on the desk, in file cabinets of all sizes and shapes. On the walls, pictures of the special people and pets in Paul's life bump against a few of the awards he has received for his contributions to the advancement of animal health and the veterinary profession. And, always, you see a can or two of Paul's drink of choice, Diet Coke, on the desk. (He drinks so much of the stuff that the company practically delivers it by the case, direct.)

On any ordinary day, Wes and Barney, the family's two terriers, wander at will, alternately begging for attention inside or barking outside at people walking along the parkway on the other side of the fence behind the house. In the next room, a crippled bird named Sunny, saved by Paul's veterinarian wife, Carla, amuses himself with toys and an astonishing repertoire of sounds.

That day, however, belonged to the cat.

With a cat's uncanny ability to know when something concerns her — or should — she was demanding our attention as we discussed the project and scribbled notes. She rubbed against our legs, purring and meowing, and then sat up on her haunches and waved her front paws at us. After that didn't work well enough for her purposes, she gathered herself and threw her sleek tabby body upward, landing in the middle of our paper. Her point finally made, she flopped down on the desktop and started to purr.

"Don't forget who's in charge here," she said, as clearly as if she could talk, her green eyes glimmering through half-closed lids.

We never have forgotten.

Cats love to be the center of attention, and Paul's cat, PC, is no exception.

What Cats Know . . . and What We Want You to Know

We wrote this book for your cat, true, but in an odd and certainly unfair twist of fate, your cat can't buy the book for himself. (Or maybe that's not so odd; after all, members of royalty never buy anything for themselves — that's what servants are for!)

Don't tell him this, but no cat can buy a book, much less read a book. Nor can a kitty make wise decisions regarding veterinary care, show you how to keep his claws in fine shape, or choose safe toys and equipment. He can't even tell you what you've done wrong with the litter box so it's just not the place to go when a cat has to . . . er, go.

He can't, but we can.

Understanding litter box problems is just the tip of the iceberg of things many of us don't know about our cats. Until very recently, cats have been sadly neglected concerning research into what keeps them healthy and what makes them tick, especially compared to the amount of attention given to other domesticated animals, such as the dog or the horse.

Reasons for this neglect exist, of course. Although cats, in their role as vermin killers, have been every bit as important to humankind over the centuries as any other of our animal partners, they've gone about their jobs in their own way and in their own style, as cats always do. Whereas horses were developed and trained to run fast, cut cattle, and pull heavy wagons, the cat caught rats and mice. Whereas dogs were developed and trained to fill a hundred jobs, from herding to hunting to guarding — plus a few modern adaptations, such as serving people with disabilities — the cat caught rats and mice.

They seemed to do fine on their own, these cats, slipping back and forth with ease across the line between wild and domesticated for hundreds of years. Cats have always had those among us who loved and admired their beauty, but others have also been uneasy with the cat's independence — to the point of hating them, in some cases. Others simply found the cat worthless and had no use for the animal.

In the study of health and behavior, unfortunately, this latter group was largely in control — until recently.

Welcome to the Age of the Cat!

Although you still hear about those who dislike cats, their voices aren't the dominant ones today. More people love cats, and are working to make the cat's life better than ever before, in areas ranging from important health studies to increased understanding of behavior, to new equipment designed to make living with a cat easier for both of you.

The cat is now the top pet in the United States. Some 60 million in number, the cat eclipsed the dog in popularity in the '80s and now holds a margin of popularity of more than 5 million. Cats hold their own as pets in other developed countries, as well.

Cat lovers old and new have one thing in common besides their love for their cats: They spend money. Pets are a $20 billion industry annually, and goods and services for cats make up a significant part of that figure. That kind of clout is fueling research into feline health and has manufacturers scrambling to get out products to serve this piece of the market.

As the pet industry has changed, so has the veterinary one. Fifty years ago, veterinary students were primarily men from rural backgrounds; now, the nation's veterinary schools are sending out graduates who come from primarily urban and suburban roots, and more of these graduates are women. This change mirrors the one in the larger population that's driving the interest in cats and changing the future of feline medicine, both in the research field and in practice. A growing number of veterinary practices are cats-only, and there is an association of veterinarians who specialize in feline care.

Taken as a whole, these changes suggest that the cat is going to reign supreme for a good long time, finally getting the attention so long deserved.

All we can say is . . . it's about time. And we're sure PC agrees.

Approaching Cat Ownership as an Informed Consumer

"Curiosity killed the cat" is a saying that has been around for years, but it's not curiosity that does in the vast majority of the millions of loving felines who die every year, some because they're homeless, others because of preventable health or behavior problems. Misinformation and unrealistic expectations are far bigger threats. A lot of myths are out there regarding cats — we dispel a few of them in Chapter 17 — and more are added every day, it seems.

You need to do your homework to avoid any surprises, and we've written *Cats For Dummies* to help you with exactly that task.

If, for example, you go into cat ownership with the sadly all-too-common belief that a cat is as easy to keep and almost as inexpensive as a houseplant, you're not going to be prepared for the costs of keeping a cat healthy — even though these costs can be quite reasonable. You're going to be surprised that your cat needs your love and attention, on a regular basis. And you're going to be shocked to find out that you need to put some effort into training your cat to avoid clawing your furniture and to use the litter box. All these surprises can easily be avoided, for the good of both you and your pet.

We want you to become a savvy consumer of feline-related goods, services, and information; to avoid falling in love with the kitten some children are peddling from a box at the flea market unless you can be sure the little scrap of fluff isn't ill; to avoid choosing *any* kitten or cat until you decide on some of the basic questions, such as longhaired or short, pedigreed or not, or active or relaxed in temperament.

We want you to know even more. The new focus on things feline is a wonderful thing, to be sure, but it also means that a lot of products are suddenly out there that may be nothing more than a waste of your money — and you need to know how to weed them out. You need to know the basics of nutrition to provide your pet with a healthy, well-balanced diet. And you need to understand the basics of litter box behavior so you can choose the products that work with your *cat's* sense of what's right (because a product that works for you but not for your pet is one that leaves you with both messes and resentment).

We want you to know it's worthwhile to take the time to learn about your cat, and about caring for your cat properly. You'll see why if you consider that a well-cared-for cat can be your loving companion for more than 15 years and that many cats live happily and healthily even beyond that milestone. These years are a gift; make them count!

Although cats offer years of love and companionship, many people put more research and effort into selecting a frozen dinner than they do into choosing the right cat and then caring for that animal properly. Your cat's love and companionship outlasts not only tonight's dinner but probably also your home computer and your car, both of which you probably researched thoroughly before buying.

Your cat may also be with you longer than a spouse, and that's truly a sobering thought. We can't help you with your marriage, but we can help you with your cat by telling you everything you need to know to make the relationship work for you both — and for many, many years.

A happy, healthy cat and a happy cat owner: We ask for no greater legacy for our work.

How This Book Is Organized

Cats For Dummies is divided into five parts. If you're looking for a cat, you may want to start at the beginning. If you already have a cat, you can skip around, checking out the chapters that address your needs at any given time. Are you moving? Check out the chapter on cats and traveling. Have you taken a homeless and pregnant cat into your home? You want to review the parts not only on care of the mama cat and her new babies but also on how to raise those babies to be good pets, as well as how to find the right homes your angels deserve when the time comes for them to leave the nest.

We've packed so much information into *Cats For Dummies,* we're guessing you're probably going to want to read it all in time. How else are you going to find out just what about catnip makes some kitties crazy, how and why cats purr, and what you need to be careful about if you're pregnant and your cat uses a litter box? All this information's in *Cats For Dummies* — and more!

No matter in what order you choose to read it, here are the basics of how this book's organized.

Part I: Starting to Think Cat

Although every cat is special and certainly unique, some are a little more distinctive than others. Many pedigreed cats fall into this category, such as the short-legged Munchkin, the hairless Sphinx, or the Scottish Fold (the cat with creased ears). Although the overwhelming majority of pet cats don't come with papers, we want to give you enough information about those who do so that you know what you may be missing.

Beyond these truly distinctive — some would call them strange — breeds, however, is plenty else to consider. Some cats are more active than others, some more talkative, some more relaxed. In coat, you need to think about hundreds of beautiful colors and combinations, not only in terms of long-haired and short. (Don't forget to think, too, how that beautiful fur may look on your carpet or favorite sweater!) You also need to know a little about where you're going to be looking for a cat — from breeders, shelters, pet stores, or friends and neighbors — so that you have your best chance at getting the right pet, one who's healthy and well socialized.

In this part, too, you find out about conducting further research on your own with our concise guide to feline cyberspace resources.

Part II: Bringing a Cat or Kitten into Your Life

After you know "what" you're looking for — for example, an adult, a spayed female, a short-haired cat from a reputable shelter — you're going to need help finding the "who" — that one special cat who's going to be your pet for the rest of her life.

In this part you find the information you need to make that choice. We include tests to help you pick out the best prospects — healthy, active, and outgoing kittens and cats. From such a pool, you can truly let your heart be your guide. Pick one — or maybe two!

We also include information on how to get your new relationship started right. How to manage introductions between your new pet and the other residents of your home, two-legged and four-legged; how to ensure your house isn't full of health hazards for an inquisitive kitten; and how to show your pet in a positive and loving way where scratching and relieving himself are acceptable.

In this section, too, we offer advice on the best cat gear available. Shop until you drop? You bet! Your cat is sure to thank you for choosing among these top products.

Part III: Maintaining a Happy, Healthy Cat

Taking care of your cat involves more than leaving out a bowl of food. In this part, we offer the latest information on good nutrition and preventive care, as well as what you need to know to spot and understand the most-common cat health problems and to select and work with the veterinarian who's right for both you and your pet.

Even as we tell you how to care for your kitten's special health needs, we give you the information you need to make your cat's senior years comfortable and happy. Helping you — and your children — through the difficult process of saying good-bye is part of this section, too.

Part IV: Living Happily with Your Cat

In this part, you find guidelines to help you cope with behavior problems that drive pet lovers crazy — and, unfortunately, send many cats on a one-way trip to the shelter. Save your carpets, your upholstery, your houseplants, and your sanity with our guide to solving feline behavior problems. And because training needn't all be about *problems,* we offer some tips on getting your cat to perform a couple basic tricks. Who knows? Your cat may even enjoy it!

From reading feline body language to health concerns to fighting, we've got the answers you need. We cover the basics of breeding, too.

What about feline activities? More people than you realize travel with their pets — and not just when they move (although we cover that, too). If you prefer to leave your pet at home while you're away, we give you tips on ensuring that he's well cared for in your absence. And what about cat shows? In this section, we offer all you need to know to start enjoying them and to start participating, even if your cat's *not* pedigreed.

Part V: The Part of Tens

From disaster preparedness to common household dangers to the best things ever said about cats, we've saved some of the very best for last. This information's all good reading — and even better with a purring cat in your lap!

Icons Used in This Book

Every *...For Dummies* book has little pictures in the margins — we call them *icons* — to help you navigate through the book, and *Cats For Dummies* is no exception. We are different in that most of *our* icons are unique to this *...For Dummies* book, and more adorable than you may find in others (except maybe *Dogs For Dummies*). Here's a rundown on what each icon means:

You don't *have* to read the information next to the *...For Dummies* guy, but we really think you should anyway. You see a lot of him in the health sections especially, where we want to give you in-depth information but also offer you the chance to skip over it and still get a pretty good basic understanding of whatever topic you're looking to find. If you're in a hurry, give him a pass. But come back, please, for that little bit of extra information. We think you're going to find it's worthwhile.

This icon flags things that are especially useful for making life with your cat easier or making your pet happier and healthier. It highlights time- and money-savers, too!

Your cat wants you to read very carefully every word next to this icon. That's because this icon marks some of the best products or services available for cats — and for those who love them.

Your cat wants you to read very carefully every word next to this icon. That's because this icon marks some of the best products or services available for cats — and for those who love them.

For related information or for a more detailed discussion of the topic, you want to follow these paw prints to another spot in the book.

We've put information that's especially amusing or intriguing in a lot of places, and we use this little symbol, the catnip of our icon family, to point out those cool cat facts for you so you're sure not to miss them.

If we think something's so important that it deserves restating or summarizing, this icon goes in to make sure you don't jump over that information. If you see this little flag, know it marks information we think is worth reading more than once.

This icon denotes some of the most common mistakes cat owners make, along with tips for avoiding them.

Some Final Words

In addition to advising people about their pets, Gina makes her living as an editor, so she's pretty fussy about the "correct" use of language. In one little area, however, she disagrees with the experts: the use of the pronoun "it" for referring to animals.

Paul agrees.

We don't like the use of "it" to describe our animal companions — and what's more, we refuse to use it! A chair is an "it." A cat tree is an "it." A car is an "it," although we can think of at least one that's named after a beautiful big cat — the Jaguar. (And don't forget the Cougar or the Lynx!) Animals, however, are living, thinking, loving beings: "hims" and "hers." And so are they alternately described in this book.

The use of "him" or "her" in any given reference applies to both genders, unless specifically noted otherwise.

How to Reach Us

We invite you to tell us about *your* cat and your tales of living with a feline companion. You can read the exploits of Gina's animals — as well as up-to-date information on animal health and behavior — as part of her weekly column, "Pet Connection," which is provided to newspapers by the Universal Press Syndicate and also appears every week in America Online's Pet Care Forum, of which Paul's Veterinary Information Network is in charge. (The keyword PETS takes you there if you're an AOL subscriber.) You can e-mail us at Giori@aol.com, but "snail mail" is just as nice to get, at the following address:

Gina Spadafori/Paul D. Pion, DVM, DACVIM
Pet Connection/Pet Care Forum
5714 Folsom Blvd., No. 211
Sacramento, CA 95819

Part I
Starting to Think Cat

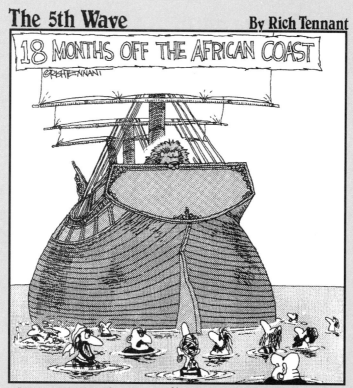

The 5th Wave   By Rich Tennant

18 MONTHS OFF THE AFRICAN COAST

@RICHTENNANT

"Let me bring him on board', you said. 'He's so cute and cuddly, he'll make a nice mascot for the trip home'. Well, <u>nice</u> mascot he's turned out to be!!"

In this part . . .

This part explains everything you need to know about selecting the perfect cat or kitten for your family. Thinking of a pedigreed cat? We tell you everything you need so you can start looking into not only the most popular breeds but also the more unusual, from evaluating personalities to finding the right breeder. The majority of people won't be getting a pedigreed pet, however, and we've got plenty of information for you if you're among them, including how to evaluate the various sources for cats and kittens.

Chapter 1

A New Appreciation of the Cat

• •

In This Chapter

▶ A surge in popularity

▶ Common misconceptions

▶ Who should have a cat — and who shouldn't

• •

Forget ancient Egypt, where the cat was honored as a god. The Golden Age of the Cat is now. More is written about cats and said about cats (and in a modern twist, posted on the Web about cats!) today than in all the generations before. Cats are the subject of musicals, of research into their diseases, of business reports that tally the billions of dollars spent to keep them healthy, clean, and amused. In the technology-heavy and time-short societies of the developed countries, more people are discovering what poets, artists, and cat-worshippers have known all along: The cat isn't just "dog lite" but is an affectionate, beautiful companion in her own right.

The cat is civilized — but never fully. As the velvety paws of a cat hide her razor-sharp claws, the sleek body, purring in contentment, conceals the wild spirit that lives in every cat ever born. The cat was given to us so that we may caress the tiger, as the saying goes, and on some level, that must surely be part of the charm. Our lives today are so far from what we were once — a people involved in the daily struggle for survival, hunters and seekers, both predator and prey. If we're haunted by our primeval memories still, our cats are not. They live theirs every day. And we share those memories a little whenever we welcome cats into our homes.

The idea is both exhilarating and reassuring.

The feline body is a perfect package of grace and symmetry, of function creating a form that has inspired humankind for generations. For a look at the feline body — and how to tell if things aren't as they should be — see Chapter 9.

Although dogs and horses, cattle, pigs, and poultry — and even tomato plants and roses — have changed enormously in our hands, the cat has not. The cat has recently expanded in physical variety — different coat colors and types, different ear shapes and body types — but all such variations are still quite definitely *cats,* more alike than different. Look at the tabby-striped African Wild Cat — thought to be the ancestor of our domestic cats — and you see an animal much like the one purring in your lap.

The cat chose domestication on his own terms and chose our companionship the same way. We're only now starting to understand fully what a wonderful gift we've been offered.

From Humble Beginnings: How Cats Became So Popular

As with the cats of ancient Egypt, changes in the way we live have prompted the cat's boom in popularity. Whereas early humans found the pack instincts of dogs useful from the beginning — both for hunting and, later, for tending flocks — the cat was of little use to humankind until our ancestors started cultivating and storing grain. The earliest evidence of domesticated cats dates from about 6,000 years ago — as opposed to 12,000 for dogs — but the most telling indications of the presence of domestic cats are about 4,000 years old.

The cat then became honored — even worshipped — for a skill we sometimes wish had been lost along the way: hunting. Before the cat stepped in, rodents had a fine, fat time in the grain storage bins. The cat's hunting prowess evened the score a great deal and opened the door for cats from Africa to take over the entire world, carried as useful workers on grain-laden ships throughout the ancient world. Farmers everywhere were grateful for their aid.

Although you still find cats plying their trade as rodent-killers on farms all around the world, the cat's greater role today is strictly as a companion. And in this, too, the cat excels.

As important as the cat's hunting skills were to our ancestors, today the sight of a half-eaten bird or mouse brought in as a gift is appreciated by few — and condemned by those who point to the cat as a factor in the falling numbers of songbirds. In Chapter 17, we set the record straight regarding a popular myth about cats and hunting.

Two things have changed in the developed countries to make the cat's rise in popularity inevitable.

First, more of us are living in smaller quarters — in apartments, in condominiums, in houses on smaller lots — than ever before. Although such conditions aren't conducive to the keeping of dogs — even though many people make it work, anyway — they're in no way a deterrent to living with a cat, especially an indoors-only one. Cats quite happily share the same environments people choose, living in city apartments and on farms, in cold climates and in warm ones, in small houses and in mansions. Marvelously adaptable, cats handle being alone much better than dogs do.

Second, many of us have little time or money for a pet — but a greater need for companionship than ever before. As children, we need someone to listen to us. As young adults, we delay starting a family — or choose never to start one at all. In our middle years, we're nearly pulled apart by the demands of job and family. Our older years may be more active than ever before but can also be lonely, spent far from our children.

Nonjudgmental listener and ever-affectionate companion, the cat makes a difference in many lives — and with relatively little investment of time and money.

Truly, the cat has found a niche again — this time, to stay.

Thank you, Edward Lowe

One other thing made the transition of the cat from pest control to pet possible — or, rather, one person: Edward Lowe, the inventor of Kitty Litter.

Prior to Lowe's brainstorm, cats either went outside to relieve themselves — as many still do — or went in boxes filled with sand, soil, or sawdust, none of them a very practical solution for easy clean-up and smell control.

In 1947, cat-lover Kaye Draper of Cassopolis, Michigan, sought sawdust for her cat's box from a local business. The firm also sold kiln-dried, granulated clay for cleaning up grease spills. Edward Lowe, son of the shop's owner, suggested that the woman take home some of the absorbent clay instead, and an industry was born.

After she came back for more, Lowe decided he was onto something. He put the clay in five-pound bags, wrote "Kitty Litter" on the front,

and suggested to a local store owner that he sell the bags of clay for 65 cents — at a time when sand went for a penny a pound. The owner laughed, so Lowe then changed strategies: "Give it away," he said, "and see how it does."

Kitty Litter made Lowe, who died in 1995, a millionaire many times over. The sales of cat-box fillers run between $600 and $700 million a year, according to *The New York Times,* with about a third of that income going for the brands Lowe founded.

For more on cat-box fillers — how to choose them and how to use them — see Chapters 6 and 12.

By the way, the name of Kaye Draper's cat somehow escaped being recorded for posterity. We think a little credit is due to him (or her), too.

Frances and Richard Lockridge knew how important cats can be to children when they observed in *The Quotable Cat* (Contemporary Books): "No cat has ever said, 'I love you,' except to the sensitive ears of children." We think many cats have expressed their love — but sometimes adults aren't listening well enough to hear them. For more wonderful cat quotes, see Chapter 22.

Some Common Misconceptions about Cats — and the Facts

Even as cats reign supreme at the top of the popularity charts, a lot of people still harbor some misconceptions about them. Many of these people would probably enjoy having a cat in their lives if they'd only open their minds and their hearts a little.

Most of the ideas about what cat's *aren't* come from comparisons to what dogs *are,* and, of course, that's not the right way to look at things. Other ideas about cats apply to those who're mostly outdoor, or semiferal. A cat who's well-socialized from birth and closely bonded with his human companions is another animal entirely.

Remember, too, that what's a fault in the eyes of some is a virtue in the eyes of others. The overexuberant affection of a bouncy big dog isn't for everyone, believe us.

For more cat myths — and the truth — see Chapter 17.

"All cats are cold fish"

No doubt about it — cats pick their moments. As they have from the first, cats choose the companionship of humans on their own terms.

Although some cat critics claim that the animals are in it only for the food, any cat lover knows otherwise. Cats are "in it" for the warmth, too. Laps, beds, and even the tops of TVs and computer monitors offer many opportunities for taking nice long naps, which cats spend most of their time doing.

Oh, but it's more than that. Cats consider the people in their life as family and show it in many ways. If they bring you prey, they're providing for you. If they gently knead you with their paws while purring, they're treating you as they did their mothers. If they play with you, they're treating you as littermates or other cat pals. If they kiss you, don't kid yourself — it's legit!

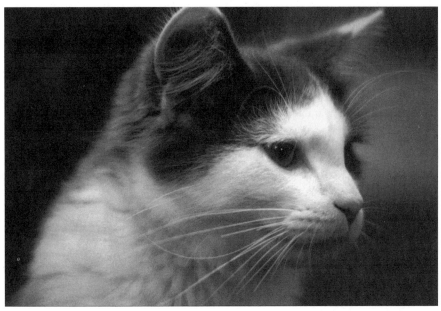

Though they are quite affectionate, cats also need time to meditate.

Grayheart — Photo courtesy of Randy Anderson.

Cats need their contemplative moments, of course, as do we all. A cat needs time to think — about how much she loves you . . . or how tasty that little mousy would be. But anyone who has lived with a cat will vouch for the sincerity and constancy of their affection.

People who don't like cats often complain that a cat chooses *their* lap out of a whole room full of cat lovers who'd love to offer theirs. This behavior is often given as an example of the independent — or even malicious — nature of the cat. The truth is that something else is at work: Cats feel threatened by direct stares and avoid strangers who take such liberties. In a room full of cat lovers and one cat hater, probably only one person *isn't* looking invitingly at the cat — and that's the one who gets the cat's vote.

"Cats love places, not people"

Well documented stories abound of cats traveling hundreds — even thousands — of miles to return to an old home after moving. This amazing behavior leads many people to believe that cats prefer places to people. Sadly, the same belief prompts some to leave their cats behind if they move, figuring that the animals are happier at the old house and hoping the new residents take them in.

Most of these abandoned cats join the sorry ranks of the ferals or are taken to the shelter to be euthanized.

That cats are very territorial and mark their own property certainly is true — they even mark *you* with their scent, as they rub against your legs, hands, or face. Their territorial behaviors don't mean they prefer places to people, but they do suggest that cats have a hard time relating to the humans they love in the context of a new home — and may try to find you in your old house.

Your cat loves you just as much in your new home as in your old one — but he needs time to adapt.

Moving a cat to a new home requires planning, patience, and care. For information on how to make the move work for you both, see Chapter 15.

"Cats can take care of themselves"

Unquestionably, cats are easy-keepers. But anyone who adopts a cat thinking that cats are like houseplants, just furrier, is in for a big surprise. Kittens and cats seek and need attention and affection. They also need both preventive and routine care for any number of common ailments. Behavior problems such as litter-box avoidance are more common than most people think. To care for your cat well, you need a few basic supplies, a high-quality diet, and a veterinarian you know well enough to ask the questions you need answers to if problems arise.

Although cats do need care, they are still low maintenance compared to a lot of other pets. Cats are wonderful pets for people who work, people who travel, and people who just want the easygoing companionship a cat can provide. Your cat always keeps up his end of the bargain — make sure that you keep up yours.

Cats are arguably the most easy-going, adaptable, and inexpensive pets you can choose, but they do have their own special needs. Your responsibility is to protect your cat and provide him with the care and love he needs. In return, you have a beautiful, loving companion for many, many years.

Can You Have a Cat If You Have Allergies?

Even as more people than ever before have come to appreciate cats, one group of cat lovers keeps its distance — and wishes it didn't have to. That's because one of the biggest barriers to keeping a cat is allergies. More people are more allergic to cats than to dogs, and cat allergies are oftentimes more severe as well. For people — and especially children — with asthma, cat allergies can be life-threatening.

The first thing you need to know about allergies is that the *fur* isn't what causes the problem; it's an element called *Fel D1* found in cat saliva and deposited on skin and fur when a cat grooms. This allergen becomes part of the *dander* — flakes of skin and secretions and saliva that a cat spreads wherever he wanders and that become airborne as he's petted, jumps, or shakes.

The second thing you need to know relates to the first: Because the allergen-laden skin flakes are what cause the problems, a hypoallergenic cat is not possible. Cats with little or no fur can't help you, allergists say — even though some breeders of cats such as the hairless Sphinx or the lightly furred Cornish and Devon Rexes insist otherwise.

Still, some people live with both cats and allergies, and if you're considering doing so — or struggling with the situation already — find an allergist who doesn't greet you with, "First, find new homes for your pets." In some cases, for some people, that unfortunately becomes the ultimate — and only — resolution of the problem. But giving up your cat needn't be the starting point for attacking animal allergies. It's your life, after all.

Here are some other tips for living with cats and allergies:

- ✔ **Don't neglect your other allergies.** Working with an allergist to get them under control may give you enough "breathing room" to make life with a cat bearable. Remember always that allergies and asthma are serious health problems, not to be taken lightly.

- ✔ **Establish your bedroom as an "allergy-free zone."** More than one-third of our lives is spent sleeping, and so making that time less stressful for the body is very important. Close off your bedroom and reduce dust-collecting surfaces by removing carpets and rugs, wall hangings, stuffed animals, and collectibles from the room. Invest in an air cleaner and keep air ducts and ceiling fans clean. Banish feather pillows and down comforters. Use zippered, dustproof covers on the mattress and pillows. Combat dust mites by washing bedding frequently in hot water.

  Make the bedroom completely off-limits to pets at all times. Although there's not a pet lover alive who doesn't enjoy a purring cat on the bed, keeping the bedroom "allergy-free" is probably a necessary compromise for allergy sufferers.

- ✔ **Try to limit exposure to other allergens.** Avoid cleaning solutions, aerosol products, cigarette smoke, and strong perfumes and consider using a mask while doing yard work and housework, especially at the height of the pollen season. Better yet: Get someone else to mow the lawn, do the vacuuming, and clean the litter box. Again, keeping *all* allergies under control can help your body handle your cat more easily.

✔ **Keep your pets clean and well-groomed.** The best situation is for a nonallergic member of the family to take over these pet-care chores. Weekly bathing of your cat in clear water is a must — it keeps down the dander levels. Add soap if your cat needs a real bath, but it's not necessary for allergen control — clear water is fine. Some commercial preparations claim to keep the dander levels downs, and more than a few people swear by them, which makes them worth experimenting with to see if they can help you.

Give your cat a bath? Are we crazy to suggest it? Check out Chapter 7 for tips on how to get kitty clean — without getting clawed.

Hope is in the air, along with cat dander. Researchers at Johns Hopkins University School of Medicine report promising results in recent trials of a new vaccine, called Allervax Cat, that reduces symptoms of cat allergies faster and requires fewer injections than standard allergy shots. The vaccine is predicted to become available commercially starting in 1998. Ask your allergist!

The Indoor versus Outdoor Controversy

With the evolution of the cat from semi-wild hunter to loving companion animal has come a change not only in how cats are loved but also where cats are kept. Increasingly, more cats are living indoors.

Still, no matter how easy and odor-free litter boxes can be, some people refuse to deal with them. Add to these folks the ones who can't believe a cat can be happy unless he runs free, and you've got half of one of the hottest controversies among cat owners:

Should cats be kept exclusively indoors, or should cats be permitted outside?

The subject is so hot that almost all reputable breeders and an increasing number of shelters and rescue groups refuse to place a cat with someone who does *not* promise — in writing — to keep the animal exclusively in-doors. With some breeds, this restriction is imperative: Imagine the tiny, nearly furless Devon Rex or the naked Sphynx trying to survive in the outdoors!

The truth, however, is that all cats are living dangerously if you allow them to go in and out at will. With correct diet and preventive care, an indoor cat can easily live for 15 to 20 years — or more. A cat with outdoor privileges is lucky to live as long, although many exceptions do exist, of course. Here's a list of the things that can "do in" the outdoor kitty:

Kelsey and Tim — Photo courtesy of Linda Stark.

You must
determine
whether
your cat
should live
indoors or
outdoors —
or both!

- ✔ **Cars.** Cats can be hit, of course, but cars also present a danger even when parked. Heat-loving kitties crawl up into the warm engine and can be seriously injured — or killed — if someone starts the car again while the cat is still there.

- ✔ **Dogs.** Some dogs are gleeful cat-killers, and woe to the cat who wanders into the territory of one of them. Some mean-spirited people even encourage their dogs to attack cats — and let the animals off the leash to do it!

- ✔ **Coyotes.** A well-fed cat is a tasty temptation to wild predators such as coyotes. And you don't need to live in a rural area: Coyotes have been found even in Brooklyn and are common in many other urban areas.

- ✔ **Poisons.** From antifreeze puddles to garden chemicals to rat poison (in baits or the stomach of dead vermin) to plants, an outdoor cat can easily get a lethal dose of something he wouldn't be as easily exposed to indoors. (Risks exist for indoor cats, too. Chapters 5 and 21 tell you how to avoid them.)

- ✔ **Disease.** Feline leukemia, feline immunodeficiency virus, and feline infectious peritonitis are three of the contagious and often lethal diseases your cat can pick up from other cats — through fighting or mating, primarily. And speaking of fighting, outdoor cats spend a lot of their time defending their turf — and you spend a lot of your time and money taking them to the veterinarian to patch up their bite wounds and abscesses. (More about infectious diseases is in Chapter 10.)

> ✔ **People.** Some people hate cats and go out of their way to hurt them. Others — such as gardeners — feel justified taking action against cats who foul flower beds and vegetable gardens. Also a threat are those who steal cats to sell for biomedical research. These people all pose a grave danger to your pet.

Enough accidental and deliberate threats are out there to make keeping your cat inside seem like a very good idea. But consider things, too, from the angle of *your* responsibility. Are you really being fair to your neighbors if you let your cat relieve himself in their yards because you don't want to deal with a litter box? If your cat carries a disease such as feline leukemia, is letting him out to infect other pets the right thing for you to do? And if you haven't spayed or neutered your pet, doesn't allowing her (or him) out to breed make you partially responsible for the surplus kittens and cats killed by the millions each year?

We leave the answers up to you and to your conscience.

As for the other question of whether cats can be happy living an indoors-only life, the answer is a resounding "Yes!" Kittens raised indoors become cats who don't miss the outdoors, and with patience, you can convert even grown cats. Toys, scratching posts, indoor gardens, and screened patios or balconies all make the indoor cat's life special — as may the addition of a second cat (or even a dog) for companionship.

For more on what you need to keep a cat happy indoors, see Chapter 6.

Chapter 2
Narrowing the Choices

In This Chapter

▶ Kitten or cat? Male or female? Longhaired or short?

▶ Should you consider a pedigreed cat?

▶ Characteristics by breed

▶ The not-so-ordinary everyday cat

▶ A guide to feline cyberspace resources

You've taken everything into account: Your home. Your time. Your finances. A cat is in your future, beyond a doubt, but what *kind* of cat? As you picture your living room, do you see a docile Persian on the couch, lush coat gleaming as the sunlight hits it? Do you picture an active Abyssinian, giving you a brief but imperious look from a perch high atop a bookshelf a split-second before executing a perfect leap to the top of the hutch? Or perhaps you see a nonpedigreed — a calico, perhaps — with a temperament somewhere in between, her tail held high in the universal cat greeting: "Hi there. Adore me."

But wait! You have more to consider. Before you get to imagine Your Perfect Cat, you must determine whether the "instant" variety of pet — a grown cat — would work better for your lifestyle than would a kitten, no matter how adorable. Before you consider breed, or color, you must consider the issue of fur: long or short? And what about gender? Do females make better pets, or do males?

The decisions you make must keep for a very long time. The cats themselves pay the price for wrong spur-of-the-moment decisions — just check out any shelter for proof.

As serious as that thought is, remember that choosing a feline companion is also a great deal of fun. You get to see oodles of beautiful cats, play with adorable kittens, and consider the incredible variety of the world's most easy-going, adaptable, and ever-more-popular companion.

Pedigreed or not, grown cat or kitten, whatever gender, fur length, color, or variety you choose, we want you to be in love with your cat for years to come. So read on.

After you decide what kind of cat or kitten you're looking for, you want to be just as deliberate about choosing a place to get your new pet and in picking out the very animal who's right for the life you're leading. We discuss breeders, shelters, rescue groups, and other sources in Chapter 3, and hints for picking out the right kitten or cat — including temperament tests and health checks — you find in Chapter 4.

Kitten or Cat — Which Is a Better Choice for You?

When people think about adding a cat to their lives, they seem to automatically think "kitten." And why not? A kitten seems to make perfect sense, a little fluffball who'll grow into your household and your heart. For some people, though, an adult cat is a better option. And even if you're perfectly set up for a kitten, you ought to consider an adult as well, for many wonderful pets exist among their ranks, and most will never get a chance to show how perfect they can be.

Don't rule out either before you consider each fairly.

Everyone loves kittens!

Even people who profess to dislike cats can't look at a kitten without saying "awwwwwww." Baby animals are all adorable, but kittens seem to have something special going for them. Maybe it's those large eyes, following every movement intently. The oversized ears, twitching to and fro. The playfulness, chasing and pouncing on everything that moves, be it your fingertip or a piece of kibble batted across the linoleum. The tousled fur a kitten can't quite seem to groom into the sleekness every adult cat considers her duty to maintain. A kitten is all these things — and more.

What many people don't think about as they're falling in love is that a kitten can be a lot of work and aggravation — and expense in some cases, because a kitten seems to use nearly all a cat's nine lives, which means you may end up seeing the nice people at the emergency veterinary clinic a time or two in the first year. With a kitten, you also need to put more effort into training, from making sure the tiny baby understands what's expected regarding the litter box to helping your kitten learn to stay off the counters. You also need to kitten-proof your home — or keep your baby confined in a safe part of the house whenever you're not watching him — and then spend months during which, every day, you're picking your little tiger off the drapes, off the kids, off the back of the couch, or off your slippers every time you walk down the hall.

For tips on "kitten-proofing" your home and training your kitten to stay off counters and use the litter box, see Chapter 5.

A kitten may be a poor choice for families with very young children or for someone who's handicapped by advanced age or illness. For all their spunk, kittens are fragile and may accidentally get hurt by young children who don't understand the concept of "gentle." Similarly, a kitten isn't the best choice for anyone who's a little unsteady on his feet or isn't able to chase or otherwise keep up with an energetic feline baby.

On the other hand, a kitten can be a dream come true to a family with older, more-responsible children, or a source of delightful amusement to an active older adult. You just need to look carefully at your living situation and consider the problems and pleasures a kitten will bring.

Finally, consider the matter of time. An adult cat does quite well on her own alone in the house while you work — as long as you provide her with diversions (although most of the time she's sleeping anyway). A kitten needs your time — for raising her and for watching over her to keep her out of trouble.

Adult cat considerations

Adult cats offer some compelling advantages and few disadvantages — the most serious disadvantage being simply that they aren't as "baby cute" as kittens!

Kittens get away with all their endearing goofiness because they measure way off the adorability scale, but if you suspect you're going to get tired of having your feet attacked, if you worry about your children not being gentle enough, or if you don't want to be figuring out what your little baby is into every second of the day and night, an adult cat is a better option for you. If you adopt an adult cat, you know exactly what you're getting. Body type, coat, and eye color are set. Laid-back or active, quiet or vocal, cuddly or demanding, an adult cat has already settled into his own persona. These considerations may not be as important in a pedigreed cat, because you know, based on your kitten's background and the breeder's knowledge and reputation, what your kitten is likely grow into in terms of body type, coat color, and temperament. But in a nonpedigreed kitten, these qualities are really anybody's guess. If you want to make sure that you're getting, say, a mellow pet, choose a cat beyond the ants-in-his-pants kitten stage. (More on pedigreed cats later in this chapter.)

The easy care and generous affection of adult cats make them perfect pets for people for whom walking dogs would be difficult or impossible. And study after study confirms the importance of a cat in the lives of those who feel isolated by age or disabilities.

One of the most compelling reasons to adopt an adult cat is that adults have little chance of getting a second chance after they hit the shelter, no matter how healthy, beautiful, and well-mannered they are. Kittens are so adorable they're hard to pass up, and so many people never even look at the cages of adult cats when they're at the shelter.

The possible disadvantage of adopting an adult cat is that you may be choosing a pet with behavioral problems — not using a litter box, for example. A good shelter, rescue group, or breeder practices full disclosure of any known health or behavior problems with the animals up for adoption. Remember, however, that many animals are given up for behavior problems that can be resolved or aren't their fault — such as the cat who's looking at a filthy litter box every day and decides to do his business elsewhere.

Litter box problems are one of the top reasons adult cats are taken to a shelter. Although keeping a cat who refuses to use a litter box is certainly frustrating, the problem isn't incurable. To understand why a cat avoids the litter box and to set up a retraining program to correct the problem, see Chapter 13.

An adult cat's personality may be set, but his affections aren't — a grown cat bonds with you just as tightly as a kitten does. We think that adult cats are even more likely to appreciate you for taking them in!

Most people — maybe even you — still choose a kitten over a cat; such is the power of packaging. But we want to make sure that you aren't automatically excluding some wonderful pets. Look at kittens, sure, but check out the cats, too. Strike a blow against ageism! We think you get brownie points for adopting an animal who has everything going for her — except kittenhood. Adopting an adult cat is also a great time- and money-saver.

She-Kitty, He-Kitty, Which One's Better?

You're not going to get a definitive answer out of us on this one, even if we had one, which we don't. Males and females make equally good pets, under one very important condition: *Altering.*

Male or female, a cat who is what the experts call *whole* or *intact* — in other words, fully equipped to reproduce — is a royal pain to live with. When females are "in season" — which happens several times a year, for a couple weeks at a time — they're yowly escape artists who attract noisy suitors from miles around. Some people think males are even worse. By the time they're sexually mature, they begin *spraying* — marking territory with a special pheromone-spiked urine with a smell that's not only foul but also nearly impossible to eradicate. They're also roamers and fighters.

Altering goes a long way toward eliminating spraying, but more is involved in curing this disagreeable behavior. For the lowdown on this smelly problem, see Chapter 13. What's involved in *altering* — commonly known as *spaying* or *neutering* — a cat? The answer's in Chapter 14.

The experts — even reputable breeders who keep intact cats for their breeding programs — all agree that neutering is the key to a cat's being a good pet, no matter the gender. An important contribution those involved in the sport of showing cats have made is to ensure that animals who can no longer breed can still compete — in classes for *alters*. This aspect of showing is wonderfully progressive and supportive of those who like to show their lovely cats but not breed them. (For more on showing cats, see Chapter 16.)

After cats are altered, is one gender then a better pet than the other? The answer depends on whom you ask. Some people believe males are a little more outgoing; others suggest that females are smarter. (We got into an argument over that one after one of us — not Paul — snorted "of course!" And then we each came up with examples of smart males and outgoing females, the latter group including Paul's cat, PC.)

Despite Paul's interest in computers, "PC" doesn't stand for "Personal Computer" or even "Politically Correct." It's short for "Prayer Cat," and it comes from the tabby's endearing habit of sitting up on her haunches and "praying" for what she wants, holding her front paws together before her. (Check out PC's photo in this book's introduction.)

Perhaps the biggest reason some people prefer one gender over another we can sum up by using the word "always" — they've *always* had males (or females), have *always* been happy with their choices, and see no reason to change.

If you're thinking about adopting a pedigreed kitten, you may not have a choice: Males may be all that the breeder is offering for sale, especially if the breed is rare or in development. That's because the females are held back to remain part of the breeding stock or shared only with those the breeder believes are willing to show and breed the kitten as she recommends.

Both male and female cats make good pets, and we can't really steer you in one way or another. If you have a personal preference, go with it. If not, make all your other decisions and then go with the kitten that best fits your criteria, male or female.

Let the Fur Fly

We need to get one thing straight up front: Almost all cats shed. The "almost" is there to apply to those cats who haven't any fur — such as the Sphynx, who still manages to carry a little down that rubs off on your clothes.

Cats can have three kinds of hair in their coats — down, awn, and guard. The *down* is the shortest, finest and softest hair. The *awn* is the coarsest, and the *guard* (sometimes called the *primary hairs)* is the longest. Not all cats have all three varieties. The Sphynx, as just noted, has only down hairs, and few of these. The Cornish Rex has only awn and down. The awn hairs are usually shorter than the guard hairs (and longer than the down), but when awn and guard hairs are the same length, as in the Russian Blue, the cat is called *double coated.*

Some cats, such as the kinky-furred Rexes, shed very little. Some longhaired cats shed a lot — or seem to, because the hair they drop is longer. Even the ordinary garden-variety domestic shorthair is going to lose enough fur to drive the overly fastidious person nuts. If you really can't stand the thought of cat fur on your sofa, your sweater, or even in your food from time to time, give this cat thing some serious thought.

Are you allergic to cat fur? The chances are good that you're really allergic to something else. For what that may be, and for strategies on coping with cats and allergies, see Chapter 1.

In considering a cat's coat, think about three things: aesthetics, fur levels, and time and money, as follows:

 ✔ **Aesthetics:** Some people like the sleek look and feel of a short-haired cat; others adore the flowing softness of the longhairs. The shorthairs have about them the air of a tiger: You can see their muscles move as they walk, see the coiled promise of power while they sleep. In longhairs, the power is even more subtle, hidden by lush thickets of lovely long fur. Do you prefer to rub your hand down a sleek pelt or bury your fingers in a longhaired one? This preference is the first of your decisions.

✔ **Fur levels:** Here is where the trade-offs start to come in. Although nearly all cats shed, the difference in shedding levels between short- and longhaired cats can be dramatic, especially in cats that are prized for the volume of coat, such as with Persians. Are you prepared to live with a lint roller in your bathroom, your glove box, and your desk drawer at work? Would you be appalled to have a friend pick one of those glorious four-inch pieces of fur off the back of your sweater? If you're on the low end of fur tolerance, you'd better stick with short-haired cats.

✔ **Time and money:** Longhaired cats require extra care. They mat easily and need to be combed out every other day or so and brushed thoroughly on a weekly basis. *Hairballs,* or clumps of fur caught in the cat's digestive system, can be a constant problem with longhaired cats, requiring medical attention. If your cat's mats get out of control, you need to have her professionally groomed — most likely shaved — and that costs money.

Longhaired cats are more challenging to live with in other ways, too. Their urine and feces can get caught in their coats (which is why many owners generally prefer to keep those areas of their cats clipped short), and litter may catch on the tufts of fur in their paws and get tracked all over the house.

For more information about good grooming, see Chapter 7. For guidelines on choosing litter, litter boxes, and accessories, see Chapter 6.

Your cat's coat also has a bearing on whether you can consider letting him be an indoor-outdoor cat. The sparse coats of some of the Sphynxes and the Rexes offer no protection against sun or cold; on the other end of the scale, although the hearty coats of the Maine Coons and Norwegian Forest Cats stand up to the elements, the silkier coats of the Persians may need to be protected from the elements.

Although coat length, type, and color are truly a matter of personal preference in terms of picking out a cat, you do need to watch out for one thing that's related to coat color: White cats with blue eyes have a high probability for deafness. Some of these cats have eyes of different colors and are deaf only on the side with the blue eye. (You can check for deafness by snapping your fingers or clapping your hands behind a cat or kitten's head.) Though a deaf cat can still be a good pet — indoors only, for her own protection — you'll still want to know what you're getting into before you adopt.

Beautiful colors, beautiful cats

Considering how little they had to begin with, modern breeders have developed an incredible variety of colors and patterns in today's pedigreed cats. The Cat Fanciers' Association lists more than 60 color patterns for the Persian alone.

Not that what they started with wasn't beautiful — and isn't beautiful still.

By far, the most common cat color/pattern is the "tiger-striped," or *tabby,* markings that you can still see in the wild ancestors of the domestic cat. The name *tabby* comes from *Atabi,* a silk imported to England long ago that had a striped pattern similar to that of the domestic tiger cat.

Tabbies comes in many colors, such as red (more commonly called "orange," "ginger," or "marmalade"), cream, brown, or gray. The tabby pattern is so dominant that, even in solid-colored cats, you can often discern faint tabby markings, especially on the head, legs, and tail.

Smoked, shaded, and *shell* describe the varying amounts of tipping that appear on each individual hair, with *shell* being a dash of color at the very tip, *shaded* a little more tipping, and *smoke,* at the other extreme, being a coat so heavily tipped that it may look solid, except as the cat moves and the lighter color becomes visible underneath. Fur can also be *ticked* — that is, banded with color, as in the *agouti* pattern seen in the Abyssinian, where dark-colored bands alternate with lighter ones on each hair shaft.

Pointed cats are those such as the Siamese, with lighter-colored bodies shading to darker, complementary colors at the *points* — the face, the ears, the legs, and the tail.

Bicolors are any other color (or pattern, such as tabby) paired with white, and *particolors* have three or more colors, as is true of calicos (commonly with patches of white, red, and black) or tortoiseshells (with swirled red, cream, and black).

Mixing these color types can have some unpredictable results. The spotted Ocicat, for example, was created as the result of mating a Siamese and an Abyssinian!

Should You Consider a Pedigreed Cat?

You should consider everything! Although pedigreed cats make up a very small percentage of the overall cat population — less than 5 percent, according to some sources — some people would never consider having anything but a pedigreed cat of their particular favorite breed.

One fan of pedigreed cats is Lilian Jackson Braun, whose best-selling *The Cat Who . . .* mysteries have charmed cat lovers for years. Braun's breed of choice is the Siamese and so, too, is her detective's. In fact, if not for that very first Siamese cat, a gift from her husband, there would probably be no such mystery series at all.

Although the development of dog breeds has been going on for as long as dogs have been around, the interest in purebred cats is a relatively recent phenomenon, starting in the last century. Probably the most compelling reason for the difference is that people needed dog breeds to perform various tasks — herding, hunting, and guarding — whereas the cat walked in perfectly suited to the needs of humankind: Then, as now, no more efficient hunter of rodents could be found. Why mess with perfection?

Some people have always appreciated cats as much for their beauty and companionship as for their hunting skills, and some of these folks have worked to preserve and develop cat breeds and to nurture the development of new — and ofttimes controversial — varieties.

What are the benefits of owning a pedigreed cat? Predictability is probably the main one: If you buy a pedigreed kitten from a reputable breeder, you know in large part what you're getting. Size, body type, coat color, and levels of activity and vocality are imprinted on each kitten at the time of conception. Although each cat is still an individual, you can rest assured that your individual Siamese is going to have more in common with other Siamese in terms of looks and personalities than it does with any Persian ever born. The Siamese is active and talkative; the Persian is calm and quiet. If your tastes in a feline companion run to either of these extremes, choosing an appropriate pedigreed cat is the most likely way to have your wish.

Pedigreed cats also offer a little more variety than the everyday cat does. If you like a long, sleek cat, certain breeds fit that profile. The same, too, is true for a thicker-set body type, called *cobby* by fanciers. Color choices, too, are broader. The slate-gray of the Korat and Russian Blue, really a dilution of the gene that produces black, is almost unheard-of outside the world of pedigreed cats, as is the glossy warm tone of the Havana Brown.

And what about the novelty factor? Only in the pedigreed ranks can you find cats with ears that fold forward or back, cats with kinky fur — or none at all — and cats with little or no tails or short legs. Some of these breeds are controversial — to say the least! — but they certainly do expand the choices when the time comes to think "cat."

Concerning pedigreed cats, cat lovers like them big, and they like them furry. Or at least that's the picture you get from the Cat Fanciers' Association, which lists the Persian at number one on the popularity parade, followed by the Maine Coon, another hefty longhair. Rounding out the top five are the Siamese, the Abyssinian, and the Exotic (the shorthaired Persian). Worldwide, there are close to 50 cat breeds, many so rare that only a few hundred representatives exist in each.

The overwhelming majority of cat seekers — more than nine out of ten — do *not* choose a pedigreed cat. For most, the choice is probably just a matter of price and convenience. Pedigreed cats can be expensive — a couple of hundred dollars, at least, and climbing into the thousands of dollars for

The Havana Brown has a distinct color that sets him apart from other breeds.

Photo courtesy of Michael Brim, Cat Fanciers' Association.

kittens of rare breeds and colors. They can be hard to find, too, if you journey past the most-popular breeds. Upkeep on the coats of some breeds may also limit many cat lovers to admiring them from afar.

Although most pedigreed cats are as healthy as their nonpedigreed relatives, some concerns do exist. The Persian, for example, is prone to respiratory problems, blocked tear ducts, and runny eyes because of the short face some breeders prize. Other problems are associated with the very attributes that make some breeds special: Skeletal defects can pop up in Scottish Fold and Manx litters, for example. Reputable breeders are aware of the genetic problems in their breed and work to keep them at bay. Anyone you're considering buying a pedigreed kitten or cat from should honestly discuss any problems in their breed and what is being done to reduce their frequency.

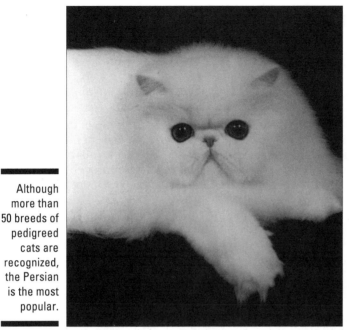

Although more than 50 breeds of pedigreed cats are recognized, the Persian is the most popular.

Photo courtesy of Michael Brim, Cat Fanciers' Association.

Do you want a chatty cat?

One trait that is highly predictable by breed is vocalization. Some breeds are so quiet you hardly know they're around, and others tell you every thought that crosses their minds, every minute they're awake.

Siamese are probably best known for being chatty, but other breeds keep up their end of the conversation, too. The Balinese, a longhaired version of the Siamese, is, not surprisingly, very vocal, as are the Oriental Shorthair and Colorpoint Shorthair, also versions of the Siamese, and the Tonkinese, a breed developed from the Siamese. Other feline conversationalists include the Bombay, the Burmese, the Rexes, and the Ocicat.

The quietest cat breeds are generally those with heavier builds and more mellow dispositions: the Persian, the British Shorthair, and the Maine Coon.

Characteristics by Breed

Pedigreed cats are roughly divided by experts into two groups that are distinguished by body type and activity level.

The breeds in the first group, the *Oriental,* are notable for their long, sleek bodies and active participation in the world around them. They're not happy unless they're supervising dinner, climbing to the top of the bookshelf, teasing that dopey dog, or seeing what every member of the household is up to. The way these cats see the world, you're not capable of running your own life without their help. Cats in this group, such as the Siamese, Burmese, and Abyssinian, are often claimed to be more intelligent and trainable.

The *non-Orientals* see things a little bit differently. If you're big and beautiful, the world comes to you with all your needs. Why interrupt a good nap to see what's on top of that bookshelf? Cats in this group, such as the Persian, Ragdoll, and British Shorthair, are generally happy to sleep in your lap while you read — and not bat at the pages as you turn them!

At first, the differences between these breeds may also seem to relate to their coats, with the sleek shorthairs falling in the Oriental group and thicker-set longhairs in the other. That assumption would be true except for the work of those who want to offer you even more options in a cat, such as longhaired versions of the Siamese (the Balinese) and Abyssinian (the Somali) and a breed that's pretty close to a short-haired version of the Persian (the Exotic).

The history and legends behind the various breeds of pedigreed cats are almost as interesting and colorful as the cats themselves. Two books that are good jumping-off points for more in-depth research into cat breeds are *Your Purebred Kitten: Buyer's Guide,* by Michele Lowell (Henry Holt), and *The Cat Fanciers' Association Cat Encyclopedia* (Simon & Schuster). Even better, check out the breed profiles on the Cat Fanciers Web site at www.fanciers. com/breed.html.

Unlike purebred dogs — who are divided roughly by purpose, sporting, herding, and so on — pedigreed cats aren't quite so easy to categorize. Not surprisingly, really, if you consider that each cat himself is unique — and if you don't believe it, just ask him!

Not happy with the two divisions the experts offer, we've tried to break down the various breeds into categories, a task almost as difficult as herding cats themselves. The breakdown's not perfect — some longhaired cats are also among the largest, for example, and some of the more active breeds are also distinctive in other ways. (In such cases, we listed the breeds twice, once in each category.) But we figured that breaking the almost 50 breeds down into categories would make thinking about what sort of breed you may want a little easier.

The go-go group

Consider the Siamese the prototype of this group. Always into everything, always looking to see what you're up to, and always loudly suggesting ways you can do it better — these characteristics are the essence of this cat, one of the world's most easily recognizable breeds with his distinctive "pointed" markings. The Siamese is such an important breed that its genes went into the development of many others, such as the Himalayan (a pointed version of the Persian); the Balinese (essentially a longer-haired Siamese); and the Birman, Burmese, Havana Brown, Ocicat, Oriental Shorthair (a Siamese in solid colors and total-body patterns), Colorpoint Shorthair (a Siamese with more options in point colors), and Tonkinese. Not surprisingly, many of these breeds — the Himalayan alone not among them — are also high on the activity scale.

A cat doesn't need to be Siamese — or related somehow to the Siamese — to be above-average in terms of being on the go. Not as talkative generally, but just as busy, is the Abyssinian, with markings that suggest a mountain lion and a reputation for being one of the most intelligent and trainable of all breeds. Other breeds with energy to burn are the Bombay, the kinky-coated Cornish and Devon Rexes, the Egyptian Mau, the Somali (a longhaired Abyssinian), and the hairless Sphynx.

You couldn't get these cats to all sit still for a photograph! If you're looking for an active breed, consider the Abyssinian, Burmese, Cornish Rex, and Siamese, among others.

Although these breeds can be a constant source of amusement with their energy and fearless ways, they can also be a handful. You should be prepared to endure cats on the drapes — the better to get up, up, up! — and kittenish behavior that endures for a lifetime. These cats never stop and are as likely to want to play at 2 a.m. as at 2 p.m. They surely want to be *with* you all the time, but *on* you? That's another matter. Lap-sitter kitties these are generally not — they've got things to do!

Still, the people who choose these breeds do so for a reason: They're fun! If one of these cats is in your future, get a good cat tree — see Chapter 6 — and lay in a huge supply of toys, because you're going to need them.

A touch of the wild

One of the many things we humans find appealing about cats is that, even in the most tame and loving of our household companions, a touch of the tiger remains. Indeed, the tiger's stripes remain on many of our pets, reminding us always of the connection — a reminder strengthened whenever you watch a cat walk, run, or leap. The grace and power are the same for big cats and for small.

Our cats may have chosen domestication, but on their own terms. And always, always, with a little bit of wildness held in reserve.

That we love this essential wildness is apparent in our long-standing interest in cat breeds that retain the look of the wild about them — not with the "ordinary" tiger stripes of the tabby but with spotted coat patterns evocative of another great wild cat, the leopard.

The Bengal, Egyptian Mau, and Ocicat evoke the beauty of the leopard with their spotted coats.

One of the most controversial of these breeds is the California Spangled, because of the decidedly unique way its creator sought to market the kittens — in the 1986 Neiman Marcus Christmas catalog. Priced at $1,400 each, the kittens were the topic of much heated debate from people who thought selling cats by catalog sent the wrong message — that cats were little more than living toys or decorator accessories.

As is true of the California Spangled, most cats with a spotted "wild look" haven't any wild blood in them at all — they're the results of breeders trying to develop coat patterns that resemble the domestic cat's wild cousins. You can put into this category the Ocicat, derived from breedings of the Siamese and Abyssinian and named for the Ocelot, which it resembles. The Egyptian Mau (*Mau* means *cat* in Egyptian) is another spotted wonder, a lovely cat bred to resemble the cats seen in ancient Egyptian artwork.

A cat of a different variety altogether is the Bengal, a cat developed through breedings of domestic cats with wild Asian Leopard Cats. Fanciers say the wild temperament has been removed by generations of breeding only the most sociable and friendly Bengals, although the look of the wild cat it came from remains.

The temperament of these "wilder" breeds generally lies somewhere in the middle between the go-gos and the more easy-going breeds, which we discuss next. They're not placid layabouts, but neither are they as active as some breeds. For those who love the look of a leopard in a manageable, loving package, these cats are perfect.

Longhaired beauties

The Persian is the other cat besides the Siamese that nearly anyone, cat-lover or not, can recognize in a crowd. The incredible coat of this breed has enchanted cat lovers for centuries. Whenever companies look for a breed that says "glamour" to use in their advertising, that they usually settle on a Persian is no accident. This cat is a glamorpuss, no doubt about it.

Perhaps no cat besides the Persian comes in as many varieties, each resplendent in that incredible coat. Tabbies of every color, torties, calicoes, every imaginable solid color and tipped coats, too. The markings of the Siamese can be found in the Himalayan, which in cat shows is considered a pointed Persian.

If you're looking for a more natural longhair, you have plenty of options. The Turkish Angora and Turkish Van are two ancient longhaired cats. The Norwegian Forest, Maine Coon, and Siberian cats are longhairs that still have the rough-and-tumble look of farm cats about them. And don't forget the Birman, the sacred cat of Burma, a breed that looks somewhat like a Himalayan, with color darker at the points, except for the perfectly white-mitted paws.

The Ragdoll is another pointed, mitted longhair of more-modern origins — it was "invented" in the 1960s — and is another choice for those seeking a longhaired cat, especially one designed to have an extremely laid-back temperament. Another lovely longhair with a relatively short history is the Chantilly/Tiffany, a cat with silky hair, commonly chocolate colored.

In the longhaired ranks, too, are a few breeds you can distinguish from their better-known relatives only by the length of their coat. Put in this class the Cymric, a longhaired version of the tailless Manx, as well as the Somali (a longer-haired Abyssinian), Balinese (a longer-haired Siamese), and Javanese (a longer-haired Colorpoint Shorthair).

The biggest challenge facing those who own longhaired cats is coat care. The long, silky coat of the Persian mats easily and requires daily attention to keep it in good form. Other longhaired coats aren't quite as demanding, but they all require more attention than the coats of short-haired cats. And they all shed rather remarkably!

Ingested hair, commonly called *hairballs,* is a bigger problem in longhaired cats, too.

For everything you need to know about grooming these longhaired beauties — including choosing a groomer for your cat — see Chapter 7. In the same chapter, you find more information on hairballs.

The temperament of longhaired cats depends on what's underneath that lovely coat. If an Oriental body's underneath — such as in the Balinese — you've got an active cat. The larger, more thickset body types, such as those of the Persian and Norwegian Forest Cat, tend more toward the laid-back end of the spectrum.

The Birman, Himalayan, and the Persian are all cherished for their stunning coats.

The big cats

Although you'll never see a pet cat as big as a St. Bernard — or at least, we certainly hope not! — a few breeds definitely warrant the heavyweight category where cats are concerned. Although most healthy cats — pedigreed and not — weigh between eight and twelve pounds, some of the big cat breeds range between 15 and 20 pounds, especially the males.

Now *that's* a cat who can keep your lap warm on a winter night!

The biggest domestic cat is thought to be the Siberian cat, with some males topping 20 pounds. This breed is pretty rare, however, so if you're looking for maximum cat, you might want to consider the Maine Coon, number two on the Cat Fanciers' Association's list of most-popular cats, or maybe the Norwegian Forest, another longhaired chunk of a cat.

Other longhaired cats with an above-average size include the Ragdoll, Turkish Van, and American Bobtail.

For a lot of cat without the fur, consider the British Shorthair, the American Shorthair, and the Chartreux.

The large cats are generally fairly easy-going in temperament and more laid-back than many other breeds. If you're looking for a more active and involved pet, these breeds are not the ones for you.

The Turkish Van, Maine Coon, and British Shorthair are perfect breeds for those who like a cat of substance.

The Maine Coon has long been popular both as a pet and a show cat. In fact, a brown tabby Maine Coon named Cosey won the first major cat show in North America, held May 8, 1895, in New York City's Madison Square Garden. The engraved silver collar and medal presented there is now the most important piece in the Cat Fanciers' Association's collection of cat memorabilia and art.

Something different

New cat breeds are created all the time, some by accident, some by design. Many cat breeds start after someone notices a kitten with something "different" — ears, legs, or other characteristics that set him or her apart from other cats.

These cats are some of the rarest around and among the most controversial. They're also among the most expensive to acquire — if you can find one at all.

Coat — or lack of it — sets some breeds apart. Primary among these breeds would be the Sphynx, a cat who's nearly hairless — nothing more than a little fuzz on his face, feet, and tail. The Rex breeds — Cornish, Devon, German, and Selkirk — all sport kinky hair, as does the LaPerm and the American Wirehair.

The short-legged Munchkin, the short-tailed Japanese Bobtail, the ear-altered Scottish Fold, and the nearly hairless Sphynx are cats sure to start a conversation — and maybe an argument!

Some breeders of Rexes claim an additional distinction for their breeds: They claim that the cats are hypoallergenic. Some people with allergies may be able to tolerate certain breeds more than others, true, but unfortunately, no such thing as an allergy-proof cat exists. For tips on making living with a cat easier on your allergies, see Chapter 1.

Tails — or lack thereof — are the talk in other breeds. The Manx is undoubtedly the best-known tailless or short-tailed cat, but others are on this list, too. The Cymric is a longhaired Manx; the Japanese Bobtail, American Bobtail, and Pixie-Bob round out the ranks of the tail-challenged.

And what about ears? Two breeds are based on an ear mutation: the Scottish Fold, with ears that fold forward, and the American Curl, with ears that arch backward.

Undoubtedly the most talked-about new breed has been the Munchkin, a cat with short legs. Although some people say that the breed is a mutation that shouldn't be developed into an actual breed, others see little difference between having a short-legged cat breed and a short-legged dog breed, of which several exist. One thing is certain: The controversy over breeds developed from mutations isn't about to abate any time soon.

Should you consider any of these breeds? Of course. If you're looking for something that's sure to start a conversation whenever company comes over, these cats are just the ticket. But be prepared, too, to hear from those who think it's a bad idea to perpetuate such genetic surprises.

The unCATegorizables

What did we tell you earlier? Herding cats is hard work, and some breeds refuse any efforts at being categorized. One, the Singapura, a Southeast Asian breed that resembles an Abyssinian, is noteworthy for being exceptionally small, which practically puts the breed in a category of its own.

And where do you put the Snowshoe, a cat with many breeds in its background who resembles a white-mitted Siamese but isn't as active? We couldn't decide.

Three other breeds are of medium size and temperament but are notable for their coats. Count among these the Korat and Russian Blue, from Thailand and Russia, respectively, both remarkable for their stunning blue-gray coats — as is the Nebelung.

The Not-So-Ordinary Everyday Cat

Most people couldn't care less if a cat has a pedigree or a fancy breed name — they just like cats and are content to adopt one that strikes their fancy or wanders into their lives.

Calling a nonpedigreed cat a "mixed breed" isn't exactly right, however, because most breeders are so careful with their pedigree cats that the possibility of an unplanned breeding is almost nil. The everyday cat really is completely *random-bred,* produced as a matter of complete serendipity with no rhyme or reason at all — at least not where humans are concerned! We like the British name for these cats — *moggies.*

Still, randomness being what it is — random — you can find some nonpedigreed cats that look very close to their show-going cousins. A big, brown, longhaired tabby that has more than a passing resemblance to a Maine Coon, for example. In the very real terms of love and affection, such cats are neither more nor less valuable than their pedigreed counterparts.

Even without human meddling, cats display a remarkable range of traits and appearances. Some of the more popular are the tuxedo-marked cats, the most famous of whom is undoubtedly White House resident, Socks. Calicoes and tortoiseshells are fabled, too, and more than one cat lover has a soft spot in her heart for a ginger tabby.

Are all calicos and tortoiseshell cats female? The surprising truth is in Chapter 17.

The point here is that *all* cats have the potential to be a special pet to someone, no matter where they come from, no matter what they look like. And cats are really more alike than they are different in terms of health, general size, and behavior.

The tuxedo, calico, and the most common pattern — the tabby — reflect the lovely variety found among nonpedigreed cats.

The differences count only in relation to what you want in a pet. You need to know your own heart before you choose to let any cat into it.

Exploring Feline Cyberspace

A great place to research cats is cyberspace. Cat lovers have taken to the Internet and commercial online services with a fever matched by few other enthusiasts — a billion pictures of cats must be on the World Wide Web by now. You can find cat-related e-mail lists, newsgroups, and Web sites on the Internet, as well as active online communities on commercial services such as America Online (where Gina's weekly pet care column, "Gina Spadafori's Pet Connection," runs in its own section of the Pet Care Forum).

What's so amazing about the Internet is the generosity of people such as Cindy Tittle Moore, who runs the `rec.pet.cats` area, and the folks behind the Cat Fanciers Web site (at `www.fanciers.com`). These people have put in an astonishing amount of work to provide cat lovers with top-rate information on cats and their care.

The Cat Fanciers Web site is one of many great sources of information on the World Wide Web.

You can have a lot of fun looking for cat-related Web sites, chatting with other cat lovers, or sharing your opinions on cats, their care, and their amazing abilities, but if you're thinking about getting a cat, the information available is incredible in its scope and is, for the most part, accurate and honest.

The online world has more to offer than research. Some of the most clever and amusing sites on the World Wide Web are cat-related and well worth a visit. For a rundown on some of the best, see Chapter 20.

You can get information on cats in many ways. We use all of them when researching or trying to come up with more ways to better enjoy life with our animals. Here's the rundown:

✔ **FAQs:** Short for *Frequently Asked Questions,* these cat-related documents on the Net range from such broad topics as choosing a cat or kitten to specific descriptions of particular breeds, to discussions of health care, genetics, and behavior. Some FAQs are lists of other Internet resources, such as e-mail lists, Web pages, online publications, and pet products suppliers. To find The Mother Of All Cat FAQs, thank Cindy Tittle Moore and point your Web-browsing software to the following address:

```
www.zmall.com/pet_talk/cat-faqs/homepage.html
```

✔ **E-mail lists:** For those who like a full mailbox, you won't find anything else quite like joining an e-mail list. Some are overwhelming, with hundreds of pieces of mail collected every day from members and distributed to everyone on the list, which may range from a couple of dozen people to several hundred. (The Cat Fanciers e-mail list has more than 850 members!) The best e-mail lists develop a sense of community, with people united by a common interest — such as a particular breed of cat or the sport of exhibiting — sharing helpful tips and warm stories of their feline companions. If you have a particular breed in mind but aren't sure what they're like to live with, a couple of months on an e-mail list should paint you as accurate a picture as you can imagine — and help you find the right breeder, if you decide to go ahead with an adoption.

You can subscribe to lists in several ways. For some, you need only to send a note to a host computer. With other lists, subscriptions are handled manually by the list owner, also called a *moderator.* Some lists have numerical limits; others screen members to keep out people who may prove disruptive. (If you believe no one should be breeding cats, you're not likely to be welcome on a mailing list of people who spend their online time discussing breeding and showing.)

After you join an e-mail list, read it for a couple of days to get the feel for the discussion before jumping in with a flurry of postings. This practice is called *netiquette,* but it's also good common sense. You don't know who's out there, reading, and you don't want to get off on the wrong foot with people who could help expand your knowledge of cats. So wait, and then, if it seems appropriate, post a low-key introduction. After you have the feel for the group, jump in!

The best list of e-mail groups is on the Cat Fanciers site, which also offers its own mailing list for the discussion of veterinary medicine, cattery management, cat-fancy politics, and the history of cat breeds. Other groups are more attuned to the interests of the adoring owner of a pet cat. Start with the Cat Fanciers mailing list information page and follow the links for lists of dozens of other cat e-mail lists, their rules, and their subscription information. To get started, point your Web browser to

```
www.fanciers.com/joining.html
```

✔ **Newsgroups:** A newsgroup is sort of like an e-mail list, except that anyone in the whole world can post to it and the information doesn't come to your mailbox — you must go get it.

Because newsgroups are open to anyone — including anonymous twits who like to cause trouble — you have less of a sense of community than you do with an e-mail list and less reason to be civil because the threat of being thrown off the subscriber list doesn't exist. The wide-open nature of newsgroups means that some people are more likely to post outrageous items — and engage in annoying *flame wars,* which are similar to the squabbles of children and just as entertaining. Even worse, the unmoderated cat-related newsgroups sometimes attract real sickos — people who think it's funny to post stories of cat killings and mutilations.

We like e-mail lists better — they stay on the subject, and sickos aren't allowed — but for more general information, newsgroups are worth exploring. Just take them with a grain of salt. The `rec.pet.cats` family includes six newsgroups: `rec.pet.cats.anecdotes`, `rec.pet.cats.announce`, `rec.pet.cats.community`, `rec.pet.cats.health+behav`, `rec.pet.cats.misc`, and `rec.pet.cats.rescue`.

For the history and charters of these newsgroups, point your Web browser to the following address:

```
www.zmall.com/pet_talk/cat-faqs/rpc-charters.html
```

✔ **Web sites:** Web sites are like newsgroups but with the added excitement of graphics and pictures. Hundreds of cat-related Web sites exist, from ones dedicated to individual breeds to ones devoted to cat pictures, cat gear, and cat showing. Most Web sites are either an individual's labor of love or a profit-minded commercial venture, so content and quality vary widely.

For a list of cat-related Web sites, point your Web browser to

```
www.fanciers.com
```

You can also check out the Yahoo! Web directory's list of cat-related sites at

```
www.yahoo.com/Science/Zoology/Animals__Insects__and_Pets/
Mammals/Cats/
```

✔ **Chatting:** Although possibilities for real-time discussions with other like-minded cat fanciers exist on other commercial services and on the Internet, America Online and CompuServe offer the easiest way to communicate "live" with other cat lovers. Regularly scheduled "chats" are part of the CompuServe Cats Forum (GO: CATS), as they are in AOL's Pet Care Forum (Keyword: PETS).

Cats 'n' computers

Two products are custom-made for cat-loving computer nerds. The first is *Catz,* a software package that produces an interactive pet to live in your computer. You choose a kitten to adopt from a handful of contenders and give him a name. You can pet him, feed him, play fetch, or take his picture. It's all great fun, and it's $19.95 from P.F.Magic. To order, call 1-800-48-ADOPT, or visit the company's Web site at www.pfmagic.com/catz.

A good deal and a good deed are the outcome if you order the second product, the Computa-Cat poster from the San Francisco SPCA.

Originally designed to promote adoptions, the work — designed and written by Paul Glassner — is a clever homage to computer advertising. A handsome tabby is in the middle of the poster, surrounded by a "product description," such as the following description for the cat brain: "Semi-programmable. Central Control Unit functions independently." The Computa-Cat poster is $12 plus $4 shipping and handling from the SFSPCA, 2500 16th Street, San Francisco, CA 94103. Proceeds go to the society's programs for helping animals and people.

Chapter 3

Considering Sources

· ·

In This Chapter

▶ First impressions — and lasting ones

▶ Shelters and rescue groups

▶ Breeders, good and not-so-good

▶ Pet shops

· ·

*Y*ou know what you want: pedigreed or not, long-haired or short, kitten or cat, male or female. You've done your homework, and you're getting closer to sharing your home with a cat. (And if you haven't narrowed your choices down yet, you may want to take a look at Chapters 1 and 2.)

Where do you find that special cat or kitten?

One thing is certain: You find no shortage of cats. During the warm months that mean "kitten season," you can find people with kittens to give away nearly everywhere — at your workplace, in front of your grocery store, at flea markets, shelters, and pet stores.

Why should you make choosing your new pet more trouble than you need to? Why not pick out that adorable little calico kitten from the neighbor cat's third litter? As for pedigreeds, does it really matter whether you seek out a show breeder or buy from a pet store or someone who's breeding for fun and a little profit? If the cat's registered, aren't the sources for pedigreeds all the same?

Buyer beware!

All sources are not the same, which is why you should take your time in getting your kitten and not just fall in love with the first fuzzy face you see.

How much should you spend?

Prices for cats and kittens vary widely: You can pay from nothing at all to the (generally) less than $50 that shelters charge, to $300–$500 for an "ordinary" but well-bred pedigreed cat from a reputable breeder, to a couple hundred more for one from a pet store, to more than a couple of thousand dollars for a well-bred "show-quality" kitten or one of a rare or red-hot breed. In general, however, a pedigreed "pet-quality" kitten of a common breed from a reputable breeder costs between $300 and $700.

The true cost of a cat is in the upkeep, but at least you get to make payments on that. The most basic, proper care — food, litter, basic gear, preventive veterinary care, boarding or pet-sitting while you're on vacation, and perhaps grooming for long-haired cats — costs you a reasonable minimum of $300 a year or so. Add in occasional veterinary emergencies and the strictly optional, but enjoyable, addition of tempting feline merchandise — lavish toys, high-end, high-tech litter boxes, books and magazines, and cat-themed goodies for you — and a cat can be a pretty pricey pet.

As a result, you should keep the cost of acquiring a cat in perspective. A $500 pedigreed kitten from a reputable breeder costs less than $34 a year if you figure the cost over a 15-year lifespan. And the cat-tree we covet from our friend's pet boutique costs $300!

The important thing is not the cost but the health and temperament of your new pal. Better you should get a friendly kitten glowing with good health from your local shelter than a sickly or shy "bargain" pedigreed from a poor-quality breeder. Pedigreed or not, go to the source that offers healthy, happy pets, and you'll save money in the long run.

You can get a good pet from any source, and many people out there can prove it. One friend of Gina's, for example, has a wonderful cat she found as a half-dead kitten in a dumpster! But your chances of getting a healthy, well-socialized kitten are best if you work with reputable shelters and rescue groups or reputable breeders. Nothing is more heartbreaking than falling in love with a kitten only to have your veterinarian tell you that your new companion tested positive for feline leukemia.

What does a feather have to do with picking out a kitten? Check out Chapter 4 for information on how to choose that one special companion from a litter of adorable babies or a shelter full of gorgeous homeless cats.

What You Need to Know about Shelters

A few years ago, Gina went to a conference for shelter workers and sat in on a seminar on making cats comfortable and keeping them healthy in the high-stress environment of a shelter. One of the presenters was a woman who'd made great changes in how her facility handled cats, and she had the pictures to prove it.

Previously, the cat facilities at her shelters had been a converted dog run with a lid on it to prevent escapes. All the cats were thrown into that run — and "thrown" is exactly how they got there. The only way a cat left that run was for adoption or death, and either way, the escape was the same: A noose on the end of a catch pole grabbed him, and he'd be lifted out, hissing and crying in terror. Imagine what a horrible impression a cat who'd been treated that way would make on a prospective adopter! (Not that the impression mattered much, however, because nearly all the cats were put to death.)

That shelter has changed today, and so have many others (although, sadly, not all). Cats and kittens are treated with more respect and caring, even at the end of their lives, and are housed in ways that make them feel more comfortable and keep them healthier, even in the challenging environment of a shelter. Clean cages in a quiet area away from dogs, or multicat "colony" housing, make their stays as pleasant as possible. For too many cats, however, the shelter's door is one-way — the numbers of kittens and cats are greater than those of adoptive homes — but the best groups do everything they can to find new homes for their animals.

Creative outreach programs working in partnership with the media and with businesses such as pet-supply superstores take pets where the people are to increase the volume of adoptions. And shelters themselves are changing — after years of listening to people talk about avoiding the gloomy surroundings, progressive organizations are giving their buildings a face-lift to make them light, bright, and inviting. The best shelters have well-trained, caring staffs and a healthy core of volunteers to keep cats socialized and counsel potential adopters as to their responsibilities to their new companion.

Today's shelter cats are more adoptable than ever before, thanks to programs that evaluate pets and perform basic health services — and some extraordinary ones — before animals are made available to the public. Forget your old ideas about shelters as nothing more than gloomy places for pets to die — *bright, clean, airy,* and *upbeat* are the words to describe many shelters today.

Making a decision about a shelter cat or kitten is difficult. You want to take them all, and the realization that some of these animals aren't going to find a new home softens even the hardest heart. But you aren't doing anyone any favors if you let your heart make your decisions here. Take a friend to help keep you from settling — and make sure that your friend isn't a bigger mush than you are, or you may both end up with the wrong pet! Play it cool.

Be aware of some potential problems with shelter pets. Shelter kittens and cats are stressed, which puts them at higher risk for contracting upper respiratory infections, which are generally treatable. They can also come into contact with sick animals and contract feline leukemia, feline infectious

Adoption centers run by shelters or rescue groups are a wonderful source for finding a pet — if you do your homework.

peritonitis, and feline immunodeficiency virus, which aren't treatable. (For more information on these diseases, see Chapter 10.) (To be fair, FIP can turn up in a cat from any source, and a kitten from any source that's not testing can turn up positive for FIV or FeLV.)

Although most shelter cats — like most cats in general — are shorthaired and of no particular breed, purebred cats do show up in shelters, although not with the frequency of purebred dogs. You may never see a rare breed of cat — such as the Devon Rex or Havana Brown — show up at your local shelter, but if you're looking for a more common Persian or Siamese, keep shelters in mind. You could get the breed of your dreams at a very reasonable price. And because purebred cats get no special considerations in shelters, you're saving a life to boot.

All shelters are not the same. Some are run by municipal animal-control facilities, some by nonprofit humane organizations — and decent shelters exist in both categories. Good kittens and cats are in any shelter, no matter how run-down the facilities and demoralized the staff. After all, a cat can't help where he's dumped. But just as you can improve your odds of buying a healthy, happy kitten by choosing a reputable breeder, you can better the chance of a successful adoption by choosing a *progressive shelter,* one that visibly cares about the animals, the adopters, and its staff.

You probably aren't offered the choice of not spaying or neutering your shelter cat, because most shelters either do it for you or require that you do it as a condition of adoption. For more on spaying and neutering, see Chapter 14.

Animal-control shelters

Municipal animal-control facilities are perhaps the easiest to figure out. Finding homes for pets was not the reason these facilities were founded and is not their primary purpose to this day — although many of them do a good job of it, nonetheless.

Animal-control departments were formed to protect people from animal-borne menaces — primarily rabies. They remove dead animals and enforce regulations, such as those regarding the licensing of animals — a rabies-control measure even cats fall under in some areas — and the number and kind of animals people can keep. They respond to calls about vicious animals, as well as calls involving animals that disturb a neighborhood because of noise or odor. These departments also serve as a "convenience" to people who no longer want their pets, disposing of the animals through adoption, euthanasia, or, in some locales, sales to biomedical research.

Don't forget the locals!

"Humane Society" and "Society for the Prevention of Cruelty to Animals" (or "SPCA") are generic terms freely used in the United States and Canada by animal organizations that have no connection to one another or to national organizations such as the Humane Society of the United States (HSUS), based in Washington, D.C., or the American Society for the Prevention of Cruelty to Animals, in New York City. And yet, local shelters are often stymied in their fund-raising efforts by people who have "given to the national organization" and consider their charitable efforts complete — even though money given to the HSUS and ASPCA is used to fund their own programs, not those of the local shelters. Which is why you don't want to forget your local animal shelter when giving.

Some national animal organizations do a great deal for animals, but others seem to exist mostly to raise money. (The same can be said, of course, of smaller, local groups.) The newspaper *Animal People* does a good job reporting on the operations of animal groups large and small. Each year, the non-profit newspaper prints an overview of how the largest animal groups spend their money. To get the "Where the Money Goes" issue, send $3 to *Animal People,* P.O. Box 960, Clinton, WA 98236. Or visit their Web site, at www.animalpepl.org/.

Animal-control shelters have never been well-funded operations, and this situation hasn't improved in recent years. With so much required of them by law and so few resources, readying animals for adoption and counseling prospective adopters can't be at the top of the animal-control director's list of priorities. And yet, because of caring people in many of these departments and in the communities they serve, volunteers fill the gap at some shelters, offering adoption counseling and assisting with animal care.

Because of these programs, municipal animal-control shelters can be good places to adopt. But many of the private nonprofit shelters have the potential to be better, because their mandate has always put helping animals at the top of their lists.

Private nonprofit shelters

Private, nonprofit shelters run the gamut from squalid outfits that serve as little more than a fund-raising gimmick for the people in charge to organizations with well-funded endowments and programs that not only help homeless animals but also work to improve conditions for all animals — and animal lovers — in their communities.

Most shelters fall somewhere in the middle: Their buildings could use some work, their budgets are always tight, and they do the best they can with what they have to provide for the animals in their community. Many good, loving pets are available at these shelters.

New buildings don't necessarily a good shelter make, but you certainly want to work with a shelter that clearly cares enough for its charges to make sure they're kept in areas that are clean and don't facilitate the spread of disease.

Shelter work is difficult and stressful, and employees and volunteers can suffer burnout quickly. A well-run shelter is as compassionate to its staff as it is to the animals, because one has a lot to bear on the treatment of the other. Look for a shelter where employees are helpful and knowledgeable and clearly interested in helping the shelter's animals find responsible new homes.

The best shelters have a good handle on a cat's history, health, and temperament before putting her up for adoption and have done what they can to enhance her chances of success in a new home through socialization and screening for the right home. They not only provide preadoption counseling but also offer behavioral advice after the adoption. Some even offer reduced-cost veterinary services for former shelter animals.

Look for ways to help the shelters that don't measure up. Usually, it's a question of money and volunteers, and you can do a lot to contribute in these categories. Contact your local shelter to find out how.

The scoop on "no kill" shelters

Those organizations that call themselves "no-kill" shelters are the subject of controversy in the animal-welfare community. Most shelters have far more pets than they can place, which sets up a grim game of "musical homes" that results in the death of millions of animals every year. No-kill shelters often get their name by refusing to accept animals that aren't adoptable or by refusing all animals if they're full. The turn-aways often end up at another shelter, one where the staff often very much resents having to be the bad guys.

To be fair, some no-kill shelters — such as the San Francisco SPCA — have a fairly broad definition of "adoptable" that includes those animals who can be made adoptable through medical care or behavioral modification.

As someone who's looking to adopt an animal, you shouldn't get distracted by policy debates. Look for a shelter offering healthy, well-socialized animals and adoption counseling to help you pick out the right one for you. The type of shelter with a well-trained staff and a solid volunteer corps is your best bet for a successful adoption, no matter what its policy on euthanasia.

Volunteer Rescue-and-Placement Groups

Thousands of small groups do what they can for cats without the benefit of a shelter building, and many of these organizations are excellent sources for pets. Made up of dedicated volunteers, these groups rescue and tame feral cats, hand-raise motherless kittens, find homes for cats and kittens who need them, and raise money to help spay and neuter the pets of people who can't afford the cost themselves, such as seniors on fixed incomes.

Don't let the earnestness of any volunteers overwhelm your own common sense. Make sure that the kitten or cat you're adopting is healthy and friendly.

For some people, though, the love of animals becomes a kind of mental illness. Humane investigators call these people "collectors," and they're characterized by an overzealous desire to "save" animals and a definite blind spot in caring for them. By the time humane officials intervene, the scene can be appalling: dead and dying animals in their own filth and animals eating other animals in a desperate attempt to avoid starvation. One collector was so adamant about not giving up her animals that she put the bodies of her dead cats in shoe boxes and stacked them on the front porch.

What do you mean I can't have a cat?

Some people are absolutely astonished — and more than a few are positively irate — if they're turned down while trying to adopt a cat, especially from a shelter or rescue group. After all, aren't they doing the shelter a favor by taking an animal off their hands?

That may not be how a shelter sees it.

Reputable breeders of pedigreed cats have always put conditions on the sale of their animals. They want to ensure animals that aren't of breeding quality don't reproduce, and they want their kittens to go to homes where they can receive the kind of care the breeder feels is necessary. Reputable breeders can lay down the rules because they're dealing with only a litter at a time — and they're prepared to keep all their cats rather than place them in a home they may feel is unsuitable.

For shelter cats, however, the alternative to adoption is too often euthanasia. Isn't any home better than that?

"No," say some shelters. Spay-neuter requirements are common — and necessary, given the overpopulation of cats — but some groups require far more. They may turn down people who work all day or who travel "too much" or have young children in the home. They may require that the cat be kept indoors and not be declawed. Written approval by a landlord may be required before an animal is adopted out to someone who rents.

Our feeling is that these restrictions, although well-meaning, are too inflexible. And, in fact, many of these regulations are created not for the benefit of the animals but to appease and appeal to donors who fund the organizations. We feel these are honorable and good people and organizations, but we suggest to many of the larger fund-raising organizations that it is time to reevaluate their policies and to look at what has driven policies to be what they are today.

These organizations need to be more flexible when it comes to adoptions. Although some children can be dangerous to a tiny kitten, for example, others are gentle and respectful. Some owners who travel take far better care of their pets than do those who're home all the time. Each person should be evaluated on a case-by-case basis.

What if you're turned down? Take a little time to consider again whether you're really ready for a cat — these rules, after all, are generally based on the shelter's experiences with people who generally don't make good cat owners. If you're still convinced that you're qualified, ask to discuss the matter with the shelter director — or go to another source.

Collectors are one reason to deal only with reputable animal groups, be they large or small. Ask to see proof of their nonprofit status, and discuss their policies with them. And if you sense that you may be dealing with a collector — too many cats, sick cats, and poor housing — call your local humane investigator.

Breeders: the Reputable, the Ill-Informed, and the Avoid-at-All-Costs

The Cat Fanciers' Association (CFA) estimates that a very small number of cats (less than 5 percent) are *pedigreed* — that is, registered with the CFA or another organization, such as The International Cat Association (TICA). Although around 50 individual breeds of cat are recognized by various groups around the world, most of these breeds are pretty rare. Many of the rarer breeds hardly show up in "ordinary" pet homes at all, because their breeders are dedicated to preserving and improving the lines and either keep most of their kittens or place them with other dedicated breeders.

The more-popular breeds, such as the Persian and Siamese, have many fanciers, including those folks who aren't the least bit interested in showing — they just want a good pet. A breeding industry has sprung up to service the market created by people who want "just a pet."

Although the fact seems pretty obvious, a lot of people don't realize that a cat is not like a piece of electronics. Finding a cat isn't a matter of searching for the right product — a multidisk CD player or a Norwegian Forest Cat — and the right brand — Sony or CFA — and then shopping aggressively for the best price and most convenient location.

Registration means nothing concerning a cat, and the breeder's knowledge and reputation mean everything. Think of a registry as being like the department of motor vehicles — you fill out the paperwork and send in the money, and the DMV sends back something that says, in effect, "Yep, it's a car." That slip of paper doesn't say a thing about the reliability of that car or whether the vehicle has a manufacturer's defect that can cause you trouble down the road. The department of motor vehicles didn't manufacture the car, and it's not guaranteeing quality.

The same is true of a feline registry, except most require even less in the way of proof that what they're registering even exists. Everything is done on the honor system, and we surely don't need to tell you that, where the possibility of making money exists, some people aren't very honorable. Others are well-meaning but just not knowledgeable enough about genetic problems and socialization to be breeding cats. You want to avoid both kinds of people if you're looking for a pedigreed cat.

Thinking of breeding your cat? In Chapter 14, we show you why breeding cats is both less profitable and more of an effort than you realize, how breeding puts your own pet at risk and makes him harder to live with, and how breeding contributes to the problems of surplus pets — even if you're thinking of breeding purebreds.

If you still want to breed cats, that same chapter includes a basic primer on matchmaking, kitten raising, and placement — the "good breeder" way.

Finding the elusive "good breeder"

A reputable breeder can be very hard to find and may not have a kitten available just when you want one — such as now. Those facts alone send many buyers to other, less-than-ideal sources.

If everything goes well, you're going to have your cat for as many as 20 years. Doesn't taking a little time to find the right breeder seem reasonable? To make a few phone calls, read a book or two, search the Web, and take a few field trips? To ask more questions of a person who's lived for years with the breed you want so that you can get more answers than a book provides?

For information on how to use the Internet to find information on pedigreed cats — and their breeders — see Chapter 2.

A good breeder is almost certainly showing her cats — because how can she know she's creating excellent examples of her breed if she doesn't have them judged?

A pet store with a selection of kittens often can't provide you with information on the breed you want, because the staff, no matter how well-meaning, can usually offer only cursory information about the breeds the store stocks. A backyard breeder with one "let the kids watch" litter can tell you what living with her Siamese is like but hasn't the expertise to talk about the breed as a whole. And neither source, of course, is offering cats bred expressly for the top-quality health and temperament you should demand.

The good, serious breeder, on the other hand, can tell you more than you could possibly imagine about the breed. The breeder's commitment to the kitten you buy doesn't end after the sale is final. You get a healthy, well-socialized kitten and technical support that would be the envy of any software company.

Shopping at the cat show

A cat show is the ultimate in window shopping for a cat lover and prospective kitten buyer. You want to find good breeders? Go where they turn up to show off their pride-and-joys. A cat show is the place.

Wander along the aisles with a smile on your face, and ask all the questions you want. Unless they're just getting ready to have their cat judged, most exhibitors are happy to talk — you're asking about one of their favorite subjects, after all: their cats!

Don't forget to watch the judging either. Cat-show judges consider education as much their job as selecting the best cat from among those they're judging. Many of these judges are wonderful to listen to as they explain the good and bad points of each cat or kitten they handle and compare each to the *breed standard* — the registry's written description of the imaginary "perfect" cat in each breed.

You probably can't get all your questions answered, however, and you're likely to want to talk to the breeders later. So ask for business cards or write down phone numbers — along with notes about the conversation you had with each one so that you remember later what you discussed. Ask about kitten availability and planned breedings, but don't get too deep into it at the show — the breeder is pretty busy. Enjoy the day and all the gorgeous cats and plan your more serious discussions for later, by phone and in person.

Cat shows are sometimes hard to find, because advertising and publicity seems to be a hit-and-miss affair with many sponsoring clubs. The general circulation magazines *Cat Fancy* and *Cats,* available at newsstands and by subscription, offer listings, as do the registries' pages on the World Wide Web. The Cat Fanciers Web page — at www.fanciers.com — is a good place to start looking. Keep an eye out for flyers at your local pet-supply store, too.

You have more fun at a cat show if you understand what's going on. Who knows? You may even decide to show your own cat — some shows even have classes for nonpedigreed household pets. To find out more, check out Chapter 16.

When you should avoid show breeders

You need to beware of some show breeders as a source for a pet, no matter how long they've been turning out winners. For kittens to be proper companions, they must be around people from the day they're born. They must be handled by children and by adults of both sexes. They need to hear the ordinary sounds of life among the two-legged.

Ask your questions about screening for genetic defects, about whether the breeder shows her cats, and about papers, contracts, and guarantees. But don't forget to ask where and how the kittens were raised.

If the breeder says "underfoot" with a smile and stresses how much they've been lovingly handled, you're on the right track.

Check out the free educational materials that may be available at the show site. You can often find flyers for upcoming shows, along with informational material on the breeds, cat care, and cat charities. The people staffing the table are happy to answer your questions and are usually quite knowledgeable.

Perusing publications

Attending a show is probably the most enjoyable way to start tracking down a breeder, but you have other options, too.

The feline magazines offer breeder advertisements, as do a couple notable annuals, *Cats USA* (put out by the *Cat Fancy* folks) and the *Dogs In Canada* annual, which has a cats section. The registries also put out publications that carry breeder advertising, such as the *Cat Fanciers' Almanac,* the *CFA Yearbook,* the *TICA Trend,* or *TICA Yearbook.* Listings for these registries are in the Additional Resources appendix of this book, or you can check them out via the Cat Fanciers site at `http://www.fanciers.com`.

These publications do not screen breeders, however, so proceed with caution. If you can't find anyone locally for the breed you want, call the nearest advertised breeder. If he's a reputable breeder, he likely belongs to a national or regional breed club and can give you a referral to a breeder nearer to you — if one is around.

Spotting the less-than-ideal breeders

A very few breeders are downright evil and fail to provide for even the basics of their animals' needs. A few more are mentally ill, living in filthy homes packed to the rafters with freely mating cats. These people are fairly easy to spot and avoid — unless their kittens are cleaned up and sold elsewhere.

The majority of "bad" breeders — "backyard breeders," as they're commonly known — are not uncaring. They're just uninformed. They don't know that many of the cats they produce can end up in shelters or spend their lives in pain from a congenital illness. They just want a litter "so the kids can see" or because "kittens are fun" or because they heard that breeding cats is an easy way to make a little money. They aren't bad people, but they're still not good breeders.

Following are a few things that should give you pause in dealing with a breeder:

> ✔ **Lack of knowledge about the breed.** Someone who doesn't know much about the breed, its history, or its standard isn't someone who's too concerned about producing kittens that are fine examples of the breed.

✔ **Ignorance or denial of genetic defects.** Many breeds have some problems, some of which can be avoided by careful breeding. A person who isn't aware of congenital defects certainly isn't planning her breedings to avoid them.

✔ **No involvement showing cats.** You improve the odds of getting a high-quality purebred if you buy from someone involved in showing or otherwise competing their cats. Such involvement suggests a level of commitment that's likely also to be present in the care of the cats.

✔ **Not letting you observe the litter, meet the mother or other cats, or see where the kittens were raised.** Healthy, well-mannered adults and a clean, well-run cattery are a breeder's best testimonial. If a person doesn't want you to see anything except the kitten she's trying to sell, you ought to be wondering why.

✔ **No documentation.** If the kitten's represented as "CFA registered," the registration papers should be available. (The same goes for other registries, too.) So, too, should the papers backing up health claims. A sales contract spelling out the rights and responsibilities of both parties is highly desirable. Such a document provides you with recourse should the kitten not turn out as promised — if it has congenital health problems, for example, or isn't suitable for showing, if that was part of your intent in buying him.

✔ **Doesn't seem to understand the importance of socialization.** Kittens need to be nurtured, loved, and handled to make good pets. Someone who can't explain what they've done in this area or who tries to sell a kitten less than 12 weeks old probably doesn't understand enough to be breeding cats.

Such caution is all about increasing the odds of success. Can you find a pedigreed kitten who's going to be a good pet from a backyard breeder advertising in your local newspaper? Without a doubt. But you're more likely to find one if you take the time to find a reputable, knowledgeable breeder.

Pet Stores: Proceed with Caution

You don't need to put much effort into buying a pedigreed kitten at a pet store. Pet stores usually stock kittens by the handful of the most popular breeds — and maybe some mixes, too. You don't need to talk to breeders, do your homework, or wait if you go to a pet store either. Pet stores may offer some health guarantees. And they take credit cards. What could be better or more convenient?

Based on what this chapter discusses, you should realize that you increase your odds dramatically of getting a healthier, better socialized kitten by dealing with a knowledgeable, reputable breeder, shelter, or rescue group. But that's not the only reason to avoid retail pet outlets: *Kitten mills* are an even more compelling one.

In rural regions across the United States, the wholesale breeding of kittens for pet stores goes on in an environment that couldn't be more different from a clean, well-lit shop in a mall. In these operations, commonly called kitten mills, breeding stock spend their whole miserable lives knee-deep in their own filth in tiny, makeshift cages exposed to the elements. Medical problems go untreated, and if the animals are no longer producing, they're disposed of. This situation is cruelty on a most appalling scale, well documented over the last two decades by humane groups, and continuing under the noses of overburdened federal investigators.

If you buy a pedigreed kitten from a pet store, you may well be supporting just such an operation with your money — and don't let anyone tell you otherwise.

Stung by public horror over the media exposés of substandard commercial breeders, the pet industry, the U.S. Department of Agriculture, and the breed registries have beefed up efforts to clean up this problem. Their efforts are to be commended and encouraged, but humane investigators say that these operations still exist.

But even if — and that's a mighty big "if" — every commercial breeder kept their kennels scrupulously clean and properly cared for every animal on site, you're still more likely to do better with a home-raised kitten from a small, reputable breeder. Kittens are not well suited to be mass-produced "merchandise," and that's what you often get if you buy from a pet store.

Some pet stores offer space to "oops" litters, and although such policies are well-meaning, they send the message to the people who produced the litter that it's easy to find homes for the kittens and don't do anything to encourage spaying and neutering. Some stores also buy their pedigreed kittens from local breeders in an effort to avoid kitten mills, which is also well-meaning but flawed. The problem is that reputable breeders insist on placing their kittens themselves — many cat clubs have codes of ethics that forbid their members from selling to pet stores. You may be dealing with a pedigreed kitten who has been raised under more-humane conditions, but still not the top-quality purebred you should be looking for.

A growing number of U.S. pet supply stores — led by the industry giant, PetsMart — refuse to sell kittens (or puppies) because of concerns over commercial breeders and pet overpopulation. Instead, they offer space in their stores to local shelters or rescue groups to reach out to prospective adopters.

Remember that finding a kitten or cat is about being an informed consumer. Some people have ended up with a pet they truly love from a retail pet store. Still, your best chance at finding a healthy, temperamentally sound, properly socialized, pedigreed kitten is not at a pet store. On this point, veterinarians, trainers, humane societies, and breed registries agree.

Your Neighbor's (Or Coworker's) Kittens

So, what about that litter of kittens a coworker or neighbor is offering up for free? You have no real reason not to consider them if they meet your requirements and they're healthy and well-socialized.

Those are pretty big "ifs," however. Take a kitten from a "free-to-a-good-home" source and you may end up with more problems than you imagined. If the kitten turns up positive for feline leukemia or a treatable health problem, do you have any recourse against the person from whom you got the kitten? Hardly. The chances are high the mother was never tested for disease and the father was unknown.

You have another reason to avoid the "free-to-a-good-home" folks, and we hope that you consider it: Every time someone accepts a kitten from someone who should have spayed the mother cat, the person taking the kitten is giving that cat owner a way out of accepting his share of responsibility for the horrendous numbers of cats and kittens killed every year just for the crime of being "surplus." Every time someone accepts a kitten from a "just-for-fun" breeder, the one accepting the kitten lets that person off the hook, because the breeder can then honestly say, "But we always find homes for the kittens!"

Consider such a litter if you want; many people have done just fine by adopting from such a source. But make sure that your kitten is healthy and socialized and try as best as you can to suggest that your pet and her littermates be the very last that the mother cat produces.

For information on how to select a healthy kitten from any source, see Chapter 4.

Adult cats are a slightly different matter. They're offered up for a lot of different reasons, some as frivolous as a change of decor, some as unavoidable as the death of an owner or the development of a child's serious allergy to cats. Many of these displaced kitties are wonderful pets, and you have no reason not to adopt one, as long as you make sure that the cat is healthy and isn't being placed for behavior problems, such as avoiding the litter box. If everything checks out, give one of these guys a chance!

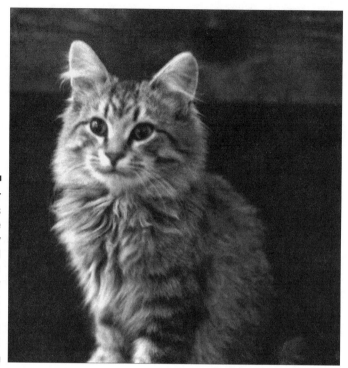

Friends or coworkers may give away wonderful adult cats for a variety of reasons; they're worth a look!

Jaymz — Photo courtesy of Dominique DeFelice.

The Cat Who Chooses You and the Shared Cat

With no other animal — not dog or fish, bird or reptile — than the cat is the chance so great that you may not be looking for a pet . . . but a pet is looking for you. Many cats come into our lives in just such a way, lured by the promise of food and kept by the giving of affection.

Gina's first cat was just such a cat. At the age of 8, she wanted a calico cat more than anything and started feeding a friendly cat without her parents knowledge. The cat — who belonged to a neighbor — divided his time between the two homes for a while but eventually settled down in the new home, where he was read to and talked to and spoiled and fussed over. The gray tabby liked the new digs enough to endure his new name: "Calico."

Some cats are "shared," never choosing one home or another, and take their meals and attention wherever suits them. Other cats become the special companion of one person and give up their far-roaming days. Taking in a wandering cat is good for your soul — and good for the neighborhood and his life expectancy if you end his outside days for good.

Part II
Bringing a Cat or Kitten into Your Life

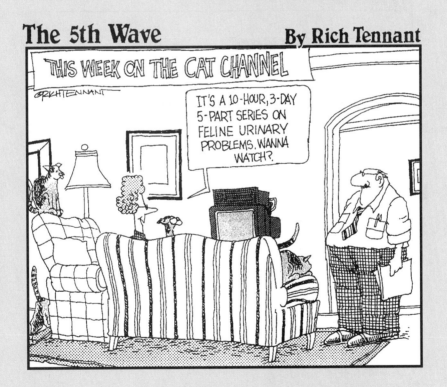

The 5th Wave   By Rich Tennant

THIS WEEK ON THE CAT CHANNEL

IT'S A 10-HOUR, 3-DAY 5-PART SERIES ON FELINE URINARY PROBLEMS. WANNA WATCH?

In this part . . .

This part explains how to test the personality of a cat or kitten to help choose the right individual for you. Should you consider two kittens at once? How about taming a wild kitten or cat? We offer both the pros and the cons. You also find out how to introduce your new pet to the current residents of your home, not only your children but also other cats, dogs, and pets of all sorts. Finally, we tell you exactly what you need in the way of supplies to keep your cat happy and healthy.

Chapter 4

Choosing Your Feline Companion

· ·

In This Chapter

▶ Making a decision for life

▶ Understanding the importance of socialization

▶ Personality-testing kittens

▶ Evaluating the adult cat

▶ Looking for signs of good health in kittens and adult cats

▶ Wild things: considering the formerly feral

· ·

*I*s the old saying about cats true, that you choose a dog, but a cat chooses you? Not really. Although many cases still exist where a cat just walks into your life and sets up housekeeping in your heart, the days are gone for most of us when all you had to do to get a cat was set a saucer of milk on the back-porch step.

This scenario is true of any cat, but it's particularly true of those with pedigrees. Although their numbers are still far overwhelmed by the "breed" some call an alley cat — but cat experts call a *domestic shorthair* (or *domestic longhair*) — the interest in pedigreed cats is growing all the time. And if you want one, you have to go to the time, and sometimes considerable expense, to track down the reputable breeder who has the kitten or adult cat of your dreams.

But where can you find an "ordinary" cat? (We use that term guardedly, because every cat is a unique work of art and love.) They're everywhere! In kitten season — summer and fall, primarily — you can hardly turn around without someone trying to give you an adorable ball of baby cat fluff. A litter of tabbies is advertised on the bulletin board at work. Your neighbor waited too long to spay her kitten, and wants you to look at a tuxedo-marked kitten, so handsome. You pause outside the grocery store to look at the kittens some children are giving away out of a cardboard box. And you know that in your local shelter the number of choices is multiplied many times over and tinged with the sense of urgency for the kittens and cats for whom time is rather quickly running out.

Choose with your head, looking for the animal most likely to fit in with your life and your expectations. Choose with your heart, for the love between you is a bond that will sustain both of you for years.

No matter your choice, however, always remember how lucky you are to be able to bring a cat into your lifestyle; living with a cat's companionship is truly one of life's sweetest pleasures — one that is soon to be yours for many years to come, if you take your time at this stage of the game.

If you haven't so much as thought about the gender of the cat you want — much less the breeding or age — take a look at Chapter 2. If you're still not sure whether you're cat material, Chapter 1 can help you decide. And finally, Chapter 3 helps you evaluate the places to get a kitten or adult cat — from your coworker to a pet store to a breeder to a shelter — in hopes of avoiding the biggest mistakes people make when adopting an adult cat or kitten.

Always remember and enjoy the fact that your new cat is yours for life.

Natasha — Photo courtesy of Elizabeth Cárdenas-Nelson.

Evaluating the Environment

The first step in choosing a kitten or adult cat is not looking at the animal herself, or her littermates, but the environment in which she has been raised. After all, you're looking to adopt an animal companion, well-socialized and healthy. Though a cat's own personality factors into this equation, the circumstances of her upbringing probably count for more.

Domestication is a product of heredity and upbringing, and few of our closest animal companions are as able to step back and forth across the line between wild and tame as nimbly as the cat. Whereas the lives of wild, or *feral,* cats are not easy — and are often, in fact, quite short — the domesticated cat is able to fend for herself on the edges of human society, hunting and scavenging and carving out a life with little human intervention, and even less human contact.

The difference between feral cats and the ones purring contentedly in the lap of human luxury can be summed up in two words: luck and socialization.

For an animal to be comfortable around humans, he must be raised around humans. For an animal to love human companionship, he must be *socialized,* carefully and frequently, from an early age. Behaviorists working with all kinds of animals have known this fact for decades; more recent research applies it specifically to the cat.

Before their eyes even open, kittens begin learning and becoming comfortable with their world. If humans (or other animals, such as dogs) are part of this world, they become better pets as a result, more loving and attentive. Without the human touch during these important stages, all the subsequent kindness and socialization in the world doesn't count for as much: Your cat will probably always be a little tentative and shy.

Although socialization is probably the most important factor to consider when evaluating a kitten, there are others. The quality of care that the mother cat gives her kittens, for example, depends upon the quality of care she herself receives. Cats are resourceful and dedicated mothers, doing their best to provide for their young under the most challenging conditions. No matter how hard a mother cat tries to care for her babies, however, the stresses of a life of deprivation can have a negative effect on her kittens. Studies have shown that when a mother cat isn't adequately fed, her kittens develop slowly physically and may never catch up mentally or emotionally.

Unless your life's dream is to have a cat who spends his days hiding under your bed, you'll probably do best eliminating those adult cats or kittens whose lives didn't get off to the best of starts. Proper care of the mother and frequent handling of the kittens are essential to the creation of a loving, outgoing, and relaxed feline companion.

We evaluate pet stores and shelters, breeders good and not-so-good, and all the other sources for kittens in Chapter 3. In this chapter, we assume that you've weighed your choices and chosen the right source, and now it's time to choose the right pet from that source. If you don't know the pros and cons — including some rather disturbing ones — of various sources, it pays to review them in Chapter 3.

Getting a read on a kitty's history

So what do you do in order to find out about a kitten's or adult cat's history? Sit down with him and say: "Tell me about your kittenhood"? Unfortunately, it's not that easy. Some cats are talkative to the extreme, but actual words tend to fail them. To find out about a cat's past, you have to be a little more observant — look and listen for the clues that suggest you have a winner.

In some cases, especially with kittens, finding out about the mother cat and that all-important socialization is easy: All you have to do is ask the owner. This is certainly true if you're buying a pedigreed cat and dealing with a reputable breeder who knows the importance of good nutrition for the mother and handling and exposure to new things for the kittens. This breeder is happy to tell you everything that went into the development of your kitten, from how she considered the mating, matching pedigree to pedigree, to what she fed the expectant mother, to how and how often she handled the kittens.

If the breeder shows her cats, she's just as interested in well-handled kittens as you are — if not more so — because the kittens she picks for competition need to be able to deal with frequent baths and grooming, car and airplane rides, noisy exhibition halls with lots of gawkers, and judges handling them thoroughly to assess their *conformation,* or physical closeness to the written blueprint for the breed, called a *standard.*

We discuss the world of cat shows — and whether you can find a place in it for you and your cat — in Chapter 16. There we explain all about enjoying and understanding the exhibition of prized felines.

But what about the kittens your coworker wants you to see? Her family, too, may have provided a perfect environment out of common sense and the kindness of their hearts. The mother may be a beloved family pet or a cat in trouble they took in to help out. Again, ask about the mother's health and consider the environment the kitten was raised in. A litter raised indoors, in the heart of a family, with children to handle them and dogs to get used to (if you have dogs), with pans rattling and people talking — and even yelling — is full of superb pet prospects.

Making special considerations

If it seems as if we're suggesting only choosing kittens whose backgrounds you can verify and whose mothers you can meet, let us assure you that's not the case. Millions of wonderful kittens and adult cats are available for adoption from shelters, from dedicated foster-and-placement volunteers, and even from adoption outreach programs that take kittens and adult cats where the people are, whether it's in the adoption center of a pet superstore or the streets of San Francisco's financial district.

In these cases, you have to rely on your observations and on trust with the (one hopes) reputable animal organization that brought the animals out (ideally after getting a read on their temperaments and health first).

You have to give these animals a little leeway, especially the adult cats. Although healthy, well-socialized kittens can play in nearly any surroundings, even the best cats may be miserable and disoriented in the cages of a shelter. We discuss more on evaluating kittens and cats individually a little later in this chapter, but for now we just want you to remember: Don't make environment count for everything. Many a kitten or adult cat has risen from unfortunate beginnings to make a great pet. You just need to spend more time observing and testing the adult as an individual, that's all.

Choosing a Kitten

Though you shouldn't automatically consider a kitten — there's a lot of good to be said about an adult cat — most people are thinking "kitten" when it comes time to bring a cat into their lives. And you certainly can't deny the charm of a kitten.

Many times people make their choices based on aesthetic reasons — although personally we think *all* cats are beautiful! Some people are drawn to gray tabbies, others to calicos and tortoiseshells. That is no problem, of course, for the beauty of a cat is one of the pleasures of sharing a life with one, and beauty *is* in the eyes of the beholder.

But make sure your kitten is more than just a glamorpuss. Make sure he has a temperament you can live with, and make sure, above all, that he's healthy. Evaluating both of these criteria takes a little time.

Should you bring your children along to look at kittens and cats? How could you not? That said, the youngest children — below the age of three or so — may indeed be best left behind, for they have yet to learn how to be gentle in their handling of animals and could scare or even hurt a delicate kitten. (After you adopt a new family pet, you need to work on teaching your child how to handle her.)

Buddha — Photo courtesy of Tim Gallan.

No matter
how
adorable
the kitten
may be,
always
check his
health and
temperament.

School-aged children can help with the personality-testing, which is, after all, really about playing with the kittens (see the upcoming section, "Personality-testing your kitten"). From the age of nine or ten or so, children can be fully involved in the process, right down to choosing the kitten and caring for her at home — both under adult guidance. Kids and cats are good together!

Adopting at the ideal age

Many breeders don't let their kittens go to a new home before the age of 14 or even 16 weeks, when the baby's immune system is fully working (more on that in the vaccinations section in Chapter 9) and the kitten has enjoyed a wonderful start in the company of her littermates and mother — as well as children, dogs, and other realities of life among the two-legged.

Kittens benefit from the extra time with their littermates for the first 12 to 14 weeks of their lives, which is why most experts suggest that kittens adopted at this age have the best prospects for becoming healthy, well-adjusted pets. We'd draw the line at 10 weeks of age (at least), which is about the time when a kitten has developed the skills he needs to use as an adult, and we consider prime adoption time to be from 12 to 14 weeks of age.

At what age do kittens open their eyes? When can they walk, and hear, and leap? You can find information on kitten development from birth on — and how you can influence it in a positive way — in Chapter 14.

Remember that you're trying to find the best feline companion you can, trying to be an *informed consumer* and make your decision as much — if not more — with your head than your heart. A person who is trying to sell or give you a kitten who's too young — especially one freshly weaned at six to seven weeks of age — is probably more interested in "getting rid of" the kittens than in finding them good homes. You have to wonder what other shortcuts were taken with the litter, especially regarding how the mother was handled and how the litter was socialized.

Looking at a litter

You want to consider the litter as a whole, from the moment you first see them and vice versa. If the first thing you see is the tails of a half-dozen terrified kittens diving for cover, you want to look somewhere else: These babies are not for you.

What should you hope to see? Playful, confident kittens, friendly and inquisitive. Glossy coats under your fingers, bright eyes looking in your direction.

Wear comfortable clothes to look at a litter, and be prepared to get down to their level to check things out. Sit on the floor with them, and encourage them with chirps and wiggling fingers to interact with you.

After you get a sense of the group as a whole, start to sort out the personalities of each individual kitten. Take your time — which should be easy, for few things are more pleasurable than playing with a litter of healthy kittens. Observe which kittens are the most active or the most tentative. The kitten who never stops may not be the best choice for you, especially if you're looking for a companion to purr contentedly in your lap while you read or watch TV. The shy one may be a poor choice, too, especially if yours is an active household, with lots of comings and goings and a constant parade of children and guests.

If the litter's a good one, though, you should have two or three kittens that are kind of "medium" — friendly and playful, but not too crazy. These are the ones you should observe most closely; one of these is likely your best choice.

You may find the entire litter a little sluggish and slow afoot. Ask the owner whether the kittens just ate, or have spent the better part of the last two hours chasing each other through the house. If that's the case, ask to visit another time so you are able to better evaluate the true personalities of the kittens when they're fully awake.

Sometimes you may not be able to evaluate a kitten in the company of her littermates. This situation is especially true in shelters, where litters are commonly split when they come in. The practice — which is a sad necessity at the peak of kitten season — involves taking one or two kittens from each litter to place for adoption and sending the rest back for euthanasia. The lucky ones may just be more handsomely marked or more playful than their littermates, but they, too, may eventually meet the same fate. It's not the shelter's fault: They're just coping with pet overpopulation as best they can.

If you can't see the whole litter, you can still pick a wonderful pet. Kittens from different litters are often placed together for companionship and space considerations, so you can still observe how well each kitten interacts with others. And the most important part of choosing — personality-testing — is still available to you.

Personality-testing your kitten

Talk about fun! Checking out kittens is really about playing with them, and that's something you can never have enough of. Following are some considerations to keep in mind:

- ✔ **Evaluate her interest level.** To do so, take the kitten away from her littermates so her focus is on you.

- ✔ **Concentrate on her as an individual.** All kittens are adorable, so try to look beyond that and such things as color or that cute little Groucho mustache. Sure, you ought to like the looks of your cat, but the personality is more important in the long run.

- ✔ **Don't hurry.** Test as many kittens as you like and enjoy the time with each one. If you rush things and take the first kitten you see, the kitten who would have been a better match for you may never find a home.

- ✔ **Come with kitten-testing tools.** Bring a feather, a Ping-Pong ball, or a cloth mouse. A piece of string, yarn, ribbon, or tinsel is fine, too, as long as you remember that none of these should ever be left with a kitten or adult cat as a permanent plaything, because they are too often eaten and can cause havoc in the feline intestine.

The feather test

We like to use a feather, but in truth it can be any of your testing toys. You're looking for a kitten bursting with good health and playfulness, one who isn't afraid of people and, better yet, considers them the source of all good things.

At this stage, you should already have weeded out the overly shy kittens, and you especially should have sadly removed from consideration the kitten who spits and hisses in terror at your approach, or who stiffens or panics in your hands. If you're working with a shelter, they've probably already selected out these poor babies, leaving only the most adoptable out. Pick up the kitten carefully, with a reassuring but gentle grip under her belly, and set her down in your observation area.

Use a feather or other attention-getter to ensure that your prospective pet is healthy and inquisitive, as a normal kitten should be.

Let her explore her new environment a little while you settle onto the floor, and then, when she's satisfied with her surroundings, chirp at her and tease her with the feather (or string, or other toy). She should pursue it eagerly, batting at it and pouncing as she goes, and sitting up on her haunches to swat at it as you tease it overhead.

This is all normal behavior for a healthy, outgoing kitten, and if yours shows it, she's passed the feather test.

A moment of calm

The kitten you want should be neither too shy nor too assertive and active. The kitten you want should be comfortable being held, enjoying your stroking and soothing voice. One who struggles to wriggle free and keep playing — even if not doing so out of fear — may grow up into a cat who is too active for you.

So spend a few moments of quiet time with each of your contenders and see how they react to you as an individual. Let your heart weigh in a little here, and be receptive to the idea that one of these little fluffballs may be the one who's meant for you.

The perfect match when it comes to cats is the animal who is friendly and well-socialized, who has an activity level you can live with, and who appeals to your aesthetic sense of what feline beauty is all about. There are millions of kittens from which to choose, and many of them meet all your requirements.

Never get a kitten on impulse. The pet you choose will bring pleasure into your life for many years, so take your time and select the kitten who's right for your family.

Should you buy a kitten you've never seen?

If you have your heart set on one of the rarer breeds of cats — such as the short-legged Munchkin — you may well have to resign yourself to letting a breeder pick out a suitable kitten and ship it to you by air.

Understandably this sort of deal involves a lot of trust on both sides, and you want to be sure you're dealing with the most reputable and experienced of breeders. (You can find information on how to find such a person in Chapter 3.) But if you are confident you're working with such a person, then you should be fine — and so should your kitten.

May we make another suggestion, though? A rare-breed kitten can set you back several hundred — or even thousands — of dollars. What's a little travel expense on top of that, when you're talking about a companion who'll be with you for the better part of two decades?

Go see the litter. Go see your kitten. And fly home with him in your care. An unaccompanied kitten must travel as baggage in the pressurized cargo hold. If you're with your new pet, he can go with you in the cabin as carry-on luggage in an airline approved carrier.

It's a much better deal for the kitten, and for the nerves of the caring people at both ends. Oh, and for more on traveling with a cat, see Chapter 15.

Considering the Second-Chance Kitty

Perhaps because kittens are so very appealing, adult cats have the lowest adoption rate at many shelters. While prospective adopters head straight for the kitten section, hundreds of thousands of adult cats purr hopefully in their tiny cages, and thrust their soft paws beseechingly through the bars as if they understand the importance of catching someone's attention.

Too many never get a second chance, and that's a real shame.

It's a tragedy for the cats, of course, but it's also unfortunate for many people who don't realize that an adult cat may, in many cases, be a better choice. You know pretty well what you're getting with a grown cat — activity level, sociability, and health. Given time in a loving environment, a grown cat forms just as tight a bond with his new people as any kitten can, and we believe that in some cases recycled pets are more appreciative, somehow, of another chance at a happy life.

With adult cats, as with kittens, knowing a little of the animal's background is important, especially if your family has children or dogs. You can ask your questions about background directly if adopting from the cat's original owner, but most shelters also try to provide some basic information, which they ask of the people giving up their pets.

What if the information isn't flattering to the cat; for example, he has become available for adoption because of his failure to use a litter box? This is a tough situation, because you don't know the contributing factors — maybe the litter box was never cleaned or was left in a spot that was conve- nient for the owner but disconcerting for the cat. (More on litter box problems — and solutions — in Chapter 13.) With so many cats available, the common-sense answer is to count this kitty out. But if the cat checks out otherwise, it's really a judgment call, another factor for you to weigh before making a decision — but only if you have the time and patience to work on solving the problem.

If at all possible, take each adult cat you're considering away from the caging area of the adoption center or influence of her previous family. Sit down with her in your lap, alone, in a quiet place and try to get a feel for her as an individual. Shelters are stressful places, so she may need a few quiet minutes to collect herself, but the most calm, confident, and outgoing of cats respond pretty readily to your attention, relaxing in your lap, pushing for strokes, and purring. This is the kind of cat you're looking for.

Recognizing Good Health in Kittens and Cats

Don't fall in love with a sick cat. So many kittens and cats are available for adoption it just doesn't make sense to take a chance on one who may cost you a great deal of money in veterinary costs — and may not be with you long, anyway.

Feral cat considerations

In every community, dedicated volunteers trap, tame, and find homes for *feral* cats — those gone wild. Although these efforts are commendable and more than a few end in success stories, in general a formerly feral cat or kitten is a poor adoption prospect.

Why? They miss out on the early handling so crucial to their development as pets so they may never be fully comfortable in the company of humans. Even those who are slowly tamed may be very choosy, hiding from all but the one person who earned their trust.

A feral cat or kitten just isn't going to be as friendly and relaxed as an animal who has spent his whole life in the presence of humans, and if you adopt a wild one, you may be missing the cat who's better-suited for your life.

It's always hard to say "no" to an animal in need, but with the sheer numbers of cats and kittens so desperate for a home like yours, you may want to think twice before you choose a pet with built-in problems.

Some signs of health are obvious to anyone; others require a veterinarian's help to pinpoint. Before you settle on a promising kitten or cat, perform your own health check, and be sure to follow up with your veterinarian within a day or so.

The outer cat

General impressions are important. You should get a sense of good health and vitality from the animal you're considering adopting. He should feel good in your arms: neither too thin nor too fat, well put-together, sleek, and solid. If ribs are showing or the animal is potbellied, it may be malnutrition or worms — both fixable, but signs of neglect that may indicate deeper problems with socialization or general health.

With soothing words and gentle caresses, go over the animal from nose to tail, paying special attention to the following areas:

- ✔ **Fur and skin.** Skin should be clean and unbroken, covered thickly with a glossy coat of hair. Bald patches may mean *ringworm,* not a parasite but a fungal infection that you can catch, too. Part the hairs and look for signs of fleas: The parasites themselves may be too small and fast for you to spot, but their droppings remain behind. If you're not sure, put the cat on a clean surface, such as a stainless-steel counter or white towel and run your fingers against the grain. Then look on the surface: If fleas are present, you see the droppings as little bits that look like pepper, but if you add water to them, they turn reddish in color — because they're made up of dried blood. You shouldn't count a cat out because of a few fleas, but a severe infestation could be a sign of a health problem, especially for kittens. (Some kittens become anemic from having so much of their blood sucked by the pests.)

✔ **Ears.** These should be clean inside or, perhaps, have a little bit of wax. Filthy ears and head-shaking are signs of ear mites, which can require a prolonged period of consistent medication to eradicate.

✔ **Eyes.** Eyes should look clear and bright. Runny eyes or other discharge may be a sign of illness. The third eyelid, a semi-transparent protective sheath that folds away into the corners of the eyes nearest the nose (also called a *haw*), should not be visible.

✔ **Nose.** Again, no discharge. The nose should be clean and slightly moist. A kitten or cat who is breathing with difficulty, coughing, or sneezing may be seriously ill.

✔ **Mouth.** Gums should be rosy pink, not pale, and with no signs of inflammation at the base of the teeth. The teeth should be white and clean of tartar buildup.

✔ **Tail area.** Clean and dry. Dampness or the presence of fecal matter may suggest illness.

The inner cat

In the best circumstances, your kitten or adult cat will come with a clean bill of health certified by the shelter or other placement service, or vouched for by the cat's own health records kept by the person trying to place him. If that's not the case, you need to have any adoption prospect checked out for serious problems you can't see. Following are some problems you should have your pet checked for:

✔ **Infectious diseases.** Feline leukemia is the biggest concern. Though many cats live with the virus well enough for years, you may want to consider carefully the added worry and health-care expense of owning such a cat. Then, too, if you already have cats, you may want to safeguard their health by not exposing them to the contagious virus. Your veterinarian can determine the presence of infectious disease with a simple test, and explain to you the results — and your options.

✔ **Parasites.** Worms are the biggest problem. Your veterinarian needs to verify their presence and prescribe an appropriate course of treatment.

Don't put the cats you already have at risk by introducing a sick animal into your home. Have your new cat cleared by your veterinarian before you bring him home.

If your prospective pet clears the health check, he should start a regimen of preventive care right away to ensure continued good health. You can find information on preventive care and choosing a veterinarian in Chapter 9.

Taking a Leap of Faith — but with Your Eyes Open!

At the beginning of this chapter we state the old saying that "you choose a dog, but a cat chooses you" doesn't hold true for most people these days, but it still happens enough for you to keep your heart open to all the possibilities. For every "rule" we've put down in this chapter — don't adopt a sick cat, don't adopt a shy cat, don't adopt a cat with a behavioral problem, don't adopt a feral cat — we know of a handful of smashing success stories that prove the exception.

But these stories of love over adversity all have in common cat owners who went into the situation with open eyes and a willingness to spend the time (and in many cases, the money) to make a healthy, happy pet out of an animal with a problem.

If you want to take a chance on a kitten or adult cat with a problem, more power to you. But be honest about what you're getting yourself into. A kitty with a problem is harder (and more expensive) to live with than one who has everything going for him. And remember, too, that if you later decide you made the wrong decision with a problem cat, you'll probably be unable to find him another home.

Many things are possible, if you try. But if you're not able to put in the extra effort, be *sure* you choose a healthy, well-socialized cat who has a better chance of working out in your life, one with whom you can more easily form a relationship that will better both your lives for many years.

Chapter 5

Getting the Relationship Started Right

· ·

In This Chapter

▶ Is your house cat-safe?

▶ How to do the how-do-you-do's

▶ Kids and kittens

▶ A purrfect name

· ·

*B*ringing home a new pet is one of life's most exciting experiences, no matter whether you're an 8-year-old girl whose parents have finally given in to your begging for a kitten or an 80-year-old man looking forward to enjoying the quiet companionship of an older cat. The moment that cat or kitten comes home is the time when you and your cat are perfectly poised between two worlds: one of promise and one of reality.

For the reality to be the happy one you dreamed of when you first selected your cat or kitten, you're going to need to work to make sure that your new pet gets off on the right paw in your household. You need to make sure your house is safe for your new cat or kitten. Your children need to be aware of how fragile a pet can be and know how to handle their new companion appropriately. If you have other pets in the household, no matter the species, you need to set up introductions so all your pets feel comfortable and are kept safe as they settle into their routines and learn to enjoy — or at least tolerate — each other's company.

Just as important, you're going to be spending the first few weeks — months, in the case of kittens — working to lay the groundwork for a lifetime of good behavior. If you want your new pet to use the litter box, choose the scratching post over your sofa, and never consider your hand a biteable plaything, you need to set the rules from the beginning and stick to them, gently but firmly. Cats love routine, and after you settle yours into a good one for both of you, you'll both be much happier.

If you've adopted an adult cat with behavior problems, don't give up! Instead, turn to Chapter 13 for help with coping with the most common problems, such as scratching furniture, spraying urine, and avoiding the litter box.

Please don't be too put off by the prospect of *work* in learning to live with your new pet. All worthwhile relationships require patience and good humor to succeed. Although the first few weeks with a new kitten or cat can sometimes be a trial for all involved, the same period can also be a very special time for you and your pet. You're learning to appreciate the unique beauty and personality of your cat, and your cat is learning to trust and to love you.

Before you know it, you're looking back fondly on those first few crazy weeks, when love was new.

If you're bringing home your first kitten, consider going back for a littermate or another kitten. If you want two cats, the easiest method is to adopt two kittens at the same time, preferably from the same litter. Kittens don't have the sense of territory grown cats have and settle down together into a new home nicely. If you have a cat already, don't worry: We give you tips for managing the introductions later in this chapter, in "Hello, Kitty!"

For preventive veterinary care for kittens and cats, see Chapter 9.

Pre-Cat Preparations

"Curiosity killed the cat" is a saying that has been around nearly as long as cats themselves. And the fact that cats, even indoor ones, can get in some real jams is quite true — and kittens, small, active, and endlessly curious, are even more at risk.

If trouble's to be found, a kitten's sure to find it, which is why you need to look at your home closely and make some adjustments before bringing your new pet home — not only for safety, but to make the transition easier for you all.

Eliminating household hazards

Four words apply when preparing your house for a feline invasion: *Think like a cat.* Look at your home in a new way: as a big place full of exciting new things for a kitten or cat. Look low at nooks and crannies your new pet can get into. Look high at things your pet can get on top of. Look at things a cat can knock over, because if he can, they're gone. And mostly, look at things your cat can get into that can hurt him — those are the ones you really need to change.

Plaything problems

If you like to sew, knit, or do any kind of needlework, invest in a hamper to keep your materials completely hidden whenever you're not working on your projects. That's because cats and kittens love any kind of string, yarn, thread, or ribbon, without regard to the grave dangers such playthings pose if swallowed. And if the idea of your kitten swallowing thread doesn't give you the shivers, think about that needle going down the same pipe.

Likewise, find a secure storage place for ribbon, balled twine, or anything similar. Don't forget the string on your blinds! Wad the cord up into a short bundle and tuck it behind the blinds, out of your kitten's view.

Kittens and cats love to play with yarn, thread, and ribbon, but these items can pose a serious danger to your pet — don't let him play with them unsupervised.

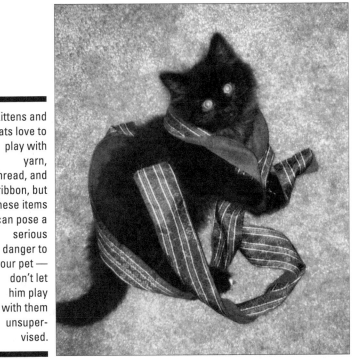

Raffy — Photo courtesy of Megan Boese.

Covered wastebaskets are a must in dealing with curious kittens and cats. The kind with lids that pop up after you step on them and close after you remove your foot are great for keeping your cat out of what he shouldn't be into — such as food waste in the kitchen and tissues and dental floss in the bathroom. Sure, you can teach your pet to stay out of wastebaskets, but sometimes the path of least resistance is the way to go. Covered wastebaskets aren't that expensive, and they pay for themselves in cleanup time and aggravation. Another alternative: Put wastebaskets out of reach under the sink or in a cabinet or broom closet.

Speaking of the bathroom, you want to make sure you hang your toilet paper in a way that makes it less entertaining — read "nearly impossible" — to unwind. Stop this delightful sport by putting the paper on the spool so that it unwinds from *underneath*. That way your pet's efforts to bat from the top gets him nowhere. If the folks in your family can't remember this advice when changing rolls — or your cat's more into shredding than unrolling — check out a pet-supply store or catalog for plastic shields that fit over the roll.

Another bathroom hazard is the toilet. Cats are fascinated by fresh water, and unless you want your kitten to take a bath — or worse, drown — remember to keep the lid down. If your home has a sump pump, make sure that's covered, too.

For plenty of ideas for cat-safe playthings — including many that don't cost you a dime — see Chapter 6.

Hiding places

Cats like to find dark, quiet places, especially if they're stressed. As long as those places are safe ones, you shouldn't discourage your cat from them. But kittens don't have as much common sense as cats and can get themselves into places they can't figure their way out of — and some of those places you may have a hard time getting them out of. Which is why, where kittens are concerned, you need to think about the places they should stay out of and work to discourage them from exploring.

If you've been through the get-into-everything stage with a human baby already, you've probably already got those nifty little devices on your cupboard that keep them from being opened by anyone but human adults. If not, take a look at your cupboards. Do they close securely, or do they fit together so poorly that a little paw can tease them open? If the latter's the case, you may want to think about kitten-proof latches — magnets, hooks and eyes, or other types. Check your local hardware store for a selection.

Your new pet may also find the area behind your refrigerator, sofa, or bookcase appealing. You may be able to block off access with cardboard while your kitten is small or put down two-sided tape at the entrance — cats hate to walk across sticky surfaces!

Another thing to look out for: chests of drawers. Although your kitten or cat may find your sweater drawer perfect for naptime, he's not going to like being trapped if you accidentally close the drawer with him in it. Even more dangerous: the kitten who likes to explore behind an open drawer who may

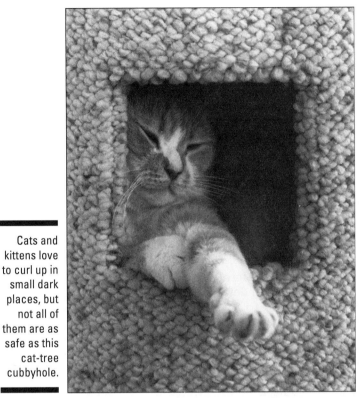

Cats and kittens love to curl up in small dark places, but not all of them are as safe as this cat-tree cubbyhole.

Scotty — Photo courtesy of Gay Currier.

get slammed against the back of the chest as you close the drawer. Remember to close your drawers immediately after you open them, and you can avoid both problems (although double-checking for your kitten whenever you close a drawer anyway certainly couldn't hurt). Be careful, too, about other areas your cat or kitten can get locked into, including closets and basements. More than a few cats have died of dehydration after being trapped, and others have died from heat after being caught in small areas and exposed to the sun. Know where your cat or kitten is: If he's not in a safe room when you leave and he's not looking at you as if to ask "Where are *you* going, pal?" find out where he is *before* you leave.

Higher and higher

Although the more relaxed breeds, such as Persians, may eventually prefer a more leisurely life on the ground, active breeds such as Abyssinians and Siamese — as well as every kitten ever born — are going to do their share of climbing. It's natural behavior, which means the best you can do is to direct it in an acceptable way — praise your cat for climbing a cat tree instead of your expensive drapes.

After your kitten first comes home, get your drapes out of harm's way while he's growing up: Tie your drapes up out of reach or fold them over their rods to get them off the floor. Encourage him to use the cat tree by staging games there and through praise and treats.

For tips on how to pick out a cat tree, see Chapter 6. For help with scratching problems, see Chapter 13.

Don't forget the trouble your kitten can cause while up high on shelves or tables. Put your most delicate knickknacks in the closet until the kitten-crazy days are past. Plants do better not on shelves but hanging from the ceiling. Don't expect miracles: If you live with cats (or any pets or children), things are going to get broken.

Bob Walker and Frances Mooney have completely remodeled their house to keep their cats happy. Bob's wonderful book, *The Cat's House* (Andrews and McMeel) shows how. But living with cats hasn't kept the couple from displaying their collection of artwork. They bolt down larger objects, such as lamps and sculptures, and use a product called Quake Hold to keep smaller things secure. Quake Hold is a putty that seals objects to their display surface. It may be hard to find outside of earthquake-prone California (where Walker and Mooney live); if so, try double-sided tape or Velcro, or ask at your hardware store whether Quake Hold can be ordered for you. Check out the Mooney's house on the Web, too, at www.thecatshouse.com.

Other things to look out for

Never question the ingenuity of kittens to get into trouble — and never forget to take precautions to keep them out of it. Here are a few more things to be aware of:

- ✔ **Electric and phone cords.** Bundle up the extra cord and tuck it out of sight — and spray anything that remains within reach of your kitten with something that tastes nasty, such as the commercial chew-stopper Bitter Apple, available at most pet-supply stores. Be especially careful if using small appliances such as irons —one good tug on the cord and your cat could get smashed. For the tangle of cords connecting your home computer to its printer, monitor, modem, or what-have-you, check at your hardware or computer store for cord-containers. The one Gina uses looks like the exhaust hose from a clothes dryer, only narrower, with a slit along its length to tuck cords into.

- ✔ **Windows.** Make sure your windows have screens that fit and are securely attached, especially on upper-story windows. Screens keep your indoor cat from becoming an outdoor cat and protect any cat from a nasty fall.

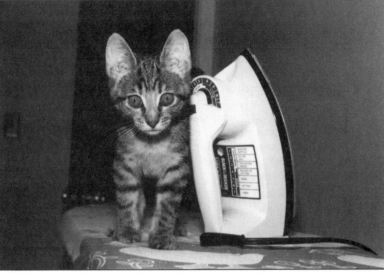

Milkdud — Photo courtesy of Beth Jenkins.

Before you decide your house is as close to cat-safe as possible, double-check it against our list of ten common household dangers in Chapter 21.

Organizing a "safe room"

With so many tempting troubles, you probably aren't surprised at our recommendation that you prepare a small place for your new kitten or cat to hang out whenever you're not around to watch her. An adult cat needs such a room, too, but for the adult cat, the idea's more about easing her into your home than protecting her from hazards.

You want to buy the equipment your cat needs before you bring him home. For information on how to pick out appropriate bowls, litter boxes, and toys, see Chapter 6.

The other reason for a safe room is *training*. Keeping your cat or kitten in a small area in the early stages of your relationship limits his options. He learns to scratch on a scratching post or cat tree and comes to understand that his litter box is the best place to relieve himself.

For more on preventing and curing behavior problems, see Chapter 13.

Indoor kitty: the conversion

If your new cat or kitten has had access to the outdoors, the best time to convert him to an indoors-only kitty is the moment you bring him home. The change requires resolve on your part and a determination to provide your new companion with everything he needs to be happy indoors — good food and fresh water, a clean litter box, a scratching post, toys, and, most important, your companionship.

What if you've had your pet for a while and are thinking of making such a change? It's still possible to do so. Pick a day — and that's that. Does such a change come easily? Not immediately, we must admit.

Cats are highly territorial, and the day you reduce your cat's territory by cutting him off from the outdoor part that he's been enjoying is the day you're going to start hearing about it — lots. Your cat is astonished at your stupidity at first: "Hey, you! I can't believe you're so dumb that you forgot how to open the door!" Later, he's positively astonished at your failure to respond: "The door! The door! Pay attention! I want something."

Don't give in. If you allow the insistent meows and pointed stares to wear you down to the point of opening the door, you've taught your cat a lesson you'd rather he didn't know: "All I need to do is put up a fuss and I get what I want." If you try to keep him inside again, he's going to be even more obnoxious.

Be patient but firm. Dissuade him from the door with a shot from a spray bottle and keep him occupied with games and attention. If he likes catnip, get a fresh supply to rub on his toys and scratching post.

Within a couple weeks, your cat starts to settle in to his new routines and you'll no longer need to worry about the dangers he faces outdoors.

A kitten's place

A bathroom — especial a spare one — is the ideal place to keep your kitten whenever you're away — it's easily kitten-proofed and just as easily cleaned. Pick up bathmats and toilet covers and put them away. Take the towels off the rack and make sure everything else from soap to razors, to shampoo bottles, to medications — *especially* medications — is safely put away. Although you may one day be able to leave toilet paper on the spool by placing it so that the paper unrolls from below — as described in the section "Plaything problems," earlier in this chapter — you may want to take the paper out completely if your kitten's little, especially if the room's a spare bath, or just put the whole thing in a cabinet or under the sink to keep the roll from getting shredded. And don't forget to close the toilet lid — a curious little kitten could drown in the bowl.

Earlier in this chapter, in the section "Higher and higher," we suggest you put up your drapes. Do the same for your shower curtain, too, tying it up or flipping it over the rod, or — better yet — remove it entirely in the beginning. If you have a shower enclosure, keep the door to it shut.

After you're done, you have a pretty sterile place, which is surely no fun for your kitten. But don't worry: We're going to tell you how to liven it up again.

Set up the room for your kitten by putting her litter box in one corner and her food and water dishes in another spot. (Put the dishes too close to the box and your cat may be offended and may choose not to eat — or may decide to "go" elsewhere.) You also need to add a sturdy, nontippable scratching post, a bed, and some toys.

You can easily understand how a safe room can keep your kitten out of trouble, but in fact, it's doing a little more than that. By keeping your kitten's options to a minimum, you teach her how to direct her natural behaviors in ways you can approve. If she has a scratching post but no couch, for example, she learns where scratching is acceptable.

So how does your cat or kitten learn where scratching *isn't* acceptable? See Chapter 13.

A cat's room

Although you can use the exact same setup for a newly adopted adult cat, you may choose a spare bedroom instead. The number-one reason for confining a kitten is to keep her out of trouble; the number-one reason for confining an adult cat, however, is to give her a place where she can feel secure while adjusting to her new home. She isn't going to get into as much mischief as a little one — although you still need to look at the room with an eye to eliminating the most-obvious hazards.

Look at the traffic patterns of your house and choose the quietest, least-trafficked room for your new adult cat. If it's a little-used spare bathroom, choose that. A spare bedroom? A den? The decision you make depends on your own home.

No matter which room you choose, you still need the same accoutrements: bowls for food and water, a litter box, a place to sleep, a scratching post, and some toys.

A "safe room" is an important part of retraining a cat with behavior problems and is also an integral part of moving your cat to a new home. For more on retraining, see Chapter 13. For information on how to move a cat from one home to another, see Chapter 15.

Kitten or cat, the first few days go more smoothly and safely if you prepare for your new pet in advance.

Bringing Your New Pet Home

The day your pet comes home is a big step for both of you. If she's a kitten, she's leaving her littermates and her mom and throwing her lot in with you, an incredibly large and, to her mind, ungainly and unpredictable creature. If she's a grown cat, she's dealing with the uncertainties of her recent life and is unsure of what the future may hold. As you would for a child visiting your home, be there for your cat but don't force yourself upon her. For four days after joining Paul's home, PC lived in a tiled sunroom, refusing to partake in any social behavior. In fact, she would jump four feet in the air every time Paul tried to coax her to interact during his cleaning and feeding time in *her* room. But slowly and surely, she acclimated to his presence and her new surroundings and her need for social interaction drew her out — on her own terms.

Try to arrange some time off after your cat first comes home, or at the very least, pick her up the first morning of a weekend. You want to spend some extra time with her, and a little extra attention here helps with the bonding.

You want the transition to be as smooth as possible, and a safe trip home is an important step. The first rule of transporting a cat: Use a carrier! The second rule: Use a carrier! You may also want to bring towels, both the paper and old bathroom variety, and a bottle of pet-mess cleanup solution in case of an accident — although don't try to clean up any mess *inside* the carrier until you and your new pet are safely home.

Did we mention that you should use a carrier to bring your pet home? Although you should never transport any cat without this important safety device, you're really engaging in risky behavior whenever you try it with a cat you don't know. We don't care how much your children want to hold their new pet — it takes only one scratch or bite for a frightened cat to get loose in your car. After that, he could go out the window — did we mention to keep them up? Please do! — or under your feet while you're driving. Even

The name game

Naming a cat is great fun, because you have no limits whatsoever to the name you can choose. Most cats probably end up with a couple of names — a longer, more formal name such as Evangeline, and a shorter, come-to-dinner name such as Evie, or Kitty-Butt, or Baby-Evie-Face.

Because your cat doesn't pay all that much attention to what you call him anyway — unless you happen to be talking about something he wants, such as dinner — you can really let your imagination go wild.

Look in atlases for interesting place names and literary references for great character names or the names of authors. Or think of names that are related to your profession or great loves, such as in the case of the friend of Gina's, an amateur hockey player, who named his cats Slapshot and Puck. Although plenty of name-your-pet books are out there — and they're all fun reading — we find that a name-your-baby book is just as useful.

Make naming your cat a family project and use this opportunity to interest your children in a trip to the library. You don't have that many opportunities in your life to name a family member, so make the most of it!

if all he does is get up under the seats, you're going to have a heck of a time getting him out of your car after you get home. Dragging him out by any piece of him you can reach, by the way, isn't going to convince him that you're a swell person and could leave you with some nasty scratches.

If you have another cat in your home, the first place you should take your new cat or kitten is the veterinary hospital. You could be risking your resident cat's life if you don't. Your new cat or kitten needs to be checked for infectious viruses such as feline leukemia and other contagious health hazards such as ear mites and upper respiratory infections. *Don't risk your resident cat's health in your enthusiasm over your new pet.* Make sure your new pet is vet-checked before attempting any introductions. If that's not possible — you save a stray on a Sunday, for example — make sure you keep the new cat completely isolated until you can get him to your veterinarian. See Chapter 9 for important preventive-care information.

Watch the birdie, kitty!

Don't forget to load up your camera with film and record the special day your new pet comes home. If you're adopting a kitten, buy lots of film, because over the next couple of months, you're going to kick yourself for missing some great shots if you don't — and hate yourself later for not having pictures of your wonderful cat as a baby. They grow up awfully fast!

Here are a few tips for taking great cat pictures:

✔ *Get your children involved.* Get them to help you with your pictures by teasing your new pet with a toy on a string, or zoom in close to get pictures of kids and cat together. On the day your new pet comes home, let the kids make some memories, too: Get them each one of those throwaway cameras. You're sure to be delighted at some of the shots you get back — and they're going to be doubly so!

✔ *Head (safely) outdoors.* Natural light — early morning is best — avoids the dreaded red-eye shot, where the flash makes your beautiful kitten come out as a monster. Taking pictures outside gives your new pet a more natural, healthy look. If your cat is a solid, dark color, use your

flash even outdoors (if your camera enables you to do so): The flash brings out the detail in your pet's face.

Caution: Make sure that your kitten or cat is out of harm's reach when taking photos in natural light. Use a screened porch or sun room if you have one available. An alternative is photographing your pet as she naps lazily in a sunny spot.

✔ *Get close.* If you want a good picture, you're going to need to go where your pet is. Shoot at just below your kitten's eye level and zoom in as closely as you can for good detail.

✔ *Watch your backgrounds.* Think neutral — a plain wall, not a cluttered cabinet. Think contrast — light for a dark cat, dark for a light one. If your tabby cat loves to sleep on the busy fabric of your sofa, consider throwing a solid blanket down first. (Or maybe always — it keeps the cat hair off your upholstery!)

✔ *Be creative.* If you want your kitten to kiss your children, do as the pros do: Put a little butter on your children, and let the kitten kiss it off.

The place where you adopt your cat, such as a shelter, may provide you with a cardboard carrier for the ride home. And that's fine for this first trip, but you want something sturdier for the long haul. Carriers made of high-impact plastic are not expensive; they last a lifetime, and they give your cat a feeling of security whenever he travels. For tips on picking out a good carrier, see Chapter 6.

Hello, Kitty!

To say that cats don't like change is an understatement — and being introduced to a new home is big change. Some hide under the bed. Some stop using the litter box. Efforts to soothe others may be greeted with a hiss or a growl — or even a swipe with claws bared.

Although these are all normal feline reactions to stress, the bad habits cats may develop while coming to terms with something new could become a permanent part of their routine. Which is why, for your new cat's sake and your own, you need to remember one word when introducing a new pet to your household:

Slowly.

Although a healthy, curious, and outgoing kitten may handle changes a little better, don't press your luck with a baby cat either. Be patient as your new pet learns to be comfortable in his surrounding and settles into the routine of your household.

The trick to introductions is the "safe room" you've (we hope) already set up, as described in the section "Organizing a 'safe room,'" earlier in this chapter. Kitten or cat, this room is a place where your new pet can feel safe — and be safe — while adjusting to his new home. How you use this room depends on the circumstances of your household, as we explain in the following sections — a frightened cat or kitten needs it more, and often longer, than does a well-socialized and correctly trained older cat.

Children

Children and cats are natural together, but you need to lay some ground rules for the safety of both from the moment your new pet comes home. Kittens can be injured by the loving attention of children, especially young ones. And with more than 600,000 cat bites reported every year in the United States, you can clearly see that some cats give as good as they get.

Does the number of cat bites surprise you? Compared to dogs — three million reported bites a year in the United States (and often more severe ones to boot!) — cats are a distant second in the bite department. But you must still take precautions for your human family members. Make sure your pet is vaccinated for rabies — more on that in Chapter 9 — and make sure you treat any bite seriously. If *your* cat's the biter, wash the wound thoroughly with soap and water and contact your doctor immediately if the skin is broken. Cat's harbor some pretty nasty bacteria in their mouths and a disease called *cat scratch fever* can even be deadly for people with suppressed immune systems. Do not take any hint of infection associated with a cat bite lightly. If you don't know the biter, contact your local animal-control and public-health officials — the cat could be rabid!

The key to keeping children and cats together safely is to make sure their interactions are supervised and to teach children how to handle and respect cats. Here are some tips, by age group:

- ✔ **Infants:** Under no circumstances should a cat (or any pet) be left unsupervised with an infant. Although the idea that your cat poses a risk to your baby has been debunked — see Chapter 17 for more information, as well as precautions for pregnant women — keeping your cat away from your baby while you're not present is just common sense. Some people have even gone so far as to put a screen door on the room to the nursery, and to be honest, this precaution isn't a bad idea.

- ✔ **Toddlers:** Children at this age can really try a cat's patience, even though they aren't being anything but normal toddlers. Children in this age group can't understand that poking, squeezing, or patting roughly aren't appreciated. Although most cats figure out quickly that children this age are best avoided, your child could be bitten or scratched if your cat is cornered or startled. Keep an eye on all interactions and consider putting a baby-gate across the entry to your cat's safe room so that he can have a place where he isn't pestered.

- ✔ **Young children:** From the time a child's in school, he can start learning to care for a pet and take an increasing amount of responsibility — under supervision, of course. One way to teach younger school-aged children to play carefully is to play the "copy-cat game." If your child pets the cat gently, stroke his arm gently to show how nice it feels. If he pokes the cat, poke him — gently! — to help him make the connection.

Teach all children to hold a cat correctly, with support under his chest and his legs not dangling. A cat who feels secure is less likely to wriggle free with a claw or a bite.

Children should learn how to hold a cat correctly, with support for the cat's legs and a reassuring hand over his body.

Anyone who lives with a cat should know that the place most likely to get you nailed if you touch it is a cat's tummy. Even cats who seem to like petting there at first can get revved up and grab on with claws and teeth. Teach your children to avoid this sensitive area and to pet in a way most cats enjoy, such as behind the ears. For more on cat body language, see Chapter 12.

Other cats

Introducing a second cat to the household is one time when patience is never more important. Despite your resident pet's initial misgivings, adding a companion can be a wonderful idea, especially for an indoor cat.

A kitten is usually an easier introduction, because most older cats accept a baby more readily than they do another adult. But even with a kitten, keep a close watch on the situation and be prepared to separate the two as described in the following paragraphs.

Territorial conflicts are greatly reduced if both cats are altered. Unneutered males, especially, don't take intruders lightly and will probably start spraying urine to mark their territory. For more information on altering, see Chapter 14.

Prepare your safe room for the new cat or kitten with a second set of bowls for food and water, a litter box, a scratching post or cat tree, and some toys. (Separate gear may be a temporary arrangement, or it may be lifelong, depending on the cats involved.) This separate room is your new pet's home turf while the two cats get used to each other's existence.

Don't forget to take your new cat or kitten to your veterinarian first. After you're sure your new pet is healthy, the introductions can begin.

Bring the cat home in a carrier, and set the carrier in the room you've prepared. Let your resident cat discover the caged animal and don't be discouraged by initial hisses. Let your resident cat explore, and after the new cat is alone in the room, close the door and let him out of the carrier. If he doesn't want to leave the carrier at first, let him be. Just leave the carrier door open and the cat alone.

Maintain each cat separately for a week or so — with lots of love and play for both — and then on a day when you're around to observe, leave the door to the new cat's room open. Don't force them together. Territory negotiations between cats can be drawn out and delicate, and you must let them work it out on their own, ignoring the hisses and glares.

Eventually, you can encourage them both to play with you, using a cat "fishing pole" or a toy on a string. And slowly — that word again — feed them in ever-closer proximity.

Bring a second cat home in a carrier and let your first cat discover the newcomer. The cats need to be kept apart during the early stages of introduction.

Most cats — but not all — eventually learn to live together happily. After you see your two sleeping together, playing, or grooming each other tenderly, you'll know the effort was worth it.

Dogs

Before you bring home a cat or kitten, make sure your dog knows two basic commands: "Leave it" and "Stay." You're going to be saying those words a lot in the first couple of weeks, so the time to practice making sure your dog knows them is *before* you bring home your cat or kitten.

Here's how to teach your dog these useful commands:

- ✔ **Stay.** Start with the "Sit," with the dog at your side, holding the leash in a straight line up from his head with all the slack out. Flash an open palm in front of your dog's nose and then say, "Stay." Step out in front of your dog so that you can block his forward motion. If he moves, snap the leash to correct him, flash your hand, and repeat the "Stay" command. If he stays, return to your position alongside him after a second or two, tell him "okay," and praise him. From there, it's a matter of building up time and distances in slow increments. If you're working at the end of the six-foot leash and your dog is staying reliably, tug on the leash a little without making a sound. If he moves, go back and correct him with a leash-pop, repeat the command sequence, and try again. If he resists the tug, return to your position alongside him, release him with an "okay," and praise.

- ✔ **Leave it.** With your dog in a sit-stay and your hand in a fist, flat surface up, offer your dog a biscuit with the other. As she reaches for it, say "Leave it" and bop her under the chin, enough to close her jaw but not lift her off her feet. Offer the biscuit again, repeating the "Leave it" command, and if she hesitates or turns away, praise her. Few dogs need this demonstrated more than twice.

For more on dog-training or anything else concerning living with a dog, you ought to buy the companion book to this one, *Dogs For Dummies*. The book was named the best general reference book by the Dog Writers Association of America as well as the best entry in the 1996 DWAA writing contest — topping more than 1,000 entries in 50 categories — and we are a little proud of it.

Bring your new cat or kitten home in his carrier, and as with the cat-to-cat introductions, put the carrier in the safe room. Bring your dog in on a leash, with the cat still safely housed, and let the two get a look at each other. Let your dog sniff, but if he's getting a little overly excited, use the "Leave it" command and praise him for minding.

New dog, old cat

Of course, sometime a cat's not the new kid on the block — a dog is! If you're planning to add a dog to your cat's world, take some time beforehand to prepare her.

Take a look at your cat's food and water dishes. Are they in a location where a dog could get to them? Because cat food is higher in protein than dog food, many dogs think it's a wonderful treat. But cat food isn't good for your dog, and your cat isn't going to be interested in sharing. So move the dishes up to a place where your cat can eat without being pestered.

How about your cat's litter box? Again, make sure that it's in a "dog-free" zone, both for your cat's peace of mind and to keep your dog from indulging in a dreadful canine vice: eating cat feces. A hooded litter box may do the trick, but a better idea is to set up the area so that the dog can't get near the box. The method you use depends on the size of your dog. Putting a cat door in the door to a spare room keeps a big dog out; putting the litter box in the unused guest bathtub keeps most little dogs at bay. (For instruction on how to teach your cat to use a cat door, see Chapter 6.)

Make these changes a couple weeks before bringing home a puppy or dog so your cat can get used to them.

Don't allow your new dog to chase your cat — keep a leash on him so that you can correct him in the early stages. Don't force your cat to interact — let him deal with the interloper in his own way and in his own time.

Although doing so may not seem fair, because your cat was there first, if your cat reacts badly to the stress — not using the litter box, for example — you may need to resort to the introduction methods for a new cat we discuss in the preceding section in this chapter and keep him sequestered in a room with his food and water, litter box, scratching post, and toys during the acclimation process.

Although canine-feline introductions don't always go smoothly at first, your pets learn to tolerate — or even enjoy! — each other's company.

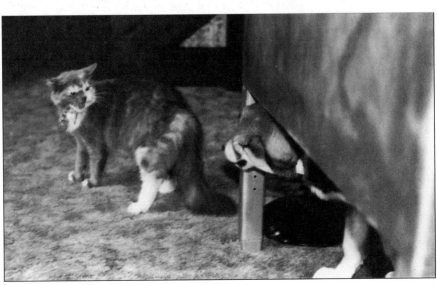

Jigsaw and Rajah — Photo courtesy of Amie Rohrer.

Then take your dog out, close the door to the safe room, and let the cat come out of the carrier when he's ready. Let the animals get used to each other's scent for a couple weeks and then put a baby-gate across the door to the safe room to keep the dog out. Let the cat choose the level of interaction.

Never tolerate aggressive behavior from your dog. Keep a leash on him until everyone's settled and use the "Stay" and "Leave it" commands to keep him under control.

Although some cats and dogs maintain an armed truce, at best, others become the best of companions. These things take time, however, so be patient.

Other pets

If you have birds, reptiles, fish, rabbits, or rodents, no introductions are necessary. *Keep your cat away!* Never forget that, although your cat may be a loving companion to you, he's still hard-wired with the instincts of a hunter, and your smaller pets are his natural prey.

Don't take chances. Make sure that, whenever you're not around to look out for them, your other pets are kept safe from your cat. Close the door to the room where they stay, and correct your cat with a squirt bottle if you see him expressing an interest.

Keep your cat away from other pets — especially those that are her natural prey.

Bonker — Photo courtesy of Aaron Springer.

Chapter 6

All the Right Stuff

In This Chapter

▶ Litter boxes and fillers
▶ Scratching posts and cat trees
▶ Travel gear
▶ All the best toys
▶ The buzz about catnip

*N*o barn cat ever imagined the way some of our cherished pets live today. Although cats have for uncounted generations relied on their own wits and skills to find food and water, a place to relieve themselves, a place to sleep, and things to amuse themselves, our increasingly indoors-only cat population looks to us to provide them with their basic needs, and to do so, you need cat gear.

But what choices you have! Forget about the old adage of making a better mousetrap: Make a better cat toy, and the world is sure to beat a path to your door today. Even more compelling: Make a perfect litter box, and you're certain to retire a millionaire, as the inventor of Kitty Litter, the late Edward Lowe, did a generation earlier.

At the basic level, cat gear takes care of your pet's needs in an inexpensive, no-nonsense way. But sometimes spending a little more can make your life easier and your cat's life more full, the latter an important consideration for the indoor cat who stays alone while you're at work.

Besides, shopping for cat supplies can be great fun!

Although we cover the kinds of dishes you need for your pet in this chapter, we tell you what to put in them in our section on nutrition in Chapter 8. Information on the best grooming supplies for your cat — and how to use them — are in Chapter 7.

Where to Find the Best for Your Cat

Never before have people had so many choices in shopping for pets. In recent years, pet superstores have popped up everywhere, with a bigger section of supplies than were carried by a half-dozen of the mom-and-pop pet stores of a generation ago. In the shadow of the retailing behemoths, small businesses have had to focus on finding a new niche, selling services such as free delivery, a higher level of pet-care advice than the superstores can offer, or niche products such as jeweled collars, wind chimes, and high-end toys and treats.

Throw into this mix supermarkets, where the emphasis is on age-old brand names and generic store brands, and the appeal is convenience. Pet supplies are one of the top categories in any grocery store in terms of shelf space, and grocery retailers and their suppliers have done a great deal in recent years to improve the quality of their pet supplies. Of course, much of the reason for this increased interest in pet supplies is because of the desire to keep their share of the multibillion-dollar sales volume intact from the onslaught of their new competitors — not only the pet superstores but also general retailers such as Wal-Mart and warehouse stores such as Costco.

And what about catalogs and the Internet? The boom in mail-order business hasn't missed the cat-supplies industry, with available catalog selections as varied as those of the pet superstores and as focused as those of high-end cat boutiques. (For a list of these companies, see the Additional Resources appendix at the back of this book.) Although still a small part of the pie, online merchants are starting to make their presence known. Even so, for the most part, the World Wide Web is used by pet owners mostly to obtain product information, not for actually ordering supplies. Experts say that this situation is bound to change, however, as more people become comfortable with online commerce.

Even though online merchants are just . . . ahem, scratching the surface of cat supplies, some innovators are offering unique merchandise on the World Wide Web. We profile a couple of them in Chapter 20. If you have America Online, you may also want to check out the online stores of the Pet Care Forum (keyword: PETS), including our friends at Reigning Cats and Dogs, an upscale pet boutique in Sacramento, California, who let us test all the new products we want.

Finally, don't forget the little guys! A lot of the most creative and attractive merchandise for cats is handmade in small quantities. Crafts fairs and farmers' markets are good places to look for these items.

You can get high-quality cat merchandise at all these outlets: superstores and small pet retailers, supermarkets, giant general merchandisers and warehouse outlets, catalogs, and online stores. Although experimenting with brand names and generic products is fine, remember always that the final determination of suitability on any product comes down to two things: First, is it safe for your pet, and second, does your pet like it?

You don't always need to think "new" when you need cat supplies. Many a top-quality cat tree or carrier has turned up at yard sales at a fraction of the cost for new, so keeping your eyes open at such sales often pays off for you and your cat. (Remember to clean "second-hand" gear thoroughly before use.)

A Place to Go

No product is more important to a harmonious relationship between you and your cat than a litter box. What behaviorists call *inappropriate elimination* — a cat who goes where he's not supposed to — is the top complaint cat lovers make about their pets and one of the primary reasons why adult cats end up in shelters.

The litter box you choose and what you put in it is one of the most important purchases you ever make, and you need to be aware that you may not get the formula right the very first time. Be aware of all the possibilities and be prepared to experiment to find just the right combination of box and filler that's right for your cat's temperament and health.

Every bit as important as choosing the right litter box and filler is making it inviting and comfortable for your pet to use. If you have a cat who's refusing to use the litter box, you want to read Chapter 13, which contains a complete section on the causes and cures for litter-box avoidance.

Litter-box choices

More choices in litter boxes exist than ever before and range from the recycling of old baking pans and dishpans to the inexpensive options of cardboard throwaways, to higher-priced models that make cleaning easier — or even automatic. The following list describes just some of your choices:

- **Disposable pans:** Small cardboard litter boxes are popular with shelters, rescuers, pet stores, and some breeders but probably aren't too practical for long-term use for your pet cat. Still, you may consider keeping a few of these on hand in case a stray walks into your life, for young kittens, or for cats who need nursing back to health. Gina once cared for a cat with a broken leg, and the smaller size of disposable litter boxes worked well with the large carrier the cat stayed in while recuperating.

✔ **Household items:** A 9 x 13-inch metal baking dish, too worn for cooking, can be a good first litter box for a kitten — its low sides making it easy for babies to hop in and out of. Plastic dishpans, with their high sides, can be a good choice for cats who like to kick their litter everywhere.

A truly novel idea in the do-it-yourself litter box category comes from feline behaviorist Kate Gamble, whose cat-behavior videos are just about the best around. (See the Additional Resources appendix for ordering information.) Gamble, who is associated with the San Francisco SPCA, uses a plastic box sold for storing blankets, cutting one side down to make an easier opening and covering the cut edges with duct tape to prevent fur snags. She says the high sides of this design is another way to combat litter-kickers; to combat tracking, she puts the box lid underneath to collect litter from her cats' paws.

✔ **Simple plastic pans:** Millions of cats have done just fine with this design, and yours may be among them. Relatively inexpensive and widely available, these pans come in a variety of shapes, sizes, and colors. Some have special rims to keep more filler in the box. Make sure the one you choose is easy to scrub clean.

✔ **Covered pans:** Manufacturers say covered pans keep odors down and prevent dogs and children from getting into the filler. Unfortunately, some owners take the approach that, if they can't smell the litter box, it doesn't need attention — and the cat who feels otherwise finds someplace else to go. If you choose this kind of pan, don't forget you must be as on top of its cleaning as you would with any other variety — and don't blame your cat for mistakes if you aren't.

Cats with asthma should not use a covered litter pan — they need the increased ventilation an open-air variety offers. For more on cat asthma and other common health problems, see Chapter 10.

✔ **Self-cleaning pans:** No one likes to clean the litter box, but some cats are so fussy that, if you let this important chore wait, your cat may turn her nose up and go elsewhere. In recent years, inventors have come up with new pans that make cleaning a nearly "hands-off" affair, thanks to the easy-clean properties of clumping cat-box filler. Some of these boxes have lift-and-sift inserts that collect used clumps as you lift them, while you roll the others over, thereby running litter through a collector that catches and holds the clumps. Although generally a little more expensive than ordinary hoodless pans, these systems may be a good option if you're so squeamish about litter-box cleaning that, as a result, you don't do it frequently enough.

Two new products are really pushing the edges of cat-box innovation — and expense! The *Sweet "P" Dry System* is a litter box that doesn't use litter at all. The system uses large granules that don't get tracked through the house, according to the manufacturer. Moisture goes through the box and is collected on absorbent pads, which are changed weekly. (Solid waste must be scooped out.) The unit costs $40 in one

Litter box choices range from simple pans to covered models, to the latest, a self-cleaning electric gadget. Whatever you choose, you must make certain that your cat agrees with your decisions or you're going to have a problem!

wholesale catalog; list price is more than $70, although, of course, you also need to factor in the savings on the litter you aren't going to be buying.

At nearly $200, the *LitterMaid system* must be considered the top-of-the-line cat box; indeed, its manufacturers promote it not as a litter box but as a household appliance. The system uses clumping litter and removes waste automatically after each use, thanks to an electronic eye that notices when a cat steps in and a 10-minute timer that ensures that he's long out of sight before the cycle begins. The machine runs a rake through the litter, catching clumps and depositing them in a sealed bin for later disposal. On the way back, the rake smoothes the litter for the cat's next visit. Ingenious!

Although no one's exactly fond of dealing with soiled litter, some people should avoid it entirely — pregnant women and people with immune systems suppressed by disease or medical regimens. That's because some cats harbor a parasite that can be dangerous to fetuses and to people with impaired immune systems. The danger should be kept in perspective, however, and does not require anyone to get rid of a cat. For the facts on the parasite and on the disease it causes (called *toxoplasmosis*), see Chapter 17.

Litter-box accessories

No matter what kind of litter box you choose, you find that you also have some additional options from which to choose — items intended to keep things neater or make cleanup easier. Here's the rundown:

- ✔ **Scoops:** These utensils range from flimsy plastic to last-forever high-quality plastic and metal. You probably need one even for self-cleaning litter boxes — scooping one mess is often easier than sifting the whole box. Skip the flimsy scoop and get something that's going to last you a while.

- ✔ **Liners:** Intended to make changing the entire contents of the pan easier, liners work fine . . . if your cat likes them. If your cat digs deep with claws extended, he may not like catching himself on them. Experiment and see what works best for you both.

- ✔ **Mats:** You find you put up with less tracking of filler if you put a mat of some sort under your cat box. You can find mats made just for this purpose in any pet-supply store or catalog, or you can use an ordinary door mat or carpet remnant.

The scoop on litter

Some experts have credited the invention and improvement of litter with being the driving force behind the cat's rise to the position of top companion animal, and certainly such a case can be made. Before absorbent filler became widely used and accepted, the alternative — sawdust and sand — left so much to be dsesired in the way of smell and ease of use that cats were often banished to the outside to eliminate their waste. After modern litter took off, however, cats became an integral part of the lives of an ever-increasing number of people, leading to the high popularity of felines today.

Many choices exist for cat-box fillers, but you must always remain aware that the decision of which one's the "right" one rests solely with your cat.

Even the best cats have accidents, and you want to keep cleaners at hand for any eventuality. The most important thing to remember: *Never* clean up a pet mess with an ammonia-based product: It makes the area smell even *more* like urine — ammonia being a component of urine — and attracts the pet back to the site for more messing.

Several good products are designed to remove stains and smell through enzyme action; one of these can be a lifesaver. Another possibility is Petsorb, a product made of absorbent crystals that absorbs the moisture of pet messes and can then be vacuumed up.

Clay litter

A half-century old and still a significant part of the market, *clay litter* is the product that started the cat revolution. Clay litter is the least-expensive option in terms of price per pound, but you need to use more of it because clay litter needs to be completely replaced weekly to combat odors — although some brands do have deodorizers built in.

Some believe that clay tracks less and is safer for the tiniest kittens. (See the sidebar "Litter health risks, real and not-so-real," later in this chapter.)

Clay is easy to use with disposable boxes and so is popular with shelters and rescuers. Liners may make replacement of the entire contents of a cat box easier.

Clumping litter

Call *clumping litter* the second revolution, if you will. And even if you won't, have no doubt about the increasing popularity of this product among cat lovers.

Clumping, or *scoopable,* litters dissolve around the moisture in urine or feces, reforming as a lump encasing the mess, which can then be easily scooped, raked, or sifted out. Because the entire mess is scooped out each time — assuming the clump doesn't break — odor problems are minimized. Furthermore, as with clay brands, some clumping litters have deodorizers in them.

Although clumping litters are more expensive per pound, they require you to use less because all you need do is replace the litter you've removed with the waste. Although clumping litter does need to be replaced eventually, that chore can wait for a month or more, depending on the quality of the litter (some brands clump better than others) and the number of cats using the box.

Does an indoor-outdoor cat need a litter box?

Are you intending to be one of those people who never deals with a litter box at all? Unless you're living on ten acres of your own private property, we think you should reconsider your decision and get your cat a litter box.

We're guessing that your neighbors are going to agree.

Letting your cat use the great outdoors as he chooses is unfair to your neighbors and unhealthy to the people who come in contact with cat waste in their own flower beds — including members of your own family.

We're not going to rehash the arguments against letting cats roam freely — they're listed in Chapter 1 already — but we do stress that, if your cat wanders the neighborhood, you need to do what you can to get him to do his business at home. Keep a litter box clean and accessible to him at all times.

According to *CatWatch*, a monthly newsletter put out by the Cornell Feline Health Center (subscription information is listed in the Additional Resources appendix), preference polls indicate that cats prefer clumping litter to other varieties, which means cats who may avoid the litter box with other types may use clumping litter without problems.

Drawbacks to clumping litter include tracking problems, because the material that sticks to moisture on cat mess clings just as easily to moisture on cat paws. A mat goes a long way to solve this problem, however.

Even worse than clumping litter's tendency to stick to a cat's paws is the mess than can develop around the genital area and back thighs of a cat with long silky hair, such as a Persian. Moisture in this area collects litter and can cause these cats problems in grooming and even defecating if the problem is unattended. To avoid these problems, keep your cat's fur cut close on his inner thighs and other areas where urine may catch, and make sure that you've set up a frequent grooming regiment to catch any granules. For more information on grooming, see Chapter 7.

Alternative litters

Coming up third in consumer preferences are various alternative fillers, including those made from wood fiber, corn cobs, pelleted newsprint, and other recycled materials. Some cats and cat owners love these alternatives; others can't stand them. Feel free to experiment until you find something that you, your cat, and your pocketbook can all be happy with.

Litter health risks, real and not-so-real

As we mention elsewhere in this chapter, hooded boxes aren't recommended for cats with asthma. The same goes for dusty litters (as opposed to low-dust varieties) and litters with deodorizers, both of which may irritate these sensitive cats.

One health risk that seems to have no basis in anything but rumor and anecdote is the purported problem with clumping litter causing intestinal blockage — and death — in kittens.

The idea traces to anecdotal reports in cat lovers' magazines, later picked up and spread through the newsgroups and e-mail lists of the Internet. To date, no scientific study has confirmed that such a problem exists with clumping litters.

To err on the safe side, some veterinarians suggest avoiding clumping litter until the kitten is out of the taste-testing-everything curiosity stage. But even that is just a precaution and isn't necessary for adult cats.

Some litters call themselves "flushable," meaning that you can put waste and filler together into your toilet for easy disposal. Whether this approach is a good idea for your household depends on your home, the age of your plumbing, and whether you're on a sewer system or a septic tank. Gina likes to offer the advice of her favorite plumber: "Don't put anything in the toilet unless you've eaten it first." If you want to experiment, consult your favorite plumber first or, at the very least, keep his number handy!

You're better off sealing waste in plastic bags and putting the bags in your trash can for pickup. One more disposal alert: Public-health officials warn emphatically that you should *never* put the waste of a cat — or any carnivorous animal, such as a dog or ferret — in your garden compost pile. (The waste of plant-eating pets such as rabbits is fine, however.)

Kitty Come Home: Collars, Tags, and More

Cat lovers are notoriously resistant to putting collars on their cats. Some just get tired of replacing the ones their cats keep slipping out of; other people are convinced that their roaming darlings may get caught on a tree branch by their collars and hang themselves.

Both groups are taking incredible chances with their pets' lives. Cat collars are an inexpensive insurance against loss, and as for the danger of being collared, your cat is many times more at risk for being lost than caught by his collar.

If you let your cat roam, give him a ticket home with some form of ID.

Traditional ID

Cat collars are made of lightweight material and designed to "give" enough to enable your cat to wriggle free should the collar ever catch on something. Don't get a puppy collar by mistake — dog collars are meant to prevent escapes, and cat collars are made to enable them. A wide choice of colors should keep any fashion sense happy, except your cat's, who'd just as soon do without. The fit should be snug but not uncomfortably so — you should be able to barely slide your little finger underneath.

After you've got the right collar, order a tag. ID tags come in high-impact plastic in a variety of colors and shapes or in metal, also in many varieties, including circles, cat's heads, reflectors, and so on. Because cat's tags are small, don't bother with putting your cat's name on it — she's not going to answer anyway. Instead, use the space to put your address and a couple extra phone numbers so that someone who finds your cat can locate you or a friend, neighbor, or relative of yours, day or night.

If you're concerned about dangling tags, look for those that attach flat to the collar.

What about a bell to slow down a feline hunter? It couldn't hurt, but some cats learn pretty quickly how to move without setting off the bird-warning device. The only sure way to keep your cat from hunting is to keep him inside. For tips on turning a free-roaming cat into an indoor one, see Chapter 5.

If your cat's constantly coming home with nothing around his neck and you're handy with a sewing machine, try Gina's quick and easy way to keep IDs on your pet. Buy $3/8$-inch elastic from a fabric store and order fabric name tags such as you'd put in children's clothes when they go to camp. Measure the elastic for a close fit, attach the label with thread or glue, and then sew the ends of the elastic together to make a collar. If you like, you can dress up the creation with rickrack or other accessories from the fabric store — just avoid anything your cat could chew off and swallow, such as sequins. Make these easy ID loops a dozen or so at a time and your cat will never lack for a comfortable collar!

Some communities require free-roaming cats to be licensed as a way to offset the costs of handling strays and to ensure compliance with local rabies-vaccination requirements. To find out whether your community is one of these with licensing requirements for cats, call your local animal-control agency. In response to concern about dangling tags, some agencies issue tags that slip over collars, and a few offer the option of tiny ear tags.

Microchips

The microchip is permanent identification no bigger than a grain of rice, which your veterinarian imbeds under the skin over your pet's shoulder blades by using a large needle. (But don't worry: One yowl is about all you hear at most, and then the job's done!)

Microchips have been of dubious value for returning lost pets in the past, however, because one company's chips couldn't be read by another company's scanner, and shelters couldn't and wouldn't cope with competing systems. That's changed recently, with moves by manufacturers toward one industry standard and with the entry of the American Kennel Club as a registry of microchipped animals in the United States and Canada — any animals, not just AKC-registered purebred dogs. The cost is anything from $20 to $50 to have your pet chipped by your veterinarian, but it's a good investment in his safety.

Check with local pet-supply stores, cat and dog clubs, shelters, and veterinarians in your area for occasional reduced-cost microchip clinics.

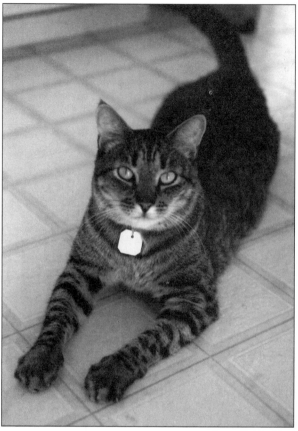

Gus — Photo courtesy of Ann Cony.

If you're going to have your cat microchipped — and we highly recommend it — find out what, if any, chip scanners are in use at the shelters in your area, and make sure that your pet is implanted with a chip that can be read by that brand of scanner. Although the industry is moving toward standardization, it's not completely there yet!

You also should register your pet with AKC Companion Animal Recovery — (800) 252-7894 — which offers 24-hour matchup service, 365 days a year. The cost to register is $9, and although the service was set up in conjunction with one manufacturer, you can register the number of whatever chip you use. If someone calls to report that they have your pet, the service releases your number so that you can be reunited with your baby quickly.

Most lost pets are found not by shelters but by neighbors, and neighbors don't have microchip scanners in their collection of home appliances. Which is why, although we highly recommend a microchip for permanent ID of your cat, we also advise you to make sure that a collar and tag are on him

---

Walking the cat?

Indoor cats can be trained to enjoy an outing outdoors on leash, and for this treat, you need a harness. (Because cat collars are made to enable cats to slip out of them, don't use a collar with a leash.)

Choose a harness designed for cats, not for dogs, in a figure-eight design. As collars do, harnesses come in many colors, with light-weight leashes to match.

Don't expect your cat to heel like a dog, however. Walking a cat really consists of encouraging your pet to explore, with you following, offering plenty of praise and maybe a treat or two.

Never leave your cat tethered and unattended, which leaves him vulnerable to attack or to a terrifying time of hanging suspended from his harness should he try to get over a fence.

---

at all times, too. In the event that someone hits your cat — a sadly common occurrence with a free roaming pet — a tag at least ensures that you don't keep wondering whether your pet is ever coming home. It's a small consolation, but believe us, knowing the fate of your pet beats spending months wondering.

A Place to Scratch

The most important thing to remember about scratching is that it's as natural a part of your cat's life as breathing. Your cat needs to scratch, and you need to provide him with a place to dig in his claws and pull.

What you need, in other words, is a scratching post, cat tree, or other scratching toy such as those that affix to corners or hang from doorknobs.

If you're going to have any success in getting your cat to scratch where you want — instead of somewhere you don't, such as the corner of your couch — you're going to need to choose a scratching place that's not only sturdy but also made of a material your pet can enjoy digging into.

Stability is important, because the first time a scratching post comes crashing down on your pet is the last time he ever uses it, rest assured. As far as material, *sisal,* a natural ropelike covering, is popular with cats, as is a carpet with loops that aren't too shaggy.

Scratching posts are usually small, less than three feet in length, and either vertical on a wide base or horizontal, like a log — mimicking what cats like in the outdoors, some scratching posts *are* logs. (Or you can bring in a log on your own.)

The best investment you can make for your pet's enjoyment is a tall cat tree with a top perch — cats love to look down on people; it reinforces their belief in their own superiority! — and a nook for those moments when a cat simply can't stand to be bothered with anyone. Some cat trees come with dangly toys attached, or you can add your own. Just make sure that anything attached or added is cat-safe — nothing that can be swallowed, such as strings or sequins.

If you're even a little bit handy, you can make your own cat tree by using scrap lumber and carpet remnants. Check out do-it-yourself plans in your local library or home-improvement retailer.

You can make a scratching place even more appealing by adding catnip. More about catnip — why it makes some cats crazy — later in this chapter, in the sidebar "Catnip and other leafy delights."

A scratching post, cat tree, or other scratching toy is an important part of training your cat to leave your furniture alone. See Chapter 13 for tips on solving scratching problems. Clipping helps keep your cat's claws in shape; see Chapter 7 for directions on how to clip your pet's nails without getting either one of you injured.

A good cat tree is stable and offers a lot of options for playing, napping, or hiding.

Sweet Dreams: Beds

Have you ever heard the old joke about the 800-pound gorilla? No? Let us enlighten you:

Question: Where does an 800-pound gorilla sleep? *Answer:* Anywhere he wants.

Now apply that to your eight-pound cat, because honestly, the answer is pretty close to the same. Within the limits of your tolerance (keeping your cat off your kitchen counters, for example) and his safety (keeping him out of clothes dryers), your cat is going to sleep pretty much anywhere he wants: Your couch. Your bed. Your dirty clothes, should you be sloppy enough to leave them where your cat can find them. Not to mention your lap, your computer keyboard, your chest, the top of your TV, your face, your bathroom sink, your feet, and the top of the book you're reading, especially if you're trying to turn the page.

That doesn't mean that you can't — or shouldn't — get your cat a bed of his own. After all, consider the matter from the infallible vantage point of cat logic: As your cat sees things, what's his is his, and what's yours is his. Got a problem with it?

One of the best beds you can offer your cat is actually on top of a cat tree, a perch perfect for snoozing high above the humans and even lesser beings, such as dogs. Cat perches that affix to window sills also provide your cat a place to nap while the world goes by, as well as offering an indoor cat the opportunity to sun himself.

Comfortable places to sleep are important to cats, who manage to spend nearly two-thirds of their lives with their eyes closed.

Soft, round "cup" or "cuddler" beds are popular with some cats, and cushions are a hit with others. You just need to experiment to see which your cat prefers.

Fabric beds can harbor flea eggs and larvae, so make sure any bed you buy has a removable cover for frequent washing. For more tips on controlling fleas, see Chapter 7.

Bowls and Waterers

As with everything else concerning your cat, her food and water bowls must be acceptable to her or you've wasted your money. In addition, they also must be made of a material that doesn't scratch — food particles and bacteria can collect in tiny gashes — and that can be completely cleaned, preferably in the dishwasher.

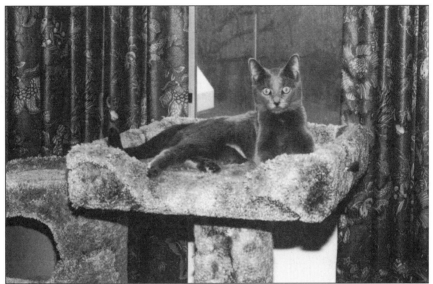

Cats love to nap or sun themselves on top of their cat trees . . .

Happy Rachel — Photo courtesy of Ellen Camm.

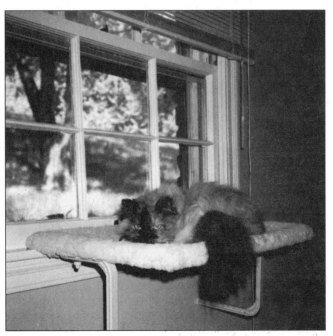

. . . or on a window perch.

Miti — Photo courtesy of Shannon Ross.

For the most part, that's going to mean stainless steel or high-impact plastic "crock" style dishes. Fortunately, the latter come in colors and patterns to fit any decor, and some specialty catalogs and boutiques also allow you to order personalized dishes.

Plastic dishes are suspected in causing some skin lesions on the face of cats. If a cat develops frontal face, chin, or lip lesions, changing from plastic bowls to another type is a good idea.

Some cats share food dishes readily, but many don't. Some share a supply of dry food from a single dish but require their own individual servings of canned food — at room temperature, puh-lease! If your cats are hissy about sharing, keep food dishes for each cat and feed your babies with some distance between them.

The most important thing about dishes is to keep them clean. Cats are fastidious, especially about their water, and many turn up their nose at any sign of old food or stale water.

Innovations abound in the pet-dish area. Some feeders allow you to leave enough food for a weekend, releasing each meal to your cat at preset intervals. Another product is designed for multicat households where one cat eats more than his share and the other one's finicky. The greedy cat wears a collar that triggers a discouraging tone if he gets near the other cat's dish!

Water dishes haven't been neglected by cat-loving inventors either. Although dishes with a reservoir of water have been available for a long time, some new water dishes play to the cat's love of water that's so fresh it's still *running.* These products constantly recycle water through the unit.

The biggest problem with water dishes with reservoirs attached is that you can too easily forget to keep them clean. These units need to be broken down daily and given a good scrubbing, because cats prefer their water fresh.

All you need to know about what to put in that fancy cat dish is in Chapter 8.

Home Away from Home: The Carrier

Every cat needs his own carrier. A sturdy carrier makes going to the veterinarian's, traveling, or moving safer and easier for your pet and offers you some options in times of disasters.

The right cat carrier can make introductions to other cats and pets easier, too. For more information, see Chapter 5.

Even the best carriers are a bargain at less than $25 or so if you shop around, and the chances are good that you can pick up one for next to nothing from yard or estate sales.

Look for a carrier that provides your cat with a feeling of security and the ability to look out at the world outside his cozy carrier. The ones we like are made of two pieces of high-impact plastic with vents along the top, the top and bottom held together by bolts, and with a grid door of stainless steel.

Don't choose the following types of carriers:

- ✔ **One that's all wire.** Your cat is made even more nervous by being exposed on all sides.

- ✔ **One made of wicker.** Although they may look attractive, you need something you can clean thoroughly if accidents happen. (And they always do!)

- ✔ **One made of cardboard.** The cardboard carrier you may have gotten at the time you adopted your cat or kitten is fine for taking him home, but it isn't durable enough to rely on in the long run.

A high-quality cat carrier is an inexpensive investment in your cat's safety. Don't neglect the purchase.

Carriers figure into many parts of your cat's life. For tips on making your cat's trip to the veterinarian easier, see Chapter 9. For information on traveling or moving with your cat, see Chapter 15. And finally, for everything you need to know to protect your cat in a disaster, see Chapter 18, in The Part of Tens.

The Ins and Outs of Cat Doors

So exactly why does the cat who just came in suddenly want to go out — and vice-versa? Is he just trying to drive you crazy? Well . . . not exactly.

Cats like to keep an eye on their territory, and if their territory includes a piece of the outdoors, they're going to want to check on it frequently. And after they're out, who's looking after the indoor turf? The cat needs in to check.

Installing a cat door can end your days as door opener, giving your cat the opportunity to come and go as he pleases. But that's not all they do. Some cat lovers have installed cat doors in interior doors as a way to keep dogs (dogs larger than a cat, that is) out of the room with the litter box. A cat door doesn't need to lead to the outdoors either: Putting one in as a gateway to a screened porch is a great way to give your indoor cat access to the smells and sounds of the world at large.

The basic cat door has a flexible plastic flap that opens as your cat pushes on it and seals shut again with magnets to keep the heat, cold, or wind out after he's passed through. Although these flaps are plenty weatherproof in sunnier climes such as California, where Gina and Paul live — with pet doors in both their houses — they may be a little drafty in areas with more-severe winters. Gina has known people who've built sort of an airlock onto their houses: a tunnel with pet doors at both ends to minimize drafts. (Although she admires such ingenuity, on the whole, such cold-climate necessities make her happy to live in California.)

You have a couple of options in installing cat doors. If you have a sliding-glass door, you can buy panels with a pet door built in that fit on the end of the slider. If you have problems with neighbor cats coming in, you can find cat doors that work electronically, opening only for those cats wearing a collar with a special, battery-operated transmitter.

Other cats aren't the only animals who can learn to use your cat's door. Raccoons and opossums can, too, and so can skunks. One of Gina's friends learned this the hard way after she walked into her laundry porch and surprised a skunk dining eagerly on dry cat food. We're not sure whether the smell ever got completely out of her house. (For information on how to get skunk smell off your cat, see Chapter 7.)

The other problem with cat doors is the things your cat can bring through them. Gina's neighbors have a black-and-white tom cat who once brought a full-grown blue jay through the cat door — and released the terrified bird in the living room!

Teaching your cat to use a cat door

After you install your cat door, just leave it be for a week or so until your cat takes its presence for granted. (Remember always that cats aren't keen on change.)

To teach him to use the door, tape the flap up securely for a few days so that he comes to appreciate the fact that he can conveniently come and go on his own schedule through this magic portal. (And we do mean securely. If your cat gets clobbered by the flap, it takes a long time to coax him near it again.)

Then put the flap down and put a little butter or margarine on the bottom edge of the flap and

encourage him with tasty treats and praise from the other side. You can also drag toys on a string through, encouraging him to chase them.

Repeat in very short intervals over the course of several days and your cat gets the hang of it, sure enough. If you have a cat who already uses the cat door, you usually don't need to do anything. Your new cat or kitten learns from the other cat. (Or even from your dog, if the pet door is shared.)

Cool Toys for Your Cat

At last, the fun part! For an indoors-only cat, toys aren't a luxury: They're an important way to keep your pet exercised, and they fight boredom and help to form a strong bond of companionship between you and your pet.

As with everything else regarding cats, the choices in cat toys are many and getting even more varied by the day, as cat-loving entrepreneurs try to create a cat toy that sells millions.

One of the earliest cat toys was invented by Dr. A.C. Daniels, who patented his Catnip Ball in 1907. The wooden ball was hollow for putting catnip in — his own special brand, preferably. The ball was followed by other catnip toys, and the company, founded in Boston in 1878, is still making cat toys today.

If you're serious about cat toys — and for your cat's sake, we hope you are — you want to get a copy of John Avalon Reed's *The Whole Kitty CATalog* (Crown), a wonderful book evaluating more than 800 toys and treats for your cat. Full of pictures, the book is a drool-fest for cats and those who love them.

The best you can buy

You can spend a lot of money on cat toys, including some pretty nifty battery-operated gadgets that whirl mice around on tracks or pull pieces of fluff around the room. Remote control mice are available, too, complete with a wireless control and batteries not included, of course.

Your cat can have some fun with all of these to be sure, but we've found that some of the best cat toys don't cost much at all. Top of the list would have to be "cat fishing poles" that have bangles, feathers, or a stuffed toy at the end of a sturdy string tied to a flexible pole. These toys allow you to play with your cat (a good thing) without letting your pet learn that pouncing on your fingers or hands is okay (a bad thing).

Little fur mice are fun, too, as are balls with little jingle bells inside. Save the squeaky toys for your dog, however, because you cat probably isn't going to like them. Other hits include toys stuffed with catnip, as well as Ping-Pong or foam balls, pipe cleaners twisted into fun shapes, or even rabbits' feet.

Knock yourself out experimenting! We guarantee that your cat's not going to mind. Just make sure that you check out every toy for safety, eliminating anything your cat can swallow.

Freebies cats love

Speaking of cat toys, some of the best things in life are free — or nearly so. When Gina ran a cat-toy poll in her Pet Connection column, the top toys all were freebies, and number one on the list were the plastic rings that hold down the lids on plastic milk jugs.

Plastic rings aren't the only popular freebie. Many cats like empty cardboard boxes and empty paper grocery bags. (Put away the plastics ones, however, because they can suffocate your cat.) Some other favorite playthings include folded empty cigarette packs (or the wrappers off them), drinking straws, the clear plastic safety ring around cottage cheese or sour cream lids, and the centers of toilet-paper, tape, and calculator rolls.

For the cat who loves to retrieve, try wadded-up tissues or paper, or the corks from wine or champagne bottles. Empty plastic film containers are great to bat around, as are nuts in their shells and even small vegetables such as Brussels sprouts or baby carrots.

Freebies that can turn dangerous are string, floss, ribbon, twine, rubber bands, or anything that your cat can swallow. You're best advised not to use these things at all in play, but if you do, make doubly sure that you put them completely away after the game is over.

More Fun Stuff

You don't find too much in the way of dress-up for your cat, mostly because your cat has too much dignity to put up with some of the really silly things dogs do. But if you want to go nuts with cat-related items for yourself, plenty of possibilities are around.

Catnip and other leafy delights

Not all cats like catnip — the ability to appreciate the herb is genetically programmed, with slightly more cats in the fan club than not.

Catnip — *Nepeta cataria* for you botanists — produces bouts of ecstasy for those cats who like the stuff. A substance called *nepetalactone* present in the leaves and stems causes the behavior, which lasts for just a few minutes and can include rolling, rubbing, leaping, purring, and general uninhibited happiness. Kittens under the age of three months do not react to catnip, and even in those cats who truly adore the "high," the plant is nonaddictive and harmless.

Valerian is another plant that makes cats happy, and the two can be grown as part of a cat garden. For more on cat-safe plants, for nibbling or for fun, see Chapter 8.

We could write a whole separate chapter on cat-themed stuff you can buy for *you*: bumper stickers and T-shirts; plates and cups; calendars and stationery; windchimes, mailboxes, and tote bags; jewelry, both kitchy and fine. You're going to find all this stuff on your own, and you're probably going to buy a lot of it. And we're not going to stop you, because we've got plenty of these things, too.

Cat shows, crafts fairs, and high-end pet boutiques are great places to look for these items — and you can have a lot of fun doing it. And no, you can't have Gina's hand-painted Siamese tile. Don't even ask.

For more information on cat shows, including how to locate one in your area, see Chapter 16. For places to buy cool cat stuff, check out the listings in the Additional Resources appendix. Happy hunting!

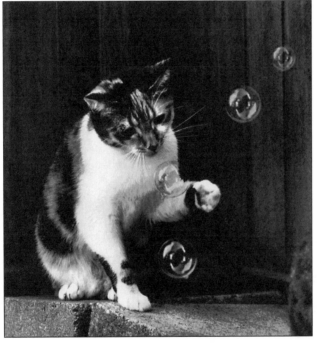

The best toys in life are often free — including bubbles!

Millie — Photo courtesy of Ron Bell.

Part III
Maintaining a Happy, Healthy Cat

The 5th Wave   **By Rich Tennant**

"We're having a few problems with him. He jumps up on counters, rips the drapes and short-sheets all the beds in the house."

In this part . . .

This part focuses on your pet's health, with everything from grooming to nutrition, preventive medicine to the most common diseases cat lovers face in their pets. You'll find information on how to choose a veterinarian in this part, too, as well as how to determine if your cat needs the help of a professional groomer. Does your cat need to see a veterinarian immediately? Our urgent-care guidelines help you decide. Special care for older cats is the focus of the final chapter, along with the facts you need about euthanasia, and pet-loss resources to help you through a difficult time.

Chapter 7

Good Grooming

*Y*ou can lose yourself in a cat's fur. Warm under your fingers, glossy-sleek to your eyes, a cat's fur can relax you, make you smile, ease the strain of a hard day before your feline companion even starts to purr. In so many lovely combinations of color and pattern, of texture and length, the coats of our cats are an inspiration to those who appreciate the gifts of nature: a supple pelt covering a body that is itself a perfect picture of symmetry, power, and consummate grace.

For a cat, a coat may seem a source of pride — so much does she preen it — but it's really much more. A healthy coat of fur can protect her from the elements and hide her from both predator and prey. Instinctively, she knows the importance of each hair and spends a great deal of her time cleaning her fur in a ritual as old as cats themselves, pulling dead hair free along with the dust from her rambles, restoring order and shine with her marvelously adapted tongue, as rough as sandpaper and handier than any comb.

Considering how much time your cat spends grooming, do you really even need to be involved in the process? Yes! Taking care of your cat's coat — as well as her claws — keeps her healthier, makes her easier to live with, and strengthens the bond between you. With some cats, human help is a must, for they have coats they can't handle alone. Pushed to beautiful extremes by selective breeding, the long silky coats of cats such as Persians need constant human attention to stay mat-free, comfortable, and oh-so beautiful.

Although many pedigreed cats *must* have help with their grooming, *all* cats benefit from human intervention. After you get the hang of grooming, you both feel better for it.

Some cats need a lot more grooming than others. For information on coat types as you're selecting a pet, see Chapter 2. Your cat's teeth need regular at-home attention as much as his coat and claws do, and we cover preventive dental care in Chapter 9. Good nutrition is important to maintaining a healthy coat, too, and for information on feeding your cat, turn to Chapter 8.

Fur, the Purrfect Complement

Your cat's coat is more than beautiful. Long or short, it provides him with protection against the elements, insulating against both cold weather and hot. The original coat pattern of cats is the tabby, still very common and much beloved, and perfect for hiding a cat in the shadows of meadow or woodland.

The protective properties of coat color are relative, of course, to the kind of life a cat leads. A dark color or pattern may be an advantage for hunting or hiding in the night, but it's a distinct disadvantage to the cat who roams the streets of city and suburb — black isn't as visible to drivers in the dark.

Most cats have three kinds of hair in their coat: short, fluffy, insulating *down;* wiry, mid-length *awn;* and longer, straighter, protective *guard.* (The specialized hairs called whiskers make up a special fourth category, the *vibrissae.*)

Not all cats have all three kinds of hair, and even those who do may have them in different proportions or lengths. The kinky-coated Cornish Rex, for example, has no guard hairs at all, and its down and awn hairs are crimped — as are its whiskers! The Persian, by contrast, has a straight coat in which even the down hairs are long by comparison to most cats, making the tendency to mat very pronounced.

Why Cats Groom

Cats do their best to keep every hair in order — and not just for the sake of appearance. Grooming has a number of advantages to your cat, as the following list describes:

> ✔ **Weatherproofing:** Separating and smoothing each hair helps to improve the fur's insulating abilities, keeping both heat and cold at bay. As a cat grooms, he also distributes the oils from his skin throughout his coat, giving it a measure of waterproofing.

COOL CAT FACTS

Grooming on autopilot

Kittens are groomed by their mothers for the first few weeks of their lives, but by the third week, they start grooming themselves as all cats do, in a very particular order, licking carefully and nibbling free any mats or dirt along the way.

Whenever cats sit down to groom, they start by licking their lips and then wetting the side of their paw, rubbing the damp paw over the side of their face; then they repeat the same sequence of motions on the other side.

After their faces are clean, they lick their front legs, shoulder and side, and then they hike first one hind leg straight up and then the other in the position cat lovers know so well, cleaning their genitals and then the legs themselves. They finish the process by licking their tail clean, starting at the base and working to the end.

What a system! The end result is a beautiful cat, ready for anything the elements have to offer.

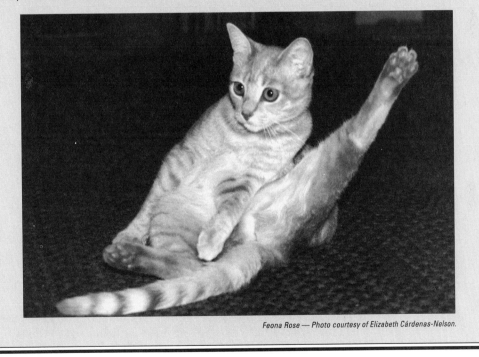

Feona Rose — Photo courtesy of Elizabeth Cárdenas-Nelson.

✔ **Scent-marking:** Grooming helps to distribute a cat's scent across his whole body, a phenomenon very reassuring to this scent-oriented animal. Scent is so important that a cat often licks himself right after being petted, both to re-establish his own scent and to drink in yours. And that's not the only grooming act that puts a cat's scent where he wants it: The act of digging his claws into a fence post (outside) or sofa or cat tree (inside) not only keeps his nails sharp, but it leaves secretions from glands in his paws on the object he fancies.

- **Parasite control:** Although your cat can't keep up with a major flea and tick infestation, he does his best by nibbling the pests from his body. (For more on your role in controlling fleas and ticks, see "Keeping external parasites under control" later in this chapter.)

- **Sociality:** In a multicat household, especially one with littermates, you often see cats grooming each other. This behavior — which is also performed on beloved humans — is a way of reinforcing a cat's connection to his family.

With so many benefits, you can easily see why, next to sleeping, grooming is one of the most important tasks on any cat's list!

Changes in the condition of your cat's coat or grooming behavior may be a sign of illness. See Chapter 9 for more information.

What's in It for You?

Many cats live their whole lives without anyone laying a brush on them, much less a set of nail clippers. And a bath? We must be nuts to even suggest it! But even if your cat isn't a high-maintenance type with silky, long hair, helping your cat with his grooming offers some benefits to you, as well:

- **Shedding:** The fur you catch on comb or brush doesn't end up on your sofa cushions, sweater, or the cream cheese on your bagel in the morning.

- **Smell:** Most cats are fairly fastidious, but some cats, especially unneutered males, can be a little offensive from time to time. Longhairs can get urine and feces in their fur, which can be uncomfortable — and unhealthy — for you both.

- **Hairballs:** More a problem in long haired cats than short, but still, no one likes listening to a gagging cat, and stepping on a coughed-up mass in bare feet is even less appealing! Regular grooming by you keeps the volume of fur swallowed by your cat as he grooms himself to the utmost minimum, and that means fewer hairballs on your lovely Oriental rug. (More about hairballs later in this chapter, in the sidebar "Help for hairballs.")

- **Bonding:** Although your cat may not like you getting involved in his grooming at first, if you're persistent, especially with the praise, your cat eventually comes to enjoy the time you spend together at this important task.

✔ **Destructiveness:** Keeping your cat's claws trimmed reduces his need to scratch, because one of the reasons cats claw is to remove the worn outer casings of the nails. (For more on scratching, however, make sure you read Chapter 13.)

✔ **Money:** Good grooming saves you money in more ways than one. By reducing your cat's need to scratch by keeping his claws in good shape, you save money on replacing things he may destroy. Grooming is also part of a preventive-care regimen: Paying attention to your pet's body not only helps him avoid some health problems, but it also helps you detect signs of illness early, which is better for both your wallet and your pet! Just the contact is good — many owners don't realize when their pet is losing weight or has new lumps and bumps or even open sores. Laying on of hands often is a great preventive care and bonding routine — aim to touch all of your cat at least once per week — do it systematically and you will find health trouble early. Getting your cat used to being touched and having his ears and mouth looked in will make the trip to the veterinarian much easier and more pleasant for all — you, your cat, and your veterinarian, too.

✔ **Allergies:** Studies have shown that good grooming, including regular baths, can help allergy sufferers cope with their pets. Some cats have allergies, too, such as to flea bites, and your attention to his grooming makes your cat's life more comfortable.

If you're allergic to your cat, you want to check out our strategies for coping with your sneezing and wheezing, described in Chapter 1.

Keeping your cat well groomed cuts down on shedding, but if you think you're going to be living in a cat-hair-free house, you're seriously deluding yourself. If you're going to live with a cat, you're going to need something to get the fur off your clothes. You can use masking tape, wrapped around your hand with the sticky side out, but we like the lint rollers that you can always keep sticky by peeling off another layer. Some pet supply catalogs sell these in bulk, and you can also find them at warehouse stores. Because you need to keep one in your home, your car, and your desk at work for your cat's entire life, shopping around for a good price pays!

Tools of the Trade

A little money is involved in the collection of the right tools to help you with your cat's grooming. Buy high-quality tools from a reputable pet supply outlet and keep them together so that you know where to find them.

Gina keeps her grooming supplies in a plastic container with a snap-tight lid, safe on a shelf in the hall closet. She keeps an extra comb in a drawer in the TV-room coffee table, so she can take advantage of a pet's good mood while everyone's watching TV.

Coat-care tools

You need a few things to keep your cat's fur clean and neat. Exactly what you purchase depends on your cat's coat type.

Grooming some cats for the show ring takes a great deal of work and years of learning how to get it right. Although we do give you an overview of cat competitions in Chapter 16, if you're really going to be competitive, work with your breeder or another mentor to learn what you need to, including show grooming. Our guidelines in this chapter are for keeping a pet cat in fine form and aren't meant to prepare your cat for showing.

Here's what you need for your cat:

- ✔ **Short- and medium-coated cats:** Start with a couple of stainless-steel combs — one with very narrowly spaced teeth, called a *flea comb,* and one with slightly wider teeth for clearing dead hair, small mats, and debris (the package will describe it as *fine*). A *slicker brush,* with its slender, bent wires, is good for applying the finishing touches to a mat-free coat; alternatively, you could buy a grooming glove — sometimes called a *hound glove* — that fits over your hand, with coat-massaging nubs on the palm so that you can pet and brush at the same time.

- ✔ **Wire-coated breeds:** Your supplies depend on the amount of coat your pet has. Some wire-hairs have crimped hair of all three varieties (down, awn, and guard) and hence a coat that's "normal" except for being wiry. Other cats have very little coat at all, and what they do have is primarily down and awn hairs. If your cat has a thick hair coat, you need the same equipment as for a short- or medium-haired cat. If your cat's fur is very sparse, you need a flea comb and a soft-bristled baby brush.

- ✔ **Long-coated cats:** Use a *pin brush* — so named because it looks like a pin cushion — instead of a slicker brush and add a medium- or coarse-tooth comb to the mix, as well as the same fine-toothed comb you need for most other cats. (Depending on the thickness of your pet's hair, a flea comb may be of little use, because it's almost impossible to pull through your cat's coat.) You also need a detangling spray and corn starch or talcum powder for mats. (More on how to use both later in this chapter, in the "Getting the gunk out" sidebar.)

Some combs don't have handles, but the kind that do are probably more comfortable to use. It's a matter of personal preference, though.

For all cats, you need shampoo. Choose one made especially for cats, or use human baby shampoo. For long, silky coats, add a cream rinse. Cotton balls keep ears dry while bathing, and balls and swabs help with post-bath ear care.

Do not use dog shampoos with flea-controlling chemicals on your cat — they're toxic. Although you can use flea-control shampoo designed especially for cats, you really don't need to: An ordinary shampoo sends fleas down the drain just as surely as one with pesticides.

Flea-control tips can be found in their own section later in this chapter, "Keeping external parasites under control."

Nail-trim aids

Your cat keeps his claws in shape by removing the worn outer coverings — called *sheaths* — and exposing the new claw below, either by chewing the sheaths off or leaving them in whatever he claws. (If you look closely at your cat's scratching post, you'll probably find old sheaths stuck in the fabric.)

Keeping your cat's claws trimmed is a good practice for two reasons: First, doing so cuts down on destructiveness by removing some — but not all — of your cat's desire to dig his claws into objects. Second, it makes things a little more comfortable for us thin-skinned humans to live with cats — as anyone with a cat who likes to "knead" with claws going in and out while napping on a lap can testify!

You have two choices in terms of nail trimmers: *guillotine* or *scissors-type*. Guillotine trimmers have a little oval guide into which you slip your pet's nail and a blade that extends into that guide after you squeeze the trimmer. The scissors-type works like scissors, not surprisingly, with the nail going between two small, crescent-shaped cutting blades. Either kind works perfectly well and is a matter of personal preference. Paul also uses human fingernail or toenail trimmers, so you can experiment with those, too.

You also need to pick up something to stop the bleeding should you nick the vein in your pet's nail. Kwik-Stop powder is available in most pet-supply stores or catalogs.

Don't be put off by packaging suggesting that either kind of clipper is for use on dogs — they work just fine on your cat, too. Some scissors clippers are made just for cats, but you may find these a little too small to use easily and prefer the regular "dog" clippers.

The Importance of Patience

Over the long haul, you're going to have very little success doing anything your cat doesn't want you to do, and you should keep this in mind in contemplating any grooming procedure.

Although some restraints on the market are designed to make dealing with a completely uncooperative cat possible — and we cover them elsewhere in the section "Cat + water + soap = Oh, my!" — neither one of you is going to enjoy using them. And if you need to fight your cat to care for him, you aren't going to bother struggling for very long — it's just human nature.

Still, you'd be surprised at what some cats are willing to put up with. Show cats, for example, are conditioned to tolerate a great deal of grooming, traveling, and handling by strangers — and with very little fuss. That's what they're used to, after all, and the show life is the only one they've known. Although your cat may never display the confidence and outgoing temperament of a seasoned show cat, you can do a lot to help him put up with some of the same grooming routines — and maybe even learn to enjoy them. The following list describes some tips:

✔ **Start early.** Get your kitten used to being handled, brushed, combed, and bathed, and prepare him for nail-trimming by gently handling his paws, pushing a claw out, releasing, and praising.

✔ **Go slowly.** Introduce new routines a little bit at a time and build up your cat's tolerance over time.

✔ **Give yourself a fresh start.** If you adopt a long haired cat or kitten who's matted, arrange to have him shaved down by a groomer (or maybe the shelter or adoption group) so you don't start out your relationship by jerking on your cat's fur. Sure, the cat looks funny, but the coat grows back quickly, and by the time it does, your cat is more used to you and to grooming.

✔ **Reward your cat.** Use treats, praise, and gentle petting to let your pet know that you approve of his behavior. You can't make a cat do anything he doesn't want to, so praise is the only way to go.

✔ **Know when to call it a day.** You'll do better if you stop before your cat becomes impatient, annoyed, or afraid, but if you miss the signs — or feel yourself becoming cross — taper off and end the session on a note of praise and petting. If you've really blown it, just let go and chalk it up to experience — and try again another time.

Never, never, never hold onto a cat who is becoming irritated. Most dogs will respond more like a child and not physically respond to an authority figure, but most cats will respond explosively if feeling cornered. The best thing to do is to let an annoyed cat get her way and to try again later. Failure to respect a cat's temper can result in serious use of claws and teeth that you do not expect from your loving pet.

Are you having trouble reading your cat's mind? The signs of a coming explosion of fear or anger are so subtle that some owners miss them. Read up on feline body language in Chapter 12.

Keeping Kitty Coats in Shape

The amount of time you spend grooming your cat's fur depends on a couple of factors, primarily the kind of coat your cat has. With their long, silky coats, Persians need daily brushing, combing, and detangling, frequent baths, and even professional grooming on occasion (see the sidebar "Does your cat need professional grooming?" later in this chapter). Other longhairs, such as the Maine Coon, have coats that don't mat quite so easily, although they, too, need more attention than the easy-care coats of the pedigreed or nonpedigreed shorthairs or the fine fur of some of the lighter-coated pedigreeds, such as the Cornish Rex.

Cats with medium or short coats are fine with weekly grooming and occasional bathing, just often enough to ensure that mats aren't forming and tails are clear of debris. More frequent attention can't hurt, however, if it helps for shedding and human allergies.

Combing and brushing

Short-, medium- and wire-haired cats are a breeze to groom after you get your cat used to the idea of being touched by the utensils. Run the comb though your cat's fur, follow with the slicker brush or grooming glove, and then step back and admire the shine!

One benefit of shorthaired cats: You can use a flea comb on them. Flea combs have narrowly spaced teeth that catch the little blood-suckers where they eat: on your cat. To use one, comb with the fine comb first, then flea comb from the skin out, a tiny bit at a time, flicking the pests into a bowl of warm sudsy water as you go. After you're done, flush the fleas away — most of them are drowned by then anyway.

Remember, however, that combing fleas from your pet does *not* solve a flea problem. See "Keeping external parasites under control," later in this chapter, for a total flea-control program.

For longhaired cats, a flea comb is hard to use, and grooming is a little more involved.

1. **Divide your cat's coat into sections with the "medium" or "coarse" comb and work through the fur slowly and gently.**

2. **Repeat Step 1, but this time use the fine-toothed comb.**

3. **Follow with a brushing, and again work with a small section at a time using the pin brush.**

   Work against the grain and then with it to put the coat back in its correct place.

4. **Don't forget lots of praise!**

Good grooming not only keeps your cat's fur in shape, but it also keeps her looking fancy, dahhling.

J.C. — Photo courtesy of Phyllis Mathias.

Pay special attention to the areas where the legs meet the body, behind the ears, and under the tails — all places that are mat magnets for longhaired cats. (For more on mats and other coat problems, see the sidebar "Getting the gunk out," later in this chapter.)

Lightly misting the part of the fur you're brushing with a little water from a spray bottle makes working the brush through the coat easier and helps keep the long outer coat from breaking. You can also try a commercial detangler — you'll probably have more luck if you choose a product in a spray bottle, not an aerosol, because the hissing sound from a pressurized can isn't going to be a hit with your cat.

If your cat's an unneutered male, you may notice his tail on top and near the base is greasy, with a brown secretion near the skin. This phenomenon is called *stud tail* and is a result of the excessive production of oil from a gland on the tail. (All cats have this gland, but usually only tomcats have problems with it.) Neutering usually solves the problem for good, but otherwise you need to control the mess by bathing.

Be aware of changes in your cat's coat, especially patches where hair is sparse or even missing. These patches could be signs of parasites, allergies, fungal infections or even hormonal problems — all of which need to be checked out by your veterinarian.

Are those . . . pimples?

If you're grooming your cat on a regular schedule, you'll find you're more observant of changes in his body, such as the subtle weight loss that can be a sign of illness. One thing you don't need to be very observant to notice, however, is *feline acne,* which is just what it sounds like: pimples or blackheads on the chin of your cat. Most classic acne cases occur in cats who are simply not good chin groomers. But be aware that there are many things that can contribute to the development and severity of feline acne and other conditions that mimic it.

The root of the problem can be as difficult to pin down as to treat. A few possibilities include the following:

- ✔ Tiny parasites called *demodex mites* that live in the hair follicles. (These are rare in cats, however.)
- ✔ Ringworm, which is not a worm but a fungus (and one that you can catch, too!).
- ✔ Contact dermatitis (a skin allergy), perhaps to a plastic food dish.
- ✔ An abscess.
- ✔ A food allergy.
- ✔ An inhalant allergy (something your cat's inhaling that he's allergic to).

You need to take your cat to your veterinarian to work out the exact problem and cure. The area needs to be kept washed, at the very least — but don't squeeze the blemishes! You may additionally get prescribed creams and pills. If you're following your veterinarian's directions and the problem shows no sign of improvement within a couple weeks, discuss a referral to a dermatology specialist.

The good news is that feline acne is more of an aesthetic dilemma than a serious health concern. As long as the area doesn't become infected, your cat won't be bothered by the blemishes.

Cat + water + soap = Oh, my!

No matter what your cat thinks, bathing can't kill him — or you either, for that matter. Cats with long, silky hair need bathing as frequently as once a week, whereas most shorthaired cats can benefit from a sudsing every couple of months.

Your cat should be combed out before bathing, because mats and tangles, once wet, can never be removed — you must cut them out. If your cat will tolerate it, tuck a little piece of cotton in both ears to keep them dry (but don't forget to fish it out later!).

Wash your cat in the sink (which is easier on your back and gives you better leverage) and use warm water. Here's what you need before you even think about wetting down your cat:

✔ **Towels.** You need them to dry your cat off afterward, of course, but also put one in the bottom of the sink to give your cat some firm footing. You can also use a small window screen to give your cat something to dig into with his claws — besides you, of course!

✔ **Spray nozzle.** Don't make your cat stand in water: Use a spray nozzle at close range to get him wet and rinse him off afterward. If your sink doesn't have a spray attachment, buy the kind that slips over the end of the faucet.

✔ **Shampoo.** Use cat or human baby shampoo, never a flea soap for dogs.

To bathe your cat, follow these steps:

1. **Take a firm hold of your cat at the scruff of the neck and ease him into the sink.**

2. **Wet him down with the spray nozzle.**

3. **Start shampooing by working a complete ring of lather around the neck and then working back from there.**

4. **Rinse thoroughly.**

5. **Repeat the process if he's really dirty.**

6. **Follow with a cream rinse if your cat has a silky coat and then rinse again.**

7. **Towel dry and then let your cat stalk off haughtily — he's earned it.**

8. **Keep him inside your warm house until he's completely dry.**

You can try to use a blow dryer on him, but it may prove more trouble than it's worth. He's already upset enough. Keep him where he's warm and let him be.

Okay, we admit it: We've made the process sound a lot easier than it is. Bathing your cat is never going to be the favorite activity for either one of you, but if you're tentative, your cat knows. Keep your grip firm, because if he senses any slackening, he's going to make the most of the opportunity to get free. If you feel yourself losing control, just let go: Better to regroup than get slashed.

Although most cats learn to tolerate bathing, especially if you start when your cat's still a kitten, you may find putting him in a mesh bag for bathing an easier way to go. You can use the jumbo-sized ones made for running delicates through the laundry or buy one especially made for bathing cats in a pet supply store or catalog. These bags keep your cat secure while you bathe him, but remember: If he's really opposed to the process, don't push it. Consider a groomer instead.

Bathing your cat from the beginning of your relationship will help keep your pet's coat in good shape for life.

Mädchen — Photo courtesy of Kristin Cocks.

TIP

Help for hairballs

Veterinarians call them *trichobezoars,* but cat lovers call them "hairballs," or, more commonly, simply "gross." Whatever you call them, hairballs — hair ingested as a cat grooms himself and then vomited back up in clumps — are a normal part of living with a cat and are usually not indicative of a health problem. If coughing up a hairball is an intermittent event — a couple times a month — and your cat appears otherwise normal, it's likely not a concern.

Your veterinarian may suggest the use of a mild laxative (mineral oil) preparation or an increase in fiber in the diet to help the hairballs "pass" in most situations. Canned pumpkin is a great way to increase the fiber in the diet.

Don't let your cat become a laxative junkie, however, as daily use may tie up and decrease the absorption of fat-soluble vitamins. These products should not be used more than twice weekly except on advice of your veterinarian. Instead of changing your cat's diet, consider combing him more frequently to remove excess hair.

If your cat's pattern of coughing up the occasional hairball changes, make an appointment with your veterinarian to find out why.

TIP

Getting the gunk out

Many things your cat gets into — or that get onto him — must be clipped out. Before hauling out the scissors, try some of these techniques:

✔ **Burrs or foxtails:** Your cat gets most of these out himself, but if you find one that he can't, try spraying a little of the nonstick cooking spray Pam on the area and then gently use your fingers to work the burr free.

✔ **Mats and tangles:** Work corn starch or talcum powder into the area and then grab the mat at the base to make sure you don't cut your pet or pull on his fur. Then use a sharp pair of scissors to oh-so-carefully slice through the center of the mat from the skin outward. If you're patient — and gentle — you should be able to tease the rest of the fur free with your fingers and your comb. To finish the job, comb through the area and then brush to remove the dirt and dead hair that caused the problem in the first place.

✔ **Paint, oil, or tar:** Cats are extremely sensitive to petroleum-based products. If your cat has gotten into more than a small patch of any of these substances, call your veterinarian for advice. A spot or two you can probably deal with on your own. *Never* use solvents to remove paint, oil, or tar: They irritate your cat's skin, are toxic if ingested, and they're flammable! Instead, wash your cat in Joy or Dove dishwashing liquid to remove petroleum-based products (which is what wildlife rescuers use to clean animals caught in oil spills). Tar may soften in mineral or vegetable oil, but still likely needs to be clipped out.

✔ **Gum or other sticky substances:** You can try a little peanut butter to lubricate the fur enough to slide the gum out. You may have to resort to clipping, though.

✔ **Skunk:** Wash with your cat's regular shampoo and then follow with tomato juice or a commercial deskunk solution (available at pet supply stores, or call your veterinarian). A cautionary note: Cats have a lot more sense than dogs do in avoiding skunks, so if your cat comes home sprayed, the first thing you should do is check his rabies vaccination status — rabid skunks can behave belligerently. If your cat is current on his shots, go ahead with the bath. If you see any new bite wounds, however, stop and call your veterinarian immediately, for your cat's sake and your own.

Keeping external parasites under control

Fleas, ticks, and ear mites are more than annoying — they can be a serious health risk, especially to cats who are very young, old, or feeble.

Persistence is the name of the game in controlling external parasites. The good news: Means of controlling some of these pests have gotten better in the last decade and especially in the last couple of years.

Fleas and ticks never go away, but you can keep them under control with regular attention.

Flea control

For effective flea control, you need to have a game plan. You need to treat your pet and his environment. You must treat to kill biting adult fleas, and you must treat to keep developing fleas from reaching adulthood. You need to do all you can to keep flea populations manageable with regular vacuuming of pet areas and regular washing of pet bedding.

And you can't let up. Not ever. Flea control is a year-round battle in large parts of the world. Even in cold regions, fleas can winter inside, just as people and pets do. During peak flea season, control and prevention is a twice-monthly affair.

A few ways exist to accomplish flea-free goals in your home and on your pet. Some possibilities include the following:

- ✔ **Your house.** Treat either with a spray or a fogger that contains both a quick-kill component, to kill adult fleas, and an insect growth regulator (IGR), which keeps immature fleas from developing. Alternatively, you can use a borate powder, which kills fleas by dehydrating them. Check with your veterinarian for product recommendations and follow directions carefully.

- ✔ **Your pet.** Program monthly liquid or pill, available only through veterinarians, is an effective part of an overall flea-control plan, but because it doesn't kill adult fleas, you likely aren't going to be satisfied with its results on its own. The product works by transmitting a chemical that prevents the eggs laid by the biting flea from developing. *Tip:* Add the liquid to a little tuna juice to encourage your pet to lap up all the medication. Two new products also available only through veterinarians, Advantage and Frontline — both liquids that are applied externally between the shoulder blades — fill the "kill gap" by providing protection against adult fleas for more than a month. Use a flea comb frequently (see the section "Combing and brushing," earlier in this chapter), but skip flea collars, sprays, and powders — they're not as effective as newer forms of flea control.

The things that don't work — although a great deal of money is spent on them every year — include electronic flea collars and various nutritional supplements such as garlic, brewer's yeast, and Vitamin B. Any evidence as to their efficacy is purely anecdotal and has not stood up to scientific scrutiny. The best "natural" flea control remedy on the market is already in your house: your washing machine and vacuum cleaner. Weekly washings of pet bedding and daily vacuuming of pet sleeping areas do a great deal to help keep flea populations down.

Flea-control efforts fail if pet owners put only minimal and sporadic effort into them: fogging the house now and then, powdering a pet on occasion. Such efforts always leave populations of either adult or developing fleas safe to reinfest treated areas.

The new prescription products — Program, Frontline, and Advantage — are so effective that many veterinarians and cat owners now believe that these are the safest, most effective flea controls.

Flea control efforts can turn *dangerous* if you use too many products and in the wrong combinations. *Always* read directions carefully, making sure that the product is safe for the use you intend, as well as around other pets in your home. If in doubt, talk to your veterinarian about your entire flea-control program. Especially if your cat's a kitten, ill, or elderly, talk to your veterinarian first about which products and combinations are safe and effective.

Ear mites

A small amount of wax in your cat's ears is perfectly normal and can easily be cleaned out with mineral oil on a cotton ball or swab. But if your pet's ears appear filthy, he's probably got ear mites — tiny pests that feed on the lining of the ear canals.

You need to see your veterinarian to be sure that it is ear mites you are dealing with and, if so, to get effective therapy. Be sure to follow directions to treat the mites: You need to treat as often as recommended for as long as recommended — even after you think the mites are gone — to prevent a reinfestation.

Ear mites are common in shelter cats and are very contagious. They can be really difficult to shake, so be persistent!

Ticks

Your cat picks up ticks in his rambles and usually dispenses with them himself while grooming, but occasionally you find one of the blood-sucking beasties in a place your cat can't get to easily, such as at the base of his ear. You probably feel the tick first as a bump while petting your cat and see it as a dark attachment. (The size varies depending on the species of tick and how much of your pet's blood it has sucked in.)

Don't touch a tick with your bare fingers. Ticks can infect you with Lyme disease if you're bitten and the tick attaches itself. Use a glove, tweezers, or a tick remover. Grasp the body firmly and pull with a steady motion. Wrap the tick in toilet tissues and flush, or if you see more than one, drop them into a small bowl of rubbing alcohol and then flush the lot after you're done. Don't worry if a piece of the imbedded head remains behind: It works its way out in time — just put a little antiseptic on the spot to prevent infection and keep an eye on the area until it's healed.

Clipping Your Cat's Claws

The hardest part of clipping your cat's claws is getting your cat to cooperate — remember what we said about patience! If you only get one claw done a night, don't worry about it, because you can get through them all soon enough.

To clip your cat's nails, push gently on his pad to expose the nail. In the center, you see a pink area coming part way down: This area is a vein, called the *quick,* and you want to avoid it to prevent bleeding. Slide your clipper to a spot just beyond the pink and squeeze the tool with a smooth, strong motion. If you can't see the quick, just cut the "hook" of the nail off and you should be fine. Don't forget to praise your pet for being tolerant.

If you do draw blood, apply a touch of Kwik-Stop powder to the tip to stop the bleeding and call it a night before your cat returns the favor.

In pet supply stores and catalogs, you find full-body restraints designed to make nail-trimming and medicating easier. Some of these are quite clever, with openings that allow you to get at one paw at a time while keeping your pet gently immobilized. These devices are fine if you can't get the job done any other way, but we think your cat would prefer you work with him slowly and gently to teach him to put up with claw-clipping instead.

A scissors-type trimmer is one of the tools you can use to keep your pet's claws clipped. Be patient and gentle and reward your cat with treats and praise for cooperating.

Does your cat need professional grooming?

If you've got a longhaired cat, you may find that the mats get out of hand from time to time, and if this happens, we feel that your cat is better off being clipped down. You can try this yourself, but your relationship with your cat is probably better if you have a professional do the dirty work.

You may also want to schedule regular professional grooming for longhaired beauties if you find that you just can't keep up. Same goes if you can't seem to keep areas that get dirty, such as the region under the tail, clipped down.

Ask your veterinarian or breeder for a recommendation to a professional groomer and check out the setup before dropping your cat off. You want to make sure that your pet is kept apart from dogs for his own peace of mind and separate from other cats for his health. A groomer who's used to working with cats — and enjoys working with cats — has a facility that makes their stay there as safe and comfortable as possible.

Also consider mobile groomers, who bathe and groom your pet in a van in front of your home or in your driveway with no other animals around.

Chapter 8

Feeding Your Cat

. . . .

In This Chapter

▶ Pet food challenges

▶ Feline nutritional requirements

▶ Choosing the right food

▶ Too fat? Too thin?

▶ A vegetarian cat?

▶ Gardening for kitties

. . . .

The very first thing you need to understand about feline nutrition is that cats are *obligate carnivores;* in other words, they evolved specialized nutritional needs that before the age of commercial cat foods could only be met by eating other animals. Human beings can do without animal-based protein, and many do so quite nicely. But a cat? No way. Everything about your cat says "hunter," from the claws on his feet to the fangs in his mouth to the way his body's put together for silent stalking on soft paws, a sudden spring, and a sharp bite to the neck of a bird or rodent.

Although some pet cats still hunt — to the detriment of many songbirds — few must do so to survive. And that brings us to the second thing you need to understand about feline nutrition: The industry that's grown to supply it is very, very big.

How big? Try billions of dollars spent for cat food just in the United States, from tiny pop-lid tins of the most delectable "gourmet" kitty paté to the biggest bags of least-expensive food that caretakers of feral-cat colonies spread in alleys, on riverbanks, and in vacant lots for the legions of the not-so-lucky.

Billion and billions of dollars are spent — and if you doubt us, visit your supermarket or pet-supply warehouse for proof. Pet food takes up as much space in your supermarket as any product line there, with the possible exception of cereals and candy — made, in many cases, by the same companies! And at the pet-supply warehouse . . . so much cat food that it must be moved around by forklift.

And don't forget your veterinarian, who likely also sells food — both so-called "premium" brands as well as therapeutic diets meant to help your cat deal with various health problems from obesity to kidney and heart disease to plaque buildup on his teeth.

So many manufacturers. So many places to buy. So many . . . *choices!* Where do you begin to find the food that provides your cat with what he needs: the essential elements of nutrition found for generations in the bodies of billions of prey animals? Can you really find such nutrition in a can, box, or bag?

We're going to guide you through all of it, of course: We tell you what's known and, more important, what isn't known about feline nutrition; what your cat needs and what's being marketed directly at *your* desires, not your cat's; how to keep your cat eating correctly after you chose the "right" foods — so that your cat doesn't get too fat or too thin.

The payoff? A cat in good health, with shiny coat, bright eyes, and energy to burn. Good nutrition keeps your cat's body purring along through the years, and choosing good food is as important as anything else you do in the hope of providing your pet with a happy, long life.

Convenience . . . at a Price?

Like the cat box and litter, commercial pet foods are a modern addition to the lives of cats, created as much — if not more — for the convenience of people as for the needs of their pets. Which is not to say that cats haven't picked up something from the deal as well. Prepared pet foods have freed cats from worrying about their next meal so that they could enjoy being pampered, thus living longer, healthier lives than ever before.

A few false steps were taken along the way, to be sure — some health problems were actually caused by nutritional deficiencies in manufactured pet foods. Two notable examples of nutrition-related health problems: *dilated cardiomyopathy* and *feline lower urinary tract disease,* or *FLUTD.* Another health problem, *hyperthyroidism* (that seemed to suddenly appear in cats around the world in the late 1970s and is still absent from some locales where commercial pet foods are not as popular) increasingly gets attention from researchers interested in feline nutrition. What will they find? Perhaps that something in foods or some other manufactured agent is responsible for the rise of this disease or, quite the contrary, that improved nutrition, health care, and other factors leading to a greater proportion of the feline population living longer are unmasking this problem of aged cats.

Maintaining the "Perfect" Cat Diet

Part of the challenge of manufacturing a cat food is that whatever you come up with as a commercially viable product that people are willing to buy is usually a long way from what you start with, especially if you consider what cats eat if left to their own devices. If cats ran the pet-food industry, in fact, the recipe for a good, nutritious meal would probably read as follows:

Take one small mouse from the freezer. Thaw. Put in a blender and hit "frappé." Serve at body temperature on a clean plate.

Yuck, you say? That's probably why instead of one fresh-frozen mouse, you're going to give your cat a dry food, where the label lists the first five ingredients as corn gluten meal, ground yellow corn, chicken, brewers rice, and wheat flour. Or a canned one that lists wheat gluten and brewers rice just a notch or two below turkey.

Rice? Wheat? Corn? What gives? Are cats carnivores or aren't they?

Yes, but not all their needs must be met by animal-based food, as they would in the wild. The commercial pet-food industry has managed to provide what seems impossible: a diet with a high percentage of plant material that, nonetheless, keeps an obligate carnivore well-fed.

As we said, this balancing of convenience, nutrition, and aesthetics (appealing to both human *and* feline tastes) is a lot harder than it looks. All in all, commercial pet food has to be considered one of the great marvels of living in a modern age — and it keeps getting better, as our knowledge of nutrition increases.

Do cats need to drink cow's milk? Not at all, although in most cases, a little dose of the white stuff is much appreciated — unless they are lactose-intolerant. Check out the facts on these and other feline myths in Chapter 17.

Fulfilling Basic Nutritional Needs

A lot of different elements (about 60) go into keeping your pet healthy, all working together to keep his body working as it should be. These nutrients each play a role, and although some seem to have a bigger part than others, each is necessary to keep your cat's body functioning. The following sections touch on the main feline needs.

Can a cat be a vegetarian?

Many people choose a diet devoid of animal-based proteins, and they want to extend their dietary choices to their cats.

No matter how opposed you may be to the idea of meat, your cat's body has a different opinion, and when your cat's health is at stake, you'd better listen.

Besides *taurine*, cats require more than a dozen nutrients including vitamins, fatty acids, and amino acids veterinary nutritionists call *essential*, because they can't be manufactured in a cat's body and must be obtained from an outside source — that is, from animal tissues.

Protein

As part of their animal-consuming design, cats naturally have high *protein* requirements — three to four times more per pound of body weight than dogs or humans do. Kittens need even more — about half again as much to support their rapid growth into adults.

Consumed protein provides the *amino acids,* which your cat reassembles into the protein parts of his body. All animals require these life-giving nutrients. Some amino acids, called *nonessential,* are synthesized in the cat's body; others, called *essential,* must be obtained from food. Variety is the important thing to remember when considering protein sources. A combination of meat, poultry, fish, dairy products, and other protein sources ensures that your cat is getting all the essential amino acids he needs in his diet.

Protein comes from both animal and plant material, and varies in *digestibility,* or the amount of protein that's available to your cat as his body makes use of the food he eats. Meat, poultry, dairy products, and eggs are highly digestible and, therefore, are high-quality sources of protein; some other parts of animals, such as feathers, beaks, and bones, are not as highly digestible. Grains are somewhere in the middle in terms of digestibility.

Carbohydrates

Carbohydrates — sugars and starches — are a source of energy, but not one cats need in their diets to survive. Of all the ingredients in prepared cat foods, carbohydrates are furthest from what they would acquire naturally in our mouse cocktail formulation.

This is not to say that cats *can't* use the carbohydrates that commercial cat foods provide, and a good thing, too, because by weight these plant products are the largest component of most commercial cat foods. Enzymes in cats' bodies break down and convert the sugars and more-complex carbohydrates into products they can use.

The fiber in foods serves another function: It aids in keeping waste products moving through the digestive system and helps prevent constipation and obstipation (total blockage), which is why canned pumpkin is a good thing to give a cat with hairballs. (For more on hairballs, see Chapter 7. Obstipation is a problem often seen in older cats, and so it's covered in Chapter 11.)

Fats

In our society, we worry endlessly about the amount of fat in our diets, which experts say is too high. But again, we must realize that cats are not people, and their dietary needs are different concerning fats — they need more than we do, about 40 percent of their calories from this one category.

Fat from animal sources carries essential fatty acids that cats can't derive from vegetable sources. Fat also is essential for the absorption and movement around the body of certain vitamins, and it also provides food with much of its appeal to the feline nose and palate.

A cat doesn't thrive on a diet of dog food, and fat is a major reason. Dogs can manufacture essential fatty acids from vegetable sources; cats can't. The protein levels in dog food are also too low for your cat's health. Most dog food also lacks enough taurine to meet the needs of your cat. Nor is cat food good for your dog, incidentally. The higher levels of protein may be troublesome for older dogs with kidney problems, and the high fat content contributes to obesity and may cause diarrhea. Even healthy dogs don't thrive on cat food — although some wish they could!

Vitamins

Vitamins are divided into two categories — *water-soluble* and *fat-soluble*. Both are important to your cat's health, and the lack of any of them in your cat's diet can have dire effects. Water-soluble vitamins include the B vitamins, niacin, panthothenic acid, folic acid, biotin, choline, and Vitamin C. Cats require niacin, which is not present in high concentrations in non-animal food sources in their diets. Fat-soluble vitamins are Vitamins A, D, E, and K. Cats also need animal products to ensure they get Vitamin A, because cats can't manufacture Vitamin A from carotene. Don't expect to feed your cat carrots to ensure good eyesight — it won't happen!

Concerns over fat preservatives

In the last few years, a lot of controversy has been generated over the use of preservatives — primarily BHT, BHA, and ethoxyquin — to keep the necessary fats in pet foods from going rancid. These synthetic preservatives have been blamed for just about every pet health problem, not to mention the increase in violence on our streets and the perceived decline in traditional values.

Many manufacturers have adopted the "if you can't beat 'em, join 'em" approach, which is why some products are now "ethoxyquin free" or "naturally preserved," usually with Vitamins C and E. And some canned products boast of being completely free of preservatives of any kind.

No good scientific evidence exists to support the decision to avoid synthetic preservatives, either by manufacturers or consumers. If the issue worries you, choose a food that doesn't have these preservatives. But be aware that you have likely fallen prey to marketing strategies and fear rather than scientific fact in that buying decision. In fact, more data exists supporting the *beneficial* effects of these products in foods (reduced cancer, reduced birth defects, and so on) than do allegations of negative effects.

This, of course, does nothing to end the controversy.

Oil-based hairball remedies can tie up the absorption of fat-soluble vitamins, which is why you shouldn't be giving them on a regular basis without talking to your veterinarian. For more on hairball treatment and prevention, see Chapter 7.

Minerals

Mineral nutrients your cat needs include potassium, magnesium, zinc, calcium, iron, phosphorus, sodium, chloride, and others. Like vitamins, they make up a small part of your cat's diet, but in the correct amounts, they're essential for good health. In the past many were concerned over excess ash (especially magnesium) in cat foods. This proved to be unfounded but continues to be a marketing gimmick many cat owners and veterinarians respond to favorably.

The important thing to remember about vitamins and minerals is that your cat needs the correct amount — but not more. "If a little is good, a lot must be better" simply doesn't apply in the case of vitamins — and nearly all other nutrients. The oversupply of vitamins and minerals can prove dangerous, which is why you should not give your pet supplements unless you've discussed it with your veterinarian first. Although excess amounts of water-soluble vitamins are passed in the urine, fat-soluble vitamins can — and do — build up to toxic levels.

Water

Do you think about nutrition as being about what your cat eats? Don't forget that what your cat drinks is just as important to her well-being. Water — clean, fresh, and in ample supplies — is essential to nearly every process of your cat's body, which is 70 percent water.

The tiniest cells of living beings cannot survive without water. Nutrients are carried and wastes removed by water. A cat can go without eating for weeks if need be (please don't test this fact, though), but without water, death comes in days.

Always make sure you supply your cat with water and encourage her to drink by keeping the dish clean and the water fresh. Some cats prefer running water, and some owners oblige by opening taps to drip for their pets.

Choosing Foods

Pet food is more complexly regulated than human food is, and most passes the testing of the *Association of American Feed Control Officials* (AAFCO). This may sound impressive, but to be honest there are two levels of claim substantiation. One is based on a chemical analysis of the food, and some

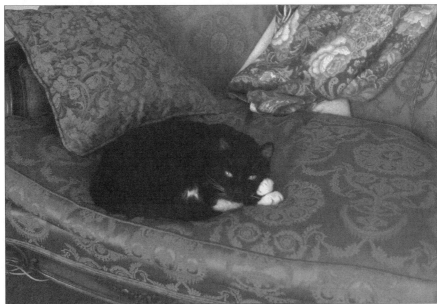

A cat who maintains a proper diet is a happy, healthy companion.

Miss Thing — Photo courtesy of Catherine Schmitz.

say that motor oil plus a few vitamins and minerals could pass — not very impressive! The second is more sound and based on feeding the food to cats. To pass these feeding tests, the pet-food manufacturers provide their products to cats and then ensure that the products are maintaining good health.

Before researching this chapter, it had been several years since Paul had reviewed the AAFCO feeding protocols. He was quite pleased to learn that they are more stringent and complete than what he recalled from past reviews. He was particularly proud to read the requirement for testing blood taurine concentration. Still, if Paul were king — and we do have to remind him on a regular basis that he is not — he'd ask that all foods be required to support two generations of normal health: in other words, that a food would be fed for several months to adults who then successfully produced kittens who were subsequently raised on the food and matured normally and produced normal litters of kittens. This testing would provide pretty conclusive evidence that nothing major was wrong in the formulation.

The problem is that these tests would take almost two years, which would be quite expensive in terms of direct costs and more so in terms of the time it would take to bring a product or reformulation of a product to market. Fortunately, the competition in the industry has heated up to the point where the major companies have decided that they cannot afford a major mistake, and many pursue what in essence amounts to these types of studies.

For these reasons, we recommend you stay with the big name manufacturers when choosing food for your cat. They are probably the only ones who can afford to do this type of extensive internal testing. For this reason, some say the most-valuable information on the bag is the company's phone number. Give them a call and ask them to tell you what they have done to ensure that you can rest assured that their food meets all your cat's needs despite the limitations of AAFCO testing.

You could perform hours of research on all the ingredients in cat food. Whole books are available on the subject; you could go to the library at your closest school or college of veterinary medicine and lose yourself in the stacks for days. We don't think you need to go to such lengths, however, to make sure your kitty's eating right. We think you can do just fine if you follow our simple guidelines:

  ✔ **Choose foods that are appropriate for your cat's age.** Although older cats can do just fine on regular adult cat food, kittens need more fat and protein and so should be fed products designed for them. Look for the words "Complete and Balanced Nutrition" on the label, as well as the AAFCO animal feeding tested statement "for all life stages" (for kittens). This does not mean you need to buy kitten food for your kitten. In fact, unless your veterinarian suggests a special food, we feel most comfortable with at least part of any cat's diet including a food with the "all life stages" statement. That way, your cat gets the variety of food he needs to ensure that all his nutritional needs are met. If your cat is gaining weight because of the calorie-dense nature of a food designed for all life stages, try mixing the food with one meant exclusively for older cats to reduce his caloric intake.

✔ **Choose foods from major manufacturers.** The older, nonpremium pet-food brands were hurt by the growth of the "premium" pet food market, but their manufacturers have done a lot to improve their product in recent years, and we have no problem in recommending them. Whether you buy your cat's food from the supermarket, a pet-supply store, or your veterinarian, as long as you're dealing with a major manufacturer's food that carries the "AAFCO animal tested" statement, you should be fine. These large companies have a huge investment in maintaining the quality of their products, and they test them constantly in feeding trials. Don't choose generic or store brands unless you specifically ask which manufacturer their food is identical to. Store brands are usually just relabelled other brands — so if they are a major brand relabelled and less expensive, who are we to suggest not saving a few pennies? Skip trendy brands from unknown manufacturers — the accountability is just not there.

Should you pop the extra dough for the more expensive "premium" foods from these manufacturers? That's up to you. Some owners like them because they often contain higher quality, more digestible ingredients that result in more absorbed, less out the rear-end in the form of smaller, neater stools — and therefore less litter-box mess. But other than that, the fact is these diets offer no proven health advantage.

✔ **Choose a variety of foods to ensure nutritional balance.** Feline nutrition is still as much defined by what we don't know as what we do. The best way to make sure your cat is getting all the nutrients he needs is to feed him a variety of food types — poultry, beef, and fish — from a variety of major manufacturers. Varying your cat's food also keeps him from becoming "addicted" to one kind — which may go off the market. Unless your cat is sensitive to changes in his diet (reacting by refusing to eat, with diarrhea, or vomiting), feed him a variety of food from a variety of manufacturers, mixed or on a rotating basis.

What type?

Even knowing what to look for in a cat food doesn't answer all your questions as you're gazing at all the choices in a pet-supply store. Cat foods come in different forms, with advantages and disadvantages to each. The following list describes the three main types of cat food from which you may choose:

✔ **Dry food.** Also called *kibble,* this variety comes in a box or bag, is less expensive than other kinds, and gives you the most options for feeding your cat. You can fill a dish with dry food and leave it out and it doesn't go bad. Dry food enables you to make sure your pet has food if you must leave him alone for a weekend. Dry food also helps reduce tartar buildup on your pet's teeth. Cats generally aren't as crazy about dry food, however, as they are about freshly opened canned food.

✔ **Canned food.** Cats love this stuff, but it's expensive to feed because you're paying for a lot of water. Canned food lasts almost forever . . . until you open it, and then it lasts about half an hour before your cat decides it's no longer fresh enough to suit him. You can refrigerate leftovers (although you need to bring them to room temperature before feeding again), or you can buy the tiniest cans, which are even more expensive. Canned food can be great for nursing ill or older cats, however, especially those whose teeth make dry food hard to handle.

✔ **Semi-moist.** Sort of a midway point between dry and canned in terms of ease of use and cost, semi-moist foods are often criticized for appealing more to humans — with clever shapes and artificial colors — than to cats.

In the interests of nutrition and cost-efficiency, we like to recommend a basic diet of dry with daily rations of canned.

When to feed?

Many people like to leave dry rations out for a cat to eat whenever she's hungry, and that's fine, with a couple of exceptions. The most obvious is if your cat is overweight — more on that later in this chapter — or is on a diet that's otherwise restricted. Called *free feeding* (also called *ad lib*), leaving dry food out at all times doesn't work if you have two cats who need to eat different foods or if you have a dog who's especially clever about getting into the cat food.

Free feeding also doesn't feel very satisfying to some people, who like the excitement their cats show as they pop open a can of food. If you're one of these people, you can compromise, if you like: Offer dry food always and canned food once daily.

What about veterinarian-prescribed foods?

Under certain conditions, your cat's doctor may recommend one of several specially formulated diets, which are available only through your veterinarian. If your cat has a health problem that one of these foods may help, your veterinarian may suggest it. These foods come in both dry and canned varieties, so you can choose the kind you and your cat prefer.

In some cases, your cat's time on these foods is temporary, whereas for other conditions your veterinarian may suggest that your pet stay on the diet for the rest of his life. Any situation that requires your pet to be on a

THE CAT'S MEOW

A sweet treet for cat lovers

Your cat's nutrition isn't the only thing on our minds — we want to make sure *you* have something special to eat, too. And so Paul has decided to share his recipe for Litter Box Cake, which came to him through his online colleagues at the Veterinary Information Network.

Children love this cake. Adults . . . well, you'd better hope your friends have a sense of humor. The editors at Gina's newspaper didn't. They thought the recipe was "too gross" to put in the newspaper. To them, we say: "Ha! Let them eat Litter Box Cake."

We wouldn't *think* of denying you the pleasure.

Litter Box Cake

1 pkg. spice cake mix

1 pkg. white cake mix

1 pkg. white sandwich cookies

green food coloring

12 small Tootsie Rolls

1 box vanilla pudding mix (not instant)

1 NEW, CLEAN litter box

1 NEW, CLEAN litter-box scoop

Prepare the cake mixes and bake according to their directions. Prepare the pudding mix and chill until ready to assemble. Use a blender on a low setting to crumble the white sandwich cookies in small batches; they tend to stick, so scrape often. Set aside all but about 1/4 cup. To the 1/4 cup of cookie crumbs, add a few drops of green food coloring and mix by using a fork.

After the cakes cool to room temperature, crumble them into a large bowl. Toss with half the remaining cookie crumbs and the chilled pudding. Gently combine. Line a NEW, CLEAN litter box with plastic wrap. Put the mixture into the box. Put three unwrapped Tootsie Rolls in a microwave-safe dish and heat until they're soft and pliable. Shape the ends so that they're no longer blunt, curving them slightly. Repeat with three more Tootsie Rolls and bury them in the mixture.

Sprinkle the other half of the cookie crumbs over the top of the mixture. Scatter the green cookie crumbs lightly over the top, too — these are supposed to look like the chlorophyll in cat litter. Heat the remaining Tootsie Rolls, three at a time, in the microwave until they're almost melted. Taper the ends as before, then plop them on top of the cake and sprinkle with cookie crumbs.

Serve with a NEW, CLEAN cat-box scoop.

Enjoy!

---

special diet for any length of time also requires you to work with your veterinarian to ensure the management of the disease in other ways, too, and to make sure your questions about the course of the disease are answered.

CAUTION

Although your veterinarian has all the best intentions in recommending these diets, you should be aware that other than those designed for patients with urinary bladder stones/crystals, obesity, and perhaps kidney disease and some causes of diarrhea, there is no scientific data to support the medicinal claims for these foods. Until such data is available, press your veterinarian for information as to why you are being asked to fork over the

Cooking for your cat

Although most people don't have the time for or the interest in preparing special meals for their cats, those who do are convinced that their pets do better for the fresh ingredients they get every day.

You can create a diet for your pet by using fresh meats or other protein sources, grains, vegetables, and mineral and vitamin supplements, but you can't plan such a diet casually. Books such as *Dr. Pitcairn's Complete Guide to Natural Health for Dogs and Cats*, by Richard H. Pitcairn, DVM, Ph.D., and Susan Hubble Pitcairn (Rodale Books), offer recipes for creating cat food at home.

We don't believe these diets are any better for your pet than a high-quality commercial food —

and worry because you have no way to know whether you're providing *all* the 60 or so nutrients in the right amounts and ratios — but if you're following the diets carefully, they aren't likely to cause any harm.

Again, Paul's clinical experience gives him a bad feeling about this practice of cooking for your cat. He has seen too many problems result. Paul says, "Buy good commercial food. You won't be sorry." Gina says, "I trust Paul on this — as you can see, he's equally skeptical of some of the products the major manufacturers produce for premium prices (such as premium and 'therapeutic' diets). His recommendations come from the heart, not from any commercial interests or affiliations."

extra money for these diets. This will in turn push your veterinarian to pressure the manufacturers to generate and provide the data, or to stop trying to convince veterinarians and pet owners that there is reason to spend the extra money. (If you can't tell, Paul has real concerns about long-term use of "therapeutic" diets.)

Treat your cat!

Giving your pet a little something special from time to time isn't going to do him any harm and can be very useful in training situations. A couple of things to keep in mind, however:

- ✔ **All things in moderation.** Treats, whether store-bought or from your dinner plate, aren't a complete and balanced diet for your pet. Make sure the majority of his diet is still high-quality, complete, and balanced.

- ✔ **Avoid some foods entirely.** Food that's heavily spiced or has onions can upset your cat's digestion, leading to diarrhea or vomiting. Onion can also lead to severe blood problems in cats. Avoid onion or onion powder in foods you prepare for your cat and in baby foods you may use as an occasional treat or for nursing a sick cat (the latter under the supervision of your veterinarian, of course).

> ✔ **Consider your cat.** If you give your cat treats from your plate, you can't complain that he's a pest at mealtime. And if your cat's supposed to be losing weight, you shouldn't give him a treat at all.

We humans tend to confuse food with love, and we extend this idea to our interactions with our companion animals. Your cat doesn't really need treats. Pet your cat, play an interactive game, or just hang out together — these activities are better options in the long run than overdoing the goodies.

Curbing Eating Problems

Although maintaining your pet's nutritional levels may not require much more than choosing good foods and standing back, in the cases of cats who are too fat or too thin, you're going to need to monitor the situation more closely.

A healthy cat generally weighs between eight and ten pounds, although some breeds are smaller (such as the Singapura), and others are larger (such as the Ragdoll). You can generally judge your cat's correct weight by his ribs: If they're too prominent, your cat is too thin; if they're too hard to find, your cat is too fat. Your cat's ribs ideally should be covered by a layer of fat, but you should be able to feel his ribs easily if you put your hands on him.

The too-much cat

Obesity is the top nutrition-related problem seen in cats, with up to four out of ten cats showing up at their veterinarian's office carrying too much weight. An overweight cat is prone to a host of related problems, including diabetes; joint, ligament, and tendon problems; breathing problems; and even skin problems in exceptionally fat cats who can't groom themselves correctly.

These cats are also more prone to a very serious and often-fatal liver problem called *hepatic lipidosis*. This condition is most often seen in obese cats that have not eaten for some reason for an extended period of time. Therefore, fasting or "starvation diets" should *never* be used as a means of weight loss in a fat cat. Talk with your veterinarian about the correct amount of food for your cat and do what you can through playing to make your cat more active.

The finicky kitty

Although some cats never met a dish of food they didn't love, others are very picky about what they eat. Feeding a variety of foods from a variety of manufacturers helps to keep cats eating, as does warming the food or feeding them wet rations instead of dry. Be aware, however, that your cat may not be as finicky as you think. If you leave dry food down all the time, he may be nibbling more than a dozen times throughout the day and thus never eating very much in any one observed sitting.

Another possibility occurs if yours is an indoor-outdoor cat: He may be picking up meals at another house besides your own — or maybe at more than one! Or perhaps he's using his natural killer instincts and "cooking" for himself!

Finickiness is not a reason for concern as long as your cat's not losing weight. A half-pound or even a pound up or down is no big deal, but more than that and you need to call your veterinarian. Weight loss is one of the first indications that something's going wrong with your cat.

A special peculiarity of cats is that unlike dogs or kids (the human kind) who we insist *will not* starve themselves to death, cats may! Some cats simply do not like to eat a variety of foods and will refuse to eat anything but their favorite. Others will simply hold out until they get what they like. Playing "chicken" with your dog or kids is fine with us. They are both great manipulators, so we wish you luck. But playing this game with cats can be serious business — especially when "played" with overweight cats. Not eating can lead to serious medical problems in cats. This is true for the sick cat who is "off-feed" and losing weight or the cat who refuses to eat. We are not talking about concern over a cat missing one or two meals. That can be normal and healthy (as long as he looks and acts healthy otherwise). What we are talking about is a cat who simply refuses to eat and is losing weight. Don't take chances. See your veterinarian.

Greens for nibbling

Many cats love to graze, some for the fiber, some because their tummies are upset, and some . . . well, they just like it.

Indulge them by planting safe greens for them to nibble or just enjoy. Here are a few winners:

✔ **Catnip and Valerian.** Most people know about the amazing effect catnip has on some, but not all, cats, but not many people know that Valerian *(Valeriana officinalis)* is another plant that tickles a cat's fancy. Plant both of these in cat-proof areas or your pet may pull the seedlings out by the root!

After the plant is large enough to stand it, trim some of it and offer it to your pet.

✔ **Alfalfa, rye, and wheat.** Always keep a batch growing in a sunny area and let your cat graze to her heart's desire.

✔ **Parsley and thyme.** Another favorite for nibbling, these plants can be grown indoors as well as in your garden.

Not all greens are good for cats. Check out our list of the deadly ones in Chapter 21.

A cat with the right amount of fat on him looks sleek, such as the cat at the top. A too-thin cat is bony (bottom left). A cat who's obese carries a pendulous belly and has ribs that are hard to feel (bottom right).

Chapter 9

Preventive Health Care
for Your Cat

Where your cat's health is concerned, one person makes all the difference in the world as to how long and how well your cat lives. Want to guess who that one person is?

Your veterinarian, you say? Great guess — and a very important person, to be sure. Now try again.

You could have — and should have — a top-notch veterinarian, someone who's up-to-date on recent advances in veterinary medicine, someone who is not afraid to say "I don't know, but I'll find out" or to suggest a referral to a specialist. You need someone with whom your cat is relaxed and you are comfortable enough to ask all the questions you need to. But unless you're living with your veterinarian, the most important health-care provider in your cat's life is indisputably *you*.

You are the person who sees your cat every day, who feeds her, and keeps her litter box clean. *You* are the one who knows where she likes to sleep and how much and how well she grooms herself. *You* are the expert on the sound of her voice, which toys are her favorites, and the way she likes to sit on the counter in the bathroom and watch you wash your face in the morning.

More than anything else, *you* are the person who knows whether anything about your cat isn't "normal." Your powers of observations are the ones that keep her healthy — and maybe save her life. And we want to help you improve those observations.

But this duty involves more than just being a keen observer. Your role in keeping your cat healthy also includes at-home preventive care, such as keeping her teeth clean, as well as the important task of choosing the right veterinarian. The latter is essential, because even though you are the most important element in keeping your cat healthy, you have a partner — and that partner is your veterinarian. Choosing the right one for you and for your cat — and learning how to work with him and his staff efficiently — is essential for your pet's well-being.

Another part of your responsibility to your cat is keeping her well-groomed. Grooming is about more than good looks — it's another part of your cat's preventive-care regimen. For the right tools and techniques to keep your cat's coat healthy, see Chapter 7.

A happy, healthy cat is the result of good preventive care, and *you* play the biggest role in ensuring he gets it.

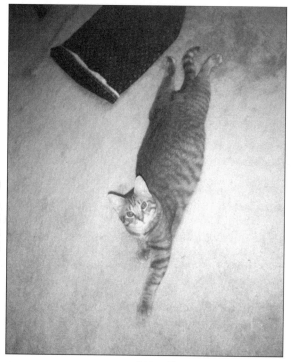

Calvin — Photo courtesy of Tammy Castleman.

Recognizing Signs of Good Health — and Bad

Because the signs of illness in cats are often subtle, a cat lover must be a bit of a detective to spot illness early. The detective work starts before you even suspect that your cat is ill and includes a few of the same kinds of basic diagnostic tools a veterinarian uses.

Make observing your pet a part of your everyday routine and integrate checking your pet for health problems a weekly must, part of an extended session that begins with petting and ends with your cat's favorite game. After all, anything that you and your pet find enjoyable you continue to do on a regular basis, and routine health checks need to be regular to be useful.

The physical cat

To identify an illness or abnormal situation, you must be able to recognize what is normal for your pet. You know your cat better than anyone else and must decide whether an abnormal situation warrants professional help. Sometimes the condition is so serious it leaves no doubt, but other times, especially in those cats who do little during the course of a normal day, the changes are so subtle you could easily miss them — and recognizing and dealing with these subtle signs of illness promptly is important.

To help you keep on track of changes in your pet, we recommend that you keep a monthly log and record your findings in each of the areas we discuss in this section. If you find that your readings match our description of what's "abnormal," consult your veterinarian. The following list describes several areas you want to keep track of:

- ✔ **General appearance.** Before starting a hands-on exam, stand back and look at your pet for a few minutes. Consider his posture, activity level, gait, coat, and overall appearance for an impression of good health. *Abnormal:* Exposed skin, thin or dry coat, ribs showing, sluggishness, outright limping or just lack of "spring" in the step, or other subtle signs you can pin down only as being "just not right."

- ✔ **Weight.** The hardest thing about weighing your cat is weighing yourself first, but you must. Step on the scale with your cat, note the weight, and then step back on alone. Subtract your weight from the total to get your cat's weight. A normal cat weighs about eight to ten pounds, but the range is wide, depending on gender and breed. Your cat is normal for his body type if a comfortable pad of fat lies over his ribs but you can still feel the ribs if you press your hands gently in, or *palpate*. (More on correct weight is in Chapter 8.) After you determine your cat's ideal weight, a difference of a half-pound up or down is normal over the course of a few months; anything more rapid or more weight loss is reason for concern. ***Abnormal:*** More than a pound of gain or loss — or less if very abrupt — or too little or too much fat overall, even if the weight remains constant; swelling of the belly.

✔ **Nose.** Moist and clean. ***Abnormal:*** Dry, cracked, scabbed, or irritated; nasal discharge; or bleeding.

✔ **Eyes.** Bright, moist, and clear, centered between the eyelids, with the pupils of equal size. The whites of the eye should not appear colored and should have only a few visible blood vessels. The pupils should shrink equally as bright light is shined into either eye and enlarge if the cat is excited or scared, if eyes are held closed, or the room is darkened. ***Abnormal:*** Eyes that are dull or sunken, that appear dry, or have thick discharge. One or both eyes not centered or pupils of unequal size. Yellow, muddy brown, or bloodshot eyes. Pupils that fail to respond or respond differently to changes in the intensity of light.

✔ **Ears.** The skin should be, clean, dry, smooth, and without wounds. The ear canal should be clean and almost odor free. ***Abnormal:*** Swelling, wounds or scabs, or any sign of a rash. Crust, moisture, discharge, or strong odor in the ear canal. Pain at the touch or an unusual way of holding the head or ears.

✔ **The mouth.** Your cat's teeth should be clean and white, with gums that are uniformly pink. Press on your pet's gum with your finger or thumb and release quickly. The color is now white at that place but should return to the same color as the surrounding tissue within one or two seconds. This exercise checks the *capillary refill time,* or *CRT,* and is a crude assessment of how well the heart and circulatory system are working. ***Abnormal:*** Loose or missing teeth, tartar (discolored, crusty buildup around the base of the teeth) or gums that are red or blue, pale, inflamed, or sore. A swollen tongue, lumps and bumps in the mouth, sores in the mouth, big tonsils visible at the back of the mouth. A rapid or slow CRT.

✔ **Breathing.** You should find that hearing your pet breathe is difficult, and his chest wall should move easily to and fro as he does. Most of the act of breathing should be performed by the chest wall. His abdominal (or stomach) wall should barely move. ***Abnormal:*** Any unusual noise heard while the pet is breathing, such as "crackles" or wheezes, could indicate a problem, especially if you haven't noticed the sound before.

Breathing that is labored, rapid, or done with an open mouth, and excessively involves the abdomen. Lumps, bumps, or masses on the chest and neck may also indicate a problem.

✔ **The abdomen.** Start just behind the ribs and gently press your hands into the abdomen, feeling for abnormalities. If your pet has just eaten, a palpable enlargement may be present in the left part of the abdomen just under the ribs. Proceed toward the rear of your pet, passing your hands gently over the abdomen. You should find no lumps, bumps, or masses, and your pet should feel no discomfort as you press gently into him. Some bumps in the abdomen are normal — they're internal organs, such as the kidneys, which is why it is so important that you do your health checks routinely, starting with a healthy cat so you learn what is normal and take note of changes that may indicate problems. Your pet's stomach should not be swollen. ***Abnormal:*** Any lump, bump, or mass that you're not used to feeling but that is consistently present when you check. Your cat groans or has difficulty breathing as you palpate. A hard, tense, or swollen abdomen.

✔ **Hydration.** Check to ensure your cat has enough fluids by pulling the skin just behind his shoulder blades into a tent and then releasing quickly. Your pet's skin should snap immediately back into position. Another good sign of hydration is that the gums just above the teeth are moist when touched. ***Abnormal:*** The skin returns slowly or remains slightly tented. The gums are dry and tacky when touched, or the eyes have a "sunken" appearance.

Vital signs

Although a hands-on exam is an essential part of determining what's normal for your cat so you can spot problems early, three other diagnostic tools ought to be in every cat lover's bag of tricks: taking your cat's temperature, heart rate, and respiratory rate. This information is useful if you call your veterinarian and can help him determine whether you need to bring your pet in and what he may be facing after you get there.

The time to learn how to take your cat's heart rate, respiratory rate, and temperature is *before* you're faced with a sick cat. Practice at home whenever you and your pet are relaxed, and if you're having difficulty, ask your veterinarian to show you how the next time you take your cat in for routine preventive care.

Here's how to start learning these important skills:

✔ **Taking your cat's temperature.** Although you can find a special thermometer for pets in any pet-supply catalog or well-equipped pet-supply store, you can also use an ordinary glass mercury or digital-readout "people" device from your pharmacy.

Lubricate the thermometer with petroleum jelly or a water-based lubricant, such as K-Y. Gently and slowly insert the thermometer about one or two inches into your cat's rectum. (If the instrument doesn't slide in easily or your cat objects, don't force it.)

Leave the thermometer in place for two minutes and then read and record the temperature. In a normal cat, the temperature should be between 100 degrees and 102.5 degrees (a little higher is fine in a normal cat on hot days), and the thermometer should be almost clean after it's removed. Call your veterinarian if your cat's temperature is below 99 degrees or above 103 degrees, or if you see evidence of mucous, blood, diarrhea, or a black, tarry stool on the thermometer.

✔ **Taking your cat's heart rate.**

Feel the your cat's heartbeat with one hand over his left side, behind the front leg. Count the number of beats in 15 seconds and multiply by four to get the heart rates in *beats per minute,* or *bpm.* A normal cat is between 140 and 220 bpm, with a relaxed cat on the lower end of the scale. Call your veterinarian if your cat's heart rate is too rapid, is too slow, or is irregular. If you find it hard to locate and count the heart rate, ask your veterinarian to show you how next time you visit with him.

✔ **Taking your cat's respiratory rate.** Stand back a bit and watch your cat breathe when he is relaxed and standing. Watch the abdomen and chest wall move. Often it is easier to count the respiratory rate when you watch the abdomen move. Count the number of movements in 60 seconds to get the respiratory rates in *breaths per minute.* A normal cat is between 15 and 25 breaths per minute, with a relaxed cat on the

Practice taking your cat's temperature before he's sick.

lower end of the scale. Don't try to count the respiratory rate when your cat is hot, or excited and panting. Call your veterinarian if your cat's respiratory rate is too rapid. If you find it hard to count the respiratory rate, ask your veterinarian to show you how next time you visit him.

You may find taking your cat's temperature and heart rate easier if someone else holds the animal, especially if you're just learning.

If you go to the trouble of measuring temperature, heart rate, and respiratory rate, write it down in a log with the date it was done. Compare future values to what you measured before. Call your veterinarian if there are sudden changes or marked and gradual changes over time.

The emotional cat

You must be aware not only of your cat's body, but also of his personality. Many times, behavioral changes are later confirmed as illnesses through the use of such veterinary diagnostic tools as blood or urine tests. Always be aware of the subtle changes in your pet's behavior, especially regarding the following areas:

- ✔ **Changes in eating habits, especially loss of appetite.** Be aware of how much your cat eats and make a mental note of any changes. More than a day without eating is reason for concern. In a multicat household of free feeders, you may have a hard time figuring who's eating what. Make a conscious effort to see each of your cats at the food dish daily, and if you give them canned rations once a day, feed them separately. Be aware, however, that if your cat is an outdoor cat, his appetite may be influenced by his hunting and by the generosity of your neighbors.

- ✔ **Changes in litter-box habits.** Many times, a "behavior" problem is really a health problem, and avoiding the litter box or using it more often than normal is one of the classic examples. A cat with a urinary-tract infection or diabetes, for example, may break his normal patterns of litter-box use.

- ✔ **Changes in drinking habits.** Cats drink more in the summer than in the winter, but even taking that into consideration, you should be aware of changes in your cat's drinking habits — too much or too little.

- ✔ **Changes in grooming.** If you notice your cat looking ill-kempt, he likely has a problem, especially if he's normally fastidious. Grooming is one of the most important parts of a cat's routine, and the cat who isn't taking care of his coat isn't well.

✔ **Changes in voice.** You know what's normal for your cat — how often he pipes up and how he sounds when he does. If your cat is noisier than usual or more quiet or the sounds he makes are different, something is going on.

For more on nutrition, see Chapter 8. Tips for solving behavior problems such as litter-box avoidance are described in Chapter 13. Grooming — your part and your cat's — is covered in more depth in Chapter 7. When does your cat need to see a veterinarian immediately? See the sidebar "Emergency!" later in this chapter.

Choosing a Veterinarian

If you're going to have a healthy pet, you need the help of a veterinarian. And although some people believe that these health-care professionals are virtually interchangeable, distinguished only by convenience and price, we feel that you're doing your pet a disservice if you don't put a little effort into choosing the right veterinarian.

The cost of veterinary care is a legitimate consideration, of course, and pet health insurance may help ease your worries if your cat becomes ill. For more information on health insurance for pets, see Chapter 10.

To work effectively with your veterinarian, you need to develop a relationship over time so she can build a history and become familiar with you and your cat. Group practices are great — two, three, four, or more heads are often better than one when your cat is ill and what is wrong and how to deal with it are not immediately obvious. However, even within a group practice, working with one veterinarian as your pet's primary caregiver is best.

Of course, many veterinarians who practice on their own aren't really alone anymore. Through the Veterinary Information Network online, a solo practitioner is part of a group practice of more than 4,500 associates who help each other with difficult cases every day. Paul has worked hard to make this service provide all the help your veterinarian needs so that she can provide the best and most-up-to-date care for your cat.

Your veterinarian should be technically proficient, current on the latest treatments, and willing to seek out more information on your pet's behalf or work with a veterinary specialist. She should be articulate, able to explain what's going on with your cat in a way you can understand, and willing to answer your questions so you can make a responsible decision on your pet's behalf. Above all, you must be able to trust your veterinarian. After all, knowing what goes on in a veterinarian's office after you leave your pet behind is impossible. An animal can never comment on treatment, and an animal lover must rely on trust to make sure a pet is dealt with fairly.

Before you choose a veterinarian, ask friends, coworkers, and neighbors for recommendations. Over the years, animal lovers can tell which veterinarians are knowledgeable, compassionate, and hard-working. Those veterinarians are always talked up by satisfied clients.

Other factors may help you narrow down your list of possibilities:

✔ **Is the clinic or hospital conveniently located, with hours you can live with?** If you have a 9-to-5 job, a veterinarian with a 9-to-5 clinic doesn't do your pet much good. Many veterinarians are open late on at least one week night and for at least a half-day on Saturday, or they're willing to make other arrangements.

✔ **Does the veterinarian consult with a veterinary college staff or independent or in-house specialists, or does he subscribe to an online veterinary service, such as the Veterinary Information Network?** A willingness to discuss tough cases with colleagues is the sign of a veterinarian who's putting in effort on your pet's behalf. Online services also assist veterinarians in getting to the bottom of a tough case, as well as offering continuing education and searchable databases of professional journals.

✔ **What kind of emergency care is available, if any?** Although emergency veterinary clinics are prepared for any catastrophe, they're not familiar with your pet. If your veterinarian's practice does *not* offer 24-hour care, does it work with one that does?

✔ **Do you feel a rapport with this person? Are you comfortable asking questions? Discussing fees?** The final call on whether a particular veterinarian is right for you comes down to intangibles. If you don't feel comfortable, you're less likely to deal with your veterinarian, and the lack of productive communication hurts your pet in the long run.

✔ **Will your cat be comfortable here?** You need a practice that runs efficiently enough so that your cat isn't stuck for very long in a waiting room full of dogs. You may also want to consider a feline-only practice. The American Association of Feline Practitioners reports that more than 350 cats-only practices are now in the United States and Canada, nearly triple the amount from a decade ago. Some of them are even staffed by one of the newest veterinary specialists: board-certified feline practitioners. None of which is to say that a general practice can't do well by your cat. We just want you to know all your options. (See the Additional Resources appendix for veterinary associations.)

Paul's company, the Veterinary Information Network, Inc. (VIN), offers a free veterinary-referral service on the World Wide Web, at www.vetquest.com. More than 25,000 veterinary practices are in the VetQuest database, and the service even shows you a street map to help you find the hospital or clinic you choose. For more information on VIN or VetQuest, see the Additional Resources appendix.

Understanding Your Veterinarian's Role in Preventing Illness

Preventive care is easier on you, your cat, and your bank account, which is why you should take advantage of all the measures available today, starting with a thorough annual examination and continuing with vaccines, dental care, and parasite control.

Spaying and neutering are also among the most important preventive-health measures. For more information on these routine surgical procedures, see Chapter 14.

The not-so-routine exam

The cornerstone of your cat's preventive-health regimen is an annual examination by your veterinarian.

This important visit is the time for your veterinarian to go over your cat from ear tip to tail tip, slowly and thoroughly, examining every inch for abnormalities, adding to your pet's medical history and comparing to his past observations. His staff may have already recorded your cat's temperature and pulse rate, but he listens to the sounds of your pet's heart and breathing and gently presses into your pet's body to ensure that internal organs feel normal and that no lumps or masses are present.

Eyes, ears, nose, and mouth all get a good look, too, and your veterinarian asks you questions about your cat's habits. Your cat can't speak for himself, so his body and his owner must speak for him.

Prepare for your cat's annual visit by reviewing your own observations regarding the condition of your cat. Write down any questions you have and make sure that you ask them while you're there.

Vaccinations

Call them "shots" if you want, but vaccinations deserve a lot of respect for cutting the rates of infectious disease in cats. A series of vaccines for kittens and annual vaccines for cats are still believed to be one of the best ways to ensure good health for your cat — even though these preventive-health measures continue to evolve as research expands the body of knowledge in feline medicine.

Be aware that the need for annual boosters beyond the initial kitten series and the first annual booster are being re-evaluated for many of the vaccines given today. The right regimen for each vaccine is not yet known. The law dictates what must be followed for rabies in each state. Let your veterinarian know that you are interested in discussing the pros and cons of vaccinations and how often they should be repeated. Recommendations for each vaccine will likely change over the next few years.

Vaccines work by putting a tiny amount of a disease-causing virus or other microorganism into your cat, challenging her immune system to create disease-fighting antibodies. Should your pet ever come in contact with the actual disease, her body then recognizes it and is already prepared to defeat it. Many vaccines are *killed,* meaning that the disease-causing organism has been rendered lifeless before injection, or *modified-live,* which means it has been altered so it no longer produces the signs of the disease. Although each acts slightly differently in the body, the result, ideally, is the same: an immune system ready to fight the "real" infectious agents should they ever turn up. (We say "ideally," because no vaccine is 100 percent effective and safe.)

Should you pass on vaccines because they're not 100 percent safe or effective? We don't think it's in your cat's best interest. An occasional cat will develop an "allergic" reaction to a vaccine, and these usually become apparent quickly and are managed by your veterinarian. To ensure this very uncommon complication does not become serious, keep your cat confined and observe her for a few hours after the vaccine is given. If you have any questions or concerns, call or return to your veterinarian.

Another concern regarding vaccines is the suggestion that some cats develop a malignant tumor at the site where the shot is given (estimates for the risk now approach one sick cat per 10,000 vaccinated). For help in protecting your cat, see the section "The risk factor," later in this chapter.

Remember the following regarding vaccines:

- ✔ Do not use cancer or allergic reactions as a reason to avoid getting your cat vaccinated. You are much much more likely to lose your cat to one of the diseases we vaccinate against, if unvaccinated, than you are to ever see a tumor in your cat.

- ✔ Kittens are especially fragile — do not even consider skipping the kitten series and first annual booster.

Ouchless vaccines may be the wave of the future. One manufacturer has introduced a combination vaccine for feline panleukopenia, feline rhinotracheitis, and feline calicivirus that's administered by putting drops into the cat's eye or nose. Alas, no needle-less vaccines currently exist for rabies or feline leukemia.

The protection factor

Several vaccines are available to protect your cat from disease; you need to discuss with your veterinarian which are appropriate and at which intervals they need to be administered. (See the following section, "The risk factor," for more information on vaccine concerns.) The vaccinations you're offered for your cat may include the following:

- ✔ The common combination vaccine, called *FVRCP,* that protects your cat against three diseases: *feline panleukopenia, feline rhinotracheitis,* and *feline calicivirus.* (The initials of the vaccine stand for Feline Viral Rhinotracheitis, Calicivirus, Panleukopenia.) Protection against an additional disease, *feline chlamydiosis,* may be part of this combination vaccine; ask your veterinarian.

- ✔ Vaccination against *rabies* is required by law in many areas but should be part of your cat's regimen even if it's not — for your health as well as your cat's. (See the sidebar "The deadly danger of rabies," later in this chapter.)

- ✔ The vaccine against the *feline leukemia virus,* or FeLV, should not be considered until your cat tests negative for the disease. Experts disagree on whether this vaccine is a good idea for indoor cats; the decision is yours after talking to your veterinarian. For cats likely to come into contact with other felines, the vaccine provides important protection against this deadly contagious disease.

- ✔ The latest addition to the disease regimen is a vaccine for *feline infectious peritonitis,* or FIP. Cats in multicat households are at the highest risk for FIP, whereas most household pets are considered at low risk. Serious concerns regarding this vaccine have been raised recently. Discuss with your veterinarian whether your pet needs this vaccine.

We provide information on common cat diseases, including FIP and FeLV, in Chapter 10.

The risk factor

In recent years, cat lovers have been horrified by reports of deadly cancer caused by something that's supposed to save the lives of their cats — routine vaccinations. Unfortunately, this disease, called *vaccine-associated feline sarcoma* or *feline vaccine-site sarcoma,* is more than a rumor, and it has claimed the lives of hundreds of cats. The tumors turn up at the vaccination site, but in all honesty, no one is sure whether this is true.

Kittens and vaccinations

For cats, vaccinations are usually an annual affair, part of the yearly checkup recommended for all cats. Kittens, however, need a series of vaccinations to protect them as they grow.

Kittens pick up antibodies from their mothers through the placenta and in the special milk, called *colostrum,* that they drink in the first two days of their lives. These antibodies diminish over time, but until they do, they not only protect the kitten against disease, but they also may block the usefulness of any vaccine.

Although it can be determined exactly when a kitten's maternal antibodies have fallen to the point where a vaccine is necessary, doing so is impractical, so veterinarians give a series of shots to ensure that the kitten is protected.

The first combination vaccine is given after a kitten first comes in to the vet's. If the first shot is given at 6 weeks, others are given at 9, 12, and 16 weeks. If the first shot is given at 8 weeks, the others come at 12 and 16 weeks of age.

Kittens are tested for feline leukemia, and if the owner decides to vaccinate, those shots come at 12 and 16 weeks. *Feline infectious peritonitis* is a controversial vaccine that should be considered only for cats in large multicat households or breeding operations. Talk to your veterinarian about when the vaccine should be given, if at all.

When to vaccinate for rabies is often determined by law; doing so at 12 to 16 weeks is fairly routine, followed by revaccinations one year later and then every two or three years.

If you are getting multiple vaccinations for your kitten, many veterinarians advise clients to spread the vaccines out and not have more than one or two inoculations given in any one visit. If too many shots are administered at one time, the potential for reactions or interactions may be greater.

Nor is anyone quite sure why this problem occurs, and the risk is low compared to the dangers of not vaccinating your cat — risks not only to your cat's health, but also, in the case of rabies, to your own. To protect your cat, you should take the following precautions:

- ✔ At your pet's annual examination, discuss with your veterinarian which vaccines your cat really needs. Because of the number of cats infected with rabies — since 1981, more cats than dogs in the United States have been diagnosed with rabies — rabies protection is not only important but is required by law in an increasing number of places. Your cat may not need to be vaccinated against feline leukemia, however, if he's kept indoors and doesn't interact with other cats.

- ✔ Discuss with your veterinarian the location of where the vaccines are injected, and ask her to use single-agent vaccines. Recent recommendations include giving each vaccine in a specific location to help confirm which vaccines are responsible and to allow for more treatment options should a problem develop.

> ✔ Make sure your veterinarian notes the vaccination sites, as well as information on the vaccines, such as the name of the manufacturer and the serial number.
>
> ✔ Be aware of any lumps at the vaccine sites. A small lump immediately after vaccination is normal, but call your veterinarian if the lump grows or persists beyond three weeks.

Keep the risks in perspective, and press your veterinarian for the most recent information available. Vaccinations still prevent many times more deaths than they cause. Veterinary knowledge is growing in this area constantly, so ask your veterinarian to keep you informed on the recommended changes in preventive care for your cat.

Two of the best ways to keep up on current veterinary information is to keep an eye on the Internet and subscribe to a newsletter. The major online services — America Online, Microsoft Network, CompuServe, and Prodigy — all have pet sections, and lots of animal-health sites are on the World Wide Web — one of the best is the Cat Fanciers page, at `http://www.fanciers.com`. (See Chapters 2 and 20 for more information about online resources for cat lovers.) Two monthly newsletters produced by veterinary schools are also a first-rate source for current health and behavior information. *CatWatch* is produced by the Cornell University College of Veterinary Medicine; *Catnip* comes from the Tuft University School of Veterinary Medicine. For subscription information, see the Additional Resources appendix.

Dental care

Ensuring healthy teeth and gums for your pet is one area where you and your veterinarian must work together.

Dental scalings and polishings by your veterinarian are an important part of preventive medicine, and keeping teeth clean between veterinary appointments is something that can — and should — be done by cat lovers.

Plaque buildup on teeth causes gums to recede, opening pockets at the root line that are paradise to bacterial infections. Left unchecked, these infections can lead to tooth loss, make eating painful, and put the cat's immune system and internal organs under pressure, causing illness and premature aging. Rotting teeth and gums can become a powerful source of bad breath that some pet owners treat with products that may temporarily fix the smell but do nothing about the real problem.

Although some groomers and cat owners scale plaque themselves, this practice doesn't address the problem at the root line, so regular cleanings under anesthesia by a veterinarian are essential to ensure dental health. In

The deadly danger of rabies

Although most people associate rabies with dogs, cases of feline rabies are becoming more common. Vaccination is so important for your cat that in many places it's required by law.

Rabies is caused by a viral infection of the nervous system. Most cases of rabies in the United States occur in wild animals. Because cats often coexist peacefully with wild animals, they're more likely to be bitten by a rabid wild animal. (Normally timid animals can become aggressive if rabid.) Most cases of rabies in cats can be traced to skunks, foxes, raccoons, and bats.

The risk of contracting rabies from your cat — or any cat — is extremely small, but the disease is so deadly that, if your cat were to contract it, he would need to be humanely killed, and you would need to have a series of inoculations for your own protection.

A cat with rabies may hide, become agitated or nervous, get weak in the hindquarters, or become aggressive. Swallowing difficulties are also common. Whether he's vaccinated or not, if you suspect your cat has tangled with a wild animal, contact your veterinarian and local public-health officials immediately. Your life depends on it! If your cat is current on his vaccination, he'll need to be quarantined, but if not, public-health officials may require that he be killed. That's because the only way to tell for certain that an animal is rabid is to test the tissues of the brain.

Need we make this any clearer? *Be sure your pet is vaccinated against this deadly, contagious disease.*

---

between, brushing two or three times a week with a child's toothbrush or fingertip brush and a toothpaste designed for pets slows the reformation of plaque and extends the time between dental scalings. This is not always easy to do, but if your cat will allow it, you can make a big difference in his oral health.

The key to getting a pet used to having his teeth brushed is to do it in small steps over time and to be patient and encouraging.

Good dental health is especially important in the care of older cats. For more information, see Chapter 11.

Parasite control

Cats pick up all kinds of parasites, both internal pests such as worms and external ones such as fleas and ear mites. Your veterinarian may ask you to bring in a fresh stool sample to check for the presence of worms and prescribes any necessary medication to eliminate the parasites, if present.

Emergency!

Anything is worth a call to your veterinarian if you're not sure what's wrong with your kitty, but some things require urgent attention. Here are some clinical signs that should have you heading for your veterinarian's — or for the emergency clinic:

✔ Seizure, fainting, or collapse.

✔ Eye injury, no matter how mild.

✔ Vomiting or diarrhea — anything more than two or three times within an hour or so.

✔ Allergic reactions, such as swelling around the face, or hives, most easily seen on the belly.

✔ Any suspected poisoning, including anti-freeze, rodent or snail bait, or human medication. Cats are also especially sensitive to insecticides (such as flea-control medication for dogs) or any petroleum-based product.

✔ Snake or venomous spider bite.

✔ Thermal stress — from being either too cold or too hot — even if the cat seems to have recovered. (The internal story could be quite different.)

✔ Any wound or laceration that's open and bleeding, or any animal bite.

✔ Trauma, such as being hit by a car, even if the cat seems fine.

✔ Any respiratory problem: chronic coughing, trouble breathing, or near drowning.

✔ Straining to urinate or defecate.

Although some problems don't classify as life-threatening, they may be causing your pet irritation and pain and so should be taken care of without delay. Signs of pain include the following:

✔ Panting

✔ Labored breathing

✔ Increased body temperature

✔ Lethargy

✔ Restlessness

✔ Crying out

✔ Aggression

✔ Loss of appetite

Note: Some cats may seek you out for reassurance; others may draw within themselves.

Don't take a chance waiting to see whether things "get better" on their own: Call your veterinarian!

Don't bother with worming medications sold at pet-supply stores; they may not treat the kind of parasites your cat has. Better you should have your veterinarian accurately diagnose and treat your cat than subject your pet to medication that doesn't fix the problem. This sort of thing is false economy!

The parasite that drives people craziest is the flea. For help in treating this persistent pest, see Chapter 7.

Chapter 10

Common Cat Health Problems

*1*f provided with the benefits of preventive health care and kept protected from accidents and infectious diseases, cats can live long, healthy lives — and many of them do.

If they get sick, the chances are better than ever before that a veterinarian can help. The growth in the popularity of cats has led to an explosion of interest in their health-care needs, with research into feline diseases ongoing at the world's top schools, colleges of veterinary medicine, and pharmaceutical companies serving animal health needs. Then, too, the science of veterinary medicine in general has advanced as the diagnostic and treatment tools of human medicine have become widely available to pets as well, and such procedures as CAT scans (appropriately!), kidney transplants, and radiation therapy are now routine at veterinary colleges and specialty practices. The ranks of veterinary specialists have grown as well — Paul is a board-certified veterinary cardiologist, for example — bringing even more knowledge and options to cat lovers in the area of veterinary care for their pets.

Another "human" entry into the pet arena, albeit still a minor presence, is health insurance to help cover not only the most expensive of these procedures but also the routine measures cat lovers have paid for years.

What do all these advances mean for you and your pet? If you're careful to practice preventive health-care measures for your pet, and you're both lucky, you may barely be touched by the revolution in veterinary medicine. But if you need help, it's there — now more than ever before — and getting better all the time.

You can help to advance the future of feline health by supporting two charitable organizations that provide grants for companion animal health research: The Winn Feline Foundation and the Morris Animal Foundation. The Winn Feline Foundation, for which Paul serves as a veterinary consultant, is affiliated with the Cat Fanciers' Association. The Morris Animal Foundation is a nearly 50-year-old organization founded by two men: veterinarian Mark L. Morris, developer of a line of therapeutic diets for pets, and Morris Frank, owner of the first seeing-eye dog in the United States. Information on contacting these groups is in the Additional Resources appendix.

Despite all the incredible advances in the diagnosis and treatment of feline illness, one of the most important elements in maintaining good health for your pet is still the laying on of hands — yours. For what you need to know to conduct an at-home examination — as well as a full discussion of other important preventive-health measures — see Chapter 9. And don't forget the importance of good nutrition! All you need to know to get your cat eating right is located in Chapter 8.

A Cooperative Approach to Cat Health

We named this section "a cooperative approach" because we've come to realize, after years of listening to both pet owners and veterinarians, that what should be a team effort to protect and ensure the health of a pet is sometimes anything but. The relationship between the client (that's you, not your cat) and the veterinarian can become adversarial if neither party respects the contributions of the other and both parties forget the reason that brought them together: to help the *patient* — in other words, your cat.

Sometimes, the task of figuring out what's wrong with an animal is like walking into a movie in the middle — for one brief moment you have no idea what the story's about and little chance of predicting the outcome. But given the opportunity to see a few more scenes, you start to understand what's going on. For the veterinarian, all too often that one glimpse is all he gets. The client wants an answer, a shot, or a pill to makes things better. He wants the problem fixed — now.

And although the client probably wants an immediate solution to his own health problems, too, he's resigned enough to say "yes" to test after test to find the right answer — as long as his insurance is footing the bill.

And there, of course, is the rub.

In the vast majority of cases, the client is footing the bill for veterinary procedures. And although veterinary costs are a small fraction of comparable procedures in human medicine, the fact that you're spending hundreds instead of thousands (or hundreds of thousands) of dollars isn't all that reassuring if your budget is stretched as far as many families' are today.

The veterinarian has bills to pay, too, and he wants to make you happy, which is why many of them fall into the habit of giving the client exactly what he wants — a shot or a pill that takes care of the symptoms, regardless of whether the problem is fixed for the long term. This sort of practice is not good veterinary medicine, and you should tell your veterinarian that you understand he may not be able to fix what's wrong right now. Let him know you want diagnostic tests (if they're needed, of course) and that you're happy with fewer medicines (if he was considering giving them just to make you think you got something out of the visit). Finally, let your veterinarian know that you value his diagnostic skills and respect his desire to investigate the problem more before acting. Your cat will receive better care as a result.

You and your veterinarian are on the same team — or you should be — together in the goal of keeping your cat in good health. Your cat deserves the best, and so do you. And so, too, does your veterinarian, who has spent years studying to be able to help your cat. So let him. Listen to him.

If you have the right veterinarian, he listens, too, to your concerns about treatments and finances. You can accomplish a lot through clear communication, respect, and trust.

Choosing the right veterinarian is about more than price-shopping and convenience. The old saying, "you get what you pay for," very much applies when you are selecting a veterinarian; the "lowest-priced" veterinarian is not necessarily the best choice for your cat, or the most truly cost-effective. For a discussion of the factors that should go into choosing a health-care professional with whom you can work for the benefit of your cat, see Chapter 9.

When Does My Cat Need a Specialist?

Although not as many specialists exist in veterinary medicine as in human medicine, you still find a growing presence in your community or within a short drive — and more are likely to turn up in the future. Your veterinarian should be open to referring you to a specialist or consulting one on your behalf, if your pet's condition warrants it.

Although many urban areas can support independent specialists or specialty practices, in less-populated areas you're more likely to find a full complement of specialists at the closest university that has a school or college of veterinary medicine. Current companion animal specialties relevant to cats include the following:

- Anesthesiology
- Behavior
- Cardiology
- Clinical pharmacology

✔ Dentistry

✔ Dermatology

✔ Emergency medicine and critical care

✔ Internal medicine

✔ Neurology

✔ Oncology

✔ Ophthalmology

✔ Radiology

✔ Surgery

What's special about "specialists"? Becoming a veterinary specialist requires additional study in a two- to five-year residency program as well as a specific examination for each specialty. The result is certification over and above that required to achieve a degree in veterinary medicine.

For veterinarians already in practice, the American Board of Veterinary Practitioners (ABVP) also offers specialty certification. This program does not require a formal residency program prior to examination but is still a very meaningful and rigorous demonstration of a veterinarian's commitment to excellence and lifelong education. Among the subspecialties of ABVP certification are a companion animal (dog and cat) and, of special note, a feline specialty.

If your veterinarian doesn't suggest a referral to a specialist, and you wonder whether seeing one may help your cat, bring the idea up for discussion. Let your veterinarian know that you aren't questioning his care but want to bring more-specialized expertise in to help your pet. If you have a good working relationship with your veterinarian, calling in a specialist is never a problem.

If your veterinarian is reluctant to refer, remember that the final decision in your cat's care is always yours. Keep the lines of communication open.

The relationship between your regular veterinarian and a specialist is a complementary one of respect for the skills of each other. Your veterinarian knows the specialist isn't out to "steal" clients, and the specialist realizes that, to get referrals, he needs to be clear on his limited role. To save time and money, your veterinarian shares your pet's medical history with the specialist and discusses your pet's case. The specialist probably requires additional tests to get the information he needs to make an accurate diagnosis and develop an appropriate course of care. A specialist doesn't practice "shotgun medicine" — if he's brought into the case, his purpose is to figure out exactly what's wrong, if he can, and work to restore your pet to health.

You can help encourage the benefits of a healthy referral system within your community by following a few rules. First, understand you're being referred for help with a special problem to someone your veterinarian believes can help. Do *not* leave your regular veterinarian for this new person unless you, the specialist, and your veterinarian agree doing so is best for your cat. Doing otherwise spoils the relationship between your veterinarian and the specialist. In fact, any specialist who'd agree to taking you on as a permanent client should be looked at as having less-than-ideal ethics and, therefore, perhaps is not the best veterinarian for your cat. Finally, do not ask that the specialist perform procedures for which you weren't referred to him — especially routine tests or vaccinations. An ethical specialist would be put in the difficult position of refusing your request out of respect for the referring veterinarian. Are these guidelines necessary? We argue "yes," for without your support and participation, top-notch specialty care for your cat could prove hard to find when your pet needs it.

Two of the greatest challenges faced by veterinary medicine are the small number of specialists and the lack of a central hospital system where practitioners have "hospital rights" in a facility with advanced diagnostic and treatment capabilities. This reality has created a system with many smaller self-contained hospitals, while limiting the "reach" of specialists and interaction among colleagues. Recent changes in technology have changed the way veterinarians share diagnostic information — and saved time and money as a result. The online world is changing the way veterinarians consult with colleagues. Members of the Veterinary Information Network have access to a contingent of colleagues and online specialists, such as cardiologists and surgeons, who, although they may be thousands of miles away, can help diagnose and treat cases. Other services accept and interpret transmitted ultrasound and radiographic images and other data. Laboratories maintain computerized databases of their animal-health records, and should your pet end up somewhere his records are not — such as at an emergency-care clinic on a holiday — the attending veterinarian can in many cases access recent test results for comparison and analysis.

Ten Common Health Problems

Although the cat has a reputation for being a pet who doesn't have a lot of health problems, the fact is that a lot of things can go wrong. Despite Paul's desire to tell you about every one of them in such complete detail that you could pass the veterinary boards after reading this book, we're going to stick to ten of the most common and give you what you need to know to make the care decisions you need to in working with your veterinarian.

The most important role you play in keeping your cat healthy is preventive. Keep on top of the preventive-care measures your veterinarian recommends, such as vaccines, and get into the habit of noticing changes in your cat's attitude, appearance, or behavior. For more on preventive medicine, see Chapter 9.

A few health problems are more common in older cats, and so we've put them in the older-cat section in Chapter 11. These problems include diabetes, and hyperthyroidism, as well as dental problems brought on by neglecting your cat's teeth and gums. Important *preventive* care for your cat's mouth is covered in Chapter 9.

Abscesses

Nearly every outdoor cat and even many indoor cats at one time or another develops an *abscess,* or pocket of pus. The most common cause of abscesses in cats is puncture wounds, often the result of a bite from another cat during a fight for territory or during mating. (Another good reason for spaying or neutering your pet — see Chapter 14 for even more information.)

A cat's mouth is full of a nasty mix of bacteria, and your cat's body starts trying to fight this bacteria after he's been bitten. At first, you may not even know your cat has been injured. Whether the inciting wound is from a sharp rock or the teeth of a neighbor's cat, the first evidence of a problem may be noticing your cat is limping or just "not doing right." Hints that an abscess is brewing may range from finding nothing but an elevated temperature to finding the abscess — either still closed and feeling like fluid in a pocket under the skin or open and draining and smelling disgusting! At the first sign of persistent (more than an hour or so) limping or "not doing right" (being less active, not eating, not drinking, avoiding or seeking out attention), you should get your cat's carrier and make a trip to the veterinarian.

The horrid bacteria in a cat's mouth is one reason (rabies is another) why being careful to wash the wound thoroughly and seek medical attention is so important if you're ever bitten by a cat.

If possible, your veterinarian opens the abscess and flushes the pus out. He may also insert a *drain* to keep the site from closing up too soon and give a shot of antibiotics or prescribe some antibiotic pills to be given at home. (For tips on giving pills and other medications, see the section "Giving Your Cat Medication," later in this chapter.)

Believe it or not, finding out that an abscess is the cause of limping or not feeling well is a good thing. An abscess is usually easily diagnosed, treated, and quickly resolved. Repeated abscesses, however, may be a sign of a problem with your cat's immune system — and that may be the first sign of a significant health problem.

The best "treatment" for abscesses is preventive. Indoor, altered cats have the least chance of being bitten by another cat; unneutered roaming males have the greatest.

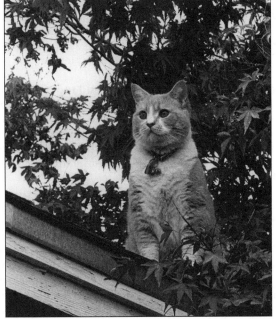

Outdoor cats are exposed to many more health problems than indoor ones, including abscesses and infectious diseases.

Scotty — Photo courtesy of Gay Currier.

Feline asthma

Gina is a lifelong asthmatic who has ended up in the hospital a few times struggling to breathe. Although she takes medication regularly to help prevent and stave off attacks, sometimes the disease gets the best of her for a while. And she's not alone. Asthma is on the rise in humans, and the experts aren't sure why. Cats frequently get what we call *feline asthma* — and in most cases, we also don't know why.

The signs of asthma in cats are very similar to those seen in humans — difficulty breathing, first and foremost. Cats with asthma also "wheeze" and may exhibit a cough that sometimes sounds like gagging. If he's having trouble breathing, a cat sits with his neck extended and inhales and exhales rapidly with his mouth open.

Asthma is not the only disease that can cause difficulty breathing, so neither you nor your veterinarian should assume that asthma must be the cause.

The signs of feline asthma can come on quite suddenly and be very serious. Like an asthmatic person who feels as if she can't breathe, your cat can panic. You must do all you can to minimize stress while your cat is having a hard time breathing. The best way to do so is by not creating stress: Now is not the time to be chasing your pet and forcing him into a carrier. Let him calm down first.

If this instance is the first time your cat has had a problem breathing, take your cat to your veterinarian or to an emergency clinic (if after hours or on a weekend or holiday) immediately. Call ahead so that the clinic can be prepared for your arrival and be prepared for a stressful wait for the answers to what's causing your cat's breathing difficulties.

Cats having difficulty breathing are quite fragile and too much handling can worsen their condition to the point where they may even die. As much as you and your veterinarian want to know the cause of the problem and begin treating immediately, often the best thing for your veterinarian to do is to rule out quickly any obvious problems, such as obstruction of the airway or air or fluid around the lungs, and avoid significant handling while giving medications and time a chance to work.

If your veterinarian has diagnosed asthma in your cat, she probably will have prescribed medications that help ease the symptoms. Whenever your cat is having breathing problems, give him the medication if you can do so without stressing him further; otherwise, wait for him to settle down. Use the time to call your veterinarian and discuss the symptoms and whether your cat needs to come in. If you're told to bring your cat in, use the carrier he feels so familiar with and, after you get to the office, walk directly to the receptionist for an immediate assessment. Your veterinarian or her staff can determine the severity of the attack, and if warranted, your cat is immediately seen to get the medications and oxygen that should help relieve his distress.

Although no one knows the cause of feline asthma, minimizing exposure to dust (remember to use low-dust litter and leave off the litter box hood), smoke, aerosol sprays, and other irritants is essential. Keep your ears and eyes open and stay in close contact with your veterinarian so that you can get the newest information relating to the cause, prevention, and treatment of feline asthma.

Three nasty viruses

The three "F" viruses — *feline immunodeficiency virus (FIV), feline leukemia virus (FeLV),* and *feline infectious peritonitis (FIP)* deserve their first initials — they are all bad news on your cat's health report card. They are transmitted cat-to-cat.

FIV

Feline immunodeficiency virus, or *FIV,* is the feline counterpart to AIDS, although you can rest assured no evidence has been found to suggest that FIV can have ill effects upon humans. Cats infected with FIV, may develop opportunistic diseases ranging from cancer to ringworm, to bacterial or viral infections.

Testing and isolating infected cats is the only way to control this disease; no vaccine or cure currently exists. Testing on kittens is unreliable, so feline health experts recommend testing of all cats more than six months old. Only by knowing the FIV status of your cat can you be certain of what you're dealing with and protect the uninfected cats in your household. Because most kittens are three months old or younger when they're adopted, any adoption brings a matter of risk. If the cats you already have are free of the disease, however, you've greatly reduced the total risk. Beyond that, the best you can do is test your kitten at six months and hope for the best.

Finding a positive test proves only that the cat is or has been infected by the virus and the infection has stimulated production of antibodies to the virus. A positive test performed by your veterinarian doesn't prove your cat is sick from the virus — even if your pet appears sick at the time of the test. Two different tests exist, and you should ask that your cat be retested with the other to confirm the results before making any decisions regarding your pet.

The good news is that infection with the feline immunodeficiency virus generally carries a better prognosis than does infection with the feline leukemia virus (also covered in this section). A positive FIV test, therefore, should not be considered a reason to change how you treat your cat except that no new cats should be introduced into your home and your cat should stay indoors to protect himself from other diseases and to protect other cats from his infection.

FIV-positive healthy cats may live for months to years — many cats live for six to ten years after diagnosis.

To help your pet live longer with FIV, work with your veterinarian to catch health problems early and treat them aggressively. Your cat doesn't have the healthy immune system of a normal cat, so you and your veterinarian must help him out.

FeLV

Feline leukemia virus, or *FeLV,* is a known killer. FeLV both weakens the immune system and directly contributes to the development of cancers in infected cats. The disease is thought to be the most important infectious contributor to the death and suffering of cats.

Although vaccines are available against this deadly disease (see Chapter 9 for more information on vaccines), they're not foolproof. As with FIV, the best way to protect your cat against feline leukemia is to know the infection status of the cats he hangs with and protect him from the infected ones — ideally, that means keeping him inside, alone or with other FeLV-negative cats.

Test all new kittens or cats before introducing them to the cat or cats you already have and vice versa. (You should test for FeLV before your new pet is vaccinated against the disease anyway.) Your cats should also be retested after exposure to potential FeLV carriers, especially if your pet has been bitten. Because FeLV is associated with many symptoms of illness, your cat should also be tested whenever he's sick. Outdoor cats or others who are exposed to potential FeLV carriers should be retested annually.

Most veterinarians have a combination FeLV and FIV test available that allows them to determine the presence of both of these viral diseases with a single blood sample, and generally for less cost than doing the two tests separately.

FeLV is serious business. Don't let your soft heart convince you to take home a cat or kitten before you know your new pet's FeLV status, especially if you already have a cat or cats at home — you're risking their lives to do so. If you find you have exposed your cat or cats to FeLV, though, do not panic. Isolate your pets from the FeLV-infected cat and have them tested according to your veterinarian's recommendations. Infection with FeLV can require long-time repeated exposure, so don't be too concerned because of one interaction.

What does having your cat test FeLV positive mean? First, realize having the virus does not equal being sick. Some otherwise healthy FeLV-positive cats live for months to years with no evidence of disease. If the infected cat is your only pet, you have no known reason to consider changing how you care for him other than not letting him out where he can expose other cats or be exposed to bad things other cats may be carrying. Take extra care to prevent exposure to diseases and work closely with your veterinarian to diagnose and treat early and aggressively any FeLV-related diseases that may develop.

The good news (yes, we think you deserve some now): Unlike with FIV, many cats can eliminate FeLV infections from their body. That's why retesting any cat who tests (and is confirmed) positive within two to three months after the previous test is so important.

FIP

Feline infectious peritonitis, or *FIP,* is a serious concern for those with multiple-cat households or catteries but is likely not a common risk to those with single pet cats. Having said that, however, we must note that FIP is a deadly disease whenever and wherever it strikes.

FIP is caused by a virus classified as a *coronavirus.* The confusing part about FIP is that many types of coronaviruses are around, some of which cause disease, and some of which do not. Most disease-causing coronaviruses cause only short-term diarrhea in young kittens. Unfortunately, we have no good way to tell which kind of coronavirus is infecting a cat — the mild kind or the deadly FIP kind. Your veterinarian can tell you your sick cat has been exposed to a coronavirus but can't tell you — until too late — whether the disease in your cat is FIP.

As if this situation weren't bad enough, evidence is accumulating that the not-so-bad coronaviruses can rapidly mutate into the very bad FIP virus. Shades of Darwin — this virus is definitely one that's not playing fair! The end result: You really can't protect your cat from FIP. The virus is pretty tough and can infect a cat after weeks to months of lying around on the floor or floating around in the air. Fortunately, the virus is easily destroyed by most common disinfectants and detergents, so basic hygiene helps a lot.

FIP is a "great impersonator" disease, meaning that it can present itself in many ways. The disease may look like a spinal or brain disease, a digestive-system disease, an eye disease, or even cancer or heart disease. The most-common clues to your veterinarian that FIP is present are found in blood tests, in the results of analysis of fluid from the chest or abdomen, or in the results of a biopsy sample after surgery to find out what's wrong with your cat.

Unfortunately, no known effective treatment exists for FIP. Available treatments are aimed at quieting your cat's immune system and prescribing antibiotics to fight the bacterial infections that may go hand-in-hand with FIP.

Although an FIP vaccine has been produced, many top veterinarians, including Paul's friend Dr. Alice Wolf, of Texas A&M University, believe that little risk of exposure to or of developing FIP in household pets exists. For your cat, then, the current vaccines seem to have little practical application.

Cats in large colonies, catteries, or breeding operations are the greatest risk for developing FIP because of the number of cats in close quarters, but even for those cats, the current vaccine may not be advisable. Studies done at Cornell University raise further questions as to the benefits and maybe even about the safety of vaccinating against FIP.

For now, if yours is a household with one or just a few cats, we recommend that you not vaccinate for FIP. Discuss the situation with your veterinarian, however, because research continues and the situation could change tomorrow.

Upper respiratory infection

Many cats catch "colds" sometime during their lives, and most of these afflictions are caused by viruses. Cats with an upper respiratory infection are lethargic, have fevers and runny eyes and noses, sneeze, and often do not want to eat or drink. These infections are quite contagious, so spreading disease through your household to other cats is a real concern. Young kittens and kittens and cats with other diseases that weaken the immune system — such as FIV and FeLV — are most susceptible to these infections.

If your cat develops an upper respiratory infection, call ahead and let your veterinarian know why you are coming in — he may want to take special precautions to help prevent exposing other cats in the waiting room to the virus upon your arrival at the hospital.

As with a cold in humans, so long as the fever is not too high (normal is 100 to 102.5 F.) and your cat continues to eat and drink, overnight (or longer) hospitalization can usually be avoided. Keeping your cat's eyes and nostrils free of "crust" by washing gently with a moist cloth helps keep their appetite up. If your cat stops eating and, especially, drinking, dehydration is a danger, and hospitalization or home veterinary care is needed.

With appropriate care, most cats recover fully in a few days to a week; however, some cases can persist for more than two weeks. If your cat has repeated bouts of upper respiratory infections, or if they are particularly severe or persistent, your veterinarian is likely to be concerned and want to test for diseases that weaken the immune system.

Urologic problems

The kidneys are the blood filters of the body. They help eliminate excess fluid if a cat drinks more than he needs, retain fluid if the cat drinks less than he needs, and eliminate waste materials ingested in food, drink, or medicine or produced by the body. The *bladder* stores urine until the cat is ready to eliminate it from the body, preferably in a litter box. The system is not foolproof, however, and some cats have problems, especially as they age.

Cat lovers are often very conscious of their cat's elimination problems, because a sick cat often stops using the litter box. Making sure a behavior problem is not a health problem is the first step toward trying to solve it. After your cat has a clean bill of health, you may need to retrain him in correct litter-box routines. See Chapter 13 for more information.

Kidney diseases

Kidney disease is mostly seen in older cats but is possible at any age. The kidneys decrease functioning to varying degrees. Initially you may notice only changes in urination or drinking (more and more often) but later may see weight loss and more-severe evidence of a buildup of toxins in your cat's body.

A preventable cause of kidney failure in cats is poisoning from the ingestion of antifreeze. Make sure you protect your pet by cleaning up spills. More information on common household dangers for your pet is in Chapter 21.

Be concerned if your cat is urinating and drinking excessively. These symptoms can mean any number of problems. Observant owners may also note reduced appetite, more frequent vomiting, less grooming, and weight loss, but these symptoms are usually later-stage results of kidney failure.

Some have proposed that chronic kidney problems are caused by bacteria entering the blood in cats with badly infected teeth. Although this is still under debate, it does suggest the importance of preventive dental care for your pet. For more information on preventive dental care, see Chapter 9.

Treatment for kidney failure can include diet changes. Current trends lean toward low-protein diets with attention to low salt if high blood pressure accompanies the problem. Don't be surprised if these recommendations change as they have many times in the past. (See Chapter 8 for more information about feline nutrition.)

You need to work with your veterinarian to monitor your cat's health, which likely includes blood tests to spot problems and changes. Your veterinarian may need to hospitalize your cat to give intravenous fluids and may even ask you to give your cat fluids under the skin at home. You can help monitor how your cat is progressing by keeping a written daily log of your cat's attitude, appetite, and weight. This record helps you notice trends that may signal a need for additional attention from your veterinarian before they become serious.

Although treating kidney failure requires long-term effort on your part, much progress has recently been made in managing this disease. Consult your veterinarian to learn the latest available options, from diet to drugs that stimulate production of red blood cells, to blood pressure control, to kidney transplantations.

Feline lower urinary tract disease (FLUTD)

Formerly called *feline urologic syndrome,* or *FUS,* the term *feline lower urinary tract disease (FLUTD)* encompasses a range of health problems.

In the mildest form, this group of diseases causes irritation to the bladder, the only sign being an increased frequency of urination. As anyone who's ever had a bladder infection can attest, irritation of the bladder results in a feeling of always having to "go." If you notice your cat is going to the litter box more often than usual, arrange an appointment with your veterinarian. It will help if you are able to tell him whether your cat is urinating more frequently with the usual volume or with more volume *and* more frequency.

You can judge volume by the wetness of the litter and how often you need to change the litter.

In its most urgent form, FLUTD causes urinary obstruction. The *urethra* — the tube connected to the bladder that takes urine out of the body — is blocked by mucus and crystal plugs. This complication is far more prevalent in male cats. It is a true veterinary emergency, because blockage of the urinary tract can result in kidney damage and ultimately death if not treated promptly.

In most uncomplicated cases of FLUTD, you will see the cat urinating frequently, voiding only small amounts of urine, clear, cloudy, or bloody, not only in the litter box but also in unusual places such as the sink or bathtub and shower. However, a cat that is fully obstructed or "blocked" will exhibit frequent straining without successful urination, and often vocalization and other signs of distress.

Until the late 1980s, the majority of cats seen with FLUTD were found to have *struvite* crystals or stones forming in the bladder. The theory then was that this condition resulted from too much *ash* or *mineral* content in food, especially magnesium. Pet-food companies responded with many diets low in ash. Later, researchers started focusing more on the effects different diets have on the *acid* content of urine. An increase in acidity of the urine helped greatly with struvite stones and crystals but along the way may have caused other health problems.

Today struvite crystals and stones have become less common, and cats found to have FLUTD now require more individual investigation to determine what is causing the problem. These conditions include a different kind of crystal or stone (including calcium oxalate, urate, and others), infections of the bladder, and a condition called *interstitial cystitis*, to name a few of the more common.

Failure to urinate is an urgent health problem that needs to be addressed immediately. Your veterinarian will take action to relieve the buildup of urine and then suggest tests to figure out what underlies the problem.

Heart disease

Heart disease is relatively common in cats. Your veterinarian generally first detects heart disease in your cat in one of the following two ways:

- Hearing an abnormal sound (a murmur, a gallop sound, or an irregular beat) with her stethoscope during a routine physical examination
- Examining your cat after you first notice your cat is breathing rapidly or having trouble breathing

In the case of a breathing problem, heart disease can appear to come on very suddenly. You may think your cat is fine and then a few hours later notice her gasping for breath.

What many cat owners see as "sudden" usually has been building to a noticeable state over time. This is why we give you the information you need to take your cat's heart rate and respiratory rate, so you know what's normal and what's not before you're faced with an emergency situation.

Other signs of heart disease you may notice are the following:

- ✔ **Changes in weight.** More than a half pound or pound weight loss or gain that occurs within a couple of weeks.

- ✔ **Coughing.** Sometimes, determining whether your cat is coughing or vomiting and gagging is difficult. If your cat demonstrates either frequently, consult your veterinarian.

- ✔ **Weakness or paralysis of one or more legs — most commonly a hind limb(s).** Some cats with heart disease develop blood clots in the heart that can then leave the heart and block the arteries that "feed" the body. These most commonly affect the hind limbs but can affect any area of the body, including the forelimbs, kidneys, brain, and so on.

- ✔ **Not feeling well.** This last one fits into the category of what Paul calls the Ain't Doing Right (ADR) cat.

Congenital heart disease is not as common in cats as in dogs but is seen from time to time. A murmur heard in a kitten should be evaluated by a specialist. Many cats with congenital heart disease appear normal until they reach several years of age.

If serious heart disease is found or suspected in your cat, the primary concern is to stabilize any life-threatening situations. Your veterinarian may suggest the removal of fluid from in or around the lungs by using medication or a needle and syringe.

If the situation is not as acute and you suspect heart disease — or if your cat was having trouble breathing and is now feeling better — your veterinarian is still going to want to know what's wrong with your cat. Diagnosis in such cases usually requires a chest radiograph (X ray) and an echocardiogram (cardiac ultrasound). Electrocardiograms (ECG) may also be helpful.

If you have limited funds, the most valuable money you can spend in this situation is often for the echocardiogram and an experienced veterinarian or specialist who knows how to read it.

After an accurate diagnosis is made, your veterinarian or the veterinary specialist works with you to determine the best combination of medications, diet, and monitoring that gives your cat the best chance at a long, healthy life. Nothing is guaranteed, however, and a cat with heart problems is always a candidate for sudden death. As hard as this fact is to deal with, you need to be prepared.

For help in dealing with the loss of a pet, see Chapter 11.

Tumors

Tumors are, unfortunately, common in cats. Many can be traced back to feline leukemia virus, but others . . . well, no one knows why they occur. Some tumors can be ultimately fatal; others are of little concern at all.

The most important things to remember about tumors is that you should carefully monitor your cat for lumps and bumps — he enjoys your loving rubbing, poking, and prodding, and the more you do this sort of thing, the more you get to know what's normal for your cat and what's a new "growth." You should also be constantly aware of weight loss or other signs of your cat not feeling well. At the first sign of a problem, consult your veterinarian. She will want to examine your cat and probably perform some diagnostic tests, including blood tests and perhaps a fine needle aspirate of any suspicious masses. If cancer is suspected, the most important test to pursue is a biopsy.

Your veterinarian may recommend a consultation with a veterinary oncologist to assess the seriousness of the tumor and the options for care. Commonly available treatments include surgery, medication, and radiation — often a combination of treatments is used. Your veterinarian, perhaps with the help of a veterinary oncologist, can help you understand what to expect from the tumor type diagnosed.

Remember that what they tell you is their best guess based on what happens to most patients and that your cat could do much better or worse than average. Your veterinarian will help you make decisions regarding treatment options based on what they believe is best for your cat.

The very vaccinations that have saved so many feline lives have ended up killing a few, who end up with malignant tumors at the injection sites. The risk is low, however, and you're putting your cat at much greater risk if you avoid vaccinations because of your worries. For more information on the risks of vaccinations — and the benefits, of course — see Chapter 9.

Veterinary Health Insurance

Money is the 800-pound gorilla of veterinary medicine, looming over every suggestion a veterinarian makes and every decision a client considers. One way to tame the beast a little is to purchase health insurance for your cat.

Americans have been slow in warming to the concept, which is well-established in Europe: In Sweden, 17 percent of all pets are insured, as are 5 percent of Great Britain's dogs and cats. Only one pet-health insurer exists in the United States, VPI Insurance Group of Anaheim, California, which covers the health of a mere 75,000 pets (out of more than 100 million estimated pet dogs and cats).

Your veterinarian may know of other health plans that may help your pet. Some veterinary hospitals are even experimenting with HMOs!

Giving Your Cat Medication

No matter how much you and your cat hate the idea, at some point in your pet's life, you're going to come home from the veterinary office with medication, and you're going to need to give that medication to your cat. Is it easy? Not really, but we can help make the process easier. Is it necessary? You bet. Seeing your veterinarian and then not following through on care instructions is worse than a waste of money: It may be dangerous for your pet.

Your veterinarian depends on you to report whether the medication given is helping or hurting. Do not hesitate to call your veterinarian and let her know if you think the medications are making a difference — positive or negative. Sometimes, the only way to know is to stop the medication. Just don't do so without talking to your veterinarian so that she knows and agrees. And don't adjust the dose — up or down — without your veterinarian's knowledge and approval. Doing so is like playing with fire. Only in this case, your pet is the one who may get burned!

Pilling your pet

Gina once asked her readers for their best tips on getting pills down their pets, and her phone was ringing off the hook for days. Most people try the sneak method, attempting to disguise a pill in a bit of something yummy in hopes that their pet doesn't notice the pill inside. You can try this approach, but honestly, it works a lot better for dogs, who're "wolfers," than for cats, who eat carefully, considering every mouthful. Sneaking something past your cat this way is hard!

Better still is the straightforward approach: Take a firm but gentle grip on your pet's head from above, pry open his jaw with the index finger of your other hand, and press the pill far enough back on the tongue to trigger swallowing. Some people have good luck with "pill guns" (available in pet-supply stores and catalogs). These plastic devices enable you to put the pill on the tip and then press it to the top of your cat's throat.

Although experienced cat lovers — and, of course, veterinarians and veterinary-health technicians — can make pill-popping look like an easy, one-person job, you're likely to find the task easier at first if you have someone else hold your cat while you pill her.

A firm but gentle approach is best for "pilling" your cat.

One of the best suggestions to come out of Gina's poll came from the fellow who "screened" his cat to pill her. He "hung" her by her claws on the screen door and then gave her the pill. Tough on the screen door but easier on the owner — and in some cases, the cat!

Liquid medication

Ask your veterinarian for some large syringes with the needles removed. These are marked on the sides to make measuring easy, and they're easier, too, at getting liquid medicine in the right place. An eyedropper works well, too. Raise your cat's muzzle with a firm but gentle hold on the top of her head and lift her lip on one side. Ease the tip between the teeth and toward the back of the mouth and then release the liquid in a slow, steady motion. Your cat will swallow naturally. Pause if she needs more time to swallow.

Ear medication

Lay a large towel across your lap and draw your pet up, relaxing her with stroking and soothing words. After she's relaxed, apply the ear drops, massaging the base of the ear gently.

Release liquid medication in the back of the throat with a slow, steady motion.

Eye medication

While restraining your pet, gently apply a line of ointment from the tube across the length of the eye, being careful not to touch the surface of the eye. Try to hit drops squarely in the center. Close the lid for a couple of seconds to let the medication distribute evenly.

As with anything your pet would rather avoid, be patient, gentle, and firm when giving medication — and follow with praise. If you're having trouble medicating your pet, have your veterinarian walk you through it — or discuss alternatives.

Chapter 11

Caring for an Older Cat

. . . .

In This Chapter

▶ Understanding the aging process

▶ Preventive health tips for older cats

▶ Coping with disease

▶ Knowing when to let go

▶ Helping your family through the grief

▶ Providing for your cat in your will

. . . .

*U*ntil recently, many people had cats who came and went — mostly went — with sad regularity. The common wisdom: You didn't "own" cats. You fed them, admired their beauty, and enjoyed their company. You let them in and out of your house with a degree of good humor and grieved for them after they disappeared, after a year or two or maybe five, but generally not much more.

The situation can be so much different now.

The popularity of cats has led to an explosion in knowledge of how to care for them at all stages of their lives, and geriatric care is no exception. Barring accidents, cats can live healthier, happier lives years longer than they ever have before — 10, 12, 14 years. Protected from the outside world, cats can live even longer, with 16, 18, and even 20 years — or more — a possibility for some.

The difference in lifespan is not in the cats themselves but in the relationship we humans have with them — the expansion of both knowledge and responsibility. The secret of your cat leading a long and comfortable life is as much in your care as in the genes she inherited from her mother and father — and we're going to help you make the most of both in this chapter.

We've focused in this chapter on preventive-care measures that are especially important to older cats and diseases that are more common in felines middle-aged or older (more on age stages later in this chapter). You should also check out our more-general preventive-care guidelines in Chapter 9, especially the section on spotting health problems early.

To live with an older cat is to share a lifetime of love in a look, a pat, a purr. The bond you've spent years building is a thing of wonder now. You know each other. You're comfortable and relaxed with each other. You love each other effortlessly. These years are special, and you should enjoy them.

Of course, these are also the years when you realize your cat isn't going to be with you forever, and these thoughts can dampen your enjoyment of this special stage.

Don't feel sorry for your cat or yourself. Take a lesson from her and enjoy each day wholly. Your cat lives in the now and has no concept that the changes in her life are part of a natural process. She doesn't know where the years lead. She lives day to day, spending her time purring in your lap or sleeping in the sun, crying for her dinner or chasing a toy across the carpet. If she feels good and is with you, she is happy. And so, too, should you be.

You're the one who has the biggest influence over your cat's lifespan. Protection, prevention, and early detection are the words to remember as your cat ages. We're not going to sugarcoat this for you: The two most important things you can do to ensure your cat a long, healthy life is keep your pet inside and take care of spaying and neutering. An indoor cat is protected from the hazards of the outdoor world, especially cars and contagious viruses. And an altered cat is protected from health problems, such as reproductive-related cancers and infections and, especially in males, the constant pressure to roam in search of mates and fight in defense of territory.

For more information on the indoor versus outdoor controversy, see Chapter 1. For more information on spaying and neutering, see Chapter 14.

How Old Is "Old"?

A general rule for determining whether a cat is middle-aged or old is that one year in a cat's life equals four in a human's. In truth, the situation is not that neat, and if you think about it, you can easily see why. Under a "one equals four" rule, a one-year-old cat would be the equivalent in terms of mental and physical maturity to a human four-year-old, and that's clearly off.

A better equation is to count the first year of a cat's life as being comparable to the time a human reaches the early stages of adulthood — the age of 15 or so. Like a human adolescent, a year-old cat looks fairly grown up and is physically capable of becoming a parent but is lacking in emotional maturity.

The second year of a cat's life picks up some of that maturity and takes a cat to the first stages of full adulthood in humans — a two-year-old cat is roughly equivalent to a person in the mid-20s.

Sammy was 19 at the time he posed for his formal portrait, a good example of the difference a lifetime of good care can make.

Sammy — Photo courtesy of Hope Harris.

From there, the "four equals one" rule works pretty well. A cat of three is still young, comparable to a person of 29. A six-year-old cat, similar to a 41-year-old person, is in the throes of middle age; a twelve-year-old cat, similar to a 65-year-old person, has earned the right to slow down a little. A cat who lives to be 20 is the feline equivalent of nearly 100 in terms of human lifespan!

As with humans, age is relative. An unloved and uncared-for cat is not going to enjoy life at six, whereas one twice that age, given proper care and nutrition, may be nearly as playful as a kitten.

Normal Signs of Aging

Aging comes in a mostly predictable way to cats, so subtle that you may not notice the signs at first until suddenly you look at your pet and think: "How long has she been losing weight?" or "When did she stop trying to jump on her favorite perch?" The thought right after that is even more upsetting: "Is this serious? Should I be worried?"

Although anything that worries you warrants checking with your veterinarian, if for nothing more than your peace of mind, knowing what's normal for your cat goes a long way toward easing the years for you both. (A keen observer of body language and emotion, your cat knows if you're upset, after all.)

Normal signs of aging are gradual. Sudden problems may be indicative of a serious health problem. If your cat changes quickly in appearance or behavior, have her seen by your veterinarian right away.

Decline of the senses

As your cat ages, her senses of hearing, vision, and smell may worsen, although different cats age in different ways. Some of these changes may be barely noticeable to you as your cat adapts to them, and others may be more obvious, such as foul breath due to dental disease that requires more-frequent attention to control with advancing age.

Other changes can be very hard to notice. We know people who didn't even know that their pets were deaf, although imagining how that could happen isn't that hard. After all, even in the best of circumstances, your cat pays attention only when she wants to!

You may suspect that your cat has a hearing loss if you think your cat isn't reacting to the sounds that always got a response, such as the whirring of the electric can opener near dinner time. To test your hunch, check by snapping your fingers behind her head.

Although your cat can get along just fine indoors if her hearing isn't as keen as it was, deafness really does put her at risk outdoors. Even the cat who has survived into old age by being street savvy can't dodge a car if she can't hear it coming.

Your cat's sense of taste may have an important effect on her appetite, which can be a problem in some older cats. Smell is extremely important to how your cat determines what's enticing enough to try, and if this sense has declined, nothing may seem worth tasting.

Heat makes smell more intense. If your cat isn't eating, your first call should be to your veterinarian. If everything checks out okay, entice your cat by serving canned food at room temperature or a bit warmer.

Changes in appearance

Because your cat's body is undergoing changes internally, you may notice changes externally. Cats lose muscle mass as they age, so your pet may seem bonier than when he was young. Other cats may become obese, eating the same amount of calories despite a reduced level of activity. (For more information on obesity, see Chapter 8.)

Change may show up in your pet's coat, leaving it feeling dryer and more sparse and the skin less supple. Your cat may not be as efficient at grooming himself as he ages — or, as he becomes more fragile, he may not be able or interested in doing the chore so diligently.

Your cat looks better and feels better if you assist him with his grooming. For more information on how to help, see Chapter 7.

Behavior changes

The temperament of healthy older cats is really something to anticipate with pleasure in many cases. Your cat may mellow over time, becoming more interested in lapsitting and less in crawling up your drapes and performing death-defying leaps from atop tall pieces of furniture. This softening of attitude may be what you notice most as you consider your older cat, but other behavior changes may appear that you should also think about.

Your cat may sleep more, but you need to watch that, too. Extreme disinterest in the world around him can also be a sign of disease, as can an increased energy level. Be aware, too, of changes in appetite or thirst — although your cat needs fewer calories and more fluids as he ages, extreme changes need to be checked out.

A new kitten?

Because older cats do so poorly when stressed, you should think very seriously before introducing a kitten to your household.

A kitten's playful ways just aren't appreciated by a geriatric cat and may prompt behavior problems such as litter-box avoidance or a loss of appetite — the latter a serious health concern in all cats, but especially in older ones.

Keep your older cat healthy by playing with him by using a cat fishing pole or toy on a string. He's going to appreciate the time you spend with him, especially because you're happy to play on his terms and leave him alone after he's had enough, not keep pestering him like a kitten.

You have plenty of time in your life for a new kitten. We think that if you have an older cat, you should hold off on adding a youngster and let your cat enjoy his senior years as he sees fit.

Many older cats tend to sleep more — and they deserve such luxury! Watch out, however, for signs of extreme disinterest.

Omar — Photo courtesy of Michael Brewton.

Because behavior changes in older cats are often the result of health problems, you need to be aware of these changes and be sensitive to how quickly they occur. The formerly sweet-natured cat who's now cranky or defensive, for example, may be acting that way because of chronic pain. Or the cat who suddenly neglects his litter-box routines may have an infection or even diabetes. Because your cat can't talk about what's bothering him, you need to listen to his body and be aware.

Special Care for Kitty Teeth

Some cats, like some people, can go a lifetime without rigorous dental care without ill effects (other than disgusting everyone who smells their breath). However, this is the exception and not the rule. A little care can go a long way toward making your cat more appealing to be near as well as preventing significant dental problems. If you've paid attention to his teeth his entire life, you've done your pet a wonderful service. If you haven't, you have some catching up to do to ensure that dental problems don't make your cat unhappy. Bad teeth can lead to pain while eating, and some believe periodontal disease can lead to ill effects as bacteria (causing disease in the mouth), entering the bloodstream and causing infection in the kidneys and other organs. Don't ignore these problems!

When your cat is comfortable and relaxed, gently raise his lip and take a look. You're sure to see the yellowing and wear that's a normal part of the aging process of his teeth, and that's okay. What you're looking for are signs of developing periodontal disease, which is a relentless chronic process that

The older-cat physical

Annual physicals are even more important as your cat ages and need to be more extensive than when she was younger. Your veterinarian may suggest blood and urine tests, for example, to determine what's normal for your cat so that subsequent changes in the test values are more apparent.

This *well-cat appointment* is a good time to address your concerns about your cat's aging and get all your questions answered. Encourage your veterinarian to discuss your cat's condition thoroughly and all the care options that are available to you.

Although feeling comfortable with your veterinarian and confident in her abilities is always important, such considerations are especially important if your cat is older. You're working together as a team to ensure your cat's health: Make sure your veterinarian is someone you trust so you can make the best decisions on your cat's behalf. (Information on choosing a veterinarian is in Chapter 9.)

inevitably leads to oral discomfort, tooth loss, and poor general health. These include plaque; a brown, brittle substance called *calculus* that builds up on the tooth surfaces, especially near the gumline; and gingivitis, which is the inflammation of gum tissue. In severely affected mouths, tooth root abscesses are not uncommon and require prompt veterinary attention.

You can keep your pet's teeth healthy by brushing them at least three times a week — see Chapter 7 for how to make the task easy on you both — but before you can start such preventive care, your veterinarian must take care of the problems that have already developed. This care likely involves a cleaning and polishing under anesthesia, along with the treatment or removal of any diseased teeth and diagnosis and management of any further dental problems.

If your cat had nothing more than plaque buildup and mild inflammation, he's likely to go home with clean teeth and dental-care instructions. From there, the task of keeping those teeth in good shape with regular brushing and an eye toward the need for further veterinary care is in your hands.

Some Common Problems

Most health problems older cats get are also seen in younger cats, with the notable exception of hyperthyroidism, which we discuss in this section. Some diseases pop up frequently in older cats, however, and we want to make sure that you're aware of them.

Because many health problems can occur at any age, please don't neglect the more-general chapters on veterinary care, especially Chapters 9 and 10, which include sections on preventive-care measures that can keep some worries from ever surfacing at all.

An excellent book-length source of information on older cats is *Your Aging Cat: How To Keep Your Cat Physically and Mentally Healthy Into Old Age*, by Kim Campbell Thornton and John Hamil, DVM (Howell Book House/ Macmillan General Reference).

Diabetes

Diabetes is a loss of control of the amount of sugar n the blood — a cat with diabetes will have a very high concentration of sugar in the blood and urine.

There are two types of diabetes: The first is called *insulin-dependent diabetes,* in which the pancreas fails to produce enough of the hormone *insulin* to regulate blood-sugar levels; the other form of the disease occurs when the body does not respond properly to the insulin the pancreas produces.

Fat cats are more susceptible to diabetes, which is another reason that preventing obesity is so important.

Cats with diabetes may appear to be losing weight while eating actively. They will also drink and urinate more frequently in large volumes. You may notice your cat's urine is "sticky," like sugar water, as a result of the high sugar content.

In more advanced cases, cats can become acutely ill, even comatose. Any markedly depressed cat should be considered potentially very ill, and veterinary care should be sought immediately.

If your cat is diagnosed with diabetes, your veterinarian will suggest dietary changes that may include controlled weight loss and high fiber diets.

Sometimes, medications can help to control the blood sugar level. In most cases, though, you will need to give insulin injections to your cat. Your veterinarian will demonstrate giving injections and discuss how you will together monitor your cat's progress and medication needs. Be sure to keep a diary of all changes to your cat's medication needs and responses; this diary will help you and your veterinarian better control your cat's diabetes.

Some cases of diabetes can be cured by finding and treating other diseases that are making the cat's system more resistant to insulin. Some cats will recover permanently or temporarily from diabetes.

Hyperthyroidism

What got into that cat? It's a question more people are wondering these days, as their cats seem to lose weight though eating more and perhaps get even more energetic as they age, instead of less.

Although having an oldster with the energy of a kitten may seem wonderful, that zooming cat may be sick with a disease that can kill if left unchecked. *Hyperthyroidism,* the overproduction of thyroid hormone, is among the most common maladies in older cats. Hyperthyroidism is certainly the great impersonator within older cats. Paul has a very focused approach to medicine and is largely not in favor of "shotgun" testing, but he does believe that every older cat should have thyroid hormone levels monitored or at least tested at the first sign of any change in health. Hyperthyroidism can present in many ways — ranging from the overactive thin cat who eats all the time to the "just ain't doing right cat" that befuddles veterinarian after veterinarian.

When a cat produces too much thyroid hormone, his metabolic rate can soar to the point where it can burn off a third of his body weight. Left unchecked, kidney, heart, liver, and other problems can develop, sometimes leading to death. However, remember that none of these symptoms *must* be present, and even overweight cats may be suffering from hyperthyroidism.

The treatment of hyperthyroidism is one of the bright spots of feline geriatric medicine. Although the disease is common, several good care options can, in many cases, cure the problem.

Veterinary medicine offers three methods for treating hyperthyroidism. The one chosen often depends on location and the overall health and disposition of the pet. Following are those options:

- ✔ **Radioactive iodine therapy.** This option is the preferred method of treatment, and you can easily see why: cure rates of 90 to 95 percent, with no further treatment. The cat gets one dose of a radioactive substance that kills the overproducing cells without directly harming other body functions. It's a one-day matter, but what follows presents a dilemma for many owners: The treatment creates a radioactive cat that must be kept on site at the clinic or college for 7 to 14 days, after which the animal is considered safe to go home. Other problems: This treatment is not available in all areas, adding travel time to the equation for those who want to pursue it. Veterinary colleges are one source of this treatment, as are specialty practices in many urban areas.

- ✔ **Surgery.** Another option is a *thyroidectomy,* the surgical removal of the offending thyroid gland or glands, which can be done by a pet's regular veterinarian. The problem: The surgery is delicate, with a chance other problems may result. Surgery is a good option if radioactive iodine treatment is not available, or if the cat hasn't the temperament to endure confinement.

- ✔ **Medication.** Hyperthyroidism can be treated with the drug Tapazole, but some cats don't tolerate the drug well, and some owners aren't up to the task of administering multiple daily pills for the duration of a

Anesthesia and the older cat

As common as anesthesia is in veterinary medicine, many misconceptions exist about its use where older animals are concerned. The idea that the risk of anesthesia outweighs the importance of preventive veterinary care (such as dentistry) is no longer valid. Yes, it is true that no anesthetic procedure is without risk. However, in the hands of a good veterinarian and his staff, anesthesia, even in the elderly patient, has become a routine and very safe procedure with risks so low that with few exceptions they should not dissuade you from pursuing necessary preventive or other surgical procedures.

The risks can be greatly minimized by a history, physical examination, and a few basic tests beforehand, including a laboratory evaluation of blood and urine, and possibly a chest X ray. Although these tests admittedly add to the cost of a procedure, they enable your veterinarian to understand fully the health status of your cat before anesthetizing him. During the procedure, placement of an IV catheter and administration of fluids can further add to the safety of the procedure. These are very worthwhile expenses that should be routine for anesthetic procedures in any but the shortest procedures in young, healthy cats. In the case of dental work, your veterinarian may prescribe antibiotics before, during, and after the procedure.

The benefits of these tests and precautionary measures may be hard for many to recognize. But the tests provide a baseline against which to compare future results, and most importantly, in the rare situation where a problem develops, you'll be glad you had the forethought to insist upon having them performed.

No discussion of anesthetic danger can be complete without a few words on your responsibilities where anesthesia is concerned:

✔ **Follow your veterinarian's instructions on preparing your pet for surgery.** If no food is specified, make sure that you deliver your pet with an empty stomach. Following this one piece of advice is one of the easiest and most basic ways to reduce risk. During anesthesia, the contents of a full stomach can be regurgitated with the unfortunate potential complication of being inhaled into the lungs. In general, you should completely withhold food the night before but continue to allow free access to water until the morning of the procedure.

✔ **Be prepared to provide special home care for your pet after surgery.** Releasing animals before sedation wears off fully may be common practice for some veterinarians. Such animals must be kept safe from hot or cold environments because their reflexes are reduced. If you do not feel comfortable caring for a sedated pet, arrange for your veterinarian to extend the care. If your veterinarian does not run a 24-hour hospital, be sure to have the number of your local emergency clinic handy in case there are complications following your cat's anesthesia.

✔ **Don't hesitate to ask questions.** Make sure that you understand what the procedures are and what to expect. Pets commonly have a cough after anesthesia, for example, because the tube used to deliver the gas may cause some irritation. If the cough does not clear in a couple days, call your veterinarian.

No matter what the age of the pet, the chances are very high that the anesthetic presents no problem if both you and your veterinarian work to minimize the risk. And the payoffs, especially those involving dental care, can be significant. Despite this, you should fully understand what and why a procedure is being recommended, and the decision to pursue that course or not should be a decision you participate heavily in.

pet's life. Because of these problems, drug therapy is often used to stabilize a cat prior to the other treatments in order to address the immediate health problems caused by hyperactivity until a long-term solution can be put into place.

Recent evidence suggests a small percentage of cats treated for hyperthyroidism develop kidney problems after being treated. This should not dissuade you from treating your cat. We expect that more information will be available on this in the near future and recommend that you discuss this issue with your veterinarian before making a final therapy decision.

Obstipation

Obstipation is the complete inability to defecate, resulting in a very painful and serious condition for your cat that needs veterinary attention. The causes of this backup are not well understood. The intestines become dilated and unable to push stool out of the body normally.

Be alert to your cat's bathroom habits. If your indoor cat is straining or crying out while trying to defecate or if you notice an absence of feces, your cat has a problem. Oddly, this blockage may initially appear as diarrhea, because your cat's body, so irritated by the retained feces, may generate lots of watery fluid or mucus to try to cope — and that may seem like "ordinary" loose stools when passed.

Any change in your cat's litter-box habits is potentially a sign of disease and must be checked out by your veterinarian to ensure that problems are caught while they can still be treated.

Your veterinarian is likely to suggest taking a radiograph (X ray) to determine what's behind the problem. Enemas are the short-term solution; drug or surgical methods may eventually be required. Long-term care may require the use of drugs or laxatives to keep stools soft, as well as an increased attention to your cat's grooming to cut down the volume of hair he swallows. Success is mixed with drugs. Surgery, to remove part of the colon, is rather extensive and can lead to problems with diarrhea; however, in many cats the surgery can be rewarding.

We've touched on just a few of the most-common health problems in older cats, but there are many other health problems that afflict cats young and old. Check out our more-general health-care information in Chapter 10, and learn the importance of good preventive care by reading Chapter 9. Above all, consult your veterinarian.

Knowing When It's "Time"

Euthanasia, the technical term for "putting a pet to sleep," is one of the hardest decisions you must ever make, and it doesn't get any easier, no matter how many times over the years you face it. Your veterinarian can offer you advice, and your friends can offer you support, but no one can make the decision for you. If you live with an elderly or terminally ill pet, you look in her eyes every morning and ask yourself: Is this the day?

To know for sure is impossible. But take solace in knowing that in more than 14 years of practice, Paul has only four times had to look at an owner and say, "Hey, it is time." Although we say to know for sure is impossible, Paul firmly believes that owners *do* know when it is time and respects their decisions without question. Asking guidance from your friends, family, and veterinarian is very appropriate, but only you can make the final decision. Good friends, family, and veterinarians will offer good "if it were my pet" advice, but they should also respect your decision without question.

Some owners don't wait until their pet's discomfort becomes pain and choose euthanasia much sooner than many people would. Some owners use an animal's appetite as the guide — if an old or ill animal is no longer interested in eating, they reason, he's not interested in anything at all. Other owners wait until no doubt remains that the time is at hand.

Each guideline is the right one for some cat and some owner at some time. You do the best you can, and then you try to put the decision behind you and deal with the grief.

Ironically, the incredible advances in veterinary medicine in the past couple of decades have made the decisions even more difficult for many people. Not too long ago, the best you could do for a seriously ill pet was to make her comfortable until that wasn't possible anymore. Nowadays, nearly every advantage of human medicine — from chemotherapy to pacemakers — is available to our pets.

If you can afford such care and have a realistic expectation that it can improve your pet's life — instead of simply prolonging it — then it's an option that you should pursue. But let nothing push you into making a decision based on guilt or wishful thinking.

Euthanasia is a kindness extended to a treasured pet, a decision we make at a great cost to ourselves. It's a final act of love, nothing less.

Euthanasia options

Should you be with your pet at the end? What should you do with the remains? The questions are all difficult, but no answers are wrong.

Euthanasia is a quick and peaceful process as performed by a veterinarian. The animal is unconscious within seconds and dead within less than a minute; the euphemism "put to sleep" is a perfect description. Those who attend the procedure come away reassured that their pets felt no fear or pain.

Some people say that staying with a pet at its death is the final gift of love, but no decision you make regarding the last few minutes of an animal's life changes the love you shared for the years that preceded those final moments. If you want to be there, by all means stay. But leaving is no less a humane and loving gesture.

Call ahead to set the appointment and make clear to the receptionist what you're coming for. That way, the practice can ensure you don't need to sit in the waiting room but instead are immediately ushered into an exam room if you choose to remain with your cat. Your veterinarian is going to do his best to make sure that all your questions are answered and that you're comfortable with everything before proceeding. He may clip the fur on your cat's foreleg for easier and quicker access to the vein for the injection of the euthanizing agent; he may also choose to insert a catheter or sedate your pet.

Remember: Crying is normal, and your veterinarian understands. So, too, we believe, does your pet.

You may want to spend a few minutes with your pet afterward, and your veterinarian understands that, as well, and is going to give you all the time you need alone to begin the process of dealing with your loss. (If your pet dies while in the veterinarian's care, you may also choose to view the body to give yourself closure and let the healing begin. Discuss this decision with your veterinarian.)

You may be more comfortable with having your pet euthanized at home. If so, discuss the matter with your veterinarian directly. Many vets extend this special service to long-time clients. If yours doesn't, you may consider making arrangements with a veterinarian who does house calls.

You can handle your pet's remains in many ways, and doing so is easier if you make your decisions beforehand. The choices include having your municipal animal-control department pick up the body, burying the pet in your back yard or at another site (where it's legal and with the land owner's permission, of course), arranging for cremation, or contracting with a pet cemetery for full services and burial. Again, no choice is "wrong." Whatever feels right to you and comforts you best is what you should do.

Several manufacturers offer tasteful and attractive markers for your yard to memorialize your pet; these items are often advertised in the back of such magazines as *Cat Fancy*. Other choices include large rocks or slabs of stone or a tree or rose bush. Even if you choose not to have your pet's body or ashes returned, placing a memorial in a special spot may soothe you.

Another way to celebrate the memory of your cat is to make a donation to your local humane society, regional school of veterinary medicine, or other favorite animal charity. A donation in a beloved pet's name is a wonderful thing to do for a friend who's lost a pet as well.

The major card companies have introduced pet lines in recent years, and among the items available are some very elegant sympathy cards. Smaller companies have been serving this niche for years, however; among them is *Litterature,* which produces a full line of animal-related cards. For ordering information, see the Additional Resources appendix.

Dealing with loss

Many people are surprised at the powerful emotions that erupt after a pet's death, and they're embarrassed by their grief. Remembering that pets have meaning in our lives beyond the love we feel for the animal may help. Often, we don't realize that we're grieving not only for the pet we loved, but also for the special time the animal represented and the ties to other people in our lives. The death of a cat who was a gift as a kitten from a friend who has died, for example, may trigger bittersweet memories of another love lost.

Taking care of yourself is important at this difficult time. Some people — the "it's just a cat" crowd — don't understand your feelings and may shrug off your grief as foolish. The company of other animal lovers is very important. Seek them out to share your feelings. The commercial online services — America Online, CompuServe, and Prodigy — encourage animal lovers to share memories of special animals with one another in their pet areas, and the outpouring of support in these virtual communities is heartfelt.

A difficult time, no doubt, but remember: In time, the memories become a source of pleasure, not pain. You're not on any set timetable, but it happens. We promise.

A handful of books and one really fine video may help you help your child with the loss of a pet. From Fred Rogers (yes, "Mr. Rogers," of the Neighborhood) comes the book "When a Pet Dies" (Putnam) and the video "Death of a Goldfish." Rachel Biale's "My Pet Died" (Tricycle Press) not only helps children cope better with pages to fill in, but also offers parents advice in special pages that can be torn out. Finally, Judith Viorst's "The Tenth Good Thing About Barney" (Aladdin) is a book experts in pet-loss have been recommending for years.

You're not alone

You may find talking to others about your pet's death helpful. Ask your veterinarian about pet-loss support groups. Almost unheard of a couple decades ago, many communities have these groups today. You may also want to see a counselor; this, too, can be helpful.

Veterinary schools and colleges have been among the leaders in creating programs to help pet lovers deal with loss. A handful now operate pet-loss hot lines staffed by veterinary students trained to answer questions, offer materials that may help you (including guidelines for helping children with loss), and just plain listen. (Paul's wife, Carla, worked at the University of California, Davis, center when she was in veterinary school.) These are wonderful programs, and they're free for the cost of the call. (If you call during off hours, they call you back, collect.)

Locations, operating hours, and phone numbers of pet-loss hot lines are as follows:

University of California
School of Veterinary Medicine
Davis, California
Hours of operation: 6:30 to 9:30 p.m., Pacific time, Monday through Friday
(916) 752-4200

Washington State University
College of Veterinary Medicine
Pullman, Washington
Hot line program in development; counseling and information on request
(509) 335-4569; 335-1303

University of Florida
College of Veterinary Medicine
Gainesville, Florida
Hours of operation: 7 to 9 p.m., Eastern time
(352) 392-4700, Ext. 4080

Michigan State University
College of Veterinary Medicine
East Lansing, Michigan
Hours of operation: 6:30 to 9:30 p.m., Eastern time, Tuesday, Wednesday, and Thursday
(517) 432-2696

Ohio State University
College of Veterinary Medicine
Columbus, Ohio
Hours of operation: 6:30 to 9:30 p.m., Eastern time, Monday, Wednesday, and Friday
(614) 292-1823

Tufts University
School of Veterinary Medicine
North Grafton, Massachusetts
Hours of operation: 6 to 9 p.m., Eastern time, Monday though Friday
(508) 839-7966

Virginia-Maryland Regional College of Veterinary Medicine
Blacksburg, Virginia
Hours of operation: 6 to 9 p.m., Eastern time, Tuesday and Thursday
(540) 231-8038

Cornell University
College of Veterinary Medicine
Ithaca, New York
Hours of operation: 6 to 9 p.m., Eastern time, Tuesday, Wednesday, and Thursday
(607) 253-3922

What If You Go First?

First things first: You can't leave your estate to your cat, because in the eyes of the law, an animal is an "it," with little more legal status than a chair. Nor can you set up a trust for your pet for the same reason. The beneficiary of a trust must be a bona fide human being, and the fact that you think of your cat as a person doesn't really matter, because the courts don't.

Although you, of course, should discuss this matter with your attorney, talking it over with your friends and family is even more important, because finding one of them whom you trust to care for your pet after you're gone is what you must do. You must leave your feline "property" to that person, along with enough money to provide for the animal's care for life. You have no real control over the outcome, which is why you need to choose someone you trust and then hope for your cat's sake that things turn out okay.

The Association of the Bar of New York City offers a low-cost pamphlet on providing for your pet if you can't. To order "Providing for Your Pets in the Event of Your Death or Hospitalization," send a $2 money order or check made out to the Association of the Bar and a self-addressed, stamped, legal-sized envelope to the association's Office of Communications, 42 W. 44th Street, New York, NY 10036.

Part IV

Living Happily with Your Cat

"I never appreciated having a cat until I went bald."

In this part . . .

This part explains how to understand your cat better, and work through the challenges that come up in your life together. We've included a chapter on the subtle body language of the cat, as well as tried-and-true strategies for resolving behavior problems such as clawing furniture, chewing houseplants, or avoiding the litter box. Have you taken in a homeless cat who's pregnant? We tell you what you need to know to help her, and raise and place her babies in loving homes. We also show you how to travel with your cat, or how to find the best care when you leave your pet behind. Finally, we give you a glimpse inside the world of cat shows.

Chapter 12

Understanding Your Cat

· ·

In This Chapter

▶ Five senses — and more
▶ Body language
▶ Communicating with your cat

· ·

Communication is at the heart of any good relationship, and that's just as true when the bond is between a person and a cat as it is when it's between two people. Learning more about the way your cat communicates can only strengthen the bond between you, making your life together more pleasurable for you both.

Understanding a cat is as remarkable as meeting a person from another planet, in a way, because the worlds you come from are vastly different. Ours is a world of words, of machines, of complex lives; our cat's is a world of nature, of body talk and sound, of simple pleasures. By understanding our cats, we can spend a little time in their world, so simple and relaxing.

But learning to "speak cat" isn't just for our benefit. If we work to understand the way our cats communicate, we can care for them better, understand what they want, avoid unecessary conflict, and catch the first signs that they're sick.

Picking up on your cat's body language is one way to spot illness, but an at-home exam is just as important. Check out our preventive-care tips in Chapter 9.

Making Sense of Cat Senses

Like most predators, cats have keen senses; they wouldn't have survived long enough to be domesticated if they didn't. Even today, when many cats have their food served to them in their own bowls, a great many don't have things so lucky. For them, a wonderful collection of natural talents is all that stands between them and starvation. That any of the wild ones survive at all, for any length of time, is a tribute to the senses of the cat.

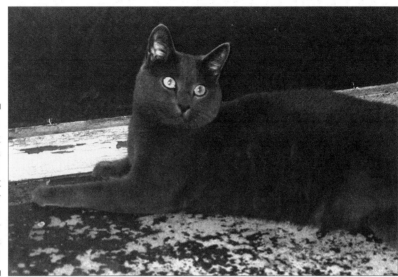

Learning to "Speak Cat" helps you and your pet better understand each other — and it's fun!

Charlie — Photo courtesy of Jennifer Ehrlich.

Smell

People and cats are living in completely different worlds in terms of the sense of smell. The cat's sense of smell is many times more powerful than a human's (and a dog's is more powerful still). Are you surprised now that the litter box you think is "tolerable" is offensive to your cat?

Of course, the litter box is a modern problem, and the cat's sense of smell is good for much more than deciding when it's not clean enough. Smell plays a role in the establishment of territory (see the sidebar "Scent-marking" later in this chapter), in the finding of prey, and in the determination of whether "found" food is safe enough to eat. Dogs are scavengers who eat just about anything; cats are true predators: fresh food, please, and freshly killed — even better. Ever wonder why your cat turns up her nose at canned food that's been out a while? Simple: It doesn't *smell* right.

If your cat is so finicky no delicacy you serve suits her — or you're nursing a sick cat — warm the food up to just above room temperature before serving: about 85 degrees (or what we humans would call "lukewarm"). Doing so makes food smell better to a cat, and therefore that food becomes more enticing. For more on feeding and nutrition, see Chapter 8.

In addition to their noses, cats use a body part called the *vomeronasal organ,* at the front of the roof of the mouth, to help them process smells, especially those of a sexual variety, such as the smell of a female cat in season. Whenever cats use this organ, they open their mouths a crack and "taste" the smell, a facial expression called *Flehmen.*

Hearing

Unlike our unmovable ears, cats can use their external ears like satellite dishes, "tuning" them independently toward any sound that catches their attention. The ears of cats can catch sounds two octaves higher than humans can hear, a range of hearing higher than the dog's. Your cat can learn to understand many of the words you use in speaking to her, such as, "Would you like to eat now?" The fact that a cat ignores most of them doesn't mean she isn't listening — she's just being a cat!

COOL CAT FACTS

Scent-marking

The correct "smell environment" is so important to your cat that he engages in various marking behaviors to make everything in his world smell like him — even you! Here are a few of your pet's scent-marking behaviors:

✔ *Rubbing.* Your cat has structures called *sebaceous glands* at the base of his hair follicles that produce *sebum*, a substance that serves two purposes: coating the fur for protection and depositing scent on objects in the cat's environment. These glands are most numerous around your cat's mouth and on the chin, lips, upper eyelids, on the top of the tail base, and near the anus and sex organs. If a cat rubs with his head (a behavior known as *bunting*), or any of these parts of his body, he's depositing sebum — and scent — on everything he touches. Our pitiful noses can't detect these deposits — and it's probably just as well.

✔ *Urine-spraying.* Although few humans mind being "marked with sebum" as our cats rub against us lovingly, we don't at all approve of another of the cat's territorial behaviors: urine-spraying. Although any cat may spray, the behavior is most common in unneutered males, who feel especially driven to mark their territory with their pungent urine by backing up to objects (or even people) and letting fly with a spray. (For information on how to deal with spraying problems, see Chapter 13.)

✔ *Clawing.* If your pet digs his claws into his cat tree (or your couch!), he's not intending to be destructive. Scratching keeps claws in shape by removing the outer layer of material and keeping the tips sharp, and it also provides your cat with the opportunity to stretch. Perhaps not many cat lovers realize that scratching is also important for scent-marking. As a cat claws, the pads of his feet come in contact with what he's digging into, and that motion leaves behind scent from the sweat glands in his feet (which is why even declawed cats "press the flesh" against objects in their territory). No matter how useful clawing is to a cat, it's a problem for many cat-lovers, one we offer solutions for in Chapter 13.

✔ *Grooming.* Your cat's attention to having "every hair in its place" has many reasons, but one of them is scent-marking. Your cat's tongue covers every inch of his body with his own saliva, which contains his favorite perfume: Eau de Me.

For a couple of final thoughts on how important "smelling right" is to a cat, consider this: Cats often groom themselves right after being petted — to cover your scent with theirs! Your cat may also pay extra attention to your scent after you've stepped out of the shower, re-marking you with sweet rubbing to make sure everyone knows you're "his."

Vision

The common belief is that cats are color-blind. Not so. Researchers believe that cats can distinguish between colors — cats have, in fact, been trained to do so — but don't see much of a reason to try.

The marvels of feline vision pertain more to the cat's ability to see in exceptionally dim light conditions — important for animals who hunt at night — and their keen edge in detecting motion and distance, important traits for a predator who needs not only to find dinner but also to pounce on prey with great accuracy.

The "night vision" of cats is made possible by a special layer of cells behind the light-gathering retina that enables the cat to "double" the ability to discern objects in darkened conditions. Whereas humans reflect back red (from blood vessels) in the dark if a light (such as a headlight) hits the back of their eyes, cats reflect back a golden or green flash because of these layers, called the *tapetum lucidum*.

Taste

Because cats prefer to consume fresh animal tissues for their nutritional needs, you shouldn't be all that surprised to find out that they haven't much of the appreciation for sweets that humans do. As can humans, cats can discern whether dishes are bitter, salty, sweet, or sour, although their interpretation of the desirability of these tastes no doubt varies from ours. Because cats have fewer taste buds than humans do, the feline sense of smell probably plays a large role in determining the desirability of food.

The rough feline tongue is an extraordinary tool, perfectly adapted for grooming (including removing fleas) and cleaning the meat off the bones of their prey.

"Biscuits" of love

Cat lovers all know the special paw motions of a happy cat in the lap, although no one seems to agree on what to call this pleasurable bit of body language. Call it "making biscuits" or "kneading," the message is the same: affection and trust.

Making biscuits is a holdover from kittenhood. When cats are babies, they move their paws against their mother's side when nursing. When your cat does this to you, she's telling you she considers you her mother, purring and kneading in a demonstration of feline love.

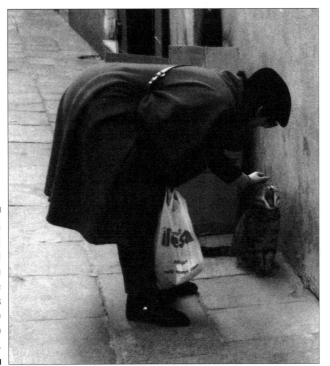

Cats love to touch and be touched — although they're sometimes too "cool" to show it.

Photo courtesy of Linda Stark.

Touch

The hairs of a cat's coat and the whiskers of his face are extremely sensitive, and complement the night vision cats enjoy when moving about after dark. Cats love to touch and be touched (the latter within certain personal cat limits), in part because touching — especially with the tongue or the head — is a way of spreading around a cat's all-important personal scent.

Speaking "Cat"

No kitten ever needed a book to understand feline body language — or human body language, for that matter. Although cats are not as adept at body language as dogs — whose wolf ancestors developed an intricate body language to keep the peace in the family structure, or *pack* — felines can communicate reasonably well with cats and other animals, too. (Consider how perfectly most dogs understand the "back off" sign of a cat with an arched back if you doubt the power of trans-species communication.)

COOL CAT FACTS

Do cats have more than five senses?

Two phenomena that have been well documented over the years suggest that cats have a few more things going for them than we mere humans can understand.

One of these is the ability to "predict" seismic events, such as earthquakes. Cats (and other animals) appear to be sensitive to signs of increasing tension below, a theory promoted by those who claim that before an earthquake, the number of lost cats and dogs increases — presumably because the animals are attempting to escape from any danger.

Another interesting skill is the cat's ability to return to what he recognizes as "home" from hundreds of miles away — after his family moves, for example. Although some of these cases are surely mistaken identity on the part of the people and cats involved, others are well documented, and experiments have shown that cats have a particular sensitivity to the earth's magnetic field and so are masters of direction — no road maps needed.

We may never understand exactly what's behind these "extra senses," but that's probably fine with our cats: They'd prefer we admire their special air of mystery!

Dogs can read cats, and cats can read dogs, and both do a better job at interpreting nonverbal cues than do the overwhelming majority of humans, who must seem perfectly stupid to their pets. Throw in the verbal language of cats — meows and caterwauls, hisses and purrs — and you may need to reconsider your view that cats "can't talk."

On the contrary, your cat could well argue that *you* don't listen.

Eyes

Your cat's eyes react automatically to light conditions, the pupils narrowing to vertical slits in bright sunlight and growing to large, black pools in darkness. Beyond those reactions, however, your cat telegraphs his emotional state in his eyes. Eyes that are opened wide but not so wide as to look "startled" suggest the polite interest of a relaxed cat. Wide eyes and large pupils suggest fear. A stalking cat (whether on the hunt for a mouse or a toy) has eyes that are open, "hard," and intensely focused. A cat who's ready to lash out narrows his eyes and focuses his pupils — beware!

COOL CAT FACTS

Although cats don't appreciate being stared at — didn't your parents ever tell you that's rude? — they do appreciate "sharing a blink." Kiss the way cats do: Catch your cat's eyes with yours and then slowly blink. Your cat may even blink back!

Ears

A stalking cat turns both his satellite-dish ears straight forward, the better to catch the slightest peep from a hidden mouse. The ears of a relaxed cat are up and usually to the side, moving around to focus more keenly on sounds that may mean the temporary end of his comfortable period. If frightened, the cat's ears take a more sideways cast. The position you should never ignore, however, is the completely backward and flattened ears of a cat who's ready to lash out with a bite or a slash, whether in defense or aggression.

Tail

Tail up and flipped forward over the back is the cat's way of saying, "Hi, how are you; nice to see you; isn't it time to get my dinner?" — a relaxed and friendly greeting of affection and trust. A cat who's uncertain puffs out his tail, holds it low — perhaps even tucked under — and moves it from side to side. If stalking, the cat's tail is held low and stiff, except for twitching at the end as if the force required to hold one's body still is too much for a cat, who must release nervous energy from the end of his tail. (This "hunting twitch" may also be seen in play.)

The tail is one of the best physical indications of a cat's impending aggression. (See the sidebar "Prelude to a hiss," later in this chapter.) A cat who's becoming agitated whips his tail from side to side; often the tail is puffed out as well. A tail wag is *not* the friendly gesture in cats that it is in dogs, for sure!

Voice

Each cat, like each person, develops a voice uniquely her own, similar to others of her kind but never quite a match. Cats have a wide range of sounds available to them to express their emotional state; here's the collection:

- **Meows.** From the short chirping sound a mother cat makes to her kittens to the longer "I want it now" noises of a hungry pet, cats manage to get a lot of variety from a couple of basic sounds. They vary them in endless ways, holding their vowels sounds sometimes and other times clipping them short. Cats even have a meow we humans can't hear, because the noise is outside our range of hearing. Live with a cat for a while and you come to understand the specific meanings of your pet's various meows, which in broader terms usually mean, "Hi ya. I want something."

- **Caterwauling.** Even people who don't have cats know this sound, a multi-octave yowl usually performed as a duet between two cats who're getting ready to rumble. The message: "Get out of here or you'll be sorry." These concerts can happen anytime two cats contest territory but are especially frequent during the spring and fall mating season.

- ✔ **Chattering.** If a cat is excited by the prospect of a kill or the possibility (for a male) of mating, you sometimes observe a rapid clacking of teeth.

- ✔ **Growling.** Really more of a softer, sustained low yowl, without the up-and-down variation of the caterwaul. Growling is the sign of a frightened or angry cat and is often punctuated by hissing and spitting — the latter two sounds being particularly useful for convincing dogs to back off!

- ✔ **Purring.** The feline equivalent of a smile. Like a smile, a purr turns up in some situations that aren't so happy, sort of an "I'm nice, so don't hurt me" message. Content cats purr, but so do injured or frightened ones, as well as cats giving birth or nursing kittens.

- ✔ **Screaming.** A cry of intense pain. We hope you never hear it, especially from your cat.

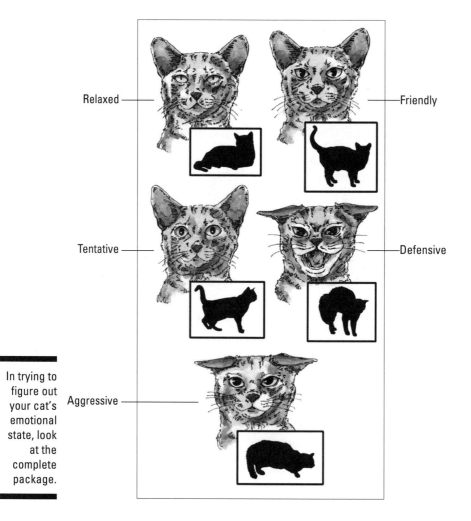

Relaxed

Friendly

Tentative

Defensive

Aggressive

In trying to figure out your cat's emotional state, look at the complete package.

Hair and whiskers

Scared or angry cats hold their hair erect in an effort to look bigger; in the early stages of fear or aggression, some cats just puff out their tail. Whiskers have a broader repertoire in expressing emotion. If a cat is curious or angry, he holds his whiskers forward (cats also do this in the dark to help them "feel" their way around). Cats pull their whiskers backward if frightened.

Most cats have 24 whiskers, divided on either side of the nose and arranged in four horizontal rows. The top rows and bottom rows can move independently of each other, and each whisker — they're technically called *vibrissae* — is imbedded deeper than normal hairs to enhance its sensory input. Another odd whisker fact: The kinky coated Cornish Rex and Devon Rex have curly whiskers as well!

Even though whiskers are important to cats — your pet may become disoriented if they're removed, which is why you never should cut them — there is no correlation between the length of whiskers and the width of a cat. If your cat gets fat, his whiskers don't grow to match!

Posture

The way a cat holds her body must be placed in context to be understood, observed along with signs from the tail, ears, eyes, voice, and fur (including whiskers) to correctly interpret your cat's emotional state. A cat who's enjoying being petted from head to toe, for example, often arches her back to maximize contact with the stroking hand. In another situation, an arched cat is one you shouldn't be touching under any circumstances, or you may get injured. The difference is context!

Study the overall cat to make sure, but the following list gives you a first impression of what different positions mean:

- **Inquisitive.** The friendly, curious, or inquisitive cat is relaxed, moving forward comfortably with tail up and ears up and slightly to the side.

- **Defensive.** A cat who's just defensive, angry, or scared arches and puffs out her fur in the classic "Halloween cat" pose. From this pose, a defensive cat makes a run for it if he can; a truly furious cat attacks. A cat who's really in trouble rolls over onto his back to bring into play his formidable defensive weapons — claws and teeth.

- **Aggressive.** A cat who's going to attack crouches low, his back a little higher than his front, ready to put his powerful hind legs to use in a leap forward. Fur on the *hackles* (over his shoulders) is up, as is the fur on his tail. This cat is one who means business; back away and let him be!

A cat in any defensive or aggressive posture is best left alone, even if he's your cat. Give him time to chill out completely before you even attempt to approach.

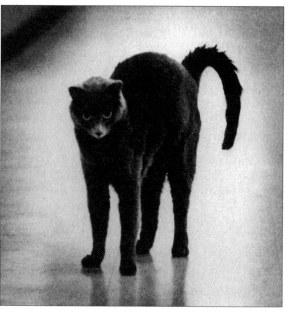

Judging from his body language, this cat clearly had more than enough of the photographer who'd been trying to take his picture.

Photo courtesy of Richard D. Schmidt.

Prelude to a hiss

Human stupidity (from the cat's point of view, that is) in misreading or ignoring body language earns more than a few cat lovers a scratch or bite from time to time — the result of misinterpreting a cat's "I've had enough" signs.

The classic example of this phenomenon is the cat who, while being petted, "suddenly" grabs the hand that pets him with teeth and claws — to the shock and sometimes anger of the human doing the petting.

In fact, these "out of the blue" attacks rarely are. Before the bite or clawing, a cat gives out subtle (to us, anyway) signs of diminished tolerance. Primary among them: an increase in the stiffness and twitching of the tail.

Often, the problem starts with petting your cat's tummy, a very vulnerable area for any animal. Your cat may even offer his belly out of love, but after you start to pet, he becomes increasingly uncomfortable with the attention.

Watch your cat's body signs: If he's tensing or that tail starts twitching, stop petting *immediately.* Not only does doing so save you claw and teeth marks, but stopping before your cat strikes also slowly builds up his trust in you and his tolerance for physical attention. (For more information on feline aggression, see Chapter 13.)

Chapter 13

Solving Behavior Problems

· ·

In This Chapter

▶ Why cats do what they do

▶ Medical reasons for "bad" behavior

▶ Litter-box avoidance and other problems

▶ When to get help — and where to find it

▶ The controversy over declawing

▶ Trick-training for cats

· ·

Cats are among the easiest of animals to live with as pets, which in part accounts for their massive and ever-growing appeal. Cats are naturally quiet, clean, affectionate, and largely self-sufficient, capable of adapting to any kind of dwelling, any definition of family.

But when things go wrong . . . they go very, very wrong from the human point of view. A cat with a behavior problem such as aggression can be a source of strife and even heartbreak in your family, with the cat the eventual loser. Other cats can ruin your belongings — covering them with the hard-to-remove stench of urine, clawing them into tatters, or chewing them into bits. Your furniture isn't safe, nor are your houseplants, nor are your own hands, for some cats seem quite deranged at times, purring one minute and biting the next.

To some cat lovers, these behaviors can seem unpredictable, unfathomable, and even spiteful, when, in fact, they're nothing of the sort. What cat lovers call "bad" behavior often makes complete sense to a cat, who's just doing what comes naturally to him, coping with boredom, illness, stress, or change in the way cats have always done. What cat lovers call "problems" are natural behaviors to cats, as much a part of their genetic makeup as super-keen hearing or whisper-soft paws.

To *solve* problem behavior, you must *understand* problem behavior.

Unfortunately, too many cat lovers don't even try to understand, reacting instead in the way that makes sense to the *human* animal — in anger that can start with physical punishment (which never works on a cat) and can end with a one-way trip to the shelter.

For your cat's sake and for your own, we offer alternatives to spare you both the confusion, anger, and resentment that feline behavior problems cause and to restore contentment and trust in your home — to help you reclaim the loving relationship you both deserve.

In this chapter, we help you understand what's causing your cat's unwanted behavior and show you how to set up a program to turn the situation into something you both can live with. Your cat's not perfect, and neither are you, and that's something to keep in mind as you work with behavior problems. Problems often take time to develop, and they also take time to fix.

The process takes patience and a certain degree of accommodation on your part. But most cat-behavior problems can be worked out to both your satisfaction. Don't give up. Read on.

The first step in solving any behavior problem is to make sure it's not a medical problem. We can't stress this fact enough. The signs of illness in cats can be very subtle — see Chapter 9 for more information — and are often disguised as behavior problems. Talk to your veterinarian before attempting to change your pet's behavior, because your efforts will likely fail if you're working with a sick cat. This advice is doubly true if your cat's behavior change is sudden — he's likely sick, especially if you can't pinpoint any other environmental changes, such as a new person or pet in the home, as a reason for the behavior change.

Your veterinarian can also guide you with your plans for changing a healthy cat's errant behavior — or refer you to a behavior specialist who can. Behavior is one of the fastest-growing areas of knowledge in veterinary medicine, a result of the profession's realization that behavior problems end up killing more animals than do diseases. This new emphasis has increased the use of drug therapy to help with behavior problems, including use of some of the same antidepressant and anti-anxiety medications used in human medicine. These medications aren't miracles, but they can give your cat a fresh start as you work to cure behavior problems.

Understanding "Bad" Behavior

Here's an enjoyable way to spend an afternoon and learn a lot about your cat at the same time: Go to your video store and rent a documentary on tigers.

You're certain to be astonished at how much the cat purring in your lap reminds you of this stunning wild cat. The way the tiger walks, with understated elegance and always the promise of power. The way the tiger hunts, still and focused except for the tiniest twitch at the end of the tail.

Now, pay attention to the part of the film about "territory," how tigers need one of their own and how tigers let each other know where one animal's hunting turf ends and another begins.

They rub against things, they spray, and they claw.

Admittedly, seeing a tiger do these things is a lot more dramatic than watching an eight-pound domesticated cat do them. A scent-marking head bump from a tiger may knock a person over. And as for the other two behaviors, you wouldn't even want to be around. If a tiger wants to leave a message (or refresh an old one) he stands up on his hind legs and digs his claws into a tree, putting deep slashes (along with his scent) on the hapless plant. And then, just to make the point a little more emphatic, he turns, faces away from the tree, raises his tail, and squirts a great blast of urine at it. And then he turns again and sniffs, with a gaping expression (called a *Flehmen response*) that looks like a sneer but is really enabling him to "taste" the smell through a sensory organ in the roof of his mouth.

With no one to yell at him for doing these things to the corner of a couch or a pile of dirty laundry, he ambles off. His world smells the way he thinks it ought to, and he's content.

Now maybe you're beginning to see the problem. The very same things the tiger does to mark territory are natural behaviors for your cat, too. And yet you want your pet to abandon them entirely? We have news for you: It's just not possible. Nor is asking fair.

Fixing feline behavior problems is like taming a tiger: You must work slowly to reshape your pet's natural behaviors in ways that you both can live with.

Looking at the Root of Unwanted Behavior

You're asking a lot of a cat whenever you bring her into your home, and the fact that, in most cases, the situation works as well as it does says a lot about the strength of the love between cats and people. You ask your cat to relieve herself where you want her to instead of anywhere in her territory. You ask her to scratch in one place instead of marking every surface in her life. You ask her to ignore her ability to jump gracefully onto tables and countertops and adjust her naturally nocturnal schedule to your daytime one.

Most cats make the compromises. For those who don't, you need to figure out why before any problem solving can begin. Here are some things to consider:

- ✔ **Medical problems.** As we mention at the beginning of this chapter, behavior problems are often really signs of illness. A cat with untreated diabetes, for example, drinks and urinates frequently, may overwhelm your efforts at keeping the box clean, and starts choosing other sites to relieve himself. A cat who suddenly starts biting may be in pain and is only lashing out to protect himself. A cat with a urinary-tract infection may find urinating painful and come to associate the pain with his litter box. Are you really surprised he's going to stop using it? All the behavior techniques in the world aren't going to cure a medical problem. You'll need your veterinarian's help for that.

- ✔ **Stress.** Cats find change stressful and can react by altering their behavior in an attempt to cope. Maybe a cat marks territory in a home that's just been "invaded" by a new pet or person. In a cat's mind, this behavior makes sense and is calming: Making the world smell like himself is comforting to him, if not to you. You need to calm your cat's stress in other ways, by limiting his territory for a while, for example, or by putting him on medication.

- ✔ **Unreasonable demands.** You need to look at your own role in any behavior problem. Are you asking something of your cat that's not possible for him to give? Your cat may not want to use the litter box you give him if it's rarely clean, for example, and asking him to leave the couch alone is really not fair if he has nothing else in the house to scratch. You need to provide him with some alternatives before you can hope for good behavior.

- ✔ **Boredom.** You've asked your cat to give up the whole world and all you're offering in return is a few hours of your presence a day and maybe a catnip mouse? *Bor*ing! Indoor cats need lots of things to keep themselves amused — lots of toys and lots of games, and lots of attention from you. You needn't spend a lot of money on cat toys — we've got a section on freebies in Chapter 6 — but you need to make an effort to help your cat play with them. If you're gone from home a great deal, another cat (or even a dog) may provide your pet with exercise, companionship, and amusement.

- ✔ **Never trained correctly in the first place.** If all you're ever doing is screaming or hitting at your cat, you're probably not teaching him anything except that you're someone best avoided. Physical correction has no place in changing a cat's behavior — cats just don't understand it. And using such correction just stresses them out, leading to even *more* problems.

Look at what has been going on in your life. How has your cat reacted to the situation, and how have you? Keep a journal of problems to help you spot and understand trends and to remove some of the emotion involved in living with a problem pet. Realizing that your cat's behavior isn't spiteful or capricious can make the problem easier for you to live with while you work on turning the situation around.

Strategies for Changing Behavior

Unlike dogs, cats don't have a built-in mechanism for working with a family. Dogs take naturally to the idea of a family, because their ancestors lived and hunted in cooperative teams called *packs,* which have a highly developed social structure. With the exception of lions, cats large and small are solitary hunters, and they're used to taking care of themselves. You can't make cats do what they don't want to do, so to change any behavior, you must offer an alternative you both can accept, even while you work to make the "bad" behavior less appealing.

Your cat loves you and enjoys your company, but if you want to convince him to do things your way, you must answer the quintessential cat question: What's in it for me?

The good news is that cats are creatures of habit. After yours learns where scratching, chewing, or relieving himself is okay, you can put away all the gadgets you've used to convince him.

Yes, kitty!

Reward your cat for good behavior with praise, with treats, with petting, and with games. If your cat uses the scratching post instead of the couch, make sure she knows you approve by playing with her with a cat fishing pole or a toy on a string. Tell her that she's good for using the litter box, for eating *her* plants instead of yours, and for attacking her toys instead of your slippers. Your cat isn't born knowing the rules of living among humans, and if you make following the rules pleasant, you have much better luck getting her to follow them.

No, kitty!

Never hit your cat, and never let her think any discipline is coming from you. Physical discipline is worse than meaningless to cats — and it can make a situation even worse by making your cat stressed out and afraid of you.

What works in cats is to make them believe that whatever they're doing wrong triggers an automatic response they don't like — and that you have nothing to do with it as far as they can tell. The couch they used to enjoy clawing is now covered with something they don't like to touch. Every time they get on the counter a tingle of static electricity tingles under their paws or a stream of water hits them in the fanny.

Following is a list of booby traps that work well to discourage cats and help you and your kitty live together in harmony:

- **Use water and loud noises:** Slyly squirting your cat with a squirt bottle, setting off compressed air in a can (with or without a horn), loudly shaking pennies in an empty soda can, and squeezing a squeaky dog toy (cats don't like the sound, but you can't use this device if you also have a dog, because they do!) are all tools to stop your cat in the middle of a bad act and convince her that maybe a repeat isn't in her best interest.

- **Take cover:** Covering areas you don't want your cat to touch with double-sided tape, foil or plastic, or plastic carpet runners with the points up is also a good plan. An electric mat called a Scat Mat (available in pet-supply stores and catalogs) that gives off a slight shock is great for furniture and countertops.

- **Set wooden mousetraps:** Wooden mousetraps are another device to give your cat the message about being where he ought not. Get a few of the kind that aren't prebaited and set them *upside-down* on countertops or in wastebaskets, with a sheet of newspaper over them. The devices aren't meant to hurt or trap your cat but just to startle him. After he bumps a trap, it jumps and closes with an eye-opening *crack,* helping to convince your pet that the area you've booby-trapped is better left alone.

- **Coat with something icky:** Coating something you don't want your cat near with a substance that tastes horrible — such as Bitter Apple or Tabasco sauce — is another form of booby-trapping that works in some cases. It doesn't take much: Your cat's sense of smell and taste is very keen!

Squirt bottles are one tool for curing problem behavior, but they work best when the water comes "out of nowhere" as far as your cat's concerned.

Calm kitty

Sometimes you need to go back to the beginning and reduce your cat's stress by giving her a smaller area for a while, the same as we recommend you do when you first bring your cat or kitten home. (See Chapter 5 for more information on introductions.) This *safe room* is not a punishment for your cat; on the contrary, it's a relief from whatever's bothering her in a new environment and a chance to refocus her on the behaviors you want — using a scratching post or a litter box. The safe room is excellent therapy for marking, because your cat doesn't have a large territory to defend.

We want you to play with her and pet her and tell her she's loved. But for short periods — a week, maybe two, followed by a gradual re-introduction to the house, room by room — a safe room can ease both your minds and get her retraining off to a good start.

Veterinarians are increasingly able to offer medications to help during the retraining of your cat, drugs that are also used in human medicine to relieve anxiety. These medications can really help, but they're usually a short-term solution. You still need to deal with the underlying problems in order to achieve long-term success. Discuss the use of these medications — or a possible referral to a veterinary behaviorist — with your veterinarian.

Fairness

You need to make sure that what you're expecting from your cat is fair in two ways: Are you being reasonable? Are you being consistent?

Being *reasonable* involves offering your cat alternatives: a litter box and a location he likes, for example, or a scratching post in a choice location. You also need to consider whether you're fulfilling your cat's needs — is he getting enough exercise and play?

If your cat's constantly in need of something to do and you're not there to play with him constantly — and few of us are — consider getting another cat for a playmate. Be aware, however, that not all cats will take to a newcomer. Some are such loners that the addition of another cat may cause more problems than it cures. Unfortunately, there's no way to predict which way your cat will go.

Consistency is about always expecting the same standards of behavior. Letting your pet on the counter while you're both home alone but expecting him to stay off after guests arrive simply isn't fair.

Adding another cat to your family can, in some cases, help to reduce stress and relieve boredom for your pet.

Camden and Cleo — Photo courtesy of Michelle Vukas.

Inappropriate Elimination

House-training problems — called *inappropriate elimination* — are the number one cause of behavior-related complaints from cat lovers — and with good reason. No one likes to deal with urine and feces in a litter box, much less in a part of the house you didn't expect to find them. Cats who can't be convinced to use the litter box all too often end up looking for a new home — and for these animals, the prognosis is grim.

Fortunately, most cases of inappropriate elimination can be solved if you're determined to look at things from your cat's point of view, make a few adjustments, and stay patient.

Although you still need to fix the underlying problems of why your cat isn't going where he should, some medications may help in the short run. Talk to your veterinarian.

Litter-box avoidance

The first step in getting your cat to use the litter box is to figure out why he's not using it. Rule out a medical problem — commonly, a urinary-tract infection. These infections give the cat a "sense of urgency" to urinate even when the bladder is not full, and urinating may even be downright painful in

Where to find help with behavior problems

Many people are reluctant to seek help if faced with a pet-behavior problem, either because they think the idea of a "pet shrink" is crazy or because they don't think the money would be well spent.

If you're one of these people, think again. Consulting a behaviorist can save you time, money, and aggravation. You save time, because someone with experience in animal behavior can quickly determine the root of the problem, without the emotional baggage that a pet owner may bring to the situation. ("He's doing it for spite!") You save money, because a consultation or two is a great deal cheaper than a new sofa. And aggravation? We don't need to explain that one if you're living with a problem cat.

More importantly, getting help can save your cat's life! Behavior problems are among the top reasons why cat owners "divorce" their feline companions. Here, divorce means giving your pet to another person or animal shelter or worse — requesting they be euthanatized (a nice way of saying humanely killed — and often the ultimate result at the adoption shelter) or abandoning your pet to the streets.

Be aware, however, that animal behavior is an unregulated field — anyone can call himself a behaviorist.

You're best off choosing a veterinarian who's board-certified by the American College of Veterinary Behaviorists. These professionals have gone through years of study in animal health and behavior and have done a residency in the field as well. Your best bet at finding one of these veterinarians is to contact your closest school or college of veterinary medicine's teaching hospital.

People with other academic degrees (such as psychology), general practice veterinarians, and people who've picked up their cat knowledge completely in the field also make themselves available for advising on behavior. You find good and not-so-good people in all three areas, which makes getting recommendations and checking references important.

In addition to checking with your closest school or college of veterinary medicine, check with your own veterinarian or local humane society, any of which may be able to refer you to someone who can help. Some humane societies even offer behavior classes or consulting.

The form the consulting takes varies. Some behaviorists consult by phone, others take appointments with or without your cat, and still others make house calls. Online help is hit and miss, with a lot of unqualified people offering advice. One exception is America Online's Pet Care Forum, where behaviorist Steve Aiken runs the cat area.

more-severe cases. Your cat may come to associate the use of the box with these unpleasant sensations and so avoids the box. If that's the case, you need to retrain your cat, perhaps by changing the box and litter so that it "feels" different, but probably by using the safe room approach. (More on that in this section.)

If your cat checks out fine, you need to experiment to make sure everything about the box is to his liking. The following list describes some things to consider:

- ✔ **Cleanliness.** Cats are fastidious animals, and if the litter box is dirty, they look elsewhere for a place to go. Think of how you felt the last time you were faced with a dirty public restroom, and you can probably empathize! Attend to the box frequently — twice a day is ideal — and make sure that it's completely scrubbed clean and aired out on a weekly basis. Another option: two litter boxes.

- ✔ **Box type and filler.** Many choices people make to suit their own tastes don't match with what their cat wants, and when you're talking boxes and litter, your cat's opinion is the only one that really counts. Many times the offending box or litter is one chosen in an attempt to reduce smell for people — but your cat can still smell just fine. A covered box may seem more pleasing to you, but your cat may think it's pretty rank inside. Likewise, scented litters may make you think the box smells fine, but your cat may disagree — not only is the box dirty, he reasons, but it's got this extra "clean" odor he can't abide. Go back to basics: a simple box, a plain litter. Many cats prefer clumping litter, and this variety makes the box easier to keep clean, too. Just skip the deodorizers.

- ✔ **Location.** Your cat's box should be away from his food and water dishes (you don't eat near the toilet, so why should your cat?) and in a place where he can get to easily and feel safe. Consider location from a cat's point of view: Choose a quiet spot where he can see what's coming at him. A cat doesn't want any surprises while he's in the box. You should also experiment with additional boxes in your house, especially if you've got more than one cat. Urine and feces are weapons in a war over territory: Some cats share boxes; many don't.

Make the area where your cat has had mistakes less attractive by cleaning thoroughly with a pet-odor neutralizer (available in pet-supply stores or catalogs) and covering with foil, plastic sheeting, or plastic carpet runners with the points up to discourage reuse of the area. Enzymatic pet-mess cleaners take time to work, so figure on keeping the area blocked off for at least a couple of weeks.

If this procedure doesn't clear up the problem, you may need to retrain your cat by keeping him in a small area for a few days. Make sure that the safe room has no good options besides the litter box — no carpet, no pile of dirty laundry. Block off the bathtub — keep an inch of water in it to discourage its use as a place to go. After your cat is reliably using the litter box, let him slowly expand his territory again. As long as you keep up your end of the bargain and keep the litter box appealing, he should keep up his end, too.

Urine spraying

The application of urine to mark territory is different from the release of urine to eliminate waste from the body. Urine-marking is called *spraying*, and the strategies for addressing it are different from those that you use in getting a cat to use a litter box. The cat who's marking territory backs up to the object he wants to mark and sprays urine backward, with his tail held high and quivering, alternating his weight on his back feet.

Although both male and female cats spray, unneutered males are the biggest offenders, followed by unspayed females in season. The first rule of dealing with this stinky problem is to make sure that your pet is neutered — this procedure takes care of the problem in 90 percent of the cases if done before sexual maturity is attained, at about six months.

For those cats who don't respond to neutering, environmental stresses — such as a new person in the house or a neighbor's cat in the yard — may be triggering the spraying. Anti-anxiety drugs may help, as can cleaning sprayed areas thoroughly and covering them with foil to discourage fresh marking. (Cats dislike anything involving foil, and the sound of urine hitting the stuff really annoys them.) Don't hit your cat for spraying, even if you catch him in the act — doing so makes him even more insecure and likely to mark.

A few days of isolation in a safe room may break the spraying routine. (See the section "Calm kitty," earlier in this chapter, and also the use of safe rooms as discussed in the "Introductions" section of Chapter 5.)

Maybe your cat is trying to tell you something with his spraying. In her entertaining book *Hiss and Tell: True Stories From the Files of a Cat Shrink* (Crossing Press), behaviorist Pam Johnson writes about a man whose cat sprayed his new wife's work clothes every evening. In the end, he discovered that the woman was having an affair with a coworker, and the cat was reacting to the smell of the other man on the wife's clothing. Pretty smart!

Attacking Other Problems

We've really given you the keys to solving most problems you may face earlier in this chapter: Make sure that your cat has no health problems and then make sure that what you want your cat to do is more attractive than what you don't want him to do. The same rules apply for other cat problems, but we've included a few more tips in the following sections to help you cope with some specifics.

Litter-munching dogs

Gina gets calls all the time from readers who are astonished that their dogs consider the contents of a litter box some kind of special treat. These folks are always desperate for an end to this disgusting habit.

As incredible as the thought seems to humans, many dogs do indeed consider cat feces to be every bit as wonderful as dog biscuits — they're drawn to the undigested protein.

Faced with constant supply and ready access, no dog can resist for long, which is why efforts to train a dog to leave the litter box alone are rarely successful. The better plan is to restrict access, which you can accomplish in many ways, including those described in the following list:

✔ **Purchase covered litter boxes.** Some cats don't like them, and cats with asthma can't use them. (See Chapter 10 for more on feline asthma.) If your cat falls into either category, this solution isn't going to work for you.

✔ **Change the litter box's location.** You must be careful not to upset your cats. But experimenting with such ploys as gradually moving the litter box to a location above the dog's reach usually doesn't hurt.

✔ **Provide barriers.** One way is to rig the door to the room containing the litter box so that it stays open wide enough for the cat but not for the dog. Another possibility is to put a cat-sized door through the door to the litter box room if your dog is medium-sized or larger. For small dogs, try a baby gate — the cat can jump it, but the dog can't.

✔ **Keep it clean.** Don't forget to keep the box scooped: A dog can't eat what a dog can't find.

Aggression

You need to do a little detective work and figure out what's causing your cat to bite or claw you. Aggression takes many forms, and the solution depends on the cause, some of which may be as follows:

✔ **Fear or pain.** If your cat is striking out because he's afraid or hurting, your best bet is to leave him alone and work on the underlying problem. A cat in pain or fear has his ears flat back against his head and his body rolled into a defensive posture low against the ground with claws up and ready. This cat is saying, "Don't come near me!" You need to let your cat calm down — hide if need be — before you can get your veterinarian to check her out. Often under these circumstances that carrier your cat seems to hate will seem like a haven. Place the carrier with the door wide open in the room with your cat. Your cat may choose to go in there and this may save you the "fight" of trying to force your cat to enter the carrier for the trip to the veterinarian. *Remember:* Don't fight with your cat. You *will lose.*

✔ **Overstimulation.** You're petting your cat and suddenly he grabs you with his claws and teeth. Not a full-powered attack, but you've still got those sharp tips around your hand. What to do? In the short run, freeze. Don't fight your cat or you may trigger a real bite. Sometimes smacking your other hand hard against a hard surface — a table top, for example — may startle your cat into breaking off the attack. If you stay still, however, he usually calms down and releases you.

That's the solution if you've gotten to the attack stage. The better option is to be familiar with your cat and his body language and stop petting before he becomes overstimulated. Cat lovers often think such attacks come without warning, but the fact is that they missed the warning signs of a cat who's simply had enough. The tail is the key: If your cat starts twitching his tail in a jerky fashion, time to call off the petting has arrived. If you watch your cat's body language — more on that subject in Chapter 12 — you can slowly build up your petting time. Three pats, then four, then five. Push up to, but never over, your cat's level of tolerance and build slowly on your successes.

Often these "I've had enough" attacks come if you've been petting your cat's belly. This is a very sensitive area for cats, and even if yours offers it to you, you're better off petting somewhere else. One reason is sexual in nature: Your male cat becomes aroused when his belly is rubbed, and reacts with a bite because that's what feline mating behavior involves. (For more on cat sex — it hurts! — see Chapter 14.)

✔ **Play aggression.** Sure, it hurts all the same, but the cat who pounces on your feet and then careens off the wall isn't trying to hurt you — he's playing. You need to increase your play sessions with your cat with an appropriate toy, such as a cat fishing pole or toy on a string — not one of your body parts — to help your cat burn off his excess energy before you try for a quiet pet session. Let him know that attacks on you are not permitted by letting him have it with a blast from an air horn or a spray bottle. A little Bitter Apple on your hand can help, too.

✔ **Redirected aggression.** Your cat sees another cat, an intruder, outside your living-room window. He becomes enraged. You walk by, and he nails you. What gives? You were just the victim of redirected aggression. This one's tough to fix. Try to discourage strange cats in your yard: Thump on the window or put the air horn out the door and give them a blast.

Counter-cruising

Use your squirt bottle, air horn, or other deterrent to discipline your cat if you see him on countertops and tables. As much as possible, try to stay out of sight so that your cat associates the annoyance with the table or counter. A Scat Mat (a plastic mat that gives off a tingle if touched) is great for this: It disciplines your cat when you're not around, and from the ground, your cat can't tell whether it's still there or not.

Even if your cat seems to be inviting the attention, a belly rub may end with a sudden bite to your hand.

Nick — Photo courtesy of Angie Hunckler.

Destructiveness

Most "interior redecoration" done by cats is a result of them doing what comes naturally — chewing, clawing, and even digging. You need to work to convince your cat to leave your things alone while offering him places where he can be a cat and not get in trouble.

Clawing

You need to start on this project by getting your cat a good scratching post or cat tree. (See Chapter 6 for information on these items.) A cat tree or post must be stable enough for your cat to climb and pull on, covered with material your cat can dig her claws into, and put in a prominent area so that your cat uses it.

After you've got the post or tree in place, encourage your cat to use it by teasing her with a cat toy and praising her for digging in her claws. If your cat enjoys catnip, rub some on the post to encourage her to spend more time there and give her treats for being on the tree as well. Make sure that she knows in no uncertain terms that climbing and clawing are perfectly fine and encouraged on her scratching post or cat tree. Don't put her paws on the post, however — cats don't like to be "forced" to do anything!

Make sure that the post you choose isn't covered in the same texture of carpet as that in your house or your cat may have a hard time making the distinction between why clawing carpet on the post is okay but not on the floor. Better yet: Choose a post or tree covered with *sisal,* a rough-textured rope material cats love to dig into.

When aggression can't be fixed

We feel you must *never* forget that the combination of agility, climbing acumen, sharp claws and teeth, and a stubborn streak larger than any one person could ever possess combine to make most any cat someone you don't want to get on the wrong side of. We do not wish to instill fear or shy you away from the joys of living with a cat, but we do want to emphasize a couple of things.

Unless you feel *very* competent at restraining cats, never attempt to force your cat to do anything using any but the most gentle of physical means. The best way to deal with a cat who has gone "over the edge" is to leave him alone. Do not try to restrain or punish him. Leave the room or let him leave the area and find a quiet place to calm down.

If you *ever* find yourself facing a vicious cat, call for help. Occasionally a cat will seem to go nuts, sometimes for no reason at all, and Paul has experienced this first-hand. The following experience is fortunately quite rare. We hesitated to even include it — but felt it our responsibility to do so.

Paul once found himself rushing to rescue his sister from her beloved cat, who had suddenly turned aggressive and imprisoned her within a single bedroom (with a phone, luckily) in her New York City apartment. Thinking this was humorous, Paul entered the apartment to find a cat who had gone crazy and quickly convinced Paul that his only safe haven was on the terrace.

Paul will never forget watching this once-friendly cat lunge at the plate-glass window trying to reach him. Talking with his sister through the bedroom window, Paul convinced her to call animal control, which finally came and captured the cat with appropriate equipment. Unfortunately, this cat never calmed down and had to be euthanatized. Although a postmortem examination did not reveal any explanation for the sudden rage behavior, Paul believes this must have been a medical problem with an unfortunate outcome. This sort of thing is very rare, but it emphasizes that, should you ever find yourself facing an uncontrollable feline, seek safety and call for help.

Now that we have scared you, let us reassure you that you are unlikely to ever face such a situation. It has certainly not caused Paul to abandon cat ownership, nor has it ever caused him to dissuade anyone from cat ownership — quite the contrary!

Make the areas you don't want your pet to touch less appealing during the retraining process by covering them with foil, plastic sheeting, or plastic carpet runners with the pointy side out. Use double-sided tape generously as well — cats hate the feel of sticky stuff under their paws. You can still use the furniture yourself by applying the foil, plastic, or what-have-you to pieces of cardboard that you can lift off if you want to sit down.

Because clawing is also a territory marker, move the cat tree into a prominent place, near that clawed corner of the couch in the center of the room, now covered with deterrents. Praise your cat for using the post instead. Move the post slowly — a few inches a day — to a place more to your taste.

If you catch your cat clawing, squirt with a spray bottle or use another distracting device. Try to stay out of sight whenever you do so and don't lose your temper. *Remember:* The idea is to get the cat to believe that the furniture itself is doing the disciplining. ("Wow, I put my claws in there and got water on me!")

Yes, your house is going to look pretty ugly for a while, with cat deterrents all over the furniture and a cat tree in the middle of the room. You must live with it until your cat's new pattern of clawing only where acceptable is established. If you're patient and consistent, that new pattern will eventually take root.

For some cats, nail tips help with clawing problems. Glued onto the nails every six weeks or so, these Soft Paws tips even come in a variety of colors.

Keeping your cat's nails trimmed is another way to reduce his destructive capabilities. For instructions on how to do this task safely, see Chapter 7.

The plant terminator

Plants and cats are natural together, at least from the cat's point of view. The leaves are good for nibbling, and if the pot has the room — and it doesn't need much — the soil looks like a suitable alternative to the litter box.

Pity that people don't see things the same way.

The key to peaceful coexistence between cats and houseplants is to give your kitty a garden of her own and make the rest of the plants as undesirable or as hard to get to as possible. We've put a list of cat-friendly plants in Chapter 8; keeping fresh greens growing takes care of your cat's need to nibble. As for your other plants, here are some tips on keeping them safe from kitty:

- ✔ **Make the pots unattractive.** Use foil or plastic carpet runners with the pointed-side up under the pots to discourage your cat from approaching, and put decorative rock over the soil to discourage digging.

- ✔ **Make the plants taste bad.** Putting Bitter Apple or Tabasco sauce on the leaves makes your cat think twice about munching.

- ✔ **Convert them all to hanging plants.** If all else fails, this strategy is by far the most successful for keeping plants untouched around a determined leaf-chewer.

Don't count on any deterrent to keep your cats from plants that are toxic — don't have them in your house, period. We've included a list of toxic plants from the National Animal Poison Control Center in Chapter 21.

Should you consider declawing?

If any one topic is sure to produce a discussion among cat lovers, it's declawing. The procedure is widely performed to end scratching and is just as widely vilified. Some breeders and humane societies refuse to place a cat or kitten with any adopter who doesn't promise not to declaw. Even Paul and Gina don't agree on the subject.

Declawing is the surgical amputation under general anesthesia of the last part of the toe — comparable to the removal of your fingertip at the first joint. The skin is glued or stitched over the exposed joint, the feet bandaged, and the cat sent home to heal for the next couple weeks. In most cases, only the front claws are removed.

Although the procedure is a successful way to curb destructive behavior, Gina feels that, too often, declawing is performed at the first sign of clawing or — worse — is considered as automatic a part of owning a cat as vaccinations. Paul believes that although perhaps not what your cat would choose, done properly, the short-lived and very controllable discomfort that results from declawing is easily justified when you consider that for many cat-owning families there is not agreement on the value of the cat to the household. To those who are not the cat lovers in the house, the cat will lose when it comes down to a choice between the leather couch or the cat.

Scratching is natural and satisfying for cats, and you owe your pet the effort to teach him to scratch in appropriate places before you opt to declaw him. But although Gina feels that declawing should be reserved for those cats who can't be reformed and are facing euthanasia because of their behavioral problems, Paul argues that many cat owners know their tolerance for destruction and many just do not want to even risk damaging their furniture and opt for declawing as a preventive measure.

Paul adds that frequent attention to trimming your cats nails — keeping the points off — can accomplish the task nearly as well, but most people just aren't religious enough about this task to stay ahead of the risk to the furniture.

By the way, Paul's cat, PC, is not declawed. She and Paul have an understanding that she abides to and so the issue has not needed to be addressed.

One thing that Gina and Paul agree on concerning declawing: If you *do* choose to declaw your cat, you *must* keep him inside — without his claws, he's less able to defend himself against dogs and other dangers; he can't swat and has a harder time climbing to safety if attacked. (Although don't ever think for a moment that declawing diminishes the threat posed by a good sharp set of cat teeth!)

The cloth chewer

Some cats like to chew and suck on clothes, especially wool sweaters — a problem behaviorists call "wool chewing." This destructive habit was originally thought to be associated with a cat who'd been weaned too young, but now behaviorists believe that the tendency is genetic and more common in some breeds or mixes — such as the Siamese or other Orientals — than in others.

Putting rocks in pots and foil around them will help teach cats to leave plants alone.

Increasing fiber in the diet (such as adding a teaspoon of canned pumpkin daily) may help, as may offering substitute chew articles such as sheepskin-covered dog toys. Regular, active play sessions also may help your cat shed some of his excess energy.

Wool chewing is one of those cases where the most effective way to change your cat's behavior is to change your own. Keep the objects of your cat's obsession out of reach in closed hampers or drawers!

The trash cruiser

You can foil the cat who gets into wastebaskets by using a single, marvelous innovation — a can with a lid. Why struggle with your cat if a pop-up lid fixes the problem? Another alternative: Put the basket behind a cupboard door.

Mousetraps in the top of the trash startles your cat, and double-sided tape along the rim discourages him. These deterrents also make using the basket a little harder for you, which is why we prefer the lid-it-or-hide-it approach.

Noisiness

Some cats are chattier than others; indeed, "talkativeness" is an adored breed trait in the Siamese and other Orientals. If you've got a noisy Siamese, to a certain extent you're just going to have to live with the problem — in other words, you can't change the stripes on a tiger!

Some noisiness is inborn: Kittens call to their moms when they want something. Some noisiness is actually *trained* into cats by humans. If you hop up and accommodate her every time your cat demands something — to be fed or let out or in — you've taught her that the squeaky wheel gets the grease. Even in the middle of the night or at the crack of dawn.

To retrain your cat, resolve not to give in to her demands. If you start out by ignoring her yowling and then give in anyway, you've taught her that all she needs to do to get her way is to make *more* noise, not less. Correct her for the noise — with a shot of air or water — and then go about your business. She gets the point soon enough that her demanding gets her nowhere. Realize that in the short run your cat will be even more insistent. If you give in, you're sunk. So don't. This, too, shall pass.

THE CAT'S MEOW

Can your cat learn a trick or two?

Some people point to the dog's ability to learn obedience commands and tricks as proof that the dog is smarter than the cat. Others point to the same as proof that the cat is smarter than the dog.

We're not going to get into that argument. The important thing to remember is that cats and dogs are *different* in how they relate to us. Dogs have an ingrained need to be part of a family structure — to have a job to do within that family. Dogs are that way because wolves are that way — survival depends on the family, or pack.

The cat came from a different place — from solitary hunters who didn't need teamwork to survive. If you want to put a good spin on it as a cat lover, you could say that dogs *need* to be with us, but cats *choose* to.

Because of this distinction, you absolutely cannot get a cat to do something he doesn't want to. Something must be in it for him. With training tricks, that something is usually food (although some cats will work for a toy, or

petting). Teach the cat an association between a word — such as "sit" — and an action by using treats and praise.

According to animal trainer Anne Gordon, in her book *Show Biz Tricks for Cats* (Adams), you start teaching the "sit" command with a hungry cat, a table, and a quiet room. Get your cat to stand up by touching her in front of her tail and then hold the treat a little over her head, saying her name and the command "sit." Slowly move the treat between your cat's ears, but not high enough for her to pick her front paws off the ground and grab the tidbit. Instead, she'll sit. After she does, praise her and give her the treat. Work in short sessions and be patient. Your cat eventually gets the idea!

Sound crazy? Gordon has trained dozens of animals — including many cats — for commercials, TV shows, and movies. Her book offers precise instructions for teaching 30 tricks, including jumping through a hoop, climbing a ladder, and rolling over. Great fun!

Chapter 14

Littering: Should Your Cat Become a Parent?

*1*f you take a kitten or cat into your life, you take on the responsibility for caring for your new pet. You ensure your pet's good health by taking her to your veterinarian, by feeding her well, and by grooming her. You keep both of you entertained through play, and you give her love and receive her love in return.

Truly, the bond between people and cats is remarkable, a pact of companionship that lasts for years, but it brings with it responsibility for making the right decisions for the good of your cat and for all cats.

Your kitten's barely settled into your house when you must make one of the most important decisions for a cat owner: Do I allow my cat to breed?

For most people, the answer is a decisive "no." And because of that answer, your cat is a better pet, remains in better health, and doesn't contribute to the tragic surplus of cats and kittens, millions of whom die without ever knowing what your cat knows: what being a loving and well-cared-for pet is like.

Still, the decision is yours to make. And sometimes it's really not your decision at all, because your young cat could end up pregnant before you expected, or a pregnant cat could end up on your doorstep. After the deed is done, you have another set of responsibilities: helping your cat through the pregnancy and birth, helping her raise her kittens, and finding them responsible homes.

The Case against Breeding

According to a 1995 survey by the American Animal Hospital Association, nearly 80 percent of the cats and dogs in the United States and Canada are spayed or neutered. What do these people know that you don't? Consider . . .

- ✔ A neutered male is less likely to roam, less likely to fight (and thus less likely to cost you money to patch him up), and less likely to spray urine everywhere to mark his territory. He's more likely to live longer, because the cat who's looking for a mate is really looking for trouble. If a car doesn't get him, infectious disease (spread by fighting or mating) or cancer may.

- ✔ A spayed female is a more attentive and loving pet, because her energy isn't constantly directed toward finding a mate. (Cats are in heat nearly all the time until they become pregnant.) If you spay your cat, you protect her from some cancers and infections and from sexually transmitted infectious diseases.

- ✔ A cat of either sex who isn't altered can be obnoxious to live with. Reproduction is their reason for living, and if you don't let them follow their instincts, they drive you crazy trying to get out and crying endlessly. If you want to live with such annoyances, that's your business, but if you truly love cats, you want to consider another reason why spaying and neutering is so important: Millions of unwanted cats and kittens are euthanized every year because not enough homes are out there for them.

- ✔ If kittens are plentiful, overwhelmed shelters can't even give them all a chance at adoption: They pull the one or two cutest or healthiest babies out and send the rest back to be euthanized. Millions and millions of kittens end up this way.

Spay or neuter your cat, we implore you. It's the right thing to do. If you love kittens, volunteer at your local humane society or SPCA. You don't actually need to work at the shelter, which some people find "depressing." Many volunteers foster orphaned or sick kittens until they can be placed in responsible homes.

If you have children, please don't feel they need to experience "the miracle of birth" and allow your cat to breed. Instead of contributing more kittens to the world — when watching a video can teach your children about birth just as well — let your children learn the lessons of caring and responsibility that living with a pet brings.

The too-many-kittens syndrome sends millions of wonderful pets to shelters each year. This one found a home, but many aren't so lucky.

Photo courtesy of Richard D. Schmidt.

Spaying and Neutering: What's Involved?

Spaying and *neutering* are the everyday terms for the surgical sterilization of a pet — spaying for the female, neutering for the male. Neutering — or *altering* — is also used to describe both procedures. The clinical terms for the two operations are *ovariohysterectomy,* for the female, and *castration,* for the male.

Both spaying and neutering must be done only by a veterinarian, and both procedures require general anesthesia.

Spaying involves the removal of the female's entire reproduction system: The uterus, fallopian tubes, and ovaries are taken out through an incision in the abdomen. Your veterinarian may require you to return to have your cat's stitches removed in about ten days, or he may use stitches that are absorbed into the body. Recovery is fast, taking just a few days, during which you should limit your cat's activities — no jumping or boisterous play. You may not notice much difference in your female's personality, unless you've lived with her through her nearly constant heat cycles and endured her noisy efforts at attracting a mate — along with the fighting, yowling, urine-spraying toms who answered her call. Those days are thankfully behind you both.

In *neutering*, the cat's testicles are removed through incisions in the *scrotum,* the pouch holding the testicles. These incisions are generally left unsutured in this relatively minor procedure. Postoperative care normally involves monitoring and keeping the incisions clean and dry. Many veterinarians recommend keeping the cat inside (if he's not already an indoor pet) and using shredded newspaper in place of litter until the incisions close, which usually occurs within three to five days.

Behavioral changes can be dramatic in neutered males. Fighting, urine-spraying, and roaming can be nearly completely prevented in cats neutered before sexual maturity — the age of six months of so. These behaviors are also dramatically reduced in older neutered males as well, although some retraining for behavior problems such as urine-spraying may prove necessary (see Chapter 13).

Spaying and neutering are among the most common medical procedures in the United States and Canada and carry very little risk for your pet. However don't for a minute think that *common* — meaning that your veterinarian is good and fast at it because he does it often — means *trivial*. Cat alterings can and do result in rapid death if done wrong. This procedure is major surgery. Don't let the common name (spay) or the low cost (a losing proposition for most veterinarians) fool you.

Given the choice, pay more for what looks like more-complete attention to details. Ask about and discuss the following:

- ✔ **Anesthesia.** What combination of inhalants or injectables are used?

- ✔ **Sterility.** Are fresh sterile instruments used for every animal?

- ✔ **Monitoring.** Is someone besides the surgeon there to monitor anesthesia? And what about afterward? Will someone check on your pet? If overnight care is not part of the plan, who will take your call if you suspect a problem? Will your veterinarian explain what you should be looking out for?

- ✔ **Emergency provisions.** Is a "crash cart" in the surgery room and trained personnel who can respond as astutely as your favorite doctors do on TV's *ER*?

- ✔ **Suture material.** What type is used and why?

Do you really need to take so many precautions? Consider this true story: In 1987, one of Paul's cats almost died after a complication from her spay done at one of the best animal hospitals in the world — the UC Davis Veterinary Medical Teaching Hospital. She survived because Paul was there to notice the problem and the excellent staff and facilities were there to provide live-saving care, without which she would have certainly died.

Spaying and neutering are *not* the areas to save a few dollars.

The Birds and the Bees, Kitty-Style

The more you know about feline reproduction, the more you're amazed that so many cats are in this world. Think about it some more, and you're even more amazed at the sheer power of instinct in the life of a cat.

Why all the amazement? Because mating doesn't seem like much fun for cats; in fact, it's *painful*. He bites the nape of her neck to start, and then he mounts her; she slashes him after the ordeal's over. They both scream to raise the dead. She rolls around ignoring him afterward, and yet he sticks around to keep another male from having her, even though doing so means that he must fight and get bitten and clawed by her other suitors. Before long, she wants him again — desperately. More biting, more screaming, more slashing. (One study counted up to 36 matings in 36 hours.)

She may mate with some other tomcat if she can; she doesn't care who. After the boys are done with her, they're after the scent of someone new; they don't care who either.

Two months later, give or take a few days, she has her kittens. The father (or fathers) is nowhere to be found.

Makes the sex scandals that rock the media seem kind of tame by comparison, doesn't it?

Choosing a mate

If you're planning to breed your cat, you need to make sure she's at least a year old. She should also be free of viral diseases, such as feline leukemia, and current on her vaccinations. Don't wait until after she's pregnant to vaccinate her, as this practice can lead to serious problems for the fetuses. Schedule a visit to your veterinarian and discuss your plans for your cat; he can advise you on necessary preventive-care measures.

You want a healthy mate as well, and to start finding him, you should talk to your cat's breeder. Don't just search for a cat of the same breed "with papers," or you could be setting yourself up for a genetic catastrophe. Reputable breeders breed "nonfolded" Scottish fold cats to "folded" Scottish folds, for example, and Manx cats with tails to Manxes without. That's because breeding "tail to tail" or "folded ear to folded ear" often produces kittens with serious congenital defects — babies that suffer and die or must be humanely killed. Understanding the genetics behind your cat before choosing her mate is essential, and the best person to help with that is an experienced and knowledgeable breeder.

If you're planning to breed your mixed-breed cat, we encourage you strongly to reconsider. We're not being elitists: Pedigreed cats must be carefully bred or their breeds may disappear. Mixed-breed cats are in such oversupply that millions of them are killed as "surplus" every year. Supply and demand is the name of the game, and no one is clamoring for more mixed-breed kittens, no matter how adorable.

Still, if you're going to choose a mate for her, insist on his getting an exam as well to establish that he's in good health and free of contagious diseases.

When in season, the female cat may cry, pace, rub, and roll to attract males, who warily accumulate on your front porch in droves and watch her until she allows one of them to mate with her.

The "oops" pairing

The truth is that many people never see their free-roaming cat being bred. Many of them meant to have her spayed but just didn't get around to it. Then, one day, they just notice that she's pregnant.

Some people are so unaware of the signs that their cats are in season — rolling, crying, pacing — that they bring them to their veterinarians, convinced they're in pain.

If you suspect your cat is pregnant — putting on weight, for example — and don't want her to be, talk to your veterinarian about your options. Otherwise, congratulations! You're going to be a grandparent.

Caring for a Pregnant Cat

About two weeks after a successful mating, a cat's nipples darken from light pink to a rosier hue, but the casual owner of a free-roaming cat may not notice a pregnancy until it's patently obvious — until the cat is nearly ready to deliver, in other words.

Older cats need good homes, too!

Kittens aren't the only ones who need responsible, loving homes. A lot of older cats do, too. If a stray turns up on your back porch and you can't find an owner, if you inherit an older cat from a sick relative, or if you end up with an extra cat for any other reason, you want to find the best home you can. Adult cats can be very, very hard to place — they have the lowest rates of adoption for all animals at the shelter. If you're patient and persistent, however, you may find a home. Here are some tips to follow:

✔ **Do everything you can to make the animal more adoptable.** The pet has a better chance for adoption if her vaccinations are current, she uses her litter box reliably, and she's altered. (If you're trying to place your own pet because of a behavioral problem, please see whether our tips for solving them in Chapter 13 can help you keep your pet instead.)

✔ **Ask a price.** People show more respect for something they've paid for, and a price tag dampens the interest of profiteers, such as those who collect "free to good home" pets for sale to research labs or to people who train dogs for fighting. (Dog fighting is illegal in most places, but still remarkably common!) A good general rule: Charge an amount to cover the cost of the spaying/neutering and vaccinations.

✔ **Don't lie about the pet's problems or why she's being placed.** Although finding a new home for a pet with behavioral problems takes longer, you can usually still do so. But the person who gets such a pet without warning is likely to bring her back, take her to the shelter, or give her away — maybe to a horrible situation.

✔ **Spread the news.** Make up flyers and take out an ad in your local newspaper. Post the flyers everywhere you can: on bulletin boards at work, at pet-supply stores, and at your veterinarian's. Give some to your friends and family to post where they work, too. Talk the cat up with everyone you know, at least briefly: Even people who don't like cats (or who don't want one) know people who may be looking for a pet. The more exposure you can get, the better. If a thousand people hear or read about the animal, you'll probably get no interest from 999, but you need only one person to provide a good home for the cat, and that's the one you need to reach.

✔ **Ask lots of questions and verify that the answers are true.** Don't forget to ask prospective adopters whether they've had pets before and what happened to them. Make sure you're dealing with people who realize that owning a pet is a long-term commitment.

✔ **Take your cat to a shelter if time runs out.** Sad to say, better a small chance at adoption and a painless death than a short life of suffering and fear. Do not take a cat "to the country" or otherwise turn him loose to fend for himself — people who live in the country can't care for the pets who are dumped. The kinder ones take them to the shelter; others shoot them, poison them, or drown them. Even in "the wilderness," the lives of feral cats are full of suffering, shortened by disease or accident. Don't put a cat through this horror: Take him to the shelter if you can't find him a home.

During "kitten season" — late spring and summer in North America — more kittens are born than find homes. Some, all, or none of these babies may have been adopted — and the remainder were likely euthanized.

Photo courtesy of Richard D. Schmidt.

To ensure a safe pregnancy and a healthy birth, your veterinarian may suggest basic blood work to establish baseline readings and spot any potential problems. An ultrasound can be useful early on to diagnose pregnancy and later to assess fetal age, viability, and development. X rays after the 45th day can be helpful in determining the number of kittens and their relative size so you know what to expect and when and can therefore better evaluate the situation as your cat's actually giving birth.

Follow your veterinarian's suggestions for prenatal care and don't give your pet vitamins, medications, or other supplements without discussing them with your veterinarian first.

Your cat becomes restless about two weeks before giving birth, searching for a safe place to have her babies. She should be confined at this time to the house — if she's not an indoor cat already — and provided with a box in which to give birth. Even better, confine her to a single room — your bedroom, ideally.

This *queening* box can be a cardboard box with one side cut down or the bottom half of a medium-sized plastic carrier. Place the box in a spot where she feels safe — a dim corner of a room that you can keep warm and dry — and line the box with newspapers. Put her food and water dishes and the litter box nearby but not right next to the queening box.

Some breeders dislike using newspapers in the queening box because of the ink. Many newspapers sell the ends of newsprint rolls at a low cost. Check with your local newspaper to see whether this clean newsprint is available.

Keep your cat sequestered in her room. If you let her out into the house, she may have her kittens in a laundry basket or opened dresser drawer; if you let her out of the house entirely, she may have them under the front porch.

Happy Birth Day, Babies

The usual length of a pregnancy is 66 days from ovulation, but because ovulation occurs after mating — and you may not know when your cat mated anyway — you may have a hard time figuring out her "due date." Let her physical symptoms and "nesting" behavior be your guide as to when to confine her.

Your cat's temperature — normally between 100.4°F. and 102.5°F. — falls two to three degrees in the first stage of labor, but most pet owners are probably better off not bothering with temperature-taking at this stage. Instead, watch for enlarged nipples and the secretion of a tiny amount of milk. Your cat may accept some food if offered, or she may just be content to rest in her box, purring and waiting.

Your cat is usually best left to her own devices, but take the time to collect a few "just-in-case" items — some clean towels, Betadine antiseptic, scissors, a spool of thread, and a baby syringe. If your cat is a longhair, trim the fur around under her tail, at the back of her legs, and around her nipples. Finally, have your veterinarian's number at hand and check to make sure she's available for after-hours calls; if not, ask her to recommend the number of an emergency clinic. Keep that number on hand, too, and know where the clinic is located in case you need to take your cat and her kittens in.

Special delivery!

The best thing you can do for your cat at the time of delivery is to ensure her maternity suite doesn't turn into a circus. Respect her privacy during this quiet time: If your children want to watch, that's fine, but have them keep a few feet away and quiet. (They may remain speechless anyway, because the birth process is so riveting!)

The active stage of labor is characterized by straining and a discharge that begins as watery but then becomes darker. The first kitten usually appears within an hour, wrapped in a translucent membrane known as the *amniotic sac,* which the mother bites to release the kitten, licking the baby's face to start his breathing.

Although you're usually best off leaving the mother alone, if she doesn't attend to her kitten within a minute or so, you can peel away the membrane and rub the kitten with a towel to start his breathing. Tie the umbilical cord off with a piece of thread about one inch out and cut the cord with scissors just outside the tie; then dab the tip with Betadine and place the baby at the mother's side. If the kitten isn't breathing, remove the fluid from his mouth with the baby syringe; then hold the kitten carefully in your hand — supporting his head carefully and securely — and swing him downward abruptly two or three times. Clear the fluid again if the kitten still isn't breathing and then swing him again. You may not be able to save the kitten, but at least you'll know you tried.

Subsequent kittens are born at intervals of 30 minutes to an hour, with the *placenta,* the tissue that attaches the kitten to the womb, coming within 15 to 30 minutes after each kitten — or sometimes all the placentas at once, if the delivery was rapid.

You need to discuss the situation with your veterinarian if your cat hasn't delivered her kittens by the 70th day after her first breeding. You need to call your veterinarian *immediately* if any of the following occur:

- ✔ Your cat has had strong, persistent contractions for more than 30 minutes or has been actively straining for an hour without the expulsion of a fetus.

- ✔ Your cat rests (with no straining) for more than four hours after the first kitten is born.

- ✔ Your cat's contractions are weak or irregular beyond two or three hours.

- ✔ Your cat starts vomiting, appearing weak, panting or breathing rapidly, or crying or showing any other signs of undue pain.

- ✔ Your cat discharges material that is yellow or white or seems exceptionally bloody.

- ✔ Your cat doesn't deliver a placenta for each kitten.

After the birth

A normal cat eats the placentas and tears the umbilical cord; if left to her own devices, she probably eats any stillborn kittens as well. As distasteful as this act seems to us, it's perfectly normal behavior. You probably want to wrap up any dead kittens in newspaper and dispose of them properly — call your veterinarian or animal-control department for guidance.

Some breeders remove the placentas as well, and that's fine, too, but make sure you have one for each kitten.

Kittens are born blind and deaf, but they have their sense of smell and they use it to find their mother's nipples. The first milk they take in is very important — called *colostrum,* it contains antibodies from the mother and other important substances that give the kittens initial protection against diseases at a time when their own immune systems are not yet functioning well.

If the family appears healthy and content, check on them but leave them pretty much alone for the first two weeks. Call your veterinarian if the mother or kittens appear agitated or listless.

If the kittens are not thriving, or the mother becomes ill, you must step in to care for them, tube-feeding and, later, bottle-feeding them. This task is an around-the-clock job, and you need to discuss with your veterinarian what and when to feed the kittens. If you're lucky, your veterinarian may know of another cat with kittens who can care for yours as well; if not, your kittens' survival is up to you!

Kitten Development

Cats have been raising kittens without much assistance from humans for thousands of years, and things usually go along just fine if you let your cat handle her babies on her own. Watching kittens develop is a rare opportunity, however, and you want to take plenty of time to enjoy the experience.

If the mama cat and her babies appear healthy and content, leave them alone as much as possible in the first two weeks.

Photo courtesy of Linda Stark.

Your role as a "grandparent"

Cats are generally wonderful mothers, caring for their kittens diligently and lovingly and moving them to safety at the first sign of trouble. They teach them to use the litter box and play nicely with their siblings, and they often teach them the hunting skills they need should they fall on hard times.

With such a capable mother, do you really need to do anything to ensure that your cat's kittens grow up to be loving pets?

Yes, you do.

A mother cat can teach her babies to be a cat, but she can't teach them everything they need to know about living in the world of humans. For kittens to become confident, outgoing adults, they need to be exposed early to the realities of life among the two-legged.

Handle the kittens after the first couple of weeks, and have other people over to handle them, too: men and women, children and adults — the more the merrier! Make sure all the interactions are positive and gentle. Kittens who miss out on human contact before the age of 12 weeks or so may always be nervous or even aggressive around people.

Supervised exposure to other pets, especially dogs, is important, too, so that your kittens can easily handle being placed in homes with other pets.

The best thing about your role as "grandparent"? It's fun! Play with the kittens all you want — it's good for you all.

Birth to two weeks

Growth is the priority these first couple of weeks, as the kittens nurse constantly and double their weight in the first week. Their mother is constantly in attendance, providing them with milk and licking them to stimulate them to release their waste, which she eats. Umbilical cords fall off in two to three days, and eyes start opening after about a week to ten days.

Leave the litter alone as much as possible, checking only to ensure that everyone is comfortable and eating well.

If you were planning to let your cat have "just one litter," don't wait long to get her spayed. The kittens are barely weaned before your cat can get pregnant again. When you take your cat and her kittens in to be checked out by your veterinarian, discuss when to have her spayed — and make an appointment!

Two weeks to eight weeks

The kittens' hearing and vision mature between two and five weeks, and by the fourth week, the babies begin to walk, run, and even jump, becoming agile and fast-moving surprisingly quickly. Still, their mother looks after them, reacting to their cries and bringing them home in her mouth if they stray too far. The first kitten teeth appear about the same time their eyes open.

After about three weeks, the mother starts to tire of nursing; this period is when you can begin to wean the kittens and step up your gentle handling of them. The mother is still involved with her babies, however; this period is when she begins to teach them to hunt.

Make solid food available to the kittens from three weeks on; softening dry food with warm water and placing a dab on a kitten's nose makes the transition easier. The mother helps by becoming increasingly unavailable for nursing, and the kittens should be completely weaned by the age of seven weeks or so.

Give the kittens access to a litter box from the age of three weeks on, and they'll learn from their mother how to use it.

Don't allow your kittens to think human fingers and feet are for pouncing, or you could be setting yourself up — or setting up your kittens' future owners — for problems later on. Stop the game if kittens attack, even in play. Better yet: Use interactive toys, such as a cat fishing pole or toy on a string, to play with your babies.

Sometimes gender is hard to determine in kittens. Lift up the tails and compare. Your veterinarian can help if you just can't make heads or tails of it.

Male on the left and female on the right.

Eight weeks to fourteen weeks

By the age of two months, kittens have teeth, all their senses, and are nimble and playful. This stage is a great deal of fun for the owner, and you hardly need to be convinced to play with your kittens, getting them used to a lot of handling.

Although some people start giving away kittens as soon as they're weaned, they're best off staying with their mother and littermates for the first 12 to 14 weeks. Kittens who're removed from their littermates and mother may have a difficult time as adults in accepting other cats.

Still, this time is good to start lining up homes for your babies. (See the section "Saying Goodbye to the Babies," later in this chapter.) Now's the time, too, to take them to your veterinarian for health checks and any vaccinations, wormings, or other preventive-health measures your vet recommends.

The adolescent kitten

If you keep any kittens, you get to continue to enjoy their development. Kittenhood ends at sexual maturity — which may come as early as five months of age — although your young one may continue to act kittenish at times for the first year.

Kittens grow up very fast and can have kittens of their own before you think possible. Discuss spaying and neutering with your veterinarian at the earliest opportunity, or you may end up dealing with a new crop of babies soon.

Saying Goodbye to the Babies

If you've done your job right, you have something truly remarkable to offer: fat, friendly, well-socialized kittens who promise a lifetime of good health and companionship. You want to make sure that the people who take them are worthy of such wonderful babies.

Kittens are so cute that you can "get rid of" them in minutes by giving them away in front of the closest grocery store, but we hope you don't want your babies to go to just anyone you aren't reasonably sure plans to take good care of them. The problem with casually acquired pets is that people are all too often casual about them — they've picked them up on impulse and may dump them just as fast.

Please take the time to place your kittens in good homes. Take out an ad in the newspaper and put up flyers, but make sure you carefully screen those people who're interested. If your cat is pedigreed and you've been working with a reputable breeder, ask for her help in placing the kittens. She may have a waiting list!

Pedigreed or just simply adorable, every kitten deserves a responsible home. Here are some questions you can ask of potential adopters to ensure your babies find one:

- ✔ **Have you had cats before? What happened to them?** Wrong answers include "lots" and "they ran away," "we moved," or "he got hit." Accidents happen to even the most conscientious of pet lovers, but a pattern of mishaps says a great deal about the way the prospective buyer treats cats — and it's not well.

- ✔ **What's your living arrangement?** Cats can handle nearly any kind of household: big families and singles, city apartments and rural acreage, stay-at-home seniors, and busy career people. What you're looking for is a person who has given a great deal of thought to the responsibility of keeping an animal and who's prepared to ensure your kitten's needs will be met. Some breeders refuse to place kittens with people who aren't willing to keep them exclusively inside, and if you feel strongly about the issue, you can do so, too.

- ✔ **Do you have children? What ages?** If you sense you're dealing with a person who doesn't care what her children do, you could be putting a fragile kitten in a very dangerous environment. Listen for the person who realizes an animal is a part of the family, not a toy for the kids.

- ✔ **Do you intend to breed your cat? Declaw her?** Again, the "right" answers depend on your own views. If you're against declawing (or against "automatic" declawing before even a sign of behavioral problems), you can use this time as a chance to educate. If you're offering pedigreed kittens who aren't breeding quality, sell them with "nonbreeding" registration or hold the papers until the buyer gives you proof of spaying or neutering. Some breeders also offer rebates on the purchase price for proof of altering. Better yet: Spay or neuter the kittens before they go to new homes. (See the sidebar "Spaying and neutering kittens," later in this chapter.)

Be cordial and informative with buyers, but be persistent. Ask to see a driver's license. Check references, including calling the person's veterinarian. A person who has owned numerous pets and *doesn't* have a veterinary reference is another to cross off your list. Don't be afraid to turn people down. Although doing so may not be pleasant, you must do what's best for your kittens! You've put a lot of effort into them, and you want them to live with someone who's going to continue to love and care for them as you have.

Remember, always, that you want your kittens to go to good homes, and the *only one* who has a chance at making that happen is you.

Look, we don't want to scare you — well, maybe a little — but we do want you to be careful. The world's full of scary people. Here's a story about one of them: A serial killer went to the same high school that Gina did, and after he was caught, the police discovered that, before he killed people, he'd "practiced" on free-to-good-home animals, including *lots* of kittens. *Please* don't make "he wanted one and came right over" the only criterion for someone adopting one of your babies!

Spaying and neutering kittens

One surefire way to make sure you're not adding to the problem of pet overpopulation is to spay and neuter your kittens before they go to their new homes.

Ask your veterinarian whether early altering is appropriate for your kittens. The procedures have traditionally been performed starting at the age of five months, but in recent years *early spay-neuters* on kittens as young as eight weeks old have been widely approved by veterinary and humane groups and breed registries. Many shelters now alter kittens before they're adopted in an effort to stop the revolving door of "kitten out, kittens in" that so many struggle with. An increasing number of reputable breeders also spay or neuter kittens they don't intend to show before they go to their new homes.

Yes, this procedure involves an added expense, but some adopters may appreciate the convenience and the sign that they're dealing with someone who has the best interests of the cats in mind. Adjust your price to cover the cost of the surgery — or ask for the cost of the surgery if you were planning to just give the kittens away.

Chapter 15

Travel and Your Cat

· ·

In This Chapter

▶ Should your cat travel?

▶ Pet sitters and boarding

▶ Traveling by air

▶ Traveling by car

▶ Easing your cat through a change of address

· ·

*I*f you left the decision to your cat, the chances are good that neither of you would ever go anywhere. Not to work. Not to a lovely getaway weekend with the two-legged love of your life. And certainly not to the veterinarian. Cats love routine, they love territory, and they *especially* love routine *in* their territory. If they had their choice, you'd be home all the time, catering to their every whim for food, play, and petting, admiring their beauty as they settle into that warm sunlit patch on the living-room armchair for the first, fourth, or tenth of the day's oh-so-essential catnaps.

A well-run home, meals on time, warm places to sleep, and the attentions of a loving human — to a cat, this is heaven.

To humans, however, such an existence is boring. We're a considerably more nomadic lot than our cats are, and most of us love an occasional change of scenery every bit as much as we appreciate the comforts of our homes. Then, too, sometimes the choice to travel is not ours, with family, friends, and work keeping us moving — to that business conference a half-day's flight away, to our friend Peg's wedding, or to our Uncle Joe's funeral.

No matter where you're going and why, you want to make sure your cat is covered and as happy as can be under the circumstances. Most times you go away, you're leaving your cat behind, but if you're taking her with you, you want to make the journey as safe and comfortable as possible for her. And if you can't have her with you, you want to make sure her needs are provided for by pet-sitters or boarding facilities so that you don't need to worry.

We certainly don't want you to worry, whether you take your cat or leave her behind. This is why we're going to tell you everything you need to know to make the right choices for your pet, whether you're going away for the weekend or picking up stakes and moving your household — cat included, of course — cross-country. You want your cat to be happy. And so do we.

Although most cats would prefer to avoid a life on the road, a few handle the challenges well. Put in this category not only top show cats, but also show-*biz* cats, who travel with their trainers for work in television, movies, and advertising. For the ultimate cat-travel story, however, check out the experiences of Peter Gether's Scottish Fold, Norton, in his books *The Cat Who Went to Paris* and *A Cat Abroad: The Further Adventures of Norton, the Cat Who Went to Paris, and His Human* (both in paperback from Fawcett). What a cat!

Most cats would rather snooze at home than travel, and Noodles is definitely one of them.

Photo courtesy of Richard D. Schmidt.

Is Your Cat Up to Travel?

Not that many cats take to travel the way dogs do, and if you want yours to have a chance at enjoying a life on the road, you probably need to start when your pet is a kitten. An adult can be more difficult to introduce to new places and people and may never adjust.

Some trips aren't avoidable, especially if you're moving. (See the section "Moving Your Cat to a New Home" later in this chapter.) How much discretionary travel you attempt with your cat is going to pretty much be up to your cat and comes down to two questions: Is your pet healthy enough to travel? Does your pet have the personality to adapt to travel?

You must answer those questions for yourself with input from your veterinarian and, of course, your cat. And maybe experiment a little with some short pleasure trips to make sure that they're a pleasure for you both. Like Norton, the "Cat Who Went to Paris," some cats are made for a life lapping cream in French cafés; others are delighted to be traveling comfortably in a well-equipped motor home. Maybe your pet is one of these vagabonds!

The trip almost no cat likes is the one to the veterinary hospital. We've put tips on making that particular journey easier — for you, your cat, and your veterinarian — in Chapter 9.

Health considerations

Before undertaking anything more than a cross-town trip with your cat, you need to take her to the veterinarian to make sure she's in good health and current on all the preventive-care measures your veterinarian recommends. A cat who's in poor health is not well-suited to be a traveling companion.

Talk to your veterinarian about your travel and your concerns for your cat. If you're traveling by air, you need a health certificate. (You find more information on air travel in the section "Taking Your Pet with You" later in this chapter.) If you're traveling by car or by air, remember to ask for a copy of your cat's vaccination record, especially rabies. The thought that your cat may bite someone or tangle with a wild creature is horrible, but in case she does, you want to have proof of her rabies vaccination with you.

If you think your cat may be better off traveling sedated, discuss this option with your veterinarian.

If your cat is a Persian or Exotic Shorthair — or any mix that has these breeds' trademark short muzzles — traveling may be a real hazard. That's because breathing is more difficult for these short-faced pets. Air travel in a cargo hold should probably be completely ruled out, and you should ask your veterinarian what can ensure your pet's safety any time that you must travel with her.

Temperament considerations

You know your cat better than anyone else. Is she shy and nervous or relaxed and outgoing? Does she adjust well to change? To noise? To changes in feed time or location? If your cat takes two days to "chill out" after a short car trip, you may need to decide that only essential trips are in her future.

If your cat is borderline, however, give her a chance. You may both enjoy the extra time together, wherever you are.

Leaving Your Pet Behind

You need to know what to do if you can't take your cat with you, which is probably most of the time you're away from home. Your cat may not be one of those rare ones who enjoys the challenge, and even if he is, you can't always take him along. Business travel is necessary, after all, and so, too, is that emergency trip cross-country to handle the estate of a relative. Another place you may need to go where your cat can't is the hospital.

Ask your friends, neighbors, and coworkers what they do with their cats when they're gone. Ask your veterinarian, too, for referrals to pet-sitters or boarding facilities, if he doesn't have his own boarding facilities.

If you have a service in mind, whether a boarding facility or sitter, call and ask for references and then check them out — a step few people take. Ask about professional affiliations, such as the American Boarding Kennel Association or National Association of Pet Sitters, both of which offer materials and training to U.S. and Canadian members to encourage a higher degree of performance from their members.

No matter what kind of care you choose for your pet while you're gone, make your arrangements early. Pet-sitters and boarding facilities are booked weeks and sometimes months in advance for peak travel times, such as summer or the winter holidays.

Prepare for emergencies

One of the easiest things to overlook in leaving your pet behind — whether with a friend, a pet sitter, or a boarding facility — is how you want him cared for should he become ill. Discuss care options with your veterinarian in advance and then clue in the person who's caring for your cat.

Setting up emergency-care arrangements works best if you have a good relationship with your veterinarian — but then, so does everything else concerning your pet's health. Gina's veterinarian knows the kind of health care she expects, and she trusts his judgment if he can't get in touch with her. In her pets' records is a note from him saying that, no matter who shows up with her animals, the hospital is to provide care, and her credit card number is on file to handle the charges.

You're well-advised to set up a similar relationship regarding your cat so that his care is something you don't need to worry about while you're away. Touch base with your veterinarian on this point at your cat's annual exam or before you leave him to go on a trip to make sure that no misunderstandings come up.

For the ultimate in preparing for a trip where you can't take your pet, see the information in Chapter 11 on providing for your cat in your will.

Pet sitters

A wide range of services is lumped under the general title of *pet sitter*, covering everything from a reciprocal agreement between friends to care for each other's pets, to paying a neighbor kid to look in on your cat, to hiring a professional pet-sitting service to care for your pet in your own home.

The benefits of having your pet stay in your own home is that she's familiar with the surroundings — which is a very important consideration where cats are concerned. And pet sitters can do more than just look in on your pet: They can take in your mail and newspaper, water your houseplants, and turn lights on and off.

Make sure you discuss services and prices beforehand, and if you're dealing with a service, make sure that they're bonded and insured.

The biggest drawback to pet sitters is that your pet is left alone a great deal of the time, because most pet sitters probably can't spend all that much time giving your pet individual attention. (An arrangement with a young person — or a house-sitter to stay in your home while you're gone — may give your pet more opportunities to be petted or played with.) If your pet becomes ill or manages to escape, a pet sitter may not come back to notice before some time has passed. And, finally, some people just aren't comfortable having people in their home while they're gone.

Informal arrangements for house-sitting — actually having the person move in while you're gone — or pet sitting — having the person just drop in once or twice a day to check on your cat — can be even trickier than hiring a professional service. Just ask the friend of Gina's who left her house and pets in the care of a friend's college-aged daughter, only to find out that the young woman had been anything but a quiet resident. She'd had guests and even parties. The house was a bit worse for wear, but at least the pets were fine! If you're going to go with a young person — and many people do, with no regrets — make sure that parental oversight is part of the picture.

We think one of the best solutions is to *trade* pet sitting. Most animal lovers have friends who also have pets, and making a deal with one of your friends to cover each other whenever you're gone can work out very well. Trading care is a solution that's both reassuring — if you have friends who love animals as much as you do, that is — and inexpensive. All the arrangement requires is your own time in return.

Boarding facilities

Boarding facilities are another option, ideal for friendly, well-adjusted cats. Despite all the recommendations in the world, however, don't leave your pet at a business you haven't inspected yourself. You should see clean, comfortable, and well-maintained facilities, and if you don't, go elsewhere.

Ask where your pet would stay and ask to see the premises. Make sure your cat would be housed completely away from dogs and separated from other cats — although your own cats can be housed together, unacquainted cats should *never* be mixed.

The facility operators should seem sincerely interested in tailoring their facility to make your cat's stay more comfortable. They should be prepared to feed your cat as you do, especially if he's on a special diet, and they should be willing to allow you to leave behind toys or articles containing your smell — a dirty sock, for example — to reassure your pet.

Boarding your cat has a few advantages over hiring a pet-sitting service. Boarding facilities are usually very secure, and the best ones always have someone on-site to check in on your cat. Some businesses make up for the fact that they're out in the sticks by picking up and delivering your pet.

If you don't have a home yet in a city you're moving to, a reputable boarding facility may meet your pet at the airport in advance of your arrival and care for her until you get there. Alternatively, you can often leave your pet while you're house-hunting and arrange for the facility to ship her after you find suitable lodgings. (See the section "Air travel" later in this chapter.) In general, we prefer to recommend accompanied air travel, but your circumstances may not permit it, and if that's the case, a reputable boarding facility can help.

Many veterinarians have boarding facilities, too, and if yours is among them, this option may well be the best boarding choice for your pet. The biggest advantage is that the staff is already familiar with your pet and her medical background — a real plus if your cat is elderly or has a chronic health condition.

Do not patronize a boarding facility that does not ask you for proof of up-to-date vaccinations. If they do not insist that *your* pet is healthy and well-protected from disease, they're not asking these questions of other boarders, either, and that puts your pet at risk.

No matter what, we don't recommend boarding a kitten who hasn't had all his vaccinations. The increased possibility for disease isn't worth the risk.

Taking Your Pet with You

No matter if by car or air, traveling with your cat is easier if you plan ahead and bring gear to make the trip easier. You need to travel a bit more lightly if going by air, but if you're heading out by car, load up!

Note: We've covered only air and automobile travel because for most people those are the only options. Most cruise ships usually don't allow animals, nor do many bus or rail lines, including Amtrak.

The following list describes some travel essentials for your cat. Check out Chapter 6 for more information on choosing pet supplies and the Additional Resources appendix at the end of this book for contact information on pet-supply catalogs.

- **Carrier.** An airline-approved travel carrier — also called a *crate* — can get you through any situation with your cat. Shop around for value but don't skimp on quality: Get a sturdy crate made of high-impact plastic, large enough for your cat to stand up and turn around in and not much more. This carrier can safely take your cat to the veterinarian and around the world, if need be, and is the most essential piece of travel gear for any cat.

  If you're going to travel cross-country in a car, you may want to get a larger carrier, sized for a medium-sized dog, so that you have room for a litter box inside the crate on a long drive. Another carrier option is a soft-sided bag (we like the ones made by Sherpa), which may be more comfortable for you and your pet if you're traveling by air — but *only* if he's with you in the passenger compartment. You need a hard-plastic, airline-approved carrier for use in the cargo hold.

✔ **Harness, ID, and leash.** A frightened or startled cat is harder to hold onto than a hot frying pan. Make sure that, if yours wriggles out of your grasp, he's going no farther than the end of a leash. Keep a cat harness with an ID tag on him and keep a leash attached to it anytime he's out of the crate. One nice leash for travel is a reel-type Flexi; the smallest size is lightweight enough for cats and gives your pet 10 feet of freedom.

✔ **Litter box and filler.** Although we generally recommend sticking with your cat's regular brand, you're likely to find that clumping litter is easiest to deal with on the road. Don't forget to pack a litter scoop and air-tight, sealable plastic bags for keeping clumps smell-free until you can put them in a trash bin. You may find disposable cardboard litter boxes easiest to deal with, especially if you're not using clumping litter — just toss litter and box as needed, even daily. Another possibility is buying a plastic storage bin with a snap-on lid. Although it doesn't fit in a crate, such a bin holds a trip's worth of clumping litter without spilling — just keep the lid on except when you're offering your pet a potty break in the bin. And keep the clumps removed.

✔ **Food and water and bowls to put them in.** Pack your pet's regular rations and, if you're using moist food, don't forget a fork and a can opener (or choose pop tops). Keep a bottle of water in the car so your cat can always have a fresh drink and offer refreshment often. Another possibility is to use a hanging bottle on the crate. These bottles come in sizes appropriate for animals from mice to Great Danes; look for one sized for a cat or a rabbit. Finally, don't forget some treats.

✔ **First-aid and grooming supplies.** Keep a basic first-aid kit at hand and pack in a comb and a brush as well. Don't forget to bring along any regular medication your cat needs, too. For more information on the contents of a first-aid kit, see the Cheat Sheet at the front of this book or buy a ready-made kit. We list a contact number for one such manufacturer, PET-PAK, Inc., in the Additional Resources appendix.

✔ **Paper towels and a spray bottle of a general-purpose cleaner.** You're going to need these, we promise. Throw in a few old towels, too. They're good for beds, restraints in an emergency — see Chapter 10 for more information on emergencies — and for any kind of cleanup. Aerosol air freshener is another good thing to bring.

✔ **A couple of your cat's favorite toys, including an interactive one such as a cat fishing pole or a toy on a string.** Hey, what else are you going to do in a motel room besides keep your cat amused?

✔ **Travel guides.** Although cats are a lot easier to get into hotels, motels, and inns than are dogs (and a hundred times easier to sneak in, in a pinch, but we didn't say so), you're still going to need a reference to find out which places welcome pets. AAA and Mobil travel guides note where pets are welcome, and many books are out there that deal exclusively with traveling with your pet.

Now, obviously, you're going to tailor what you bring to the kind of trip you're taking. You aren't going to pack everything for a short air trip, but you need the lot if you're traveling hundreds of miles by car.

Air travel

Although horror stories make the news, the truth is that airline travel is relatively safe for most pets and it can be for yours, too, if you play by the rules, plan carefully, and are prepared to be a little pushy on your cat's behalf.

Animals move through the airline system in two ways: As cargo or as accompanied baggage. Your cat is better off if you're traveling with him so that you can make sure he's well-cared-for.

Some airlines allow animals in the passenger cabin if their carriers can fit in the space beneath the seat, which is true in the case of most cats. *This is by far the best way your cat can fly, because he never leaves your care during the course of the trip.* Not all airlines allow animals to travel in the cabin, however, and others put a limit on the number of pets in the cabin, so making your arrangements far in advance pays. *Check and double-check.*

If your cat isn't allowed in the cabin, he flies below, in a pressurized cargo hold. This situation isn't ideal, but many cats do fine with it. The Air Transport Association estimates that more than a half a million dogs and cats are transported on commercial airlines each year, and the industry group insists that 99 percent reach their destination without incident.

To make sure your pet is one of them, pay careful attention to the following tips:

- **Talk to the airline.** Some carriers — especially the new, no-frills companies — don't take animals at all. Even those that do have limits to the number of animals on a flight, both in the passenger cabin and the cargo hold. You also need to know where and when your pet must be presented and what papers — health certificate and so on — you need to bring.

- **Make sure your pet is in good health and isn't one of the short-nosed breeds.** These cats find breathing a little difficult under the best of circumstances, and the stress of airline travel may be more than they can handle. Talk to your veterinarian in advance about any concerns.

- **Make sure your cat is traveling in an approved carrier that has contact phone numbers for where you can be reached at both ends of the journey.** (Your home number doesn't help if you're not at home.) Whether you carry your pet on board into the passenger cabin or must check him as cargo, make sure that the carrier has ID on it. By law, the carrier should be just big enough for your cat to stand up and turn around in.

The best way for your cat to fly is in the passenger cabin with you, and if his carrier fits under the seat, many airlines allow it.

Make sure all the bolts securing the halves of the carriers are in place and tightened before checking in your pet. Don't forget to put a safe harness and ID on your pet. In addition, you may want to consider having him microchipped before travel. (See Chapter 6 for more information on microchipping.)

✔ **Don't ship your pet if the weather is bad or when air traffic is heaviest.** Avoid peak travel days such as around the Christmas holidays and make sure you choose flights that are on the ground when the temperature is neither too hot nor too cold, not only at the departure airport, but also at the connecting and arriving airports. Although temperature doesn't make a difference if your pet's up top with you, it makes a big difference below: Cargo holds aren't heated or cooled. In summer, a night flight is likely better, while the reverse is true in the winter. Be aware that there are regulations regarding the range of temperatures when a pet may be shipped. If the temperature on the ground in your departing, connecting, or arriving city falls outside these limits, you may run into unexpected delays or cancellations of your pet's travel plans. Plan ahead.

✔ **Choose a direct flight; if that's not possible, try for a route with a short layover.** Most pet fatalities occur on the ground, when animals are left in their crates on the hot tarmac or in stifling cargo holds. Direct flights eliminate layovers, and short layovers reduce the time on the ground.

> ✔ **Remember that your cat's life depends on the attentiveness of airline personnel if he's not in your care in the passenger cabin.** Most of these employees are excellent and caring, but mistakes do happen. You should be prepared to pester airline personnel to confirm that your pet has been loaded and has made the same connections you have. If your pet is flying unaccompanied, talk to freight-handling personnel at every airport your cat visits. Be polite but persistent; don't take "I'm sure he's fine; have some delicious honey-roasted peanuts" as an answer from a flight attendant. Make the staff *check* and report back.

Contrary to popular belief, you're generally better off *not* having your cat tranquilized before flying. The combination of high altitude and limited oxygen is a challenge your pet's body is better prepared to meet if she's not sedated. Still, your pet may be an exception. In the end, you and your veterinarian should decide on this issue.

The Air Transport Association has a free booklet, *Air Travel for Your Dog or Cat*. The booklet is available by sending a self-addressed, stamped, business-sized envelope to: ATA, 1301 Pennsylvania Blvd. N.W., Suite 1100, Washington, D.C. 20004.

Car travel

We know you love your cat's company. We know that you love his purrfect puss. We also know that, for safety's sake, your pet should be out of sight whenever the car is moving, appropriately confined in his carrier. A loose cat in a car is a danger that shouldn't be risked — even if he doesn't get under your feet, he could get up so far under the seat that you have a very hard time getting him out after you stop.

Your cat may be more comfortable — and certainly more quiet — if you cover his crate with a towel while the car is in motion. Experiment to see which method your cat likes best. If your cat doesn't stop crying no matter what, bring along a squirt bottle and give him a shot of water whenever he pipes up. Either that or bring plenty of headache remedy, because after a few minutes of listening, you're going to need it.

Your cat can go for as long as you can without stretching his legs. After you stop, put on his leash for safety before you let him out into the car and offer him water and a litter break — unless both are already available in his crate. Food is probably best left for morning and night in your motel room.

Never leave your cat unattended in a car — if the heat doesn't get him, a thief may. If you're traveling with your cat, your meals are mostly going to be of the drive-through variety. If you absolutely must leave your cat in the car — for your bathroom break, for example — park in the shade, roll the windows down a little, and be *quick* — and we mean like five minutes. Even better, take your cat and his carrier inside the stall with you. He has seen you in there before; he's not going to be shocked.

If you want to kick around for a while, shopping and sightseeing, and still make sure your cat is safe, look up a local veterinarian in the phone book and see whether you can make arrangements for a few hour's boarding. Gina has done so for years and found most veterinarians very amenable to helping out — usually at a very reasonable cost. You can also leave your pet in your motel room — but always in a crate for safety.

Moving Your Cat to a New Home

For many cats, one of the most stressful events of their lives is a pretty distracting time for their owners as well — changing addresses. Combine traveling with suddenly being in unfamiliar surroundings — which may even smell like former animal occupants! — and you can easily understand why more than a few cats spend a very long time freaked out and hiding under a bed after a move.

Your cat thinks the place you're in now is just perfect, but because he really doesn't get to vote, you need to make sure you make the move as easy on him as possible. The key to success is to keep your cat secure before, during, and after — to anticipate problems and make sure your cat is as comfortable as possible at every stage of the game.

One way to up the security factor is to order an ID tag with your new address and phone number as soon as you know them. That way, you can make sure that the new information is securely on your cat's collar before any packing begins. If you're traveling a long distance to your new home, use paper-key tags (available very cheaply from your local hardware or variety store) for temporary ID — jot your daily information, such as the name, phone number, and room number, on the tag and put it on your cat's collar. (More information on collars and ID is in Chapter 6.)

Using a safe room for moving

The best way to move your cat is to confine him to a *safe room* before and after the move. The ideal is a room where your cat isn't going to be disturbed — a spare bathroom is perfect — and outfit it with food and water, a litter box, a scratching post, a bed, and toys. Don't feel bad about confining your pet: He's more comfortable in a small space, and he isn't subjected to the stress of seeing people — perhaps strangers! — tromping out of the house with his belongings (a definition which, after all, applies to everything in your — um . . . we mean *his* — house).

Keeping
your cat
confined
before and
after you
move
makes the
transition
easier and
safer.

Confining your cat also prevents his slipping out, which is a danger at both the old home and the new. Your cat could easily become scared, take off, and get lost, even in his familiar neighborhood, if he gets disoriented. Even if your cat turns up back at your old place, a reunion can be hard to arrange if you need to leave before you find him, especially if you've moved to another city.

A safe room is also good for bringing a new cat into your home and for retraining any cat with furniture-destroying or litter-box-avoiding habits. For more information on how to use a safe room while introducing a new cat to your home, see Chapter 5. For help with feline behavior problems, see Chapter 13.

Your cat should be confined in his safe room the day before packing begins, moved to his new home in a carrier, and then confined again in his new safe room until the moving is over, the furniture arranged, and most of the dust settled.

A carrier is one of the best investments you can make in your cat's safety. For more information on choosing one, see Chapter 6. A carrier plays a crucial role in disaster-preparedness for pets; more information on planning for an emergency is in Chapter 18.

After everything's settled, open the door to the safe room and let your cat explore at will, on his terms — but just within the limits of the house. He still needs to be kept completely inside for a couple of weeks if he's not a completely indoor cat, to start him forming a bond with his new surroundings.

Trying to force a scared and stressed-out cat to do anything he doesn't want to is hazardous to your health. After you arrive at your new home, don't pull your cat out of his carrier. Instead, put the carrier in his safe room, open the carrier door, and let him come out into the room when he wants to — even if it's not for an hour or more. After he's a little calmer, you can coax him out with some fresh food or treats if you want, but don't rush him, and don't drag him out — or you may be bitten or scratched.

Leave the carrier in the safe room with the door removed. It is the most familiar place in your new home in your cat's mind and will likely be his chosen spot for a while until this new house becomes his new home.

Moving to a new home is a great time to convert your cat to an indoor-only pet. In your old home, he'd complain to the skies if you denied him access to his outside territory (until he got used to the fact that you're not letting him out, that is), but in a new home, his new territory is what you let him have and no more. The transition to his being an indoor-only cat isn't very hard on either of you and is certainly better for your cat in the long run.

Anticipating problems

Another good reason to start your cat off in a safe room after a move: Refreshing his training about your house rules, especially regarding destructive clawing, urine spraying, and litter-box avoidance — all behavioral problems that can spring up if your cat is stressed and disoriented.

By limiting your cat's options to the litter box and scratching post in his safe room, he quickly redevelops the good habits he had in your old home. After you start letting him out of the safe room to explore the rest of the house, add another litter box or two throughout the house to make the transition easier — you can gradually reduce the numbers later, after you're sure your pet's going where you want him to.

Although your cat's likely to settle back into his old, good habits in a couple of weeks if you keep him confined and allow him to relax, talk to your veterinarian about any problems that continue. Your cat may be ill, or he may need anti-anxiety medication to help him settle in. And don't forget to check out our section on behavior problems in Chapter 13.

Lost . . . and found, we hope

Although any cat can turn up missing at any time, moving is a time to be especially vigilant in protecting your cat.

Preventing a missing cat is a lot easier than trying to find one, which is why confinement indoors — permanent, ideally — is the number one way to keep your cat from getting lost.

Even indoor cats can slip out, though, which is why all pets should carry a current ID tag on their collar and even an imbedded microchip for permanent ID. (See Chapter 6 for more information on both.) Another just-in-case measure: Keep clear pictures of your cat on hand in case you need to throw together a "lost cat" flyer.

If your cat doesn't show up for dinner one night, don't just figure he's going to turn up in a day or so — take action! Place an ad in your local newspaper and get flyers made up for distribution using the picture, a description, and a reward, if you're offering one (and we recommend that you do).

Post the flyers around the neighborhood and take some to area shelters and veterinarians and especially to emergency clinics. Scan "found" ads in the paper and start checking the shelter every other day, in person.

Don't give up too soon: Pets have turned up weeks after their disappearance, so keep checking — and keep hoping.

Allowing time for readjustment

Your cat probably needs a couple weeks to settle into his new routine — to come out of the safe room, become familiar with the house, and use his scratching post and litter box normally again. Don't rush him. Be observant of the signs that your cat is becoming less tentative and more confident in his explorations, and above all, don't allow him outside until he's comfortable with the inside of your house.

Cat body language can be very subtle. Learn how to tell when your cat's relaxed, playful, or unhappy by reading Chapter 12.

If you're planning on letting your cat outside, take him out on a harness and leash and follow him around as he becomes familiar with the new area. Coax him back in by using praise and treats — let him walk in, if you can, instead of carrying him — and follow each outing with special play or petting time so that he develops a positive association with your new house and is therefore more likely to recognize it as home.

When is the right time to just let him loose? To be honest, it's always a gamble. Do your best to give your cat all the time he needs to settle in and then let him explore the outside for another week or more under your supervision. In the end, however, if you insist on letting your cat outdoors, you just must chance it and hope for the best. If you've taken the time your cat needs to adjust, he's probably going to stick around.

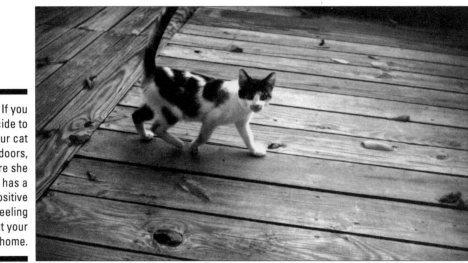

If you decide to let your cat outdoors, be sure she has a positive feeling about your new home.

Billie — Photo courtesy of Kathy Schutte.

The home-again cat

Because cats bond to places as well as to people, some cat lovers find that their free-roaming pets keep showing up at their old home after a move, especially if the new home isn't more than a couple miles from the old one.

If your pet is one of these home-again cats, the best suggestion we have for you is to convert your cat to an indoor pet, because crossing streets to go "home" considerably ups his risk factor — which is already much higher than an indoor cat's. (See Chapter 6 for the gear you need to keep your cat happy indoors.)

If permanent confinement is not possible, bring your cat inside for another couple weeks — you may have let him outdoors too soon. Dedicate extra time to playing with him, especially interactive games such as with a cat fishing pole or toy on a string. This extra time helps to relieve him of some of his stress or excess anxiety and helps him form new attachments to his new home and you in it.

Because unneutered males roam the most, having your cat altered if you haven't already done so is also a good idea.

After you let your cat outdoors again, make sure the new people at your old home aren't encouraging your cat to stay. Ask them not to feed him or pet him and to use a squirt bottle or other deterrent if they see him around.

Gina has an interesting case of a "home-again cat" who believes that her home is still his — fortunately, his new one is right next door. George, a marmalade tabby, was once owned by the former owners of Gina's house, who left him with the next-door neighbor after they moved. Although George and Gina's dog, Andy, are sworn enemies, the cat always knows when the dogs aren't home and Gina is — and he often pops in the pet door to say hello. Finding George's scent in the house later drives Andy crazy, which no doubt delights the gregarious tabby.

Chapter 16

Showing Off: You, Your Cat, and Feline Exhibitions

. . . .

In This Chapter

▶ The reason for cat shows

▶ An alphabet soup of cat registries

▶ Enjoying a show as a spectator

▶ How cat shows work

▶ Is your cat showable?

. . . .

A cat show must be one of the more pleasant ways a cat lover can spend an afternoon. From regional shows with a couple hundred entries to international events that draw more than a thousand top felines from several continents, a show is the place to see cats at their loveliest. With breeds ranging from the slender Siamese to the rugged Maine Coon, from the silkiest Birman to the near-naked Sphinx, a cat show is *the* place to see a variety of cats — to witness the preservation of the oldest of breeds and the ofttimes controversial creation of new ones. A show is also a place to talk cats with those who love them, to investigate a new breed or renew a love for an old one, to meet breeders, and to see the newest in cat gear at the vendors' tables that are a part of nearly every show.

For some, an afternoon at a show is just the beginning. Bitten by the show bug and pride in their own feline companion, they enter the next time, perhaps with a cat of no certain ancestry, and win a ribbon for their efforts. From there, the jump is natural to increased involvement, to weekend traveling for shows, to weeknights spent preparing cats for the ring, and to the eventual and seemingly inevitable founding of a cattery, with its own registered name and a considerable investment in breeding stock, housing, and cat care. A few people even become judges!

People who're involved in the sport of breeding and showing cats — known as the *cat fancy* — come from all backgrounds and every corner of the world, sharing only their firm belief that the cat is the most beautiful of all beings. For some, the sport is both an obsession and a love.

Whew! Don't say we didn't warn you if you end up a show judge! In the meantime, read on about the always fascinating, often confusing sport of cat shows.

Check out our introduction to the world of pedigreed cats, from Abyssinians to Turkish Vans, in Chapter 2.

The cat fancy is very progressive in welcoming *all* cats to its shows. You can find classes for *alters* (cats that have been spayed and neutered) as well as for *household pets* (not registered or random-bred cats) at most shows. These classes make cat shows a celebration of all things feline.

Why Do Cat Shows Exist?

People love to share their hobbies, both for the competition with and companionship of others who enjoy the same avocation. This fact is true whether a person is involved in restoring classic cars, raising roses, building models, or showing off domestic animals, be they cats, dogs, horses, or hamsters. Pride, competition, and companionship are part of the game if you're involved in cat shows — but that's not all.

One thing that show breeders don't get out of their hobby is rich. Breeding and showing top-quality pedigreed cats is an expensive proposition that the occasional sale of kittens can't begin to offset! Truly, this sport is an expression of love for cats — and pride in winning.

Preservation and development of breeds

Cat shows, like dog shows, have their modern roots in nineteenth-century England, where one of the pastimes of the land-owning classes became the preservation, refinement, and development of animal breeds — and cats were no exception. From country fairs to the first large urban shows held to the enthusiastic approval of high society, the idea of showing animals grew around the world.

The period of relative peace and affluence after World War II brought with it an explosion of interest in purebred animals, seen as a status symbol among the middle class. Some fanciers shifted into high gear by preserving old breeds, many of which had been decimated by war, while others made their own name developing new breeds, a process that continues to this day in breeds such as the controversial short-legged Munchkin cat.

Without cat shows, no place would exist for rewarding the best effort of breeders to develop and refine pedigreed cats.

Judging of breeding programs

Although you may think all the action in the cat fancy is as a cat show, these events are only the tip of the iceberg for the work of reputable breeders. You may think cats are being judged at these shows, but what's really under the judge's fingertips is a living representative of all the work that goes into producing a top show cat.

Behind every ribbon lie untold hours spent studying genetics and pedigrees in hopes of producing cats that are as near the standards of perfection as possible. (See the section "What judges look for," later in this chapter, to find out what judges are looking for.) Keeping cats well-cared-for and happy is another time-consuming part of living with show cats, as is enduring the extra annoyance of cats who exhibit the difficult personality traits that come from not being spayed or neutered.

Add to these labors of love the raising of kittens to be healthy, outgoing, and well-socialized for both pet homes and showing. Breeders are very picky about who gets their kittens, and the placement process takes time, too. As for the kittens they keep, breeders must raise them to be shown, getting them used to being handled and groomed.

The show ring is where it all comes together in just a few minutes that can seem much, much longer when you're watching your cat being judged and too very short after it's done. The cat-show judge is not an arbiter of capricious taste, but rather another tool to help the breeder steer her breeding program to the further good of her cats and her chosen breed.

Educational and charitable outreach

The cat fancy is interested in the welfare of all cats, not just pedigreed cats and not just domestic cats either. Many cat shows use their events to host educational seminars for the general public, where the ins and outs of cat-show judging are explained along with the correct ways of caring for cats. Printed information abounds as well, most of it free, not only on the various breeds but on general cat concerns as well.

Many shows also are benefits for various cat-related charities, from rescue-and-placement groups to organizations that work for the largest cousins of our domestic cats, such as endangered tigers. Other shows donate their proceeds from entry fees and renting floor space to vendors to health studies for all cats or disaster relief and shelters.

Two charitable organizations are affiliated with the Cat Fanciers' Association: the Winn Feline Foundation and the Cat Fanciers' Foundation. The Winn Feline Foundation, for which Paul is a veterinary consultant, is dedicated to raising money for studies to improve feline health. Since its founding

Cat shows are not only fun, but the judging is a valuable tool in steering breeding programs in the right direction.

Photo courtesy of Michael Brim, Cat Fanciers' Association.

in 1968, the foundation has raised more than $1.5 million for research on the health of all cats. The Cat Fanciers' Foundation was established in 1990 as a way to preserve for the public works of literature and art related to cats. The first major historical donation was the silver collar and medal given in 1895 to Cosey, the Maine Coon winner of the first major North American cat show. For information on contributing to either of these groups, see the Additional Resources appendix.

Cosey may have been the first cat to win in a large show in the United States of America, but the Madison Square Garden event wasn't the world's first modern cat show. Credit for that goes to the United Kingdom, where, in 1871, a cat show was held at the Crystal Palace in London. According to feline expert Desmond Morris, in his book *CatWorld: A Feline Encyclopedia* (Penguin Reference), the show was so successful that another was quickly organized, drawing nearly 20,000 spectators to the one-day event.

Who Gives Shows?

Unlike the dog-show world, which is dominated by massive and powerful national organizations such as the Kennel Club in the United Kingdom or the American Kennel Club in the United States, cat shows are run under the

Enjoying a day at a show

You don't need to know the difference between a Grand Champion and a Triple Champion or a Maine Coon Cat or Norwegian Forest Cat to enjoy a day at a cat show. Bring your natural curiosity, your love of cats, and your credit card, and you can have a wonderful time. Here are a few tips to make the day easier:

✔ **Wear comfortable, casual clothes with a little flexibility.** Show halls are notorious for being too hot or too cold, no matter the outside temperature. Wear something light and carry a sweater and you're covered either way. Comfortable shoes are important; you're going to be on your feet a lot. Carry a backpack or big purse as well as a notepad and pen. You're sure to run across freebies or buy toys to take home to your cat, and you may meet a breeder you want to talk to after the show. A pad for taking notes and a place to put business cards is a must.

✔ **Be aware of the demands on exhibitors.** Most in the cat fancy love answering questions and talking about cats to the general public, but not in those tense moments before they're going to the show ring. Your first question to any exhibitor should be: "Is this a good time to ask a couple questions about your cats?" They'll let you know, and if it's not, they can tell you when will be. Never bother an exhibitor who has a cat in her arms — she's almost certainly headed to or coming from the judging ring. And step aside: Cat-show etiquette — and common sense — demands that a person carrying a cat has the right-of-way.

✔ **Be respectful of the health and safety of the cats.** Don't ask to pet a cat, because you almost certainly aren't going to be allowed to. Breeders are very concerned —

and rightly so — about the spread of disease, and so the only people who touch any cats at a show are the people who brought them and the judges, who are careful to sanitize their hands and the judging platform between each cat they handle. On occasion, an exhibitor you're talking to may ask if you'd like to touch her cat. She's likely to ask you to clean your hands before and after, which is a small price to pay for the privilege of petting a cat in silky-soft show condition.

✔ **Watch at least one class being judged.** Unlike dog-show judges, who never share their thoughts with the spectators (or even the competitors, really), cat-show judges consider education an important part of their job. They often discuss the good and not-so-good points of each animal as they judge, and many are not only articulate and knowledgeable but witty as well. After the judging is over, most are happy to answer a question or two. Some shows also have separate rings set up for educational talks.

✔ **Don't forget the vendors.** Nearly every show has people on hand to sell cat-related merchandise. You find not only free cat-food samples from major manufacturers but also hand-crafted toys, grooming tools, scratching posts, and cat trees direct from the people who make them. Some of the merchandise is more for cat lovers than for the cats themselves — clothing and jewelry, artwork and books. Neat stuff!

Best of all, a cat show is a special opportunity to see dozens of beautifully groomed cats — not only of the more common breeds but also of some of the rarest in the world.

auspices of a number of associations that are often international in scope. The New Jersey-based Cat Fanciers' Association, for example, has more than 650 member clubs in North America, Asia, Europe, Russia, and South America. Based in Texas, The International Cat Association, better known as TICA (pronounced TEE-ka), likewise boasts of activities around the world.

The honor for the largest international cat show goes to the CFA, which says that its annual event attracts more than 1,000 cats from around the world. To qualify, the animals first compete in regional shows held not only in the United States, but also in Europe and Asia. The show is held each November in the United States, although locations vary. The largest national show is the National Cat Show, held in London every year, with more than 2,000 entries.

Governing bodies

The cat fancy is a fractious lot, with different groups of people holding vastly different — and incredibly strong — opinions on most aspects of breeding and showing cats. As a result, many different bodies, called *registries,* govern the sport, with different rules and titles and different policies for the recognition of new and developing breeds and colors of cats. Registries exist primarily to register cats, grant titles, and maintain rules for cat shows. In addition, some registries are involved in public education. Each group has its own registry and rules.

How to find a cat show

Local newspapers are pretty hit-and-miss in promoting upcoming events so they aren't that reliable to use for finding a cat show. In your community, you may be able to find flyers on upcoming events at your pet-supply outlet; your veterinarian may also have a bulletin board for notices.

Your best bet, however, is to pick up magazines such as *Cats* and *Cat Fancy,* both of which offer listings of upcoming shows. The listings include the date; the name of the show-giving club and its affiliation (CFA or TICA, for example); the place the show is being held; and the name, address, and phone number of the person to contact for more information. If you're thinking of entering, this person is also the one you need to call for an entry packet. Magazines put out by registries, such as the CFA's monthly *Cat Fanciers' Almanac,* provide more detailed listings of upcoming shows (as well as results on past shows).

With so much information on the World Wide Web, that you can find out about upcoming cat shows there, too, should come as no surprise. The Fanciers home page (www.fanciers.com) lists upcoming shows and links to the show-giving clubs' own sites, if available. Some clubs have made the most of the technology by offering entry forms online — just fill out, print out, and mail with the entry fee!

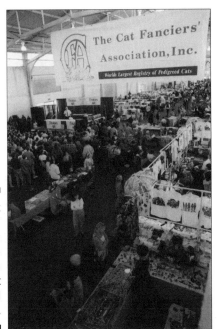

The Cat
Fanciers'
Association
claims to
have the
largest
international
cat show.

Photo courtesy of Michael Brim, Cat Fanciers' Association.

The Cat Fanciers' Association is probably the best known of the bunch, considered to be roughly the equivalent of the American Kennel Club, albeit with a much more international presence than the canine organization. The CFA was founded in 1906 as a "club of clubs," and its affiliate clubs produce more than 400 shows each year with more than 86,000 entries. The CFA recognizes 33 breeds of cat; the Persian, with an incredible 54 different color varieties, is tops in terms of registration.

Other registries differ from the CFA in policies, titles, and in the speed of recognition for new cat breeds or varieties.

The Canadian Cat Association/Association Feline Canadienne (CCA/AFC), the Federation International Feline (FIFe), the American Association of Cat Enthusiasts (AACE), the American Cat Association (ACA), the American Cat Fanciers Association (ACFA), the Cat Fanciers Federation (CFF), the Governing Council of the Cat Fancy (GCCF), and the World Cat Federation (WCF) are among the other registries, each with a piece of the pedigreed cat world.

Because of the number of show-governing bodies, we're going to stick to the CFA as we explain how cat shows work. For complete show rules for other organizations, write to each registry; the addresses are in the Additional Resources appendix.

Show-giving clubs

Although the registries do put on some shows — such as the CFA's annual international show or the Governing Council of the Cat Fancy's Supreme Show — most events are produced by affiliated clubs. And although you may think that who gives a show really doesn't matter, being active in a local or breed cat club is one of the best ways to learn the sport. Besides, if not for these dedicated fanciers, we wouldn't have any cat shows at all!

Breed clubs

Clubs dedicated to a single breed or a related group of breeds exist to promote and educate others about their cats, provide breeder referrals for kitten shoppers, and encourage high standards of breeding and ethics in those who're involved in the club and the breed. These clubs sometimes produce shows just for their breeds; are often national in reach; and are usually affiliated with a particular registry, such as TICA or CFA.

Local or regional clubs

Most shows are produced by local or regional all-breed cat clubs. These clubs are the backbone of the cat fancy, the source of a mostly volunteer army that sets up the shows and affects the course of policy at the various registries.

How Shows Work

The show world is a confusing one of many different classes, different colored ribbons, various points toward different titles, and a variety of awards for regional and national competition. And that's just in the CFA, which we're using as our "general" example of how a cat show works. Add in the varied titles and rules of other registries, and we'd need a whole book the size of this one to explain everything — or maybe several.

The important thing to remember about shows is that at no point in the pedigreed ranks is a cat solely competing against another cat. What each cat is being judged on is how closely he conforms to the written ideal, called a *standard,* of the "perfect" cat for his breed, gender, and color or pattern. (You find more information on standards in the section "What judges look for" later in this chapter.) The cat who most closely — in the judge's view, of course — meets the ideal for his type is awarded ribbons and points over cats who don't measure up as well.

Competition divisions

At most CFA shows, the cats are entered into one of the following three basic classes and then subsequently divided into longhairs and shorthairs, breed, color group (for example, tabby and white), and gender. The first two classes are for registered pedigreed cats; the third is for kittens, cats of mixed breeding, "pet" quality pedigreed cats, or purebreds of unknown breeding.

- ✔ **Championship:** For *whole* (not spayed or neutered) registered, pedigreed cats.

- ✔ **Premiership:** For *altered* (spayed or neutered) registered, pedigreed cats.

- ✔ **Non-Championship Classes:** For every other eligible cat, the non-championship classes include: Kitten, for pedigreed cats between four and eight months (no cat younger than four months is allowed into a show hall, and the kittens may or may not be altered); Any Other Variety (AOV), for a registered cat or kitten who doesn't conform to the accepted standard, such as a longhair in a shorthaired breed; Provisional Breed, for a registered cat or kitten in a breed that has not achieved eligibility for championship status; and Miscellaneous, for registered cats or kittens in a breed not accepted for provisional standing. The Non-Championship division also includes Household Pets, for any healthy altered cat, whether random bred, or pedigreed with a disqualifying fault.

Cats in each class don't compete against cats in other classes. Kittens do not compete for titles, nor do household pets in the CFA (although the latter can in other registries). Cats in championship and premiership categories compete for show titles and regional and national awards based on the number of cats they defeat over the course of their show careers.

What judges look for

At a CFA show, cats are given numbers to make judging easier and are assigned cages in the display, or *benching,* area, along with others of their breed. (The benching area is so named because the cages are on long tables or raised platforms called, appropriately, *benches.*)

At the designated time of judging, the announcer calls the cats to a ring, where the exhibitors place them in cages behind and alongside the judge, matching the number their cat was assigned to the number on the judging cage. The exhibitors then nervously take seats in the audience, or *gallery,* and the judge takes the cats out one by one — carefully sanitizing hands and the judging platform between each cat. (Between classes, the cages are sanitized, too.)

Judges are long-time exhibitors and breeders who've been determined by the registry to be knowledgeable about the "ideal" for each breed they judge. What goes into the judging is different for pedigreed cats and for household pets.

Pedigreed cats

Pedigreed cats are judged against a breed standard determined by the registry under whose rules the show is run. The Cat Fanciers' Association breed standards are all based on a numerical system in which a "perfect" cat of any particular breed gets 100 points.

For example, the CFA standard for the Russian Blue gives 20 points to the head and neck, 20 to the correct body type, 5 for eye shape, 5 for ears, 20 for coat, 20 for color, and 10 for eye color. Beyond the point scale, the standard reveals the ideal for each category; in the case of the Russian Blue, a cat defined by a distinctive coat color, the CFA standard calls for a cat whose coat is an "even bright-blue throughout, [with] lighter shades of blue preferred . . ." and further outlines what's not acceptable in the breed, such as tabby markings.

The standards vary, of course, depending on the breed. One may call for a certain kind of tail, and another may call for no tail at all (as in the case of the Manx).

Cat-show judges evaluate each cat individually in comparison to the ideal for its breed, called the standard.

As the show progresses, the level of competition gets keener within the three pedigreed divisions. A cat in the championship division (so called because that's where champions are "made") may initially compete against only other nonchampion male tabby Persians; if he's a winner, he goes on to compete against other tabby Persians, male and female; then he competes against other Persians of all color types and both genders; then he goes up against others in the longhair group; and then, he competes in an *allbreed* competition against winners from other breeds. The final winners are named in reverse order, with the top cat finally held aloft by the judge to applause from the gallery.

In each ring along the way, however, the measure of a cat is the same: How well does this particular animal compare to the ideal for the breed — the standard?

Breed standards are subject to change, and current versions are usually available at shows and always available by writing to the registry.

Household pets

Obviously, a cat of mixed breeding can't be defined by a breed standard, so in household pet classes, judges are looking for something else. Household pets must be at least four months old and, if older than eight months, must be altered. Under CFA rules, the cats' claws must be clipped, but declawed cats are not eligible to be shown. (These last two rules also apply to pedigreed entrants.)

Household pets are given "merit" ribbons by the CFA for meeting the preceding rules, as well as for being healthy (free of parasites and current on vaccinations) and well-groomed (bathed, combed, and brushed; with clean ears, eyes, and teeth). Cats are further judged on personality and beauty. The first refers to a cat who's relaxed, self-confident, and happy; the second has as many interpretations as you find judges.

Your "ordinary" cat can become a show winner by competing in household pet classes.

Mac — Photo courtesy of Kathie Schutte.

In other registries, household pets compete for titles at shows. And one organization, the Happy Household Pet Cat Club, though not giving shows, recognizes wins in other registries with points and gives out titles as points accumulate. (For information on contacting the HHPCC, see the Additional Resources appendix.)

Champions, Grand Champions, and more

In the CFA, as pedigreed cats are judged and ranked according to how closely they match their breed standards, ribbons are the obvious sign that a competition is going on. In fact, invisible to most spectators is what exhibitors are even more keen to claim — *points* toward various show titles and regional and national awards.

CFA shows offer two kinds of points: Those awarded toward Grand Championships or Grand Premierships, and those awarded in competition for regional and national awards. Points are awarded according to the number of cats bested in competition. The show-giving clubs report to the CFA the points given out at shows, some toward titles and some toward awards (such as top cat for the year in the region or nation), and the CFA keeps track of the tallies and grants titles and awards as appropriate.

To become a *champion* or *premier,* a cat must win six "winners" ribbons against others of its breed, gender, and color variety or type within the general category for either whole adult cats or altered adult cats. From there, the animal competes against other champions or premiers for points toward "grand" titles as well as for regional and national awards. In the CFA, a cat needs 200 points to become a grand champion and 75 points to become a grand premier. (Fewer premiers are in competition, so the number of points required is smaller.)

The CFA also gives awards, called Distinguished Merit, for cats who may not be going to shows at all anymore. The award is made for cats who are considered outstanding breeders, based on the competitiveness of their offspring. A male must sire 15 grand winners to get the designation, whereas a female must give birth to five.

Most titles go before a cat's *registered* name — that is, the name by which a cat is known by the registry. You may call him Jack, but to the registry, he's known by the name you put on the paperwork: CaraMia's Jackson Gold, for example. (The first name is generally the name of the cattery that bred the cat.) As your cat, Jack, continues in his show career, the initials add up (if you're lucky!) until he may end up with a registered name like GRC, RW CaraMia's Jackson Gold, DM. (Translation: Jack is a Grand Champion, a

Regional Winner, and he has sired at least 15 other Grand Champions, earning him the Distinguished Merit award.) Titles, except the DM, go before a cat's registered name; the DM goes after.

The titles and examples we've used here illustrate CFA show rules. Other registries have different titles and different rules for attaining them. If the way it all works seems confusing to you, you're in good company: Many people exhibit for rather a long time before they understand the point systems without rereading the rules a few dozen times. And even then, experienced exhibitors work out the details with a calculator!

Is Your Cat Showable?

If your cat is in good health and can handle the stress of being looked at and handled by strangers, you're welcome to enter him in the next cat show that comes up in your area. Before you do, however, read the cat magazines to see what kinds of shows are common in your region (CFA, TICA, and so on) and write to the registry for show rules to make sure that your cat is fully eligible. In some registries, for example, declawed cats are not allowed, whereas in others, your breed may not be recognized to compete at all.

After you've read the rules, attend a show as a spectator (as described in the sidebar "Enjoying a day at a show" earlier in this chapter) and pick up all the information you can find. Look for flyers on upcoming shows and pamphlets on how to exhibit, and buttonhole every friendly exhibitor you can to get all your questions answered.

Your cat doesn't need to be a registered, pedigreed animal to compete at most cat shows. Many people happily show in the household pet competition, but for others, household pet is just the beginning, and they eventually choose a breed (or more than one) to compete for other awards and to develop a breeding program.

One way to determine whether your cat may be show material is to consider how she does on her trips to the veterinarian. If she's relatively easy to handle and friendly, she's probably okay for showing. If she's terrified, spitting and slashing, you probably need to resign yourself to attending cat shows as a spectator, at least until you add a more amenable cat to your family.

Entering a show

After you've attended a show or two and determined that your cat is eligible, find an upcoming show and write or call for an entry form. (See the sidebar "How to find a cat show," earlier in this chapter, for details.) You receive the form in the mail, along with information on the names of the judges, the classes offered, and the cost to enter. (Generally, the entry fee is $30 to $40 or so, with discounts for "early bird" and multiple entries. The fee usually includes the use of a benching cage, litter, possibly food, and a show catalog.) If you don't understand the form, which calls for various information about your cat, call the contact person and ask.

What to bring

The entry confirmation tells you a great deal about the show — the time you need to be there, how to get there, and what sort of paperwork you need for your cat — bring all the paperwork asked for, including the confirmation material you received at the time you entered.

But that's just the beginning of the list of things you need in order to show your pet.

To start with, you need to bring your clean, well-groomed cat, of course, and yourself. For his own safety and comfort, your cat needs to be brought into the show in a carrier — Chapter 6 explains how to pick out a good one. You need materials to keep your cat comfortable and relaxed — something to rest on in the cage and favorite toys to bat around.

Even though food and litter may be provided, you may want to provide your own, especially if your cat is very fussy. Some exhibitors even provide their own custom cages, and although that's not necessary, you *do* need to provide cage curtains on the sides and back to keep your cat from being stressed out about the cat next to him, plus a cage floor to make him comfortable. Curtains can be as simple as towels held in place by safety pins and floors can be a piece of carpet remnant, but some exhibitors go all out to make their areas look as beautiful as their cats (and often complementary to their animals as well). Some shows even give an award for the best-designed entry in the benching area.

Some other items to bring include grooming supplies for touching up your cat, a bottle of cat-safe disinfectant, and a roll of paper towels. (Don't use pine-based cleaners, which are dangerous around cats; ask your veterinarian for a brand recommendation.)

You want to dress comfortably, bring a pen for making notes in the catalog (a notepad's a good idea, too), wear a watch, and throw in something light to read while waiting for your cat to be judged. Food and soft drinks in a small cooler are probably something you'd be happy you brought, too.

Although you can get by with very little in the way of showing supplies, experienced exhibitors load up on things to make their day — and their cats' day — easier. Watch what these people bring, ask questions about why they brought them, and finally, find out where they got them (and the price). You may find the extra gear worthwhile.

What to do

Leave yourself with plenty of time to get to your show and check in. Your confirmation package includes directions to the show site and information on what time you need to check in with the show clerk, but remember the old adage "Anything that can go wrong, goes wrong," and leave yourself plenty of time to cope with the expected.

As you check in, you're given your cat's number and benching assignment; your first course of action is to set up your cage and make your cat comfortable inside.

Listen for your cat's number: It's the call to the judging ring. Before your designated judging time, you probably want to neaten up your cat's grooming and even figure out where you're suppose to go for judging.

Never leave your cat unattended. Although most people want to do nothing worse than pet your cat (which can lead to an escape), you always face the risk of someone wanting to harm or steal your pet. The best idea is to bring a friend or family member along to keep you company, but if that's not possible, introduce yourself to your "neighbors" and trade cat-watching duties with them.

After you're called to the ring, place your cat in the appropriate judging ring and grab a seat in front of the judge to watch. Don't talk to your cat and don't remove him from the ring or the show until you're told to do so.

Getting competitive

Showing your pet, whether he's a mixed-breed or pedigreed cat, is a wonderful way to find out whether the sport of cat showing really interests you. If you're going to start winning, however, you're probably going to need a more competitive cat — a *show-quality* animal.

Because breeders want their best cats to compete, they generally don't sell show-quality animals to people who aren't already exhibiting. As you discover more about the sport and compete with your pet, you probably find yourself drawn to a breed you want to start showing more competitively. Make yourself known to breeders as a serious show home and soon you can buy that kitten who can start you on your way to ribbons, titles, and awards galore.

Although you need to become friendly with breeders to get the cat you need to compete more effectively, you also need their help to learn what winning takes. In this chapter, we've condensed into a few short pages what, for some people, is a lifetime of study. If you're to be successful, you need to develop a mentor relationship with people who know more than you do. Fortunately, cat-show people are like any others in a competitive arena: They're happy to help a novice — until you start winning!

And when that happens, you need to remember to help out the next generation of newbies for the continued good of the sport.

Part V
The Part of Tens

The 5th Wave   By Rich Tennant

"Well, she's fast on the keyboard and knows how to load the printer, but she just sort of 'plays' with the mouse."

In this part . . .

This part has a little bit of everything, and is truly what is meant by the saying "last, but not least." In these chapters we debunk some old myths about cats, tell you how to protect your cat should a disaster strike your community, and clue you in to common dangers your pet may face in your own home. Then, just for fun, we take you on a tour of some of the best cat-related Web sites on the Internet and offer you some of the best things ever said about cats.

Chapter 17

Ten Cat Myths — Debunked

The cat was worshipped as a god in ancient Egypt, vilified as a demon in medieval Europe, and is treasured as a companion around the world today. Despite all that change, the cat herself is not much altered in form or temperament. She is much the same creature she was when first she chose to associate herself with our kind.

We now know more than ever before about our cats, but a surprising amount of information that's just plain *wrong* still hangs about in our culture and, worse, keeps popping up in strange new places, such as popular movies, and so passes on anew.

Researching the myths of cats is an interesting way to discover how our feline companions have been viewed throughout the ages, but in no way should these myths and legends take the place of modern knowledge in caring for your cat.

From the earliest mousers through the mysterious origins of the Manx and Maine Coon to the legends developing about cats today — Virginia C. Holmgren investigates them all in her fascinating book, *Cats in Fact and Folklore* (Howell Book House/Macmillan General Reference). Did the medieval church's hatred for cats — who were tortured and killed by the thousands — bring about the Great Plague after mouse and rat populations swelled without cats to keep them in check? Did cats live in the New World before the Europeans arrived? Holmgren argues "yes" to all and tells the whole tale in a most entertaining way.

Enjoy the old stories — they make fine reading with your cat on your lap on some wintry evening. But remember always to keep fact and fiction separate for the good of your cat.

Here are a few enduring myths — and the facts to counter them.

Cats Have Nine Lives

Cats are survivors, no doubt of that. More so than any other domesticated animal, they keep their wildness about them, slipping back and forth across the line that separates the feral from the tame. On city streets and in country barns alike, cats live as they did thousands of years ago, dispatching rodents with efficiency, breeding prodigiously, and accepting whatever handouts come their way without giving up one ounce of their independence.

The efforts of humankind have changed cats' bodies hardly at all, except in the cases of the more extreme breeds of purebreds, such as the heavy-coated Persian and near-naked Sphinx, which are poorly equipped for a rough-and-tumble life. The cat known commonly as an "alley cat" — but more formally as the *domestic shorthair* — is seemingly well-equipped to handle the challenges of outdoor life. Finely tuned to the slightest hint of danger, he can run fast, climb faster, and, if cornered by an adversary, defend himself with a formidable array of claws and teeth. The slender, lithe bodies of cats — celebrated in word and art throughout the centuries — can fit through the tiniest hole or balance on the most slender plank. And if his high-wire act isn't quite up to snuff, the cat can miraculously right himself on the way earthward, often landing unhurt and on his feet from a surprising height.

With so much going for her, is it any wonder people came to believe that the cat had not one chance at life but nine?

The truth of the matter is that cats are more fragile than we think. Cats as a species have proven resilient, but as individuals, they are every bit as mortal as we ourselves are — and they are very vulnerable in the world. Although a well-cared-for indoor cat can live into his late teens, a cat exposed to the outdoor life is lucky to live as long. The dangers of modern life — cars, predators, ill-intentioned neighbors, communicable diseases — are just too many, and they claim the lives of even the more-street-smart cats by the thousands.

Cats have but one life, and they need our love and protection to make that life a long, healthy, and happy one.

For more on the controversy over indoor versus outdoor cats, see Chapter 1. For tips on how to make your home a happy one for your indoor cat and for information on the best cat gear around, see Chapter 6. Some household hazards to avoid appear in Chapter 21.

Cats Need to Drink Milk

Gina's mother has a soft spot in her heart for a wandering cat, offering the wild ones who come up from the creek near her home a safe place to eat and drink and to watch the birds and squirrels that she also feeds. Her yard is a spa for wayward kitties, and one of the items on the menu is always milk.

"Cats love milk," she says. "It must be good for them."

Cats *do* love milk, as anyone knows who's ever been around an old-fashioned cow barn at milking time — or, let's get real, seen one on TV. Cats young and old line up for a squirt of the real thing: warm, tasty, and oh-so-fresh. Mmmmm!

But is cow's milk the perfect food for cats? Hardly. In fact, milk can prove a very messy proposition for you and your pet, causing gastric disturbances and, um, diarrhea. Although that possibility may not bother Gina's mom, with her collection of half-wild wayfarers that she doesn't need to clean up after, it may bother you plenty if your kitty is an indoor cat and you must clean out the litter box (or other, unsanctioned, toilet location).

Mother's milk — from their own cat mama — is the perfect food for kittens, and while they're little, they get everything they need from it, including important antibodies. After the age of 12 weeks or so, however, a few cats lose the ability to digest the lactose in the milk; for those cats, milk isn't recommended. For the others, it's a source of protein, minerals, and vitamins that they can also find in a well-balanced commercial diet.

In the wild, kittens never drink milk again after they're weaned, and yours have no reason to either. If your cat likes and can tolerate milk, however, feel free to offer it as an occasional treat — but remember that it's never a substitute for fresh water, which should be kept available at all times.

If you never, ever set a saucer of milk down for your pet, however, you may rest assured that he does just fine without.

Liquid nutrition is very important to orphaned kittens; in fact, getting handfed is their only chance at survival! For more on what and how to feed a kitten in need, see Chapter 14.

Cats Purr Whenever They're Happy

Purring is one of the most special elements of a cat, as far as most humans are concerned. Caressing a purring pet has proven to relax the one doing the stroking and lower the blood pressure, too. A purring cat or kitten is sure to bring a smile to the face of any human, young or old, and cats have made a real difference in the lives of those in nursing homes or other institutional settings, just by the simple act of being a cat.

But careful observers of the cat know that purring isn't just a sound of contentment. Cats also purr if they're injured, while giving birth — even when dying. British zoologist Desmond Morris has observed in his masterwork *Catworld: A Feline Encyclopedia* (Penguin Reference) that purring is "a sign of friendship — either when [the cat] is contented with a friend or when it is in need of friendship — as with a cat in trouble."

Kittens start purring even before they open their eyes, rumbling while nursing in what must be a reassuring sound to their mother — who's likely purring herself.

Our cats have one thing to lord over the "King of Beasts" and other more formidable felines. A cat can purr; the lion can't, nor can any of the other big felines. The tiger can rumble a friendly greeting but only on the exhale. No big cat can get his motor running the way our household kitties can, purring constantly as effortlessly as breathing, both in and out. To even things out, however, big cats possess the ability to roar. On the whole, the little cat got the better part of that deal, at least where humans are concerned.

Although the experts are pretty clear on *why* cats purr, they're not yet certain as to *how*. The most common explanation has the sweet sound originating in the voicebox, with what are called the *vestibular folds,* or false vocal cords. The passing of air across these structures is thought to produce the purr all cat lovers adore.

Cats Eat Plants if They're Sick

Cats are so fond of chewing on greenery that many cat owners have widely assumed plants to be an important part of the feline diet. And the idea makes sense, too, if you look at all the undigested plant matter in the "gift" your cat leaves on your carpet (why never on the tile or hardwoods?) after a kitty gagfest. You probably figure that your cat eats plants to help bring up whatever's upsetting her tummy.

Although the experts debate how much plant matter is necessary in a cat's diet, one thing is obvious to anyone who's ever tried to maintain both houseplants and a house cat — kitties nibble on greens simply because *they love to.*

For a cat, "just because" is usually reason enough.

For a discussion of what your cat needs to eat and why, check out Chapter 8. We also tell you which plants are cat-friendly in Chapter 8 and what you need to know about catnip in Chapter 6. Plants can be deadly, too; to avoid any cat-astrophes in your home, check out the list of toxic plants in Chapter 21.

Cats Are Dangerous around Babies

This old chestnut got polished up for laughs a couple of years ago for the Hugh Grant movie, *Nine Months*, in which an expectant couple are told by a doctor to get rid of their cat.

Humane societies and cat fanciers everywhere were *not* amused and did their best to counter the effect of so much bad information.

You *don't* need to find a new home for your pet if you become pregnant, no matter what well-meaning relatives and friends may say to the contrary. Cats do *not* maliciously smother or suck the breath out of babies, as the myths hold. Still, to best protect your baby, you do need to be aware of the facts and exercise a little caution.

Cats don't suck the breath of infants, but the myth that they do probably came from their natural curiosity to investigate a new addition to the family, coupled with the tragedy of Sudden Infant Death Syndrome, or SIDS. We can easily understand how, hundreds of years ago, people may have seen a cat in the crib — perhaps sniffing at a baby's milk-scented breath — and later found a dead child and then tried to find an explanation for the loss by linking the two events together.

Common sense dictates that no animal be left unattended with a small child. This advice is for your baby's protection *and* for your cat's. The Humane Society of the United States, which keeps statistics on injuries inflicted by animals on people, knows of no documented case of a cat smothering an infant by resting on the child's face. Other experts, however, point out that such a scenario, although unlikely, is *feasible* and suggest taking precautions — which makes perfect sense: You don't want your baby to be the first to be harmed in such a way.

After your child is older, you still want to remain on the lookout for problems. Toddlers don't understand that pets need gentle handling, and although most cats catch on very quickly to the notion that small children are best avoided, a possibility always exists that your pet, if cornered, could scratch or bite your child or even be hurt himself.

Cats are wonderful family pets, and don't let anyone tell you otherwise. A cat is the perfect pet for many families — a little more flexible and self-sufficient than a dog but still an affectionate and nonjudgmental companion. Just be aware that small children and cats have the potential to hurt each other; so keep an eye on them while they're together.

Pregnancy and your cat

One of the other reasons pregnant women are often advised to find a new home for their cats has to do with the transmission of the protozoan parasite *Toxoplasma gondii,* which causes the disease called *Toxoplasmosis.*

The disease presents little danger to healthy adults, but if a fetus contracts it through the placenta from a newly infected mother, he or she faces a risk of death or spontaneous abortion, as well as birth defects in those fetuses that survive.

Cats are a cause for concern because they're an important part of the life cycle of this microscopic entity, shedding the infectious stage of the creature in their feces. Cats aren't the only way you may come in contact with the disease, however: Raw or poorly cooked meat is another.

About half the human population of the United States is already carrying the parasite. In any event, transmission of the parasites is oral — you become infected by eating the creatures by accident.

If you're already a carrier — your doctor can test you to see — you can't pass the parasite on to the child you're carrying. The danger is in becoming infected for the first time *while* you're pregnant.

The risk is great enough that pregnant women *must take precautions* to protect the child they

carry. Ideally, someone else should take over the maintenance of the litter box for the duration of the pregnancy and even before the pregnancy in the case of couples who're attempting to conceive.

If no one except you can maintain the litter box, wear gloves and a mask, dispose of the contents in sealed plastic, and then wash your hands thoroughly. Experts also recommend wearing gloves while gardening (to avoid cat feces in soil), taking care to keep children's sandboxes covered, if not in use, to keep cats out of them, and being careful in handling raw meat — clean the cutting boards, wash your hands, and cook the meat thoroughly before consuming it.

These same precautions apply to people who have impaired immune systems, such as those who are HIV-positive or are receiving cancer treatments. Although healthy adults usually have no problems should they become infected, those with immune-system problems can be at grave risk. In some urban areas, well-organized volunteers take over the tasks of pet care, so the important social benefits of keeping a cat aren't overshadowed by the potentially dangerous physical ones.

If you have questions about your cat and Toxoplasmosis, consult your physician, veterinarian, or local public-health officials.

Cats Can Be Kept from Using Their Claws

Oh, don't you wish! Despite all efforts to keep cats from clawing up the furniture — and you can read about all of them in Chapter 13 — the best you can do for your cat and your possessions is redirect your pet's scratching effort, because he needs to scratch.

Scratching is an important part of feline behavior, as much a part of being a cat as purring. Scratching stretches your cat's muscles in ways that are both important and satisfying to him. Cats live in a world of smells, and marking things for their own — including you — is also very natural, important behavior. Digging claws into the corner of your sofa is one way your pet makes himself feel at home, leaving his own reassuring scent behind from scent glands in his feet.

Some have said that to live with a cat is to caress a tiger, and scratching is one trait your pet shares with all his wild kin. It's healthy and it's natural, and you *can* deal with it in a way that satisfies you both, likely *without* declawing, which is also discussed in Chapter 13, by the way.

A Well-Fed Cat Doesn't Hunt

The ability to hunt is hard-wired into all cats, but the level of desire varies by an individual's genetics and early experiences, not by the rumbling in his belly. The play of kittens is really hunting behavior. Pouncing and leaping on any little thing that moves, from your finger to a leaf, is an early sign of the prowess that has kept the welcome mat out for cats throughout human existence.

Although the desire to hunt may be undeniable, whether your cat *kills* may have more to do with hunger than anything else, argues zoologist Desmond Morris in his book, *Cat Watching* (Crown). He says that the cat's much-observed tendency to play with its prey is really a matter of the animal's not being hungry enough to eat it but still instinctively driven to hunt. And so the cat pounces again and again. In mother cats, the desire to keep prey half-alive concerns her duties to her babies: She uses the little creature to teach them hunting skills.

Morris argues that your cat is seeing you as a kitten if she brings freshly killed prey back to you. She recognizes that you're a hopeless hunter, and she's trying to help you out.

The fact that you find such love offerings appalling are rather beside the point, and no amount of yelling can change your cat's behavior. (Punishment *never* works with cats, anyway, so save your breath.) Just do your very best to accept the gift as civilly and graciously as you can and dispose of the poor creature with all proper precautions — use a newspaper to pick it up, and wash your hands thoroughly afterward.

Hunting behavior in cats is very controversial, especially if the prey is songbirds or endangered rodent species. *Belling* (fitting your cat's collar with a small bell or other noise-making device) your cat has little effect on his ability to hunt; turning him into an indoor-dweller is the only way to protect wildlife from him — and you from his thoughtful "gifts." An indoor cat is also protected from what that wildlife can do to *him* — transmit parasites and injure him with bites.

A factory cat in Lancaster, a male tabby, is touted as one of history's greatest mousers, catching more than 22,000 mice in 23 years. Another claim is made on behalf of a female tabby, also in England. She was said to have killed more than 12,000 rats in six years, or five or six rats a day.

Both are amazing accomplishments, certainly, but we'd like to know one thing: Who on earth counted all those dead rodents?

Cat Fur Causes Allergies

If people are allergic to animals, their bodies are reacting not to fur but to proteins in skin secretions and saliva, commonly known as *dander*. These particles are applied generously to a cat's fur by the act of grooming and are liberally applied to every surface she rubs against. Every shake puts the particles airborne, where they're easily inhaled into the sensitive tissues of the lungs or sinuses.

More people are allergic to cats than to dogs, and the allergies to cats are often more severe.

Myths persist about "hypoallergenic" breeds of cats, such as the nearly naked Sphinx or lightly coated Devon or Cornish Rex. Many of these breeds are actively promoted by their fanciers as being good for allergy-sufferers, but allergists argue otherwise. All warm-blooded pets have saliva and skin secretions; all warm-blooded pets, therefore, are potential problems for allergy sufferers.

Their allergists may not approve, but many cat-allergic people wouldn't dream of giving up their pets. For strategies that may make possible juggling allergies and cats — as well as the future for treating allergies to animals — see Chapter 1.

Black Cats Are Bad Luck

Black may be an unlucky color all right — for a cat. Black cats have been associated with the forces of evil for hundreds of years, and humane societies warn that this myth has cost many of them their lives. Black cats are often the targets of those who want to practice Satanic-like rituals that include the torture and killing of animals. Such horrors are especially clustered around Halloween, humane groups warn, adding that the perpetrators aren't especially picky; if a black cat isn't available, any cat may serve their purposes in a pinch. So even if your cat usually chooses whether he's in or out, you should keep him inside until this particular holiday is past.

Black may be an unfortunate color for another reason: visibility. Thousands of cats are killed by cars every year, and the difference between a hit or a near miss may be the driver's ability to see the cat darting across the road before him. At night, patches of light-colored fur are a distinct advantage to a kitty.

If a black cat crosses your path, are you likely to see this event as a sign of good or bad luck? Depends on where you live. In the United States, a black cat is typically thought to bring bad luck, but in England, the opposite is

How can anyone feel unlucky to have such a wonderful pet?

Andrew — Photo courtesy of Johanna Bader.

true. Although Americans tend to think that the sign of a black cat is a bad omen, the Brits believe that seeing "the devil" in person is a sign they've been spared any bad luck.

Either way, the claims for black cats of special powers to the good or evil are nothing more than superstitions.

All Calicos Are Females

Almost all calico (and tortoiseshell — often called *torties*) cats are female, but not quite all. According to a study by the College of Veterinary Medicine at the University of Missouri, about 1 in 3,000 so-marked cats are male . . . well, sort of.

The gene that governs how the red/orange color in cats displays is on the X, or female, chromosome. Any cat, male or female, can be orange, but in males, that color is usually expressed in one way: the tabby pattern, often called a "ginger tom" or marmalade tabby.

Females, however, can be orange tabbies, torties, or calicos. (The last two are genetically similar, except that the calico has white spotting.)

Because orange females are divided among calicos, torties, and tabbies, people often think that most orange tabbies are males, and statistically, males do make up the majority of orange tabbies. But for females to be orange tabbies is a lot more common than for males to be either calicos or torties.

That's because, for a cat to be a calico or tortoiseshell, it must have two X chromosomes, which means that, in the overwhelming majority of cases, the animal is female. If the calico or tortoiseshell pattern exists in males, the reason is that the cat actually has an extra chromosome — two X and one Y — a genetic rarity that occasionally pops up in cats (and in people, too). These so-called *Klinefelter* males are usually — but not always — sterile.

Chapter 18

Ten Things You Need to Know to Prepare Your Cat for a Disaster

*H*urricanes, earthquakes, floods, twisters, fires, and even volcanoes have brought home to us all in recent years that a disaster can happen at any time, to any community. In the aftermath of such natural calamities has come a new awareness of the need for disaster planning for our pets, both on a communitywide level and in our own homes.

Although animals aren't allowed in disaster-relief shelters, an increasing number of animal shelters and veterinarians are better prepared now than ever before to take in animals during an emergency.

In fact, a model program started by the California Veterinary Medical Association has a veterinarian in place in each county to help coordinate animal-relief efforts. Other regions are starting to see the light, too, with veterinarians, shelter groups, and specially trained disaster teams from the United Animal Nations Emergency Animal Rescue Service, based in Sacramento, California, prepared to do for animals what the Red Cross does for people.

Behind the changes is a growing realization that animals need help, too, and that some people choose to put their lives in danger rather than abandon their pets.

We both live in Northern California, and even as we were writing this chapter, we were making evacuation plans for our families as floodwaters drove many people in our area from their homes — including Gina's brother and his family. In the end, our families were all safe, animals and all, but in the counties just north of our homes, hundreds of animals died or were displaced, and we saw firsthand the incredible work of the United Animal

Nations Emergency Animal Rescue Service. This outstanding group responds to disasters across the United States and Canada and is deserving of the support of every animal lover. Consider a donation to the work of this group; for more information, see the Additional Resources appendix in the back of this book.

Have a Plan

Prepare for all possibilities, including that you may be away from home when disaster strikes. Make sure that everyone in your family — children, too! — is prepared in the event of an emergency. Make a plan and go over it until everyone knows what to do.

People need to rely on each other during emergencies, and this fact is just as true for your pets. Get to know your neighbors, and put a plan in place to help each other out. Find out from local shelters and veterinary organizations what their emergency response plans are and how you fit into those plans in case of a disaster.

Ask your veterinarian if he has a disaster plan and how he plans to work with other veterinarians in an emergency. If he's never thought about the situation, pushing him a little on the subject doesn't hurt.

Corral Your Cat

Obviously, you're not going to get advance warning of some disasters, such as earthquakes. But if you know that a worrisome tropical storm is just off the coast or that the rivers are starting to rise, find your cat, *now!*

Even if your cat is a "combo kitty" — coming and going as she pleases — make her an indoor one while trouble is in the air. If you leave your cat outside to fend for herself during a disaster, she's going to run and hide as best she can; in the aftermath, she may not be able to find her way home through the mess — and you may not be there even if she *can* find her way home.

You can't evacuate a cat you can't find, so make sure that you know where yours is and can put her in a carrier whenever you think you may need to leave in a hurry.

Maintain Your Cat's Permanent and Temporary ID

Most animals survive a disaster. But too many never see their families again without a way to determine which pet belongs to which family. That's why pets should always wear a collar and identification tags. Better still is a permanent identification that can't slip off, such as an imbedded microchip.

Keep temporary ID tags at hand, too, to put on your pet if you're forced to evacuate. (Your pet's permanent ID isn't much use if you aren't home to answer the phone.) One of the easiest forms of ID: key tags on which you can jot a current number, slip it into a plastic housing, and then attach to your pet's collar.

A lot of people refuse to put a collar on their cats, worried that the kitty may get caught on some branch while jumping and then strangle. Others find that their cats give so many collars the slip that these owners give up trying to keep collars on their pets.

You have a much better chance of being reunited with your cat if he is wearing the appropriate tags.

Dante — Photo courtesy of Heather Dismore.

A collar can save your pet's life. Remember these words from an animal-control officer: "Every day, I put to death a dozen lost kitties who obviously belong to someone — animals we can't match up with the families who're missing them. I wish they had collars and tags, so I could locate their owners. I've put to death more lost pets than I can count, but I've never, ever been called out to remove the body of a cat hanging by his collar in a tree."

A collar and tag and a microchip are among the most important safety measures you can take on your cat's behalf. Find out more about these items in Chapter 6.

Keep Vaccinations — and Records — Current

Infectious diseases can spread from cat to cat in the high-stress environment of an emergency shelter, which is why keeping pets' vaccinations as up-to-date as your veterinarian recommends is essential.

Prepare a file with up-to-date medical and vaccination records, your pets' microchip numbers, your veterinarian's phone number and address, feeding and medication instructions, and recent pictures of your animals. Trade copies of emergency files with another pet-loving friend; having someone else who knows about your pet is a good idea should *anything* happen to you.

Have Restraints Ready

Even normally laid-back cats can freak if they're stressed. Consequently, you need to be prepared to restrain your pet — for his safety and the safety of others.

Keep carriers and restraints ready for emergencies. *Ready* means *at hand* — the means to transport your pet shouldn't be something you need to find and pull from the rafters.

Cat carriers are probably the least-thought-of pieces of emergency equipment for pet owners — but are among the most important. Sturdy carriers keep pets safe and give rescuers more options in housing pets. They give *you* more options, too, in the homes of friends or relatives or in shelters outside of the area. Depending on weather conditions, you may also safely leave pets in their carriers overnight in vehicles in an emergency.

Sturdy, cat-sized carriers belong on the list of "must-haves," and even a top-quality one made of high-impact plastic — which we recommend over cardboard — costs you only about the same as a nice dinner out: around $25, tops. And the carrier lasts forever. If you are hesitant to use a carrier because it is always a fight to get your cat in it, don't be. Cats who resist getting in the carrier at home often find it the most comforting retreat during times of stress or when away from home. To them it represents the "way home." For more on choosing the right one, see Chapter 6.

A terrified cat is a danger to anyone who tries to handle her — a whirling menace of flying claws and slashing teeth. Make sure that restraints and a muzzle are part of your emergency-care kit. Cat muzzles are made to fit comfortably over the entire face, including the eyes. The Cat Sack is a comfortable way to secure an unhappy cat: The nylon sack encloses the body but provides select access through a handful of well-positioned openings in case your cat needs emergency treatment. Both items are available through K-V Vet Supply, listed in the Additional Resources appendix.

If nothing else, throw a large old bath towel in with your emergency supplies. In a pinch, you can wrap up a panicky cat in that with no harm to either one of you.

If you need to hold onto a cat in an emergency, grasp him firmly behind the neck in a hold that veterinarians call *scruffing*.

Rotate the Supplies Your Cat Needs

Keep several days' worth of food and safe drinking water as well as any necessary medicines packed and ready to go in the event of a disaster. Rotate your supplies so that they don't get stale. If your pet eats canned food, make sure that you keep an extra can opener and spoon tucked in among the emergency supplies — or use cans with flip-top lids.

Your emergency kit should also include disposable litter boxes and at least a week's supply of litter, as well as a scoop and sealable plastic bags for disposing of the waste.

In an emergency, you can restrain your cat by "scruffing" him. A muzzle is another item for your disaster kit.

Keep First Aid Supplies on Hand — with Directions

Pet-supply stores sell ready-made first-aid kits, or you can put your own together fairly easily. The important things to remember about a first-aid kit are to keep the kit stocked and keep it handy.

Keep a first aid book with your supplies, but give the book a quick read before you store it. Veterinarians Roger W. Gfeller (who's board-certified in critical care) and Michael W. Thomas have put together a good one, *First Aid: Emergency Care for Dogs and Cats*. The book is available for $22.45 ($19.95 plus $2.50 shipping and handling) through the Veterinary Information Network, Inc. (VIN). You can order it via the Pet Care Forum on America Online (keyword: PETS) or by mail or phone from VIN. (We list the address in the Additional Resources appendix.)

We list the ingredients of a feline first-aid kit in Chapter 9.

PET-PAK, Inc., manufactures animal first-aid kits in five sizes, all neatly packed in a plastic container. (The four largest have handles.) The kit contains the basics for emergency care, along with a pamphlet on using the supplies. For more information, see the Additional Resources appendix.

Know the Locations of Other Veterinary Hospitals — and Animal Shelters

Your veterinary hospital may become damaged in the disaster, which is why having some backup plans for boarding and care is a good idea. Know where to find other veterinary hospitals in your area, as well as animal shelters and animal-control facilities. Photocopy the appropriate pages from your local Yellow Pages and tuck them in with your emergency supplies.

If you lose your pet, these facilities are going to be the first places you look in hope she turns up.

Keep a "Lost Kitty" Kit Ready

In case of a disaster, you may not be able to get flyers made, so prepare some generic ones and keep them with your emergency supplies. In the biggest type size you can, center the words "LOST CAT," along with a clear picture of your pet. Then, below the picture, include a description of your pet, along with any identifying marks, and leave a space to add the phone number where you can be reached, as well as any backup contacts, friends, relatives, neighbors, or your veterinarian. Print up a hundred copies and keep them in a safe, dry, and accessible place.

A staple-gun allows you to post your notices; keep one loaded and with your supplies, along with thumbtacks and electrical tape.

If your cat becomes lost, post flyers in your neighborhood and beyond, and distribute them at veterinary hospitals and shelters. Although relying on the kindness of strangers is nice, offering a reward makes many just a little bit kinder.

Be Prepared to Help Others

You may be lucky to survive a disaster nearly untouched, but others in your community may not be so lucky. Contact your local humane society and veterinary organization now to train as a volunteer so that you can help out in a pinch. Disaster-relief workers do everything from distributing food to stranded animals to helping reunite pets with their families — and help find new homes for those who need them.

Volunteering in a pinch is not only a good thing to do — it feels good, and it's the *right thing* for anyone who cares about animals and people.

Chapter 19

Ten Sets of Questions to Ask When Choosing a Kitten

*W*ith feline births outnumbering human ones by a factor of at least ten, you shouldn't be surprised to discover plenty of kittens and cats from whom to choose whenever you decide to adopt a kitten. You find tons of tabbies, countless calicos — and no paucity of Persians either. Such an abundance is not good news for the cats themselves — many of whom never find the loving home every one of them deserves — but for you, the cat seeker, so many cats means you can pick up a special cat without too much trouble at all.

We want you to take a little trouble, however, not because we're trying to make your life more difficult but because we think the decisions you make in choosing a cat are important and should be treated with a little respect — and because we love cats as you do. We realize, too, that the decisions you make can have an effect beyond your household, where your new feline companion is going to live for the larger part of the next two decades if fortune smiles on you both.

If you're looking for a purebred kitten, you should look for a reputable breeder. If you're dealing with a shelter or rescue group, your choice should be one that truly has the best interests of its animals in mind. And if you're dealing with a private individual, you need to make sure you're not causing as many problems as you solve by offering a home to the kitten or cat who takes your fancy. You don't want to be encouraging people who are producing sick kittens or who are adding to the ranks of unwanted random-bred cats.

When adopting from a shelter, be sure to deal with a reputable one that has its cats' best interests in mind.

Photo courtesy of Richard D. Schmidt.

Before you get close enough to ask any questions of a breeder, shelter, or rescuer, you need to ask a lot of questions of yourself — and have the answers in mind. You need to decide what you're looking for in a cat — activity levels, age, coat type, gender, pedigreed or not, and, if pedigreed, the breed — before you can go to any cat or kitten source. Chapters 1 and 2 contain the information you need to make these decisions, and Chapter 3 provides the facts on how different sources for cats and kittens stack up.

Not all the questions in this chapter apply to every situation. A couple apply to pedigreed kittens and cats only. But although a question about "breeding operations" may not seem to apply to the coworker with a litter of kittens to give away, ask anyway. If your coworkers or neighbors are letting their cats reproduce willy-nilly, you have a choice of a more ethical kind to make regarding the kittens they're offering. So do your best to ask all these questions — and make sure the answers are good ones, no matter how adorable the kittens are. Remember, too, that sometimes you get your answer in no answer at all: The breeder of pedigreed kittens who's never heard of congenital defects or the kitten-pushing neighbor who can't imagine what relevance socialization has on a kitten's suitability as a pet are people about whom you ought to think twice.

If, instead of adopting, you're finding new homes for kittens or cats, you need to know a few other questions so you can screen out a less-than-desirable home. For some tips, see Chapter 14.

If you've already scanned our list of questions, you may have noticed an apparent glaring omission: The question "How much?" doesn't appear. That's intentional. Although the cost of a kitten or cat may be of immediate concern — especially if you're looking for one of the more "rare" or "hot" pedigreed kittens, with prices in the hundreds or even thousands of dollars — price is simply not that important over the long run. Consider: A purchase price of $600 for a pedigreed kitten from a reputable breeder breaks down to $40 a year over a 15-year lifespan — less than you're likely to spend annually on veterinary care, food, litter, or maybe even cat toys! So ask the price, but keep things in perspective: A healthy, happy, loving kitten is the goal here, and those qualities are not necessarily guaranteed by a hefty price tag — or lack thereof.

Many cats and kittens are around, and the time to fall in love with any one of them is *after* you make a careful, intelligent decision regarding the one with whom you're going to be sharing your life. *Take your time!*

How Long Have You Been Breeding Cats? How Many Breeds Do You Have? Do You Show? Why or Why Not?

Although these questions seem applicable only to the person offering pedigreed cats or kittens, they may extend beyond that narrow focus. After all, the definition of a breeder mentions nothing about the pedigrees of the animals bred; a breeder is simply the person who owns the mother of the kittens — nothing more.

You're looking for someone with experience and knowledge, not someone who breeds animals for the money — and so may be cutting too many corners on health and socializing. Neither are you looking for people who breed their pets because they can't be bothered to get them spayed.

To do a good job at breeding involves a lot of work — considering pedigrees, honestly appraising cats before they're bred, and evaluating the kittens for their best placements, whether in show homes or pet homes. To do the job well, a breeder shouldn't be going in too many directions at once and should focus on just one breed or on two similar breeds, such as the British Shorthair and Scottish Fold. Weigh carefully the risk of doing business with someone who has a lot of breeds or who has been "in" many breeds over a short time: You may be dealing with a poor-quality breeder.

One of the most important reasons for breeding pedigreed cats is to preserve the breeds themselves, and that job is best accomplished by the person who tries to produce animals who are good examples of their breed in appearance, health, and temperament. One of the main purposes of showing is the evaluation of breeding stock by knowledgeable individuals — show judges, in other words. You ought to wonder why a person is breeding her cats if she's not trying to perpetuate and improve the breed by having her animals judged against others.

What Congenital Defects Are in This Breed? How Are You Breeding to Avoid Those Defects?

These questions are also for the person selling pedigreed kittens; after all, the person with an "oops" litter usually doesn't know the background of the mother or even know the *identity* of the father!

Although many pedigreed cats are just as healthy as their random-bred relations, a few breeds have health problems tied to those very traits that set them apart — such as the spinal problems that can be associated with the tightly turned-down ear of the Scottish Fold or the taillessness of the Manx. Other problems are a matter of extremes, such as the breathing, tear-making, and eating problems associated with the most severely short-faced varieties of Persians.

The breeder you choose should be able to honestly and openly discuss the potential problems with the chosen breed and just as honestly and openly explain how she works to avoid problems. Listen for signs that the breeder has a grasp of genetics and the patience to apply that knowledge. The person who ignorantly breeds a Scottish Fold with "correct" ears to another fold with the same type of ears, for example, is courting with health disaster for the animals she produces. You want to work with someone who knows that, in this breed, healthy cats come from pairings of folds with folded ears to "folds" with nonfolded ones.

How Large Is Your Breeding Operation? Where Do Your Cats Spend Most of Their Time?

How can someone with three dozen cats give your kitten the attention she deserves during her formative weeks? That's one good reason (among others) for working with someone who runs a small, caring cattery. Running a top-quality cattery is *expensive,* and the tendency to cut corners may be a little too tempting for some.

The other reason to work with a small cattery involves the interaction between a breeder and her cats. Rare is the person who can handle dozens of loose cats in the house, and most breeders who have more cats than their own comfort levels allow start caging the animals to preserve their own sanity.

Cage-raised kittens are not good pet prospects. And although cats may sometimes need to be caged for health or breeding reasons, the breeder who loves cats is going to want hers around her.

If you're dealing with a person who has more cats than she can properly care for or more than she can tolerate living with, you may be dealing with the wrong person.

Are Your Cats Tested for Infectious Diseases? May I Have the Kitten Checked Out by My Veterinarian before I Adopt?

Contagious diseases claim many felines lives, so you want to deal with a breeder who's doing his best to keep his cats healthy — and to produce healthy kittens. The three diseases with which you should most concern yourself all start with the letter *F: FeLV* (feline leukemia virus); *FIV* (feline immunodeficiency virus, sometimes incorrectly called "feline AIDS"); and *FIP* (feline infectious peritonitis).

A reputable breeder keeps his cattery clean of FeLV and FIV by making sure the diseases don't exist among his cats in the first place and by never allowing cats who haven't tested negative for these diseases to interact with his cats. FIP isn't quite so "easy" to deal with, however (and we get to that in a moment).

Infectious diseases are why cat shows so rigidly control who touches a cat and how. Don't be offended if your request to pet a cat at a show is politely refused: For anyone other than an owner or a judge to touch a cat is almost unheard of. Judges use disinfectants on their hands and on the judging table between handling cats, and cages are cleaned thoroughly between classes. For more on the sport of cat shows, see Chapter 16.

FIP is harder to control, however, because the test for this disease is inconclusive. The *coronavirus* that causes FIP can be present in perfectly healthy cats, and the test that shows its presence merely means the animal has been exposed to the virus — perhaps merely in its common, nonlethal version. (The diagnosis of FIP can be a tricky one for veterinarians and must be based not only on the FIP test but also on the clinical signs of the disease.)

Because of these diseases, a reputable breeder should be more than willing for you to have your own veterinarian examine your kitten and perform any recommended tests. This precaution is just as critical — and maybe even more so — if you're adopting a pet from a shelter, rescue group, or private individual with an "oops litter." *Make sure you're working with a source who is as interested in a healthy pet as you are.*

Chapter 10 provides information on FeLV, FIV, and FIP. For the most-current recommendations on vaccinations for these diseases, see Chapter 9.

How Have You Socialized the Kittens?

Part of this question goes back to finding out where the cats are kept, but now's your chance to take things a little farther. Kittens need to be handled by people of both genders and all ages, and they need to be exposed to the normal sounds, sights, and smells of life with us two-legged animals. Consider the kind of household you have — kids, dogs, what-have-you — and ask the breeder whether your potential pet has been exposed to any of these things.

This is one area where an otherwise reputable breeder may not stack up as well as the person with an "oops" litter raised underfoot in a noisy family with children and other pets. A good breeder works to overcome these deficiencies: Give her the opportunity to explain how she did.

What Sort of Health Guarantees Do You Offer? What Happens If the Kitten Gets Sick?

Not even the most reputable of breeders can offer a 100 percent guarantee that your kitten is going to stay healthy. Your pet may become ill within days of your bringing her home, or she may manifest congenital health defects months or even years later. A reputable breeder, shelter, or rescue group is going to want to play fair and is prepared to compensate you for some of the financial loss — although sadly, not the personal one — should your new kitten become ill or die.

Well-
socialized
kittens
are
generally
those
raised
underfoot.

Katie and Maggie — Photo courtesy of Heather Dismore.

The person giving away a "free to a good home" kitten isn't offering you anything; the risk is all yours. Contracts vary among breeders, shelters, rescue groups, and pet stores, but a "replacement policy" is probably the most common. Should your kitten die within a set period, such as two weeks, you're entitled to adopt another, without charge. A reputable breeder may even spell out the kind of replacement — for example, the color or coat type and whether the animal and the replacement are show quality or pet quality.

Other contracts may provide a mechanism for providing veterinary care or for your recovering some or all of the costs of making your new pet well. Understand the policy and make sure you're comfortable with it. The time to make any changes is now.

What Restrictions Does Your Contract Put on Me?

Some people are stunned to find out about the rules *they* must play by to take home a cat or kitten from a reputable breeder — and even more surprised at the requirements placed on them by a shelter or rescue group. Rules such as: "Your cat must be kept indoors only. You must spay or neuter your cat. You can't declaw the cat. You must call the breeder or rescue group first if you must give up your pet and give them the opportunity to take the animal back and find him a new home."

What gives? Aren't you doing some of these people a favor by taking the cat in the first place? That depends on how you look at it. Given that indoor cats generally live much longer, healthier lives than ones who come and go at will, some shelters and rescue groups have decided they aren't doing an animal any favors if it goes to a new home and gets clobbered by a car within six months. As for breeding, what good does adopting out ten cats a day do if fifteen *litters* come in the same shelter's doors during the same period?

Okay, you say, but what about declawing? Isn't that meddling a little too much? Again, this one depends on how you feel about the procedure. Some animal groups and breeders are outraged at the idea of declawing, which they view as a mutilation. They consider anyone who doesn't agree with them, by definition, an unfit cat owner.

All these conditions are signs of a source that cares about the animals being offered — people who care enough to take responsibility for the entire life of the animals, not simply until your check clears.

Still, room exists for disagreement between reasonable people, especially on the subject of indoor-outdoor cats and declawing. The important thing is to know what your responsibilities are if adopting a cat from a certain breeder or group; if you're not comfortable with the restrictions, you do have other possibilities.

You find more on the debate over "indoor versus outdoor cats" in Chapter 1. Information on what declawing involves — and the options you should explore before considering the procedure — is in Chapter 13.

May I See the Litter? The Mother? Your Other Cats? Your Cattery?

Even if you're so specific about your desires — a certain breed, a specific color, a male, show quality or pet quality — that a breeder has only one kitten who fits your specifications, you still want to see that kitten with his littermates. You also want to reassure yourself that the breeder's cats are well cared for and that you like the temperament of the cats she's producing.

Looking "behind the scenes" is a reasonable request, but a breeder or rescuer may put some restrictions on you before permitting you to do so. You can most certainly expect to be asked to wash your hands, and you're not going to be allowed near any cats kept separate from the others for health reasons — such as those who are being isolated for a while before being brought into the breeder's colony of cats.

If the breeder refuses to allow you a look, be cautious. You're justified in wondering what she may really be hiding — cats in cages, unsanitary conditions, or other circumstances best avoided by the careful cat shopper.

What Makes this Kitten "Pet Quality" or "Show Quality"?

Most people looking for a pedigreed cat end up with "pet quality" because of the large expense associated with acquiring "show quality" cats and because breeders prefer to place their "best" cats with people whom they know intend to show them. A knowledgeable, reputable breeder can honestly assess a kitten's show potential and explain what "defect" classifies the animal as pet quality.

A pet-quality cat is in no way a lesser companion. Very few cats are born with the traits they need to be truly competitive in the show world. Their markings may be wrong, or their coats may not be lush enough. Their ears may not fold forward or curl back as their show standards dictate, or their "expression" may not match the ideal for their breed. These missing traits don't mean those kittens aren't beautiful or loving. As long as their faults aren't health- or temperament-related, such cats are wonderful prospects for purchase or adoption.

Look for breeders who patiently and knowledgeably explain what's right and what's wrong with their kittens — or any of their cats.

What Are You Doing to Help Reduce the Overpopulation of Pet Cats?

This is a question that may get the fur flying. We think it is important to ask, however, for a couple reasons. First, no one should breed cats unless they love the animals and have the best interests of cats at heart. These people are the ones with whom you should do business, because their love of all cats translates into how they treat their own cats and kittens — one of whom, after all, could end up as your feline companion.

Second, asking this question is your chance to express *your* love of all cats while you're making a decision about just one of them. If you buy from a less-than-ideal source, you're encouraging the continued survival of that source, whether it's the neighbor who never spays her cat, the breeder who doesn't care about congenital defects, or the pet store that buys from those commercial breeders known by humane groups as *kitten mills,* where the miserable, short lives of "breeding stock" are spent in small, filthy cages.

Some animal rights activists don't think that anyone should intentionally breed pets at all, purebred or pedigreed or not, arguing that every kitten bred intentionally takes a home from one who *needs* a home. We disagree. Some people will always prefer pedigreed cats over random-bred ones, and we feel the incredible variety pedigreed cats bring to the feline family is well worth preserving — as long as the cats aren't abused in high-volume breeding operations and the kittens don't have congenital health problems. The cats and kittens reputable breeders produce make up a negligible number of those animals who are put to death as surplus at shelters. This is in part because the numbers of pedigreed cats and kittens is so small — less than 5 percent of the cat population in the United States consists of recognizable breeds, as compared to a majority of dogs — and in part because reputable breeders take responsibility for the lives of their cats. If a cat produced by a reputable breeder ends up without a home, she'll take the animal back.

Many reputable breeders also help the community of cats, donating money, time, or goods to further the health and well-being of those animals they didn't breed.

We'd like to think that the world would be better for all cats if no one ever adopted a kitten from an "oops" litter without the assurance that the mama cat was being spayed to prevent a recurrence; if no one bought from a retail outlet that got its "stock" from a kitten mill; and if no one bought from a breeder who didn't care or know enough to raise healthy, well-socialized kittens.

We think you care and know enough about cats to at least raise the issues.

Chapter 20

Ten Cat-Related Attractions on the Information Superhighway

In This Chapter

▶ Web browser's delights

▶ Cat pictures by the millions

▶ Pampered cats — and needy ones

▶ Goodies galore

▶ A place for remembering

*F*irst, a confession: We're serious online geeks. Paul has spent the last seven years building and running the Veterinary Information Network, Inc., the world's largest online service for veterinary professionals and the content provider for America Online's Pet Care Forum. And Gina uses the Internet to do research and to stay in touch with animal-loving friends and fellow writers around the world.

Still, the worldwide network of computers called the Internet is an incredible resource for cat lovers. With a computer and a modem to hook into your phone line, you can shop for your cat, research breeds and health topics, enjoy some kitty humor, or just plain look at cat pictures, of which the Internet seems to have more than a million — and the numbers climb every minute. *Internet for Cats* (No Starch Press) author Judy Heim observes: "There's a popular saying on the Internet: No one knows you're a dog, but everyone knows what your cat looks like."

Although lots of possibilities for cat lovers exist on the Internet — and we discuss how to hook into them all in Chapter 2 — one of the easiest ways for beginners to poke around is to use the graphical part of the Net, called the World Wide Web.

A list of ten sites can't begin to hit all the best cat sites on the Web. A hundred wouldn't do the job, nor would a thousand. If you feed the word *cat* into the AltaVista *search engine,* a site that searches the Web (at `www.altavista.com`), you'll find that the subject triggers about a million and a half suggested places to look on the Web. And that's just when *we* did it. By the time you read this book, you're likely to find up to two million such references, such is the Internet's speed of growth. If sex-related topics are the No. 1 draw on the Internet, we think that you can make a good case that cats are No. 2.

Try out our humble offerings and don't be shy about exploring on your own. Many pages offer connections, called *links,* that take you to other cat sites if you click them with your mouse; in fact, some pages are nothing *but* links. Curiosity may have killed the cat, but it never hurt a Web-browser. Following some of these links can turn up some real gems.

Don't forget to make sure your cat is comfortably in your lap as you begin.

For more on surfing feline cyberspace — finding FAQs, newsgroups, e-mail lists, and chats — see Chapter 2. We also think you'll enjoy some of the *...For Dummies* books on the subject, such as *The Internet For Dummies* and *World Wide Web Searching For Dummies* (both published by IDG Books Worldwide, Inc.).

We love Judy Heim's book *Internet for Cats* (No Starch Press), and we think you may, too. Word is that her cat, Bubbles, is the true author of this text for tabbies, but any Net-savvy human should get a kick out of the book as well.

A Link for Everyone

The Cat Fanciers site (at `www.fanciers.com`) is the best starting place on the Web for cat lovers. This site is page after page after page of links to breed descriptions, to general information, to cat clubs, to cat shows and registries, to veterinary medical resources, to breeders, to rescuers and shelters, and to every other cat-related site the creators of the page could find.

Cat Fanciers is a real treasure trove, no doubt about it, assembled by people who love and respect cats and want the very best information on them made available to us all. Bravo!

You could spend weeks exploring all the links — and the links' links — from the Cat Fanciers site, but we think you should save some time to explore another site that charms us: Felines Are Us! (at `www.awod/gallery/wgd/savage/cats.html`). FAU! has a considerably more-eclectic collection of links, ranging from home pages for various cat-lovers to veterinary sites to the Federazione Italiana Associazini Feline (which Gina uses her college Italian to translate as "Italian Cat Page" . . . or something like that).

In any case, set up your unlimited-time Internet account before checking either of these sites, because time surely does fly when you're having the kind of fun we had looking at them.

Pictures! Get Your Cat Pictures Here!

"The Web was originally designed to make it easier for scientists to send information to each other," explains our paisan John Scalzi, a humor columnist for AOL, "but the minute they figured how to send pictures through the pipe, you just know that some scientist posted the Very First Cat Picture on the Web."

And your point, John?

Because so many cat pictures are on the Web, we're guessing you could spend the rest of your life looking at them and not see them all. Fat cats. Skinny cats. Young and old, of every imaginable color and pose and background. Cats on couches; cats on cars; cats in laundry hampers. *Meow!*

Almost any cat-related site has cat pictures, and even those that don't have pictures link to other sites that do. We decided that our favorite was The Amazing Cat Picture Page! (at www.islandnet.com/~jensal/cats.html). And we're not alone: More than 129,000 people dropped in before us, and many of them left pictures of their own cats behind. You can, too, and the folks behind this lovely creation tell you how — and why — you should do so:

- ✔ "Earn big suck-up points with your feline. ('Look, that's you!')"
- ✔ "You probably don't have anything better to do anyway."

You don't need an excuse to enjoy this site. Or to put your own cat out there for everyone to see, because, be honest, doesn't the world deserve to see your cat? How can you deny people such joy? Even John Scalzi couldn't resist. His cat, Rex, is on display at members.aol.com/jscalzi/rex.htm. We find Rex a lot more entertaining than John's wedding pictures.

Your cat is likely to get tired of looking at other cats long before you do. If that happens, check out with your cat The Amazing Fish Cam! (at home.mcom.com/fishcam), a constantly changing view of an aquarium full of real, plump — and probably yummy — fish.

A Visit to the White House

Speaking of fishbowls, we need to show a little respect for Socks, the White House Cat in Residence, America's favorite feline. Here's this nice tuxedo cat, thinking he's living the high life in Little Rock, cattin' around, coming and going as he pleases, and the next thing he knows, his family's heading for Washington, D.C. — and taking him with them!

His devil-may-care days behind him, Socks (named by Chelsea Clinton for his white feet) is now The Leader of the Free Cat World, and, in the biggest irony of all, he never goes outside without a leash! Socks is a good cat, however, and has taken on his new responsibilities with typical feline nobility. He keeps his thoughts on the matter to himself.

The White House home page (at whitehouse.gov) doesn't pay enough attention to Socks in our opinion. The front page doesn't even have an obvious link to him, and you must sniff around a little to even find him. We searched the photo archives first and found the picture "President Bill Clinton Takes a Walk with Socks the Cat." Socks, leash attached, doesn't look too comfortable on the big guy's shoulders, and Mr. Clinton looks as if he's ready to sneeze.

We were ready to leave at that point, but we kept digging.

A cartoon Socks, we discovered, leads the White House tour in the children's area, but the better choice is the "Family Life at the White House" page, which offers a couple better pictures and, if you click one of the sound icons, a recording of Socks' meow.

Yes, but . . . why doesn't the official First Family photo include the First Cat? We demand a Congressional investigation!

A Place for Pedigreeds

The world is full of cat registries, and you can link to many of them from the Fanciers directory, mentioned in the section "A Link for Everyone," earlier in this chapter. The Cat Fanciers' Association — no relation to the Fanciers Web site — is the world's largest registry of pedigreed cats, and its Web site (at www.cfainc.org/cfa) deserves a visit.

Everything you want to know about pedigreed cats you can find there: official CFA breed standards, pictures of top-winning cats, cat-care guidelines, and a tour of the organization and what it stands for. A pretty basic site, to be sure, but if you're interested in pedigreed cats, this one is a great place to visit.

Help for the Homeless

Feral cats are everywhere, from the alleyways of big cities such as London, Rome, and New York to the edges of rural encampments everywhere. Ferals are domestic cats gone wild — former pets and the offspring of former pets: animals abandoned in the mistaken belief that cats can fend for themselves.

They can't. The ferals survive by scavenging, by hunting, and by handouts, but no individual cat can live this life for very long. They die miserably, and they die young.

San Diego's Feral Cat Coalition is a group that's trying to deal with the problem by stabilizing feral populations through its catch, neuter, and release program. As do many feral cat advocates, they argue that maintaining stable, nonbreeding colonies of cats is a more humane and cost-effective way of dealing with the problem than the constant effort people expend to exterminate wild cats.

The coalition's Web site (at www.feralcat.com) is a resource for those who feel the same way, with information on why the trap, neuter, and release program is a viable solution, along with articles on how to set up such a program in your community. The site also contains fact sheets for veterinarians on how to treat ferals and information on rabies, trapping, and relocation. The site's a must-see for the compassionate cat lover.

Many nonprofit rescue and sheltering organizations have set up sites on the Web, and we feel they're all sites worth looking at — and the organizations are worthy of support. But the San Francisco Society for the Prevention of Cruelty to Animals is one of the most progressive and innovative humane groups in the world, especially with cats. No adoptable animal has gone without a home in the city named for the patron saint of animals, thanks to the SFSPCA's Adoption Pact. The SFSPCA works to make pets who are borderline fully adoptable through medical and behavioral treatment and works with new owners to keep pets in place. Read all about the organization at www.sfspca.org.

The North Shore Animal League of Port Washington, New York, is another super shelter, and we think that its site (at www.nsal.org) is worth visiting in any case — but *especially* for the story of Scarlett. Scarlett was a feral cat who was hideously injured in a Brooklyn fire, going back into a burning building to bring out her five kittens. She and her kittens were saved by a firefighter, David Giannelli, who took them to North Shore. Scarlett and all but one of her kittens survived, and they're all in loving homes now. This story is wonderful, and we encourage you to read it — and see pictures of the heroic calico and her babies. Click the link called "Scarlett's Web."

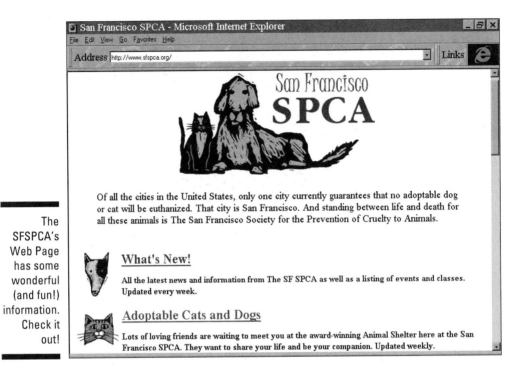

The SFSPCA's Web Page has some wonderful (and fun!) information. Check it out!

Where Tradition Lives on

You don't need to be much more than a casual observer to have noticed that fashions change in cats as well as in clothing. And in no case is this change more apparent than with the Siamese.

A few decades ago, the Siamese was a robust creature, with a solid body and an "apple head," as its fanciers described it. That cat is a far cry from the Siamese shown today, a slender creature with a wedge-shaped head. The only apparent similarities between the two styles is the cats' "chattiness" and the characteristic Siamese markings: light-colored body with darker "points" on the face, ears, legs, and tail.

The change was not popular with some people, and one of them, Diana Fineran, decided to do something about the situation. In 1987, she started working for the preservation of the "traditional" Siamese, which she believed was not only more attractive, but also healthier. She found some breeders with "apple head" Siamese and put together an organization, the Traditional Cat Association, to support them. The association now also includes "traditional" Burmese, Colorpoint Shorthairs, Persians (which have gone from the older, "doll-faced" variety toward extremely short-faced cats with health problems), Himalayans, Bengals, Nebelungs, and Chantilly/Tiffanys.

The TCA Web site (at `covesoft.com/tca`) offers standards for the older types of these breeds, as well as pictures, breeder referrals, and a membership organization.

For Serious Lovers of Cats and Books

Annette K. Gaskins is a book hound, if you'll pardon the description, and a very dedicated cat lover. She has combined her two loves in her "Cat-Lover's Bibliography" site (at `www.wam.umd.edu/~agaskins/clb.html`).

Her home page is the perfect spot to visit if you're planning a trip to the library or attempting to expand your home reference collection on cats. Her lists are fairly extensive and include both fiction and nonfiction, as well as magazines, videotapes, and cat organizations.

Because Gina loves reading fiction about animals, she especially appreciated the list of cat-related mystery writers (although she'd add the "Midnight Louie" series from Carol Nelson Douglas to the page). The listings of cat books with poems, biographies, pictures, essays, and humor is commendable, as is Gaskins' research into basic care and training books.

The willingness to share information in the online community is one of the best things about the Internet, and to find such a generous effort on behalf of cats and those who love them is really inspiring. Good job!

Veterinary Resources

As mentioned early in this chapter, Paul runs the Veterinary Information Network, Inc., an online service that offers its subscribing veterinary professionals access to continuing education, top-quality specialty consultants, bulletin boards for discussing cases with colleagues, and searchable databases of dozens of professional journals. Through the Pet Care Forum on AOL (keyword: PETS), these professionals share their veterinary expertise with pet lovers, especially in The Veterinary Hospital, where veterinarians respond to questions on the many bulletin boards.

Although VIN has been online since 1990, the Network is just now moving to establish a Web presence, at `www.vin.com`. A health-resource area for cat lovers is also growing on the site, at `www.vin.com/feline`.

Probably the best-known veterinary site on the Web is NetVet (at `netvet. wustl.edu`), put together by Dr. Ken Boschert, a veterinarian in Washington University's division of comparative medicine, in St. Louis, Missouri. His cat section offers a lot of solid information and many good links.

Two other sites are worth exploring. The first is the U.S. Food and Drug Administration's Center for Veterinary Medicine (at `www.cvm.fda.gov`), which keeps its visitors up-to-date on the latest approved drugs for veterinary uses. The site also offers links to other animal-related government resources, as well as U.S. colleges of veterinary medicine. (The colleges themselves often offer links to veterinary schools worldwide.) One of these universities, Cornell, in Ithaca, New York, has a site for its Cornell Feline Health Center (at `web.vet.cornell.edu/public/fhc/FelineHealth.html`). You don't find a whole lot on this site, but the information that's there is first-rate.

Shopping for Kitty

Enough of this serious stuff! Time to go shopping. You can find almost as many cat-toy vendors on the Web as you can cat pictures, and you can get a list of these sites from the Cat Fanciers site or find links to them from practically every other cat site on the Web. You can also put the words *cat* and *toy* into a search engine and let it rip.

We found a couple vendors we like a great deal, and we'd like to suggest them to you. All you need is a credit card to buy some great cat stuff.

The first is Cat Faeries (at `www.catfaeries.com`), and we like this one not only because it's a cool site (which it is) or because it offers cool toys (which it does), but also because we like Gail Colombo, the person who makes it all go. Gina met Gail at the Cat Fanciers' Association International show and knew in a second that Gail was a cat-loving woman — and not just because she was wearing a fuzzy cat-shaped backpack. Cats adore her, and the feeling is clearly mutual, as her well-chosen collection of fabulous cat toys and accessories attests. Cat Faeries stocks organic catnip, and each order comes with a note from the boss, Betty the Rushin' Blue cybercat (pictures of whom appear on the site, of course!).

To access the Fat Cat, Inc., Web site (at `www.kittyhoots.com`), you must pet the cat by clicking it with your cursor. Seems only fair to us! After you're inside, you can browse the Fat Cat collection of cool cat toys, including those in the shape of prey, politicians, or dogs. Would your kitty like Toss Perot or Revenge Rover? You may need to get them both to find out. The site also offers a bulletin board for talking with other cat lovers and — big surprise, huh? — CAT PICTURES! The best thing, when we visited, were free cat finger puppets. Print them out, color them, tape them to your fingers, and have a puppet show. The Fat Cat people seem to think they're for children, but all we can say is that they don't know us very well — and who took our crayons?

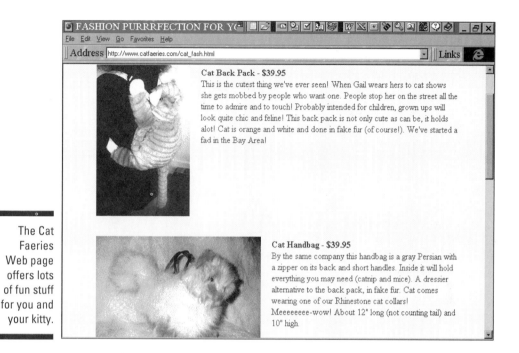

The Cat Faeries Web page offers lots of fun stuff for you and your kitty.

A Memorial Space

One of the saddest places to find cat pictures on the Web is on sites dedicated to the memory of beloved pets who've passed on. We found such places sad, true, but we also found them beautiful and inspiring. One such site is the Rainbow Bridge Tribute Pages (at `www.primenet.com/~meggie/bridge.htm`).

The Rainbow Bridge refers to a lovely story that has given many pet lovers comfort over the years. After our animal companions die, the story goes, they're restored to health and vigor and are well cared for in a special place. They're happy, except for the fact that they miss us. After we die, we see them again and cross the Rainbow Bridge together.

A wonderful story, and we hope it's true, for we'd like to see many, many animals again.

The site offers stories, poems, and pictures, each and every one guaranteed to tug at your heartstrings. The last page notes that this site was "made with love," and we have no doubt about that. Creators Meggie O'Brien and Kathie Maffit are providing a much-needed service to us all.

Chapter 21

Ten Common Household Dangers to Your Cat

*O*ur friend Dr. Stuart Turner has a full-time job running the Pet Care Forum on America Online, but he refuses to let that stop him from practicing hands-on veterinary medicine. So he works a half-dozen grave-yard shifts a month at a nearby emergency clinic.

There, he sees it all.

He sees people who bring in healthy pets with minor health problems — such as worms — that could wait for morning or even next week. He sees people who bring their ancient pets in to be put to sleep, because after they finally make this heart-breaking decision, they want to act on it. He sees cats mauled by dogs or by other cats. He sees cats sick with feline leukemia. He sees animals deliberately injured by people — shot with BB guns, set afire, kicked in the ribs, the latter cases as good an argument as you can find for keeping cats indoors.

Although every animal lost is a tragedy, some of those are a little harder to take than others. Into this class falls those pets whose deaths were the results of something an owner could have done to protect them but didn't know about.

We want you to know about them, so with Dr. Turner's help, we've as-sembled in this chapter the most-common household dangers your cat may face.

What constitutes a veterinary emergency? Chapter 10 offers the information you need that may save your cat's life.

Strings and Similar Things

What would you call a kitten with a ball of yarn? A Hallmark moment? A prize-winning picture? How about an accident waiting to happen?

Kittens and cats love playing with yarn. And string and ribbon and anything that twists and dances. They like to stalk, to pounce, to flip their slender prey in the air, and to start stalking again. That's all good, clean fun, but the chances are good that a cat doesn't stop there and goes on to eat the fuzzy line. And that's where the fun stops, because any sort of yarn, ribbon, Christmas tinsel, or string can cause havoc in your cat's intestines, causing a problem that may need to be surgically treated.

If you knit or sew, put your supplies securely away after you're done with them, and if you're opening or wrapping packages, make sure your cat isn't involved. Packing material such as foam peanuts can be a health hazard for your pet, too.

Even if your pet's not really the playful type, she may find one kind of string irresistible: juice-soaked string from a roast or turkey. Make sure that you dispose of these tempting dangers carefully, putting them in a container your cat can't get into.

Cats love to play with all types of string and ribbon, but you should let them do so only if when you're at the other end. Put it away afterward.

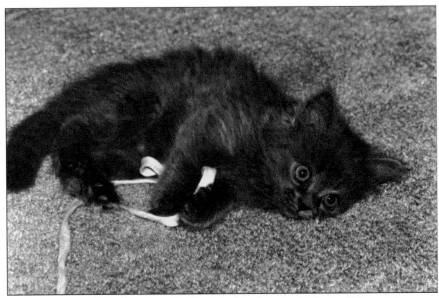

Nick — Photo courtesy of Angie Hunckler.

Antifreeze? Anti-Cat

If you're a shade-tree mechanic, you want to be extra careful changing your car's coolant. That's because most antifreeze poses a severe risk to animals — and to children! Every year, nearly 120,000 pets in the United States are poisoned by antifreeze, and more than 90,000 of them die.

And it doesn't take very much to do in a cat. Less than a teaspoon is all it takes.

Make sure you clean up carefully with a rag after changing coolant, and always be alert for puddles on your garage floor.

Less-toxic kinds of antifreeze are now available, which are made from propylene glycol instead of the ethylene glycol of conventional coolants. Sierra antifreeze is one of the new ones and is available at most auto-supplies outlets. Make the change!

The Warm and Deadly Dryer

Cats love warm, dark hiding places, and a dryer full of freshly warm clothes is a favorite. You'd be surprised how easily you can throw a few extra clothes in, close the door, and turn on the dryer without noticing your cat is inside. One of Gina's friends lost his cat in just such a way.

Prevention is simple: Keep the dryer door closed and always check for your cat — just in case. Keep an eye out, too, in the washer, dishwasher, or oven. This situation is one case in which the saying "curiosity killed the cat" can prove to be tragically true.

If you find your cat in the dryer, oven, washing machine, or dishwasher, take a deep breath and do something that seems cruel but has your cat's best interest at heart: Scare the fur off him. Close the door with him inside, and then pound on the appliance for a few seconds, making a racket that could wake the dead. Then open the door and let him make his escape. You can't always be sure everyone in your house remembers to keep appliance doors closed or checks for a cat before hitting the "on" switch. Convincing your cat to avoid such sleeping places provides another kind of insurance against tragedy.

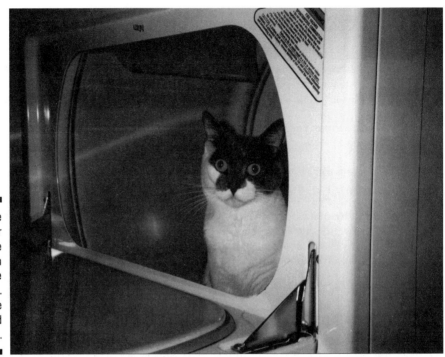

A favorite place for cats, the dryer can be quite dangerous. Keep the door closed at all times.

Bitsy Bob — Photo courtesy of Johanna Bader.

Pain Medicines That Kill

Here's an easy rule to remember: Never give your cat *any* medication without calling your veterinarian first.

That's a good rule to remember in general, but in particular, it applies to pain-killers. Although you can safely give aspirin to arthritic dogs, the smaller size and different metabolism of cats makes aspirin a dangerous proposition for them. Acetaminophen, the active ingredient in Tylenol, can kill your cat, as can some of the newer, longer-lasting pain-killers available in nonprescription form for human use.

If your cat is in pain, call your veterinarian immediately. Cats are very stoic, and if you're noticing your pet's discomfort, he's really suffering and needs immediate care. As for chronic pain, your veterinarian can prescribe something that's effective and cat-safe.

Attack of the Killer Plants

Cats love to nosh greenery. Some experts suggest that cats crave the half-digested plant matter in the bellies of their vegetarian prey, but just as good an explanation is that cats eat plants simply because they *want* to.

Indulge your cat with plants he can nibble on — the elements of a cat-friendly garden appear in Chapter 8 — but make sure he isn't munching on anything that can make him sick. You can discourage cats from chewing on houseplants, but you can't stop them, so your best bet is to make sure that anything your cat can get into isn't going to hurt him.

Although you obviously can't control what your outside cat is eating on his rambles, you should be aware of signs of illness. Check them out in Chapter 10.

The poinsettia has long been considered a poisonous plant, but that's no longer thought to be the case. No less an authority than the National Animal Poison Control Center says that the holiday plant is no longer considered deadly, although ingesting a considerable amount of it may still give your cat a tummyache.

A Shocking Experience

Chewing on electrical cords is more of a risk for inquisitive kittens, but protecting your grown-up cat against them wouldn't hurt either. Make sure cords are tucked out of the way, and if you notice any you can't hide and that are attracting kitty teeth, coat them in something nasty, such as Bitter Apple (available at pet-supply stores) to convince your cat or kitten to chomp somewhere else.

Cords aren't the only things cats love to chew on. For help with getting your pet to leave your sweaters (and other cloth objects) alone, see Chapter 13.

Four-Wheeled Menace

Probably the biggest danger cars present to cats is when the vehicles are in motion. The meeting of a two-ton car with a ten-pound kitty never comes out in favor of the feline. But even a stationary vehicle can become a deadly temptation for a cat.

Toxic plants

Cats can be deadly to plants, but more than a few plants are quite capable of getting revenge. Here what the ASPCA/National Animal Poison Control Center, a resource for veterinarians, says are some of the bad seeds. Most "just" make your pet sick, but a few of them can kill. If your pet has tangled with any of these, call your veterinarian. And don't forget: Even "good" plants can cause problems if they've been sprayed with insecticide.

Aloe Vera (Medicine Plant)
Amaryllis
Andromeda Japonica
Apple (seeds)
Apricot (pit)
Asparagus Fern
Autumn Crocus
Avocado (fruit and pit)
Azalea
Baby Doll Ti
Baby's Breath
Bird of Paradise
Bittersweet
Branching Ivy
Buckeye
Buddhist Pine
Caladium
Calla Lily
Castor Bean
Ceriman
Cherry (wilting leaves and seeds)
China Doll
Chinese evergreen
Christmas Cactus
Christmas Rose
Chrysanthemum
Cineraria
Clematis
Cordatum
Corn Plant (all Dracaena species)
Crown Vetch
Cyclamen
Daffodil
Daisy
Day Lily
Devil's Ivy

Dieffenbachia (all varieties; commonly called Dumb Cane)
Dracaena Palm
Dragon Tree
Elephant Ears
Emerald Feather
English Ivy
Fiddle-leaf Fig
Flamingo Plant
Foxglove
Fruit Salad Plant
Geranium
German Ivy
Glacier Ivy
Gladiola
Glory Lily
Hawaiian Ti
Heavenly Bamboo
Hibiscus
Holly
Hurricane Plant
Hyacinth
Hydrangea
Impatiens
Indian Laurel
Indian Rubber Plant
Iris
Japanese Yew
Jerusalem Cherry
Kalanchoe
Lilium species (includes Easter lily, Japanese Show lily, Oriental lily, Tiger lily, etc.)
Lily of the Valley
Marble Queen
Marijuana
Mexican Breadfruit

Miniature Croton (and other varieties)
Mistletoe
Morning Glory
Mother-in-law's tongue
Narcissus
Needlepoint Ivy
Nephthytis
Nightshade (Solanum species)
Norfolk Pine
Oleander
Onion
Peace Lily
Peach (wilting leaves and pit)
Pencil Cactus
Philodendron (all varieties)
Plum (wilting leaves and pit)
Plumosa Fern
Pothos (all varieties)
Precatory Bean
Primula
Privet
Rhododendron
Ribbon Plant
Sago Palm (Cycas)
Schefflera
String of Pearls/Beads
Sweet Pea
Taro Vine
Tomato Plant (green fruit, stem, and leaves)
Tulip
Weeping Fig
Yesterday, Today, Tomorrow plant
Yucca

Cats are heat-seekers, and many of them discover that engines are warm for a long time after they're turned off. These cats slip into the engine compartment from underneath, snuggle against the warm metal, and settle in for a catnap. On a cold snowy night, such a protected place must seem a godsend.

A running engine is no place for a kitty to be, however, and the cat that's still inside after the car's turned over can get badly injured.

Even if your cat's an indoor one who never has access to the engine compartment of your car, you can save another cat's life by getting into one simple habit: Before you get into your car — especially on a cold morning — pound on the hood for a couple seconds. If a cat's in your engine compartment, she's sure to wake up and take off at the sound.

Garage Dangers

Most people just aren't very neat in their garages. In addition to ignoring the drips and puddles coming from their cars — which can include deadly antifreeze, of course — folks can be careless about storing insecticides, paints, cleaning supplies, and fertilizers, all of which can be toxic.

Although cats are considerably more discriminating in what they eat than dogs are, making sure you safely store household chemicals and clean up all spills promptly is still a good idea.

Another garage danger: the door. A garage door in the open position makes a nifty high hiding place for a cat, but that secure perch can injure your pet if you set the door in motion while he's there.

And while you're at it, don't forget about other places cats get into — and sometimes shut up in — such as basements and closets.

Towering Danger

Paul's a city kid, and he did his residency at New York City's Animal Medical Center, the largest hospital in the world for companion animals. While he was there, he saw a lot of cats who'd fallen — or jumped — from high-rise apartments. Some make it. A lot of others don't.

Did they fall or did they jump? No one knows for sure, although most speculate these falls are generally accidental. Although cats are very good at landing on their feet, the impact can be deadly.

Prevention is the key to avoiding such accidents: Keep screens on your windows, and never let your cat out on your terrace.

Paul has seen some kitties survive from pretty high up, as high as 15 stories or more. And, in fact, studies of "high-rise syndrome" in cats reveals that the cats most likely to survive a tumble are the ones who started at the intermediate floors. From the lower floors, a cat hasn't time to prepare himself for impact by righting himself. From the highest, the fall's too great to survive. In between, however, is a margin of survivability —although few cats walk away unscathed.

Don't Do Doggie Dips

You may think a flea product designed to be safe for dogs and puppies is likewise safe for your cat. As solid as that reasoning may seem, however, it's wrong — dead wrong.

Never use a flea product designed for dogs on your cat. Many people tend to take them lightly, but these insecticides are designed to walk a very fine line: enough toxins to kill the parasites but not enough to endanger the pet. A product engineered to meet these challenges for dogs may not do so for cats. Check the label. Ask your veterinarian. Call the manufacturer *before* using any product. Your cat's life is at stake.

For safe, effective flea control in cats — including the latest new products available from your veterinarian — see Chapter 7.

Chapter 22

Ten of the Best Things Ever Said about Cats

*W*ith their beauty and their mysterious ways, cats have inspired creative souls of all kinds for centuries — poets and essayists, novelists and playwrights, painters and sculptors, photographers, and even advertising copywriters. The legacy of these cat-loving people has been passed down through the generations. And although the media have changed — witness, for example, the feline explosion on the World Wide Web — the cat has not. The words of such as Geoffrey Chaucer ("And if the cattes skyn be slyk and gay;/she wol nat dwelle in house half a day"), Edgar Allen Poe ("This [cat] was a remarkably large and beautiful animal, entirely black, and sagacious to an astonishing degree"), and Oscar Wilde ("Come forth my lovely languorous Sphinx! and put your head upon my knee! /And let me stroke your throat and see your body spotted like the Lynx!") strike a chord of recognition in cat lovers today.

Those who celebrate the cat's special — some would say "superior" — qualities have always been around and always will be. Today, writers such as Desmond Morris, Roger Caras, the late Alf Wright (better known as James Herriott), and mystery writers Lilian Jackson Braun, Rita Mae Brown, and Carole Nelson Douglas provide cat-loving readers with plenty from which to choose in libraries and bookstores. Brown even credits her cat, Sneaky Pie, as coauthor!

Maybe *you're* the next great cat writer! If that's so, you want to consider joining the nonprofit Cat Writers' Association, an organization founded in 1992 to promote and support those writers, editors, artists, and photographers who look to cats for their inspiration. The CWA offers an annual conference as well as a yearly writing competition, with more than $5,000 given out to the winners. For information on the CWA, send a self-addressed, stamped envelope to Diane Smith, 1759 Lake Cypress Drive, Safety Harbor, FL 34695; or visit the group's Web site, at `http://www.geocities.com/Heartland/Hills/5272/cwa.htm`.

The cat as inspiration

I look on the cat as a poem waiting to happen, its pause mere prologue to prankish delight, its purr a sweet river of song. A cat touches the soul. Whispy whisker-kisses, moist nosebumps — these are gifts beyond measure. To artists, a loving cat is an eternal muse.

— *Amy Shojai*

The cat as cybernaut

Most Internet flame wars are started by cats who did not get what they wanted for supper.

— *Judy Heim*

The cat as an individual

Cats must have three names — an everyday name, such as Peter; a more particular, dignified name, such as Quaxo, Bombalurina, or Jellyorum; and, thirdly, the name the cat thinks up for himself, his deep and inscrutable singular Name.

— *T.S. Elliot*

The cat as playmate

When my cat and I entertain each other with mutual antics, as playing with a garter, who knows that I make more sport for her than she makes for me? . . . Who knows but that she pities me for being no wiser than to play with her; and laughs, and censures my folly in making sport for her, when we two play together.

— *Montaigne*

The cat as companion

There is something about the presence of a cat . . . that seems to take the bite out of being alone.

— *Louis J. Camuti*

The cat as wild

As dogs of shy neighbourhoods usually betray a slinking consciousness of being in poor circumstances — for the most part manifested in an aspect of anxiety, an awkwardness in their play, and a misgiving that someone is going to harness them to something, to pick up a living — so the cats of shy neighbourhoods exhibit a strong tendency to relapse into barbarism.

— *Charles Dickens*

The cat as superior

It is easy to see why the rabble dislike cats. A cat is beautiful; it suggests ideas of luxury, cleanliness, voluptuous pleasures.

— *Charles Baudelaire*

The cat mourned

Pet was never mourned as you,/Purrer of the spotless hue,/Plumy tail, and wistful gaze,/While you humoured our queer ways, . . . Never another pet for me!/Let your place all vacant be . . .

— *Thomas Hardy*

The cat as honest

A cat has emotional honesty: Human beings, for one reason or another, may hide their feelings, but the cat does not.

— *Ernest Hemingway*

The cat as perfection

The smallest feline is a masterpiece.

— *Leonardo da Vinci*

Appendix
Additional Resources

Breed registries and show-governing organizations

American Association of Cat Enthusiasts
(AACE)
P.O. Box 213
Pine Brook, NJ 07058
201-335-6717
info@aaceinc.org
www.aaceinc.org/

American Cat Association (ACA)
8101 Katherine Avenue
Panorama City, CA 91402
818-781-5656

American Cat Fanciers Association (ACFA)
P.O. Box 203
Point Lookout, MO 65726
417-334-5430
info@acfacat.com
www.acfacat.com/

Canadian Cat Association/Association Feline
Canadienne (CCA/AFC)
20 Advance Blvd., Suite 101
Brampton, Ontario L6T 4J5
Canada
905-459-1481
office@cca-afc.com
www.cca-afc.com/

Cat Fanciers' Association, Inc. (CFA)
P.O. Box 1005
Manasquan, NJ 08736-0805
908-528-9797
cfa@cfainc.org
www.cfainc.org

Cat Fanciers Federation (CFF)
P. O. Box 661
Gratis, OH 45330
513-787-9009
www.cffinc.org/

Federation International Feline (FIFe)
FIFe General Secretary
Penelope Bydlinski
Little Dene
Lenham Heath
Maidstone, Kent GB-ME17 2BS
England
Jubatus@dk-online.dk
www2.dk-online.dk/users/kriste_m/
        fife/fifemain.htm

The Governing Council of the Cat Fancy
4-6, Penel Orlieu
Bridgewater, Somerset TA6 3PG
England
127 842 7575
GCCF_CATS@compuserve.com
ourworld.compuserve.com/homepages/
        GCCF_CATS/

Happy Household Pet Cat Club
Lauretta Nawojski, Secretary
6364 Montcalm Avenue
Newark, CA 94560
510-791-2646
slewis@best.com
www.best.com/~slewis/HHPCC/

The International Cat Association (TICA)
P.O. Box 2684
Harlingen, TX 78551
210-428-8046
www.tica.org

Traditional Cat Association (TCA)
18509 N.E. 279th Street
Battle Ground, WA 98604
lgil@cts.com
www.covesoft.com/tca/

World Cat Federation (WCF)
45307 Hubert Strasse 280
Essen, Germany
201 55 07 55
WCFI@aol.com
members.aol.com/wcfi/wcfh.htm

Veterinary groups

America Association of Feline Practitioners
Kristi Thomson, Executive Director
7007 Wyoming N.E., Suite E-3
Albuquerque, NM 87109
505-343-0088

American Animal Hospital Association
P.O. Box 150899
Denver, CO 80215-0899
800-252-2242
AAHAPR@aol.com
www.healthypet.com

American Veterinary Medical Association
Public Information Division
1931 North Meacham Road, Suite 100
Schaumburg, IL 60173-4360
847-925-8070
73711.555@compuserve.com
www.avma.org/

British Veterinary Association
Mr. James Baird
7 Mansfield Street
London, WIM OAT
England
101643.3370@compuserve.com

Canadian Veterinary Medical Association
Dr. John McGowan
5 Camwood Crescent
Nepean, Ontario
Canada K2H 7X1

VetQuest (a veterinary referral service)
Veterinary Information Network, Inc.
1411 W. Covell Blvd., Suite 106-131
Davis, CA 95616
916-756-4881
www.vetquest.com
www.vin.com

World Veterinary Association
Lars Holsage, Executive Secretary
Rosenlunds Alle' 8
2720 Vanlose
Denmark

Magazines and newsletters

All About Cats
21 C Heathman's Road
London SW6 4TJ
England
717 384 3261

Cat Fancy
Fancy Publications
P.O. Box 6050
Mission Viejo, CA 92690
714-855-8822

Cat Fanciers' Almanac
Official Journal of the Cat Fanciers' Association
P.O. Box 1005
Manasquan, NJ 08736-1005
908-528-9797

CatNip: A Newsletter for Caring Cat Owners
Tufts University School of Veterinary Medicine
P.O. Box 420014
Palm Coast, FL 32142-0014
800-829-0926

Cats: Official Journal of the Governing Council of the Cat Fancy
5 James Leigh Street
Manchester M16 6EX
England
161 236 0577

Cats Magazine
2 News Plaza, Box 1790
Peoria, IL 61656
800-521-2885

Cats U.S.A.
Fancy Publications
P.O. Box 6050
Mission Viejo, CA 92690
714-855-8822

CatWatch: The Newsletter for Cat People
Cornell University College of Veterinary Medicine
P.O. Box 420235
Palm Coast, FL 32142
800-222-9860

Cat World
Avalon Court, Star Road
Partridge Green, West Sussex RH13 8RY
England
140 371 1511
ashdown@ashdown.co.uk
www.ashdown.co.uk

Cat World International
P.O. Box 35635
Phoenix, AZ 85069
602-995-1822

I Love Cats
457 Seventh Avenue, No. 1701
New York, NY 10123
212-244-2351

Kittens U.S.A.
Fancy Publications
P.O. Box 6050
Mission Viejo, CA 92690
714-855-8822

Natural Pet
Fancy Publications
P.O. Box 6050
Mission Viejo, CA 92690
714-855-8822

Pet Life
Magnolia Media Group
1227 W. Magnolia Avenue
Garden Level Suite
Fort Worth, TX 76104
817-921-9300

PETS Cat Care Guide
10 Gateway Blvd., #490
North York, Ontario M3C 3T4
Canada
416-696-5488

*TICA Trend: Official Journal of The International
Cat Association*
P.O. Box 2684
Harlington, TX 78551
210-428-8046

Your Cat Magazine
Meredith Custom Publishing
1912 Grand Avenue
Des Moines, IA 50309-3379
515-284-3000

Pet-supply sources

Cherrybrook (general pet supplies)
Route 57, P.O. Box 15
Broadway, New Jersey 08808
908-689-7979
800-524-0820
www.cherrybrook.com

Direct Book Service
Dog & Cat Book Catalog (pet books, including
rare and hard-to-find)
P.O. Box 2778
Wenatchee, WA 98807-2778
509-663-9115
800-776-2665
dgctbook@cascade.net
www.dogandcatbooks.com

Discount Master Animal Care (general pet
supplies)
Humboldt Industrial Park
1 Maplewood Drive
Hazleton, PA 18201-9798
800-346-0749

J-B Wholesale Pet Supplies (general pet
supplies)
5 Raritan Road
Oakland, NJ 07436
800-526-0388
www.jbpet.com
jbpet@intac.com

K-V Vet Supply (general pet supplies)
P.O. Box 245
Route 1, South Highway 15 and 92
David City, NE 68632
800-423-8211

Litterature (cat greeting cards;
pet sympathy cards)
RR 1, Box 1234
Grafton, NH 03240
603-523-7877
www.litterature.com
lisashaw@litterature.com

LitterMaid (self-cleaning cat box)
5980 Miami Lakes Drive
Miami Lakes, FL 33014-2467
1-800-LITMAID
1-800-548-6243, ext. 1 (in Canada)
www.littermaid.com

Oaken Shaw Grange (general pet supplies)
Doncaster Road
Crofton, Wakefield
West Yorkshire, WF4 1SD
England
019 24 8630 37

Pedigree (general pet supplies)
1989 Transit Way
P.O. Box 905
Brockport, NY 14420-0905
800-548-4786

PET-PAK, Inc. (pet first-aid kits)
P.O. Box 982
Edison, NJ 08818-0982
908-906-9200
800-217-PETS (7387)
sjcinc61@aol.com
www.petpak.com

Pet Supply House, Ltd. (general pet supplies)
208 Wyecroft Road, Unit 12
Oakville, Ontario L6K 3T8
Canada
800-268-3716 (Canada only)
905-842-2030

Pet Warehouse (general pet supplies)
P.O. Box 310
Xenia, OH 45385
800-443-1160
937-374-2524
www.petwhse.com

PF.Magic (Catz software)
501 Second Street, Suite 400
San Francisco, CA 94107
800-482-3678
415-495-0400
www.pfmagic.com

R.C. Steele (general pet supplies)
P.O. Box 910
Brockport, NY 14420-0910
800-872-3773 (in U.S. only)
800-424-2205 (in Canada only)
716-637-1408

Reigning Cats and Dogs (gift items for cat lovers)
5617 H Street
Sacramento, CA 95819
916-455-5619
ReCatsDogs@aol.com

San Francisco SPCA
(Kate Gamble feline behavior videos, Computa-
Cat poster)
2500 16th Street
San Francisco, CA 94103
415-554-3009
www.sfspca.org

Valley Vet Supply (general pet supplies)
East Highway 36
P.O. Box 504
Marysville, KS 66508-0504
800-360-4838

Veterinary Information Network, Inc. (online
service for veterinarians; source for
*First Aid: Emergency Care for Dogs and
Cats* book)
1411 W. Covell Blvd., Suite 106-131
Davis, CA 95616
916-756-4881
vingram@aol.com

Wholesale Pet Supply (general pet supplies)
P.O. Box 325
Topsfield, MA 01983
800-473-8872

Animal charities

United Animal Nations
Emergency Animal Rescue Service
5829A South Land Drive
P.O. Box 188890
Sacramento, CA 95818
916-429-2457

Morris Animal Foundation
45 Inverness Drive E.
Englewood, CO 80112-5480
303-790-2345
800-243-2345
www.morrisanimalfoundation.org

Winn Feline Foundation
P.O. Box 1005
Manasquan, NJ 08736-0805
908-528-9797

Cat Fanciers' Association Foundation, Inc.
P.O. Box 1005
Manasquan, NJ 08736-0805
908-528-9797
cfa@cfainc.org
www.cfainc.org/cfa/

(**Authors' Note:** As you consider charitable
giving, please don't forget your local humane
society, SPCA, or other shelter or rescue group.
These local organizations are in the front lines
of helping cats, and they deserve your support.)

Index

(continued)

(continued)